PROPAGANDA

MAIN TRENDS OF THE MODERN WORLD

General Editors: Robert Jackall and Arthur J. Vidich

Propaganda
Edited by Robert Jackall

Metropolis: Center and Symbol of Our Times
Edited by Philip Kasinitz

Social Movements: Critiques, Concepts, Case-Studies
Edited by Stanford M. Lyman

The New Middle Classes: Life-Styles, Status Claims and
Political Orientations
Edited by Arthur J. Vidich

Propaganda

Edited by

Robert Jackall

Willmott Family Professor
of Sociology and Social Thought
Williams College
Williamstown
Massachusetts

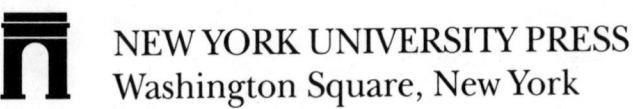 NEW YORK UNIVERSITY PRESS
Washington Square, New York

Selection, editorial matter, and Introduction © Robert Jackall 1995
Series Preface © Robert Jackall and Arthur J. Vidich 1995
Chapters 7, 11, 13 and 15 © New York University Press 1995

For other individual chapters please see the Acknowledgements.

First published in the U.S.A. in 1995 by
NEW YORK UNIVERSITY PRESS
Washington Square
New York, N.Y. 10003

Library of Congress Cataloging-in-Publication Data
Propaganda / edited by Robert Jackall.
p.   cm. — (Main trends of the modern world)
Includes bibliographical references and index.
ISBN 0–8147–4196–7. — ISBN 0–8147–4197–5 (pbk.)
1. Propaganda—History.   I. Jackall, Robert.   II. Series.
HM263.P763   1995
303.3'75—dc20   94–7500
                                          CIP

Printed in Hong Kong

10   9   8   7   6   5   4   3   2
03   02   01   00   99   98   97   96   95

Contents

Series Preface

Main Trends of the Modern World is a series of books analyzing the main trends and the social psychology of our times. Each volume in the series brings together readings from social analysts who first identified a decisive institutional trend and from writers who explore its social and psychological effects in contemporary society.

The series works in the classical tradition of social theory. In this view theory is the historically informed framing of intellectual problems about concrete social issues and the resolution of those problems though the analysis of empirical data. Theory is not, therefore, the study of the history of ideas about society, nor the abstract, ahistorical modeling of social realities, nor, as in some quarters, pure speculation often of an ideological sort unchecked by empirical reality. Theory is meaningful only when it illuminates the specific features, origins, and animating impetus of particular institutions, showing how these institutions shape experience and are linked to the social order as a whole.

Social analysts such as Karl Marx, Max Weber, Émile Durkheim, Sigmund Freud, Georg Simmel, Thorstein Veblen, and George Herbert Mead, whose works we now consider classics, never consciously set out to construct paradigms, models, or abstract theories of society. Instead they investigated concrete social phenomena such as the decline of feudal society and the emergence of industrial capitalism, the growth of bureaucracy, the consequences of the accelerating specialization of labor, the significance of religion in a scientific and secular age, the formation of self and the moral foundations of modern society, and the on-going rationalization of modern life. The continuing resonance of their ideas suggests the firmness of their grasp of deep-rooted structural trends in Western industrial society.

Later European and American social thinkers, deeply indebted though they were to the intellectual frameworks produced by the remarkable men who preceded them, faced a social order marked by increasing disarray, one that required fresh intellectual approaches. The social, cultural, and intellectual watershed was, of course, the Great War and its aftermath. The world's first total war ravaged a whole generation of youth. In Europe it sowed the seeds of revolution, militarism, totalitarianism, fascism, and state socialism; in both Europe and America it signaled the age of mass propaganda. On both continents the aftermath of the war brought economic and political turmoil, cultural frenzies, widespread disenchantment and disillusionment, and social movements of every hue and description that led eventually to the convulsions of the Second World War. These later social thinkers grappled with issues such as:

- The deepening bureaucratization of all social spheres and the ascendance of the new middle classes.
- The collapse of old religious theodicies that once gave meaning to life and the emergence of complex social psychologies of individuals and masses in a rationalized world.
- The riddles posed by modern art and culture.
- The emergence of mass communications and propaganda as well as the manufacture of cultural dreamworlds of various sorts.
- War, militarism, and the advent of totalitarianism, fascism, and state socialism.
- The deepening irrational consequences and moral implications of the thoroughgoing rationalization of all life spheres.

Emil Lederer, Hans Speier, Joseph Schumpeter, Kenneth Burke, Robert MacIver, Harold Lasswell, Walter Lippmann, Robert Park, W. I. Thomas, Florian Znaniecki, George Orwell, Hannah Arendt, Herbert Blumer, and Hans H. Gerth are only a few of the men and women who carried forward the theoretical attitude of the great classical thinkers in the course of working on the pressing issues of their own day. In this tradition, social theory means confronting head-on the social realities of one's own times, trying to explain both the main structural drift of institutions as well as the social psychologies of individuals, groups, and classes.

What then are the major structural trends and individual experiences of our own epoch? Four major trends come immediately to mind, each with profound ramifications for individuals. We pose these as groups of research problems.

BUREAUCRACY AS THE ORGANIZATIONAL FORM OF MODERNITY

- What are the social and psychological consequences of living and working in a society dominated by mass bureaucratic structures? How do these structures affect the private lives of the men and women exposed to their influences?
- What is the structure and meaning of work in a bureaucratic society? In particular, how does bureaucracy shape moral consciousness? What are the organizational roots of the collapse of traditional notions of accountability in our society?
- What is the relationship between leaders and followers in a society dominated by a bureaucratic ethos? What are the changing roles of intellectuals, whether in the academy or in public life, in defining, legitimating, challenging, or serving the social order?

THE TECHNOLOGIES OF MASS COMMUNICATION AND THE MANAGEMENT OF MASS SOCIETY

- What role do public relations, advertising, and bureaucratized social research play in shaping the public opinions and private attitudes of the masses?
- What is the relationship between individuals' direct life experiences (with, for example, family, friends, occupations, sex, and marriage) and the definitions that the mass media suggest for these individual experiences? What illusions and myths now sustain the social order? What are the ascendant forms of this-worldly salvation in our time?
- What are the different origins, dynamics, and consequences of modern political, social, and cultural mass movements with their alternative visions of justice and morality?

- What social, economic, and cultural trends have made many great metropolises, once the epitomes of civilization and still the centers and symbols of modern life, into new wildernesses?

THE ON-GOING SOCIAL TRANSFORMATIONS OF CAPITALISM

- What are the prospects for a transformed capitalism in a post-Marxist, post-Keynesian era?
- How has the emergence of large bureaucratic organizations in every sector of the social order transformed the middle classes? What is the social and political psychology of these new middle classes?
- What transformations of the class and status structure have been precipitated by America's changing industrial order?
- What are the social, cultural, and historical roots of the pervasive criminal violence in contemporary American society? What social factors have fostered the breakdown of traditional mechanisms of social control and the emergence of violence as a primary means for effecting individual or group goals?

THE CLASH BETWEEN WORLDVIEWS AND VALUES, OLD AND NEW

- How has science, particularly in its bureaucratized form, transformed the liberal doctrines of natural rights, individual rights, and concomitant conceptions of the human person, including notions of life and death?
- How have the old middle classes come to terms with mass bureaucratic institutions and the subsequent emergence of new classes and status groups? What social forces continue to prompt the framing of complicated social issues in terms of primal antagonisms of kith, kin, blood, color, soil, gender, and sexual orientation?
- What are the roots of the pervasive irrationalities evident at virtually every level of our society, despite our

Enlightenment legacy of reason and rationality and our embrace of at least functional rationality in our organizational apparatus? To what extent is individual and mass irrationality generated precisely by formally rational bureaucratic structures?

In short, the modern epoch is undergoing social transformations every bit as dramatic as the transition from feudalism to industrial capitalism. The very complexity of the contemporary world impedes fixed social scientific understanding. Moreover we may lack the language and concepts necessary to provide coherent analyses of some emerging features of our social order. Nonetheless this series tries to identify and analyze the major trends of modern times. With an historical awareness of the great intellectual work of the past and with a dispassionate attitude toward contemporary social realities, the series fashions grounded, specific images of our world in the hope that future thinkers will find these more useful than speculation or prophecy.

Each volume in this series addresses one major trend. The book in hand analyzes the origins and ethos of propaganda, which is now a pervasive feature of all institutions in modern society.

ROBERT JACKALL
ARTHUR J. VIDICH

Introduction
Robert Jackall

The term "propaganda" has distinctly religious origins. On 22 June 1622, Pope Gregory XV (1621–23) issued the Papal Bull *Inscrutabili Divinae* establishing the Sacred Congregation *de Propaganda Fide*.[1] The new congregation's organizational predecessor was a "cardinalitial commission" of the same name begun by Pope Gregory XIII (1572–85) some forty years earlier. The congregation's "mission," from the Latin *mittere* meaning literally a "sending forth," was "to reconquer by spiritual arms, by prayers and good works, by preaching and catechising, the countries . . . . lost to the Church in the debacle of the sixteenth century and to organize into an efficient corps the numerous missionary enterprises for the diffusion of the gospel in pagan lands. . . ."[2] From the earliest days of the mission movement in non-European lands, the Church showed an ability to integrate local customs and even beliefs into its encompassing framework. Propaganda, as the new congregation was called colloquially, quickly became one of the most powerful institutional arms of the Church. In 1627, Pope Urban VIII (1623–44) established the *Collegium Urbanum*, an international seminary for the education and socialization of young priests of all lands for the worldwide Counter Reformation against the Protestant revolt. The young "propagandists," as the alumni of Propaganda's college were called, developed great affection for the congregation, which they called the "great mother," and they served her with the passion of those who need to believe.[3]

The congregation's sons included a great many distinguished ecclesiastics, as well as many martyrs, men whose personal belief in and commitment to their mission was so profound that their record of self-abnegation, indeed self-immolation, remains unparalleled. Propaganda thus mobilized talented intellectuals of every sort into a vast social apparatus to persuade men and women all across the globe to believe in Christian doctrine or, if perchance they had fallen astray, to rekindle their faith.[4]

The history of the Sacred Congregation *de Propaganda Fide* still suggests some touchstone meanings about the nature of "propaganda" as a phenomenon, though modern propaganda scarcely requires the personal belief of its practitioners. Propaganda is the product of intellectual work that is itself highly organized; it aims at persuading large masses of people about the virtues of some organization, cause, or person. And its success or failure depends on how well it captures, expresses, and then rechannels specific existing sentiments.

Despite the great efforts of Propaganda and the Counter Reformation, the Church's grip on the masses and on society itself, at least in Europe, inexorably loosened with the emergence of modern economic, social, and especially democratic political institutions. The waning of Church influence also heralded the demise of political absolutism, though the twentieth century saw its re-emergence in totalitarian form.

The erosion of religious and political absolutism in Europe was slow, uneven, and largely dependent on the emergence of mediating institutions that helped transform traditional forms of domination. The rise of printing and the rapid spread of literacy underpinned, of course, all subsequent cultural developments. But the real catalysts of the emerging secular democratic order, as Hans Speier points out in Chapter 2 of this volume, were institutional milieux, marginal public spaces, that gave rise to new publics. Coffeehouses in England and Germany, salons in France, reading societies and lending libraries in other European countries, along with many other similar institutions, helped lay the foundation for the emergence of public opinion, through which the emerging middle classes articulated their worldviews and clamored for a voice in shaping the new order. To some extent the English Civil War, and certainly the French Revolution, had their origins in democratic ideas and conceptions of the social order first voiced in such marginal public spaces that later found their way into pivotal public arenas. The triumph of the middle classes and the new secular order they established owed a great deal to emerging public opinion first voiced by articulate, relatively cohesive publics.

The rise of modern bureaucratic societies and states in the nineteenth and early twentieth centuries transformed both the middle classes and the character of public opinion. In Part I of this volume, on the social groundwork of modern propaganda, Harold Lasswell, Walter Lippmann, Israel Gerver and Joseph Bensman, and C. Wright Mills all detail different aspects of this development. Essentially, the bureaucratization of industry, commerce, and government gradually displaced the old independent middle classes of farmers, free professionals, artisans, and gentlemen statesmen, and gave ascendancy to new middle classes of clerks, technicians, managers, and bureaucrats, all dependent on the large organizations they served. Specialized experts of every sort proliferated, especially substantive experts with increasingly arcane knowledge and skills, as well as administrative experts to coordinate the work of the substantive experts. The unchecked multiplication of such refined expertise in every institutional arena of our society has accelerated in our day. Specialized knowledge and techniques produce, of course, their own particular and peculiar habits of mind, values and goals, and ways of seeing the world. Bureaucracy not only splits work and knowledge into bits and pieces, but it fragments culture and life-worlds as well.

Increasingly, our society consists of self-contained little worlds, sealed off from one another; what happens in one world becomes increasingly inaccessible and incomprehensible to someone in another. But, at the same time, the extraordinarily complicated division of labor that marks our social order makes people more interdependent on each other than ever before. Interpretive experts, intellectuals skilled at fashioning representations of reality, become indispensable brokers on two fronts, first, between varieties of experts themselves, and, second, between organizational experts and the masses of people affected by their work. Of course, the representations that interpretive experts fashion bear only a passing resemblance to the substantive realities that they portray; but, once they are internalized by audiences, such representations come to supplant realities.

Moreover, just as the growth of giant bureaucracies transformed the middle classes into masses of individuals connected principally through impersonal bureaucratic rules and especially through abstract representations, so it also altered the way public opinion is formed, as well as the influence it has. Increasingly, public opinion means the vague, ill-formed, often volatile sentiments on a particular issue shared by socially unconnected people who lack the expertise to understand the substance of most important issues.

Specialized individual publics, which we now call interest groups, still fashion particular viewpoints in order to press claims in the public arena, but they prevail only when their own interpretive experts succeed in making their claims resonate with current public moods and vocabularies. The larger mass public, as Walter Lippmann points out in Chapter 3 of this volume, acts only "by aligning itself" and then only "when events have been melodramatized as a conflict." Moreover, "[t]he public will arrive in the middle of the third act and will leave before the last curtain, having stayed just long enough perhaps to decide who is the hero and who the villain of the piece." Until the mid-1930s, practitioners of such attempts to mobilize mass public opinion referred unabashedly to their craft as "propaganda," borrowing, wittingly or not, the name and its original meaning from the Sacred Congregation.

The total wars of the twentieth century, as well as the sustained ideological struggle called the Cold War, framed and paced what I call the axial age of propaganda, which is treated in the second part of this volume. The exigencies of war in this century coincided with the maturation of some mass media and the invention of still others. Print media, already well-advanced, flourished with widening distribution networks. The First World War, called the Great War since it was "the war to end all wars," hastened the development of telephone and wire services and of the radio for military uses, although commercial radio began only in 1923. The film industry, in its infancy at the beginning of the Great War, heralded the orgy of visual images yet to come, not only in film but also in television.

State propaganda machines were particularly crucial in bringing propaganda to its zenith. From the Great War through the Cold War, all major world powers competed, first and foremost, for the allegiance and good will of their own civilian populations. Without civilian morale, the vast industrial apparatus that produced ships, weaponry, and bombs and thus made total war possible, could not have functioned. In Chapter 6 Cate Haste examines the British government's propaganda organization during the Great War that helped whip up war sentiment not only among the British population, but in crucial American circles as well. Robert Jackall and Janice M. Hirota explore the vast and sprawling Committee on Public Information (CPI), the American counterpart to the British operation. As it happens, the CPI was the organizational crucible that honed the skills of a whole generation of experts with symbols for later propaganda in civilian endeavors, becoming indeed a secular rebirth of the *Collegium Urbanum.* When the Nazis came to power, one of their first coordinating actions was to centralize all communications and begin an unrelenting program of propaganda, as Z.A.B. Zeman discusses in Chapter 8. Joseph Goebbels greatly admired the Allied propaganda efforts during the Great War. Leonard W. Doob's essay on Goebbels (Chapter 9) suggests how well the master Nazi propagandist internalized and extended the lessons of his predecessors.

Along with the other extremist social movements that prospered during the 1930s, the Nazis gave propaganda a bad name, and, although some well-established groups used the term without a hint of defensiveness until well into the 1950s,[5] the term generally became synonymous with the deceitful manipulation of symbols, and not just that perpetrated by the state.

In 1937, a group of American intellectuals established the Institute for Propaganda Analysis in New York City to educate the American public to the dangers of propaganda. The Institute's newsletter, an early issue of which is reprinted here, systematically analyzed all kinds of propaganda, ranging from the radio speeches of the Catholic fascist, Father Coughlin, to the public relations campaigns of Henry Ford. The commonplace feel of the Institute's ideas today disguises the remarkable insight of its work at the time.

War propaganda holds great allure for those with the talent and expertise to manufacture and manipulate mass symbols. The stakes are high and the opportunity to pit one's wits against equally talented enemy practitioners is exhilarating. For instance, film propaganda came of age during the 1930s and the Second World War. The Nazis recruited the remarkably gifted Leni Riefenstahl to produce *Triumph of the Will*, a visual paean to Hitler's movement. Partly in response to Riefenstahl's work, various branches of the American military sought out the best American film directors such as John Ford, Frank Capra, and John Huston, to fashion images of democracy and of heroic men at war. In Chapter 11, Jessica A. Meyerson discusses this period in the history of propaganda. The military sometimes got more genius than it bargained for. One of John Huston's films, "Let There Be Light," presented such a dark, brooding vision of the effects of war on fighting men that the Army refused to release it and the film was screened publicly for the first time only in 1980. Whenever propagandists are not taken in by their own symbolic devices, the rapier-like intelligence that enables them to turn reality upside down to legitimate a social order can just as easily be used to etch their portraits in irony. Indeed, self-conscious propagandists usually produce the most effective propaganda. To the extent that they become "technicians in sentiment," as Robert K. Merton describes them in his analysis of a famous radio war bond drive (Chapter 12), their distance from their work enables them to determine in an emotionally uncluttered, if morally ambiguous, way exactly which symbols will resonate with particular audiences. Finally, the extraordinary military expenditures and national security demands of the Cold War required the constant invention of new rationales both to legitimate the economic sacrifices necessary to sustain the arms race and to mobilize and harness the emotions of the civilian population. In Chapter 13, Guy Oakes describes how the latter was done in a major propaganda campaign in the United States, that is, the paradoxical effort to convince the American people of the necessity to steel themselves emotionally to the horrors of nuclear war so that, if the worst happened, life could go on as normal, provided that one obeyed the advice of civil defense planners.

All modern societies are inundated with propaganda from every quarter. The vast bureaucracies that dominate all institutional arenas generate their own propaganda, for both internal and external consumption. Bureaucracies produce propaganda, among many other reasons, to divert attention from unpalatable hard choices; or to dress up organizational performance when soliciting appropriations or investment; or to mollify employees wary of organizational aims. Bureaucratic propaganda is of special interest because the internal exigencies of bureaucratic organizations themselves demand an orderly, rational accounting of experiences and events that are in reality almost always messy and ambiguous. Actors in bureaucratic contexts then anticipate the necessity for such accounts in order to achieve organizational rewards, though this often requires that they engage in behavior that is wholly irrational, when seen from another perspective. Using the case of battle efficiency reports during the war in Vietnam, David L. Altheide and John M. Johnson in Chapter 14 explore how official reports, the lifeblood of bureaucracies, create layers of representations that obfuscate and alter the meaning of actual experiences, which the reports presumably detail, while creating completely new, and often wholly false, "realities"' for the report's audiences.

The paradigmatic propaganda-manufacturing experts in modern societies may be found in the worlds of advertising and public relations. Few areas of our social lives are untouched by the visual images, narratives, jingles, rhetorics, slogans, and interpretations continuously produced by these experts with symbols. Although these experts do their symbolic work principally for commercial interests, they have often, as those who worked with the Committee on Public Information, loaned their services to states during wartime. In Chapter 15, Janice M. Hirota explores the structure and meaning of work in the advertising world, providing a detailed look at the actual work and organizational context within which the symbols that surround us are constructed. She also examines the particular and peculiar habits of mind that work with mass symbols both requires and shapes in its practitioners. Among others, these include a commitment to storytelling rather than to any notion of "truth" and a promiscuous affectivity that enables one to borrow and dramatize material from any arena of experience, sacred or profane, to make products of all sorts into heroes. In

Chapter 16, I examine the ethos of public relations work with special emphasis on propaganda created by interpretive experts for various corporate causes. This form of propaganda, often disguised behind elaborate fronts, finds its way into the hands of journalists who print and broadcast it as if it were "news." Virtually all organizations, from colleges to churches, from organized criminal rings to police departments, now have on staff public relations wizards and media "spindoctors" who manufacture and feed stories to ever-hungry media in order to protect interests, remove stigma, confuse opponents, create and embellish reputations, or mobilize public opinion for specific goals.

But propaganda is not the monopoly of well-established forces in society. Indeed, advertising and public relations have been the generating milieux of persuasive techniques and habits of mind that have migrated far beyond the professional boundaries of these disciplines. Social movements of every political stripe use exactly the same techniques of mass persuasion in crafting their rhetorical appeals. The frequent shamelessness of movement leaders' manipulation of the media suggests how deeply the propagandist's ethos has penetrated our entire society. In Chapter 17, Charles J. Stewart, Craig Allen Smith, and Robert E. Denton, Jr. examine the use of slogans in social movements. Slogans are in many ways prototypical propaganda – pointed, succinct, simplistic, appealing to emotions instead of reason, and offering simultaneously a rationale for action and a framework for interpreting it. Indeed, some slogans implicitly contain whole ways of seeing the world along with vocabularies that articulate those stances. Finally in Chapter 18, George Orwell, one of the most trenchant analysts of propaganda, examines the crucial political uses of the English language, whether voiced by spokesmen or spokeswomen for states, businesses, political parties, or movements of the left, right, or center. His essay not only alerts us to the systematic, deliberate misuse of language in modern society, but provides us with a first line of defense against the pervasive doublethink and doublespeak embedded in most propaganda.

Notes

1. The congregation's official name is "Sacra Congregatio christiano nomini propagando." Its original members consisted of thirteen cardinals and two prelates.
2. See Peter Guilday, "The Sacred Congregation De Propaganda Fide," *Catholic Historical Review*, vol. VI, no. 4 (January, 1921), p. 480. See also, "Propaganda, Sacred Congregation of," in *The Catholic Encyclopedia* (New York: Robert Appleton Company, 1911), vol. XII, pp. 456–61.
3. The College had many customs that helped bind its students to herself. Every year on the feast of the Epiphany, the College held an *Accademia Polyglotta* where Propaganda students from all over the world recited poems in their native languages. Moreover, every graduate of the Urban College had to write each year to the cardinal prefect of Propaganda describing his work and the state of his soul. The cardinal always answered immediately offering paternal encouragement. For a great many years, the congregation gave each of its employees, and presumably its students as well, a gift of a fan at the start of summer, a custom that dates back to Propaganda's earliest days when missionaries in China sent fans back to Rome.

   Propaganda also had a valuable museum, called the Museo Borgiano, which contained many ethnological artifacts sent by missionaries from foreign lands. For many years, the congregation ran the famous Polyglot printing press that issued liturgical and religious instructional books in a great many alphabets. The Propaganda Press still publishes annual statistical reports on missionary activities all over the globe.
4. In 1822, the Society for the Propagation of the Faith was founded in Lyons, France, and, in 1908, Pope Pius X withdrew the United States, along with some other countries, from the Sacred Congregation's regimen. Sacred Congregations, each headed by a cardinal, are part of the official institutional apparatus of the Church's vast bureaucracy and are centered in Rome. Societies, though Church-sponsored, often headed by high-ranking prelates, and sometimes national in their scope, such as the American Society for the Propagation of the Faith based in the New York Archdiocese, are ultimately local, self-supporting organizations. Their principal purpose is to provide moral support and money for missionary activities in other countries.
5. For instance, until late in the 1950s, the Advertising Council, the public service arm of the advertising industry, had a Committee on Overseas Propaganda to help thwart the perceived communist threat in foreign lands.

Part I

The Groundwork of Modern Propaganda

1 Propaganda*
Harold D. Lasswell

Propaganda in the broadest sense is the technique of influencing human action by the manipulation of representations. These representations may take spoken, written, pictorial or musical form. The expected disproportion between the specific consequence and the general reaction which is behind some political assassinations justifies the category "propaganda of the deed." Many official acts of legislation and administration derive their significance from the general as distinguished from the circumscribed results anticipated; these are the propaganda aspects of public policy. Both advertising and publicity fall within the field of propaganda. The word was first given general currency by the Roman Catholic church to refer to the dissemination of its doctrine and was later adopted and adapted by Marxists. Modern revolutionaries use propaganda to mean the spreading of doctrine; incitement is agitation.

It is true that techniques have value implications, even though values do not necessarily depend upon technique. Nevertheless, the processes by which such techniques as those of spelling, letter forming, piano playing, lathe handling and dialectic are transmitted may be called education, while those by which value dispositions (hatred or respect toward a person, group or policy) are organized may be called propaganda. The inculcation of traditional value attitudes is generally called education, while the term propaganda is reserved for the spreading of subversive, debatable or merely novel attitudes. If deliberation implies the consideration of a problem without predisposition to promote any particular solution, propaganda is concerned with eliciting such predispositions.

The antiquity of the practise of propaganda, as distinguished from its name, is apparent from the fact that much

* Reprinted from Edwin R. A. Seligman (Ed. in Chief), *Encyclopaedia of the Social Sciences*, 1st edition, vol. XII (London: Macmillan, 1934).

classical Greek and Roman literature is the more or less accidental residue of propaganda. The walls of Pompeii were found to be covered with election appeals. Frederick the Great was ever anxious to influence European public opinion. Napoleon subsidized a London newspaper, Metternich and the Rothschilds employed Friedrich von Gentz and Bismarck used Moritz Busch to spread favorable press comment. In the American Revolution committees of correspondence fostered anti-English sentiment. During the American Civil War the federal government sent perhaps a hundred agents, including Henry Ward Beecher, to England to plead its cause and added the dramatic touch of a shipload of foodstuffs to mitigate the sufferings of unemployed textile workers. It is estimated that in 1905 the czar's government spent in France alone nearly 1,700,000 francs on counter-revolutionary propaganda. In the [First] World War the battle on the propaganda front was as intense as on the military front. In the United States a federal Committee on Public Information spent nearly five million dollars. The chief of the American Red Cross in Russia spent a million dollars in an effort to keep the revolutionary government in sympathy with the Allies.

In every city hall and in every state and national capital congeries of propaganda organizations and agents speaking for every conceivable vested interest or general sentiment swarm about the legislative and administrative organs of government. Specialized promotional agents include "public relations counsels," who advise clients on broad implications of their activity in relation to the community, advertising agencies, individual press agents, vice presidents in charge of public relations and publicists who produce interested "news" and opinion. Perhaps five hundred rather important propaganda institutions are organized nationally and usually have offices in Washington, D.C., or New York City. They include social and professional organizations, such as the United States Chamber of Commerce, the American Federation of Labor, the American Farm Bureau Federation, the National Educational Association and the American Medical Association, and trade associations, such as the Cotton Textile Institute, the National Retail Drygoods Association, the Institute of American Meat Packers, the American Railway Association, the National Electric Light Association, the New England Council. In every community city clubs, community chests and other associations appeal on civic and patriotic grounds to classes or to sectional, age, sex and prestige groups. In Germany, France, Czechoslovakia, Great Britain and elsewhere there are in addition authorized economic councils that have an advisory relation to the government. Even where fascists and communists hold a legal monopoly, there is no end to propaganda; indeed new regimes are particularly dependent upon this instrument for the consolidation of power.

Propagandas are particularly prominent in intergroup and therefore in international politics. Some promotional enterprises exacerbate intergroup relations by imperialistic pretensions, militaristic provocations and separatist demands. Others stress the advantages of conciliation, of pacific methods and of cooperation without the sacrifice of independence. A chief executive, a popular aviator or artist travels abroad to demonstrate national friendship. Professors, fellowships, statues, are exchanged. Friendship propaganda is institutionalized in such associations as the English Speaking Union, the Alliance Française, the Friends of the Soviet Union. Hatred propaganda is always necessary in war time to arouse and intensify animosity against military and diplomatic rivals and to attract neutral support. In 1914 the United States became the seat of one of the most famous propaganda battles in history, with the British working through native sympathizers, Rhodes scholars and other cultural and business affiliates and the Germans rather through German nationals with such unhappy results as the so-called Dernberg episode. Some of the most prominent post-war campaigns have been prestige propagandas. "The myth of a guilty nation" has been persistently attacked by German propaganda to wipe away connotations of responsibility in both the legal and the invidious moral sense.

Intragroup propagandas may be classified as unity or disunity, revolutionary or counter-revolutionary, reformist or counter-reformist. Considered from the standpoint of its purpose, the huge network of organizations to keep German sentiment alive in Silesia, Alsace and other abodes of former German nationals or the promotion by the Italian

Fascist government of pro-Italianism among oversea emigrants
is propaganda of cultural unity. While the propagators,
too astute to avow practical political aims, usually dwell
among the somewhat diaphanous clouds of the spirit, it is
often impossible to avoid a strong irredentist tinge, which,
even when due to local exuberance rather than to central
policy, reveals that a propaganda of cultural unity is in its
effects also one of political disunity.

Propagandas that threaten the fundamental patterns of
a given group are revolutionary and invariably call counter-
revolutionary propagandas into existence. Antigovernmental
monarchists in France and Germany are confronted by
progovernmental activities. The revolutionary propaganda
of the Third International is opposed by the propaganda
of all identified with the capitalist political and property
system. Reformist propagandas work for limited changes
in the social order. As the term is used in America, reformist propagandas are those which set out to modify
conditions in the name of moral standards, as, for example,
efforts to prohibit the drinking of alcohol or recreation on
"the Lord's Day." As the term is used in Europe, reformist
propagandas are those directed at broad or deep political,
economic or social changes by gradual modifications of
an existing structure rather than by its replacement by a
new one.

Propagandas may be classified from other points of view.
Some are carried on by organizations, like the Anti-Ciga-
rette League, to promote a limited objective; others, like
those conducted by many civic associations, are for "general" purposes. Some promotional efforts are essentially
temporary, like a booster group for a favorite son.
Propagandas may be manned by amateurs or by professionals.
Those directed by persons who hope to reap direct, tan-
gible and substantial gains for themselves may be called
profit propagandas; others, such as some civic propagandas,
are headed by persons content with deriving general or diffuse
advantages for their group or class. Some propagandas
depend upon a central staff, others upon numerous local
branches. Some operate in secret, others invite publicity.
Some exist to organize an attitude toward a person or group,
others toward a policy or institution, such as free trade or

democratic government, still others toward a specific mode of participation, as buying war bonds, joining the marines, contributing to the community chest or crossing streets cautiously.

Military writers were among the first to see how greatly the displacement of cults of simple obedience by democratic assertiveness complicated the problem of eliciting concerted action. Warfare reached a phase calling for the cooperation of the whole population in military action, munition production and the supply services. As older sentiments gave way to nationalism, the spread of schooling augmented the prestige of national heroes, legends, virtues and emblems at the expense of local symbols. It did not release the masses from ignorance and superstition but altered the nature of both and compelled the development of a whole new technique of control, largely through propaganda.

Since the [First] World War accelerated social change has fostered new perplexities, disintegrated old loyalties and spread a new self-will. Merely automatic and historically hallowed ways of handling social adjustments have been rendered obsolete by shifts in technology and by strange new conditions of human contact. The programs of contending leaders, duly sanctified by theocratic or aristocratic connections, are confuted by one another. When lords fall out, commoners come into their own. Simultaneously with the fading away of old loyalties, the scale of collective activities has broadened. As proposals for action along new lines arise to compete for the moral and physical support of masses, propaganda attains eminence as the one means of mass mobilization that is cheaper than violence, bribery or other possible control techniques.

The significant symbols of propaganda may often be circulated free of expense to the propagandist. The skilled manipulator makes events so interesting in themselves that attention is spontaneously turned in their direction. For example, an insurance company recently received plentiful free space in the press when it announced that a former president of the United States had become one of its directors. Not only would the cost of an equivalent amount of regular advertising space have been enormous, but it would have been difficult to obtain headline space through a simple commercial transaction.

The propagandist's task is to intensify attitudes favorable to his purposes, to reverse obstructive attitudes, to win the indifferent or at least to prevent them from becoming antagonistic. In general, his problem is so to control the presentation of an object that a desired act will be elicited toward it on the part of selected persons. He must have a clear working conception of his goal, which is sometimes definite (to secure a majority of votes, to secure the enlistment of fifty thousand soldiers within a given period, to double the sale of a product within six months) and sometimes diffuse (to increase "good will" toward private owners of a public utility enterprise in such measure as to render impotent demands for government ownership or operation, to create a favorable atmosphere for the conduct of an international conference, to modernize community taste in public monuments).

The propagandist requires an inventory of existing facilitating and retarding factors in order to discover which hold the "balance of power." To some, which he cannot change, he must adapt. In a war problem there are some relatively immovable conditions: communication networks, similarities and differences in customs and institutions, interpenetration of population, economic ties, relative military power, organized prejudices. Allowance must also be made for factors tending to modify the general reactivity level, such as that condition of adaptation or maladaptation variously described as public anxiety, nervousness, irritability, unrest, discontent or strain. In a community with a high reactivity level a very small match can touch off an explosion.

The propagandist's creative ingenuity is tested by his selection of modes of representing a social object that will accomplish his ends. Any particular group has vested values, ranging from claims upon property to claims for ceremonial deference; hopes of increasing its non-sharable assets; and universalized patterns of right and wrong, of propriety and impropriety (mores), which it tends to defend. The propagandist must redefine the significance of social objects in terms of these various value constellations.

Thus for the mobilization of national hatred the enemy must be represented as a menacing, murderous aggressor, a satanic violator of the moral and conventional standards, an obstacle to the cherished aims and ideals of the nation as a whole and of each constituent part. Through the elaboration of war aims the obstructive role of the enemy becomes particularly evident. The maintenance of hostility depends upon supplementing the direct representation of the menacing, obstructive, satanic enemy by assurances of ultimate victory, thus preventing diversion of attention. The preservation of friendly relations depends upon representing an allied nation as strenuously prosecuting the war and thus protecting common values. The ally must appear to assent heartily to the cherished war aims of the nation and to conform to all the mores.

The propagandist may pursue his task not only on the ordinary "common sense" level but also on a level leading to the underlying emotional life of those whom he desires to influence. To elicit acts severely condemned in the culture, such as lynching, the problem is to divide each conscience against itself, thus weakening its inhibiting capacity. Emphasis upon the aggressiveness, immorality and impropriety of the "enemy" is a sop that loosens the restraining grip of the conscience upon destructive impulses. The effective choice of appropriate representations, or symbols, demands careful attention to the relativity of culture. A cartoon of a burly officer beating his wife will not stir anger in a population of peasants to whom wife beating is a sign of virility. Due account must also be taken of the continual process of redefinition of patterns of morality (mores), immorality (countermores) and expediencies and of the continual modification of the vocabulary of opprobrium and encomium, taking place in all cultures.

Numerous problems of organization arise in propaganda work. It is advisable for the propaganda specialist to be in constant touch with those responsible for policy. The experiences that create sensitiveness to the psychological implications of particular acts are quite different from those of the usual military man, engineer or scientist. Judgment on these matters is so difficult to "objectify" that it is important for comments about psychological implications to be made by forceful personalities in the immediate presence of policy determiners. Propaganda must be coordinated with information and espionage services that can supply material to the propagandist and report progress of propaganda work. That propaganda can be effectively correlated with diplomatic, military and economic pressures was abundantly demonstrated during the [First] World War.

The importance of proper personnel is shown in the relative success of the British and German propagandas in America during the war. British civilian propagandists made no such mistakes as did German military propagandists, who complained of sniping by the Belgians, forgetting that the American civilian mind approved sniping as the sly and plucky act of an underdog. Propagandists should ideally be individuals with a capacity to view themselves as objects in a world of objects. They must maintain contact with the reactivity of the community and expose their minds to experiences that impinge upon it. Adroit public relations counsels read popular novels and attend popular plays and have great capacity for identification with others. It is doubtful that nonintrospective personalities will be successful propagandists.

Increasing attention is now being given to the problem of devising precise means of assessing the influence of propaganda. Working propagandists are accustomed to proceed by the "trial balloon" method, which consists in trying out public responsiveness to material that can be disavowed. The "official spokesmen," the "unofficial spokesman," the "semi-official organ," are instruments of this technique. Advertisers have tried pre-testing, choosing matched communities and varying details of their product to discover relative popularity. Speeches may be tried out on selected groups much as plays are tested in the "provinces." Nonverbal indicators of response (pulse rate, psychogalvanic reflex and involuntary muscle innervation) are being adapted to measurement purposes. Changes in registering or voting behavior in response to different stimuli have been studied by matching precincts and varying the stimuli. Efforts have been made to hold the audience constant while changing from periodicals as a medium to radio and back again. Straw ballots, questionnaires, interviews and "listening" are regularly employed to gauge reaction.

Very little in the way of successful generalization has so far come from these preliminary studies. But certain limitations upon the role of propaganda are clear. Many fundamental social changes never pass through an active phase of propagation. New standards of courtesy and new codes of personal integrity may rise and spread unnoticed by those in the midst of the drift. Many changes come to pass because someone invents a new practise and communicates it to a very small circle necessary to its propagation. Even if it were known what proportion of significant social changes passes through active propaganda phases, some questions would remain unsolved. Since propaganda is used for and against, as was the case with repeal of prohibition in the United States, the question arises whether propagandas cancel out, leaving other factors in control.

The complaint is made against the specialized function of advocacy that is the propagandist's that it distorts judgments by exalting scoring values at the expense of welfare values. Just as the criminal prosecutor keeps a "batting average" in terms of cases won and lost rather than in terms of sound social acts furthered or retarded, the propagandist substitutes scoring values for human values. His propensity to do this is fostered by the peculiar circumstances attending his field of operation. Unlike the lawyer who works within the purview of a judge, the propagandist appeals to the public at large. And if a judge cannot always be relied upon to possess the acumen, the facilities or the motivation to subordinate tricks of professional advocacy to the necessities of just litigation, the public is much less likely to impose rules of evidence upon often anonymous advocates. The propagandist in fact operates on a jury without a judge and frequently without the cognizance of the jury.

Propaganda as a mere tool is no more moral or immoral than a pump handle. That it may be employed for subversive, fraudulent, libelous and lascivious purposes is evident. Popular confidence in such words as "bonds," "preferred stocks" and "securities" may be abused to the tune of many billions of dollars worth of "lamb's wool." The name of science may be prostituted on behalf of germicides that do no damage to the germs and tooth pastes with very little or very dubious value. A rich manufacturer may ride his anti-Jewish hobby in a prolonged press campaign and ultimately withdraw from the field with a simple apology.

There are, however, correctives for the irresponsibility of the propagandist. Some campaigns face handicaps that can be overcome by no amount of financial subsidy, a fact that is revealed by a study of public utility propagandas. Anonymous propaganda is vulnerable through exposure, and the best public relations counsels are careful to reveal to interested parties their relation to their clients. Current suggestions for the control of propaganda range from requiring the registration of propagandists to fatuous generalities about wiping propaganda off the social map. The only effective weapon against propaganda on behalf of one policy seems to be propaganda on behalf of an alternative. Legal regulations to enforce publicity, to censor or to punish for fraud, libel and slander can be effective when there is a consensus upon the meaning of integrity. The rectification of objectionable conditions may remove the provocation to subversive propaganda. But repression unsupported by concession and propaganda merely drives hostile propaganda underground.

Propaganda is surely here to stay; the modern world is peculiarly dependent upon it for the coordination of atomized components in times of crisis and for the conduct of large scale "normal" operations. It is equally certain that propaganda will in time be viewed with fewer misgivings. At first sight its practise by specialists would appear to clash irreparably with some fundamental canons of a society that calls itself democratic. Such are: (1) the theory that the individual is obliged to participate openly and continually in ascertaining the general will, and (2) the theory that one who regardless of his private opinion propagates a view for a client commits a breach of obligation. The propagandist can show, however, that even a democratic society permits exceptions. Such are the diplomat and the lawyer, whose functions, being regarded as a necessary adjunct of litigation (a substitute for violence) and a guaranty that thorough deliberation will be fostered by interested representation, have social advantages that outweigh the disadvantages of deviation from the democratic rule. The importance of keeping channels of communication (press, post, radio, platform, cinema, theater) open to all on equal terms is at once apparent.

Any comprehensive appraisal would ascertain the magnitude of the effect of propaganda considerations upon the policies of typical individuals and groups. The public relations counsel is no mere errand boy who discharges quantities of mimeographed releases in all directions the moment his client pays him a retainer. He may interact powerfully with the policy determiners of a given enterprise and extensive changes may result. No detail of operation (commodity appeal, marketing policy, labor policy, credit practise) is immune from review and criticism by an expert objectively engaged in discovering a profitable sphere of activity for a client. That propagandists have induced important policy changes is well known, but what is unknown is whether the usual effect of those who specialize in assessing currents of public favor and disfavor is to make clear to determiners of business policy the advisability of adopting broad interpretations of self-interest.

One of the consequences of propaganda in the international field is that international legal conventionalities are becoming demonstrably more archaic. The modern state system rests upon the presumption that people who happen to be living within a certain territory are the sole determiners of their own interests, and that they will abstain from interfering with the affairs of people who live elsewhere. This presumption has less validity as the economic system becomes more integrated on a world scale. Propaganda is the tool upon which most interests with ramifications in several states rely to make themselves effective within what is technically a foreign jurisdiction. Propaganda thus assists in making a fiction of the national state and in fabricating new control areas that follow activity areas, intersecting old control areas in every direction. Thus propaganda on an international scale is one important medium for transmitting those pressures that are tending to burst the bonds of the traditional social order.

The modern conception of social management is profoundly affected by the propagandist outlook. Concerted action for public ends depends upon a certain concentration of motives. The propagandist is accustomed to go directly to the springs of motivation and to utilize governmental patterns only incidentally as expedience dictates. Accidents and fire hazards, for example, have been reduced by concerted movements that involved a minimum of government collaboration. The propagandist outlook in fact combines respect for individuality with indifference to formal democracy. The respect for individuality arises from the dependence of large scale operations upon the support of the mass and upon experience with the variability of human preferences. The newspaper, the cigarette, the tooth paste, all depend upon a daily mass referendum. The possibility always looms that a new combination of appeals will supersede the old and push old tracts of fixed and specialized capital out of use.

This regard for men in the mass rests upon no democratic dogmatisms about men being the best judges of their own interests. The modern propagandist, like the modern psychologist, recognizes that men are often poor judges of their own interests, flitting from one alternative to the next without solid reason or clinging timorously to the fragments of some mossy rock of ages. Calculating the prospect of securing a permanent change in habits and values involves much more than the estimation of the preferences of men in general. It means taking into account the tissue of relations in which men are webbed, searching for signs of preference that may reflect no deliberation and directing a program toward a solution that fits in fact.

Such an approach places a premium upon candor and hard thinking rather than upon hypocrisy and formality. The older democratic doctrines allowed the nominal leader to escape his task of leadership by some procedural rigmarole: a "general will" was supposed to be "out there," and the leader's duty was to watch carefully for it to manifest itself through the machinery of balloting and legislative discussion. The focus of attention was shifted away from administration and reflection to hocus pocus, and behind the scenes or under the surface played the really determining forces. The removal of the recurrent sources of strain in interpersonal relations depends upon finding the relations that do in fact remove the strains, and this may involve mass consultations on a scale not implied in pure democratic theory.

With respect to those adjustments that do require mass action the task of the propagandist is that of inventing goal symbols that serve the double function of facilitating adoption and adaptation. The symbols must induce acceptance spontaneously and elicit those changes in conduct necessary to bring about permanent adaptation. The propagandist as one who creates symbols that are not only popular but that bring about positive realignments of behavior is no phrasemonger but a promoter of overt acts.

It follows that the management ideal is control of a situation not by imposition but by divination. The job is not to "put something over," but to find out what will stay put in social practise. This involves the cultivation of sensitiveness to those concentrations of motive that are implicit and available for rapid mobilization when the appropriate symbol is offered. The history of many social innovations, like the Boy Scout or the Girl Scout movement or the spread of parent–teachers associations and child guidance classes and clinics, is not a record of social imposition. Diffusion was due to the fact that their relevance seemed somehow to be self-evident on statement. [T]he invention of goal symbols that are popular, and that actually make an overt difference, is the act of legislation itself.

The propagandist takes it for granted that the world is completely caused but that it is only partly predictable, and he believes that one of the most potent causes of social change is the problem attitude itself, which so often produces the goal symbols capable of guiding adjustment. This means that the propagandist is able and anxious to apply the methods of scientific observation and analysis to the processes of society but that he is content to direct his creative flashes to final guidance in action.

2 The Rise of Public Opinion*
Hans Speier

Public opinion is often regarded as opinion disclosed to others or at least noted by others, so that opinions that are hidden or concealed from other persons may be called either private or clandestine opinions. The criterion for distinguishing between private and public opinion thus appears to lie in the realm of communication. In expressions like "public good," "public ownership," "public law," however, our point of reference is not communication but rather a matter of general concern, more precisely, *res publica*. This political meaning of the word is older than the meaning we customarily associate with the term "public opinion."

Thomas Hobbes, for example, distinguishing public worship from private worship, observed that public is the worship that a commonwealth performs "as one person."[1] According to this usage, the distinctive mark of private worship need not be secrecy; it might rather be heresy. Hobbes mentions indeed that private worship may be performed in "the sight of the multitude," which is an old-fashioned, if more concrete, way of saying "in public." Private worship performed in public he regarded as constrained either by the laws or by the "opinion of men." Correspondingly, in considering the nature of heresy, Hobbes remarked that it "signifies no more than private opinion."[2] If we follow the lead Hobbes gives us, we may arrive at an understanding of public opinion that makes political sense and is useful for the purposes of this historical review.

Let us understand by public opinion, opinions on matters of concern to the nation freely and publicly expressed by men outside the government who claim as a right that

* Reprinted from *Propaganda and Communication in World History*, vol. 2, edited by H. D. Lasswell, D. Lerner, and H. Speier (Honolulu: University Press of Hawaii, East–West Center, 1980).

their opinions should influence or determine the actions, personnel, or structure of their government. In its most attenuated form this right asserts itself as the expectation that the government will publicly reveal and explain its decisions in order to enable people outside the government to think and talk about these decisions or, to put it in terms of democratic amenities, in order to assure "the success" of the government's policy.

Public opinion, so understood, is primarily a communication from the citizens to their government and only secondarily a communication among the citizens. Further, if a government effectively denies the claim that the opinion of the citizens on public matters be relevant, in one form or another, for policy making or if it prevents the free and public expression of such opinions, public opinion does not exist. There is no public opinion in autocratic regimes; there can only be suppressed, clandestine opinion, no matter how ingenious or careful the government may be in permitting an organized semblance of truly public opinion for the sake of democratic appearances. By way of illustration, no German public opinion existed in occupied Germany after the Second World War under the rule of military governments, despite the speedy liberalization of press and radio in the Western zones, and despite the expression of many opinions in public. This was because the Germans were neither free to act politically according to their own decision, having been deprived of sovereignty, nor free to criticize the actions of the military governments or of the Allied Control Council.

Finally, for public opinion to function, there must be access to information on the issues with which public opinion is concerned. This means, above all, that the actions of the government must not be kept secret. Thus, Jeremy Bentham demanded full publicity for all official acts so that what he called "the tribunal of public opinion" could prevent misrule and suggest legislative reforms. Public communication of governmental acts (*Oeffentlichkeit*) was demanded by the political philosophers of enlightenment. The practice of submitting a budget to popular representatives, if not to the public at large, was established in England by the time of the revolution in 1688 and in France at the time of the French Revolution of 1789. The more democracy progresses and the more intensely public opinion is cherished as a safeguard of morality in politics, the louder become the demands for the abolition of secrecy in foreign policy as well. After the First World War such demands led to the so-called new diplomacy. Under the system of the League, international treaties had to be registered so as to prevent the inclusion of secret clauses.[3]

If public opinion be regarded primarily as a public communication from citizens *to their government,* it may be distinguished from policy counseling by policy advisers or governmental staff members, which is one of the processes of communication bearing on decision making *within the government* (whether it is democratic or not). Public opinion is also distinguished from diplomacy, which may be regarded as communication *among governments.* Finally, one may speak of governmental information and propaganda activities as communications *from a government* to its own citizens, other governmental personnel, or foreign audiences in general.

Public opinion can of course be studied also with a view to what I have called its secondary communications process, that is, with respect to the communications it involves *among the citizens.* In this context questions of the relations between opinion leaders and followers arise, as do problems of the size and anonymity of the public, the competence and representativeness of its organs, the direction and intensity of the interest taken in matters of public concern, the level and organization of public discussions, and so on. On many of these aspects of public opinion our historical knowledge is limited. In the history of public opinion the most conspicuous landmarks are the dates when governments ceased to censor the public expression of political dissent. In France, free communication of thought and opinion was proclaimed as "one of the most valuable of the rights of men" during the Revolution of 1789. In England, censorship in the form of licensing was abolished with less fanfare about a century earlier (1695).

Older discussions of our subject do not differ much from modern writings in estimating the influence popular opinions exert upon the actions of men; they differ in assessing the influence popular opinions have or should have upon the actions of statesmen and philosophers. It was common knowledge among older writers that opinions hold sway over the success, conduct, and morals of men. Shakespeare called opinion a mistress of success, and Pascal regarded it as the queen of the world. John Locke pointed out that men judge the rectitude of their actions according to three laws, namely, the divine law, the civil law, and the law of opinion or reputation, which he also called the law of passion or private censure. He attributed overwhelming power to the third law, the law of opinion, because man fears the inexorable operation of its sanctions. Dislike, "ill opinion," contempt, and disgrace, which violators of the law of censure must suffer, force men to conform. When Locke was attacked for his allegedly cynical view of morality, he defended himself by saying that he was not laying down any moral rules but was "enumerating the rules men make use of in moral relations, whether these rules are true or false. . . . I only report as a matter of fact what *others* call virtue and vice."[4]

Locke did not advance the view, however, that popular opinion should govern the actions of government. Characteristically, he used the phrase "the law of *private* censure" as a synonym for "the law of opinion." Moreover, he described the law of opinion "to be nothing else but the consent of private men, *who have not authority enough to make a law.*"[5]

Locke did not say that he shared popular opinions about morality. He knew that independent minds examine such opinions, although they cannot lightheartedly provoke the censure of others in whose company they live by showing disregard for what others consider to be right and wrong; the philosophers would otherwise "commit the fault of stubbornness," as Montaigne charmingly put it.[6]

Sir William Temple's essay *On the Original and Nature of Government*, written in 1672, has often been cited as an early discussion of public opinion. Temple observed that it cannot be that "when vast numbers of men submit their lives and fortunes absolutely to the will of one, it should be want of heart, but must be force of custom, or opinion, the true ground and foundation of all government, and that which subjects power to authority. . . . Authority rises from the opinion of wisdom, goodness, and valour in the persons who possess it."[7]

But Temple did not speak of public opinion. He spoke of opinion or "general opinion." In fact, he used the old term "vulgar opinion" when he wished to designate opinions critical of authority. "Nothing is so easily cheated," he said in his essay *Of Popular Discontents*, "nor so commonly mistaken, as vulgar opinion."[8] Temple's concern was with the nature and stability of government. He opposed the contractual theories of government, no matter whether they advanced a sociable or a bellicose view of man in the state of nature. If men were like sheep, he once wrote, he did not know why they needed any government; if they were like wolves, how they could suffer it. Contending that political authority developed out of habits and feelings formed in relation to the father of the family, he regarded opinion as a conserving force that helped the few to govern the many. The word "public," however, he reserved for the common good or the common interest of the nation: the "heats of humours of vulgar minds" would do little harm if governments observed the public good and if they avoided "all councils or designs of innovation."[9] It was precisely such innovation with which public opinion was concerned when it came to be called "public opinion" in the eighteenth century.

Even Rousseau, who put public opinion in its modern political place, demanding that law should spring from the general will, still spoke of opinions also in the traditional, predemocratic way. In his *Nouvelle Héloïse* he equated "public opinion" with vain prejudices and contrasted them with the eternal truths of morality; and in his *Considerations about the Government of Poland* he said: "Whoever makes it his business to give laws to a people must know how to sway opinions and through them govern the passions of men."[10]

The discussions of popular opinions up to the eve of the French Revolution lay much stress upon the power of opinions as means of restricting freedom, upon their prejudicial character, their changeability as to both time and place; they also indicate that men of judgment, whether philosophers or statesmen, deal prudently with popular opinion. Especially during the eighteenth century there are discussions to the effect that governments should take account of popular opinion instead of merely imposing their laws on the people. Finally, in the traditional views popular opinion was seen in close relation to imagination and passions rather than to intelligence and knowledge. Jacques Necker, who was the first writer to popularize the notion and the term "public opinion" throughout Europe at the eve of the French Revolution, still spoke of "imagination and hope" as "the precious precursors of the opinion of men."[11]

It did not occur to older writers that the "multitude" should know more about government than a good ruler, an experienced counselor, or a political philosopher. Only when economic and social inequalities were reduced and the rising elements in the population became unwilling to put up with political inequality could the claim be advanced that the government should make concessions to public opinion. Public opinion is a phenomenon of middle-class civilization. At the end of the ancien régime in France, Count Vergennes, one of M. Necker's colleagues, wrote in a confidential report to the king: "If M. Necker's public opinion were to gain ascendancy, Your Majesty would have to be prepared to see those command who otherwise obey and to see those obey who otherwise command."[12] With reference to Locke's remark about "the law of opinion" one might say that Count Vergennes warned the king of public opinion, because the people who formed it had gained enough authority to make a law.

In his fierce criticism of Edmund Burke's ideas on the French Revolution, Thomas Paine remarked that "the mind of the nation had changed beforehand, and the new order of things has naturally followed the new order of thoughts."[13] The observation that the habits of Frenchmen had become republican while their institutions were still monarchical is well sustained by modern research, although it should be borne in mind that it was a numerically small class that had slowly changed its habits.

Lord Acton attributed the growing influence of public opinion in eighteenth-century France to the rise of national debts and the increasing importance of the public creditor.[14] It is curious that this important insight into the ori gin of public opinion has not led to more detailed research by the historians of public opinion. The history of public opinion has been written primarily with reference to channels of communication, for example, the marketplace in ancient Greece; the theater in Imperial Rome; the sermons, letters, ballads, and travels in the Middle Ages; pamphlets, newspapers, books and lectures, telegraph, radio, film, and television in modern times. We know more about the history of literacy, the press, the law of sedition, and censorship than about the relationship between the struggle for budgetary control and the history of public opinion or about the emergence of social institutions, other than the press, that were instrumental in the political rise of public opinion.

In some older sources the close interconnection between public finance and public opinion is fully recognized. In the French ancien régime publicists and financiers no less than the middle classes at large condemned public loans. Bankruptcy was demanded by courts of justice and by political philosophers like Montesquieu. "It was a reaction against these proposals of bankruptcy that the French constitutions at the end of the eighteenth century proclaimed that the public debt was sacred."[15]

Jacques Necker had occasion to observe as minister of finance that his contemporaries were much concerned with his fiscal policies. He, in turn, regarded it as the "dear object" of his ambition to acquire the good opinion of the public. He contrasted the "extensive horizon" of the public with the court at Versailles, the place of ambition and intrigue, and made the interesting observation that the minister of finance could not consider the court as a "suitable theater" for himself; Versailles, he said, was a place appropriate perhaps for ministers of war, the navy, and foreign affairs, "because all the ideas of military and political glory are more connected with the pageantry of magnificence and power."[16] By contrast, the minister of finance "stands most in need of the good opinion of the people." Necker recommended that fiscal policies should be pursued in "frankness and publicity" and that the finance minister "associate the nation, as it were, in his plans, in his operations, and even in the obstacles that he must surmount."[17] Necker's great contribution to the history of public opinion was not so much what he wrote about its power but rather his important innovation of publishing fiscal statements (*compte rendu*) so that the merits and faults of governmental policy in this field could be appraised in public. He did so "to calm the public which began to distrust the administration of finances and feared that the income of the treasury would not offer any security to the capital and interests of its creditors."[18] Mme de Staël, Necker's daughter, regarded this innovation as an important means for pacifying public opinion. The government, she observed, was forced by its need for public credit not to neglect public opinion; but Necker did not yet hold the view that the general will of the public should take the place of the government. He represents a transitional phase between the predemocratic and the revolutionary–democratic views of public opinion.

The institutional changes that preceded the restriction of absolutist rule and contributed to the rise of public opinion can be stated in this historical sketch only in bare outline. Gains in economic power of the middle class and the gradual spread of literacy are merely two aspects of this process.

The first impetus toward increasing literacy was given by the Reformation, which created a broad reading public seeking edification without the mediation of priests in religious literature written in the vernacular. As Sören Kierkegaard noted with extraordinary perspicacity about Luther, he "unseated the Pope – and put 'the public' on the throne."[19] During the eighteenth century, popular religious literature gradually was replaced by secular reading materials. Content and style of fiction changed in the process. The novel of manners and the epistolary novel, both primarily addressed to women, made their appearance, and the moral concern of the readers was shared by their authors. It became possible for them to earn a livelihood by writing. The professionalization of writing was furthered by the breakdown of the patronage system and its replacement by the collective patronage of the anonymous public.[20]

Parallel with the formation of a broader literary public, the middle classes transformed musical life. Public concerts to which an anonymous audience paid admission fees took the place of concerts given by the personal orchestras at the courts of European rulers and in the luxurious residences of distinguished aristocrats.

The expansion of the reading public was accompanied by the development of related social institutions such as reading societies, reading clubs, circulating libraries, and secondhand bookstores. The establishment of the first circulating library in London coincided with the publication of Richardson's *Pamela*. Secondhand bookstores appeared in London during the last third of the eighteenth century. European reading societies were influenced by the model of the American subscription libraries, the earliest of which was founded by Franklin in Philadelphia in 1732. Thirty years later there were several *cabinets de lecture* in France, and the first German reading circle seems to have been established in 1772.[21] In addition to fiction – the favorite literature of the ladies – books on history, belles lettres, natural history (that is, science), and statistics were read in these circles. But the favorite reading matter was political journals and scholarly magazines. In fact, the reading societies of the eighteenth century must be considered as the collective patrons of the moral weeklies that contributed so much to the articulation of middle-class opinion on matters of moral concern.

In German social history one looks in vain for the social institutions that contributed powerfully to the formation of public opinion in England and France, the coffeehouse and the salon, respectively. Germany's middle classes lacked the commercial strength that made the coffeehouse so important in England. In Europe, coffeehouses date back to the middle of the seventeenth century; they became popular as centers of news gathering and news dissemination, political debate, and literary criticism. In the early part of the eighteenth century, London is said to have had no fewer than two thousand coffeehouses. Addison wanted to have it said of him that he had brought philosophy out of closets and libraries "to dwell in clubs and assemblies, at tea tables and in coffee houses."[22] The English middle classes began to accomplish their own education in the coffeehouses.

Like the history of the coffeehouse in England, that of the French salon goes back to the seventeenth century and even farther to the Italian courts of the Renaissance. In the history of public opinion the French eighteenth-century salons were important because they were the gathering places of intellectually distinguished men and women who cherished conversation, applauded critical sense, and did not regard free thought or irreverent ideas as shocking unless they were advanced pedantically. During the second half of the eighteenth century the salons governed opinion in Paris more effectively than the court. Men of letters were received regardless of their social origin and met on terms of equality with the most enlightened members of society. The salon, a place where talent could expect to outshine ancient titles, was an experiment in equality that assumed paradigmatic importance within a hierarchically organized society.[23] As d'Alembert said in his *Essay upon the Alliance betwixt Learned Men and the Great,* "the man of quality, whose ancestors are his only merit, is of no more consequence in the eye of reason, than an old man returned to infancy, who once performed great things."[24]

In Germany the salon never exercised the influence on the dignity and the literary style of authors or on the manners and opinions of their public that it did in France. Germany was a poor, divided, and in part overmilitarized country; it had neither a Versailles nor a Paris. The social institutions that helped to pave the way toward the social recognition of the ideas of enlightenment in Germany were the predominantly aristocratic language orders of the seventeenth century and the stolid moral and patriotic societies of the eighteenth century in which civil servants played an important role. Both of them may be regarded as forerunners of the Masonic lodges in Germany. They practiced egalitarian rituals, opposed the conventional customs of the courtier, extolled merit and virtue as the new principles of prestige, read and discussed John Locke, and cultivated mutual confidence as a bulwark against the dangerous intrigues in politics.

These institutional changes in European society that led to the emergence of public opinion as a prominent factor in politics may be summed up without regard to national differences as follows. A closed, restricted public gradually developed into an open one, enlarging both its size and its social scope as illiteracy receded. This movement ran its full course only during the nineteenth century. It extended to the lower classes much later than the late eighteenth-century attempts to parade the Third Estate as the nation would make us believe. From the end of the eighteenth century we have glowing accounts of the widespread eagerness of people to read and to learn, but illiteracy was still widespread. It has been estimated that about 57 per cent of the men and 27 per cent of the women could read and write in France at the time.[25]

Geographically, the process of diffusion spread out from urban centers, with the United States, England, and Germany taking the lead over France, where printing presses as well as the socially influential circles were concentrated in Paris.

The economic and technical landmarks of this process of diffusion are reflected in the cost of mass communication to the poorer classes of society. Here again progress was made more rapidly during the nineteenth century than the eighteenth century. Taxes on newspapers and advertisements were fairly high until 1836 and partly until 1845; the poor could not afford to buy them. Even postal service was not readily available to them until 1839, when penny postage was introduced. Harriet Martineau said at the time that the poor now can "at last write to one another as if they were all M.P.'s."[26]

As regards the men of letters and the publicist, the prerequisite of their wider influence was the recognition of merit as a criterion of social status, so that authors could climb the social ladder regardless of origin merely on the strength of performance. It might be added that the rise of public opinion presupposed a redefinition of scholarship and a program of its missionary diffusion to laymen, a process in which "the world" took the place of "the school" and education became a technique for the establishment of a classless society.

One of the earliest and most radical instances illustrating this missionary zeal can be found in Christian Thomasius' *Einleitung zur Vernunftlehre*, published in 1691. Thomasius believed that it was the result only of differences in social status that not everybody arrived at wisdom; science ought to be the common property of all mankind. Everybody was capable of becoming learned, and the scholar should disseminate rather than attain knowledge.[27] It has been said that Thomasius repeated "the Lutheran teaching of general priesthood in the secularized form of general scholarship."[28]

Thomasius' notion of scholarship is close to Condorcet's doctrine of education or Sieyès' views of public opinion. Condorcet's aim was to render it impossible through education to use the masses as "docile instruments in adroit hands" and to enable them to avoid the "philosophic errors" on which he believed "all errors in government and in society are based."[29] And Sieyès wrote: "Reason does not like secrets; it is effective only through expansion. Only if it hits everywhere, does it hit right, because only then will be formed that power of public opinion, to which one may perhaps ascribe most of the changes which are truly advantageous to mankind."[30]

The elimination of prejudice, ignorance, and arbitrary government that the advocates of enlightenment wrote upon their banner in order to base the commonwealth upon reason and civic virtue is frequently regarded as a rationalistic program in which no cognizance was taken of the so-called irrational factors of human nature. For this reason, propaganda has often been presented as a counterpart to the process of public opinion. It is erroneous, however, to believe that the advocates of enlightenment neglected or overlooked the emotional facets of life.

The advocates of enlightenment themselves proposed the equation of government with adult education. They suggested, for example, that the government should engage orators for political instruction as it paid priests for religious service (Weckherlin); that attendance of courses on the nature of society should be made obligatory for the acquisition of citizenship (Mercier de la Rivière); that the government should control and publish newspapers to increase loyalty to the sovereign (Quesnay); and that historical works should be written to increase patriotism and national pride (Voss).

Perhaps even more important than these suggestions of political indoctrination were the proposals for the organization of public spectacles and celebrations in order to evoke enthusiasm for common causes and enlist the sentiments of those who did not think. Dupont de Nemours in *Des Spectacles nationaux* developed a theory of national celebrations based on the idea that the desire for pleasure is the driving force of mankind. The people should be brought to develop their patriotic virtues by way of exaltation over public celebrations in which they were to participate – an idea, one might say, that was realized in both the institutionalized public celebrations of the French Revolution and in the Nuremberg festivals of the Nazis or in May Day celebrations. Other writers who pointed to the educational function of national festivals and public plays were Diderot, Condorcet, and Rousseau, and, in Germany, among others, Stephani, Voss, and Zachariä.

In view of these facts it cannot be maintained without qualification that the modern advocates and practitioners of totalitarian government propaganda have superseded the theory and practices of the reformers who helped public opinion on its way to political prominence. It would be more correct to say that the participation of large masses of the population in public affairs, characteristic of both government by public opinion and modern tyranny, is spurious in character under totalitarian regimes in that it is demonstrative rather than determinative of governmental action. It may also be said that in totalitarian regimes mass participation in politics is regarded by the intellectuals as a design to conceal the truth about power processes, whereas in the eighteenth century such participation was considered as a measure toward the ultimate elimination of the irksomeness of power, if not of power itself.

It was believed that man guided by reason and inspired by rectitude would reduce politics to a calculation in happiness and do away with war. Nevertheless, the French Revolution gave rise to war and to war propaganda, and it lifted many restrictions on warfare. It created what William Pitt called "armed opinions" and Jomini "wars of opinion." Liberty, equality,and fraternity were not merely the aims of Frenchmen; they were held to be rights of man regardless of political and national affiliation. The French revolutionary armies did not wage war against other countries but for the liberation of man from old, oppressive governments.[31] Foreign exiles in sympathy with the new regime were admitted to the French clubs, the national guard,and the public departments. They could be found even in the Ministry of Foreign Affairs.[32] They were organized in foreign legions fighting the battle for France. Indeed, the foreigners fighting on the side of the French for the ideas of the French Revolution may be regarded as the prototype of the armed contingents that, hailed by their respective "governments-in-exile," joined the British, American, and Soviet Russian forces of World War II in "the crusade" to end Hitler's tyrannical rule. Similarly, the Girondists imagined that foreign nations in their desire to be delivered from the tyranny of their rulers and priest would rally in support of revolutionary principles. Robespierre's program of 24 April 1793 envisaged a universal republic in which all citizens in all countries would unite against the aristocrats and the tyrants.[33] As Burke pointed out, before the time of the French Revolution there had been no instance "of this spirit of general political factions, separated from religion, pervading several countries, and forming a principle of union between the partisans in each."[34]

It was not only the conquest of foreign territory and the subsequent provisioning of the French armies by plunder, but also revolutionary, cosmopolitan enthusiasm and the leveling of social inequalities that enabled 25 million Frenchmen to defeat a coalition of 75 million enemies. The royalist adversaries put twice the number of soldiers in the field as did the young republic. But although the French armies lost two thirds of their nine thousand royalist officers through defection, the *levée en masse* mobilized hitherto untapped human resources for war. As the Committee of Public Safety decreed in 1793:

> The young men will go to battle; the married men will forego arms and transport food; the women will make the tents, garments, and help in the hospitals; the children will cut old rags into strips; the old men will place themselves in the public squares to influence the courage of the warriors, incite hatred against the kings, and recommend the unity of the Republic.[35]

The most important change in military tactics brought on by revolutionary enthusiasm was the emergence of the *tirailleurs*, marksmen, who aimed their shots at a target instead of relying on volleys, as the disciplined armies of the ancien régime had done. The new tactic was known only from the American War of Independence and, in Europe, from the fighting of the notoriously cruel Pandours of Croatia. Advocates of the old Frederician tactics regarded the behavior of the *tirailleurs* as "militarily superfluous," "politically odious"[36] and indicative of "the scoundrel hidden in every man."[37] Indeed the new tactic was adopted by the conservative enemies only after their defeat, in Austria (1806) and in Prussia (1809 and 1812).

The leveling of social distinctions in the French nation also affected the status of officers and had repercussions in the logistics of war. In Prussia every lieutenant had two horses, one for riding and one for his baggage, captains could not do without three to five baggage horses each. In the French revolutionary armies no such luxury existed. Privates had to shift without tents, whereas no less than sixty pack horses carrying tents followed each Prussian regiment.[38] In 1806, the French baggage train was one eighth to one tenth that of the Prussians.[39]

In the international turmoil following the French Revolution, the enemies of France were incapable of restricting the war to its former, military dimensions. They responded to the ideological challenge. In October 1793, His Majesty's Government sent a declaration to the commanders of the British forces in which France was accused of attacks on "the fundamental principles by which mankind is united in the bond of civil society."[40] And William Pitt found the most eloquent expression for the ideological issue raised by the French Revolution. On 7 June 1799 he spoke in the House of Commons, moving that the sum of £825 000 be granted to His Majesty to enable him to fulfill his engagements with Russia. Pitt pointed out that this subsidy would be used for the deliverance of Europe. In reply Mr. Tierney contended that the funds were to be used against the power of France "not merely to repel her within her ancient limits, but to drive her back from her present to her ancient opinion." Mr. Pitt rose once more and said, among other things:

> It is not so. We are not in arms against the opinions of the closet, nor the speculations of the school. We are at

war with armed opinion; we are at war with those opinions which the thought of audacious, unprincipled and impious innovations seeks to propagate amidst the ruins of empires, the demolition of the altars of all religion, the destruction of every venerable, and good, and liberal institution, under whatever forms of policy they have been raised; and this, in spite of the dissenting reason of men, in contempt of that lawful authority which, in the settled order, superior talent and superior virtue attain, crying out to them not to enter on holy ground nor to pollute the stream of eternal justice; admonishing them of their danger, whilst, like the genius of evil, they mimic their voice, and, having succeeded in drawing upon them the ridicule of the vulgar, close their day of wickedness and savage triumph with the massacre and waste of whatever is amiable, learned, and pious, in the districts they have overrun.[41]

After the Congress of Vienna the utilization of public opinion in international affairs became, as it were, respectable also among statesmen who did not pursue any revolutionary cause. Once the importance of public opinion was discovered as a new factor in international relations, it became tempting on moral as well as on expediential grounds to utilize it. Neither Canning, who believed that public opinion should be invoked in the pursuit of British foreign policy, nor Palmerston, who held that public opinion founded on truth and justice would prevail against the force of armies, realized that they were continuing to revolutionize European diplomacy by their actions. A diplomat of the old school like Metternich was appalled by Canning's enthusiasm and could see only preposterous folly in the Englishman's notion of public opinion as "a power more tremendous than was perhaps ever yet brought into action in the history of mankind."[42]

The art of arousing public opinion nevertheless became a valued skill during the nineteenth century even of statesmen like Bismarck, who failed to respect public opinion, remained indifferent to its moral claims, and made no attempt to raise its level of competence. Bismarck condemned policies inspired by sentiments or moods. He regarded public opinion as dependent, to a large extent, on mood and sentiment, incapable of the calm calculations that had to precede political decisions. Nor did he believe in the political insight of public opinion. "As a rule," he said, "public opinion realizes the mistakes that have been committed in foreign policy only when it is able to review in retrospect the history of a generation."[43] Given the political constitution of Prussia and the Reich, Bismarck could afford to make foreign policy against public opinion, if he regarded such action as necessary and if he had the confidence of his monarch. Thus, in 1866 he waged war against the will of almost all Prussians, but he also refused to risk war against Russia by interfering in Bulgaria, a course rashly sponsored by the liberal press. Similarly, in the Boer War, Chancellor von Bülow disregarded German public opinion, which strongly favored interference, in the well-considered interest of the country.

The scope of governmental influence upon public opinion was limited throughout the nineteenth century and, if compared with recent activities in this regard, had an almost patrimonial character. In nineteenth-century Europe public opinion was a synonym of opinions expressed by the political representatives of the electorate, by newspapers, and by prominent members or organizations of the middle class. In England their faith in the beneficial effects of discussion and the persuasiveness of liberal opinion upon conduct of domestic affairs grew particularly under the influence of Bentham and his followers.[44] Toward the end of the nineteenth century, Lord Bryce pointed out that in England the landowners and "the higher walks of commerce" not only form the class that furnish the majority of members of both houses but also express what is called public opinion. He held that in Germany, Italy, and France as well public opinion was "substantially the opinion of the class which wears black coats and lives in good houses."[45] He contrasted these conditions with those prevailing in the United States, where he believed government by public opinion to exist, because "the wishes and views of the people prevail even before they have been conveyed through the regular law-appointed organs."[46]

Like de Tocqueville and other nineteenth-century writers,[47] Lord Bryce recognized the decisive importance of class distinctions in limiting participation in public opinion, although he failed to appreciate the limiting influence upon public opinion exercised by pressure groups in the United States. He also lacked the perspicacity of de Tocqueville, who detected the threats to freedom of thought that public opinion in conditions of social equality presents. Reactionaries, romantics, Saint-Simonians, and Marxists attacked liberal convictions and threw doubt upon the morality, disinterestedness, and representativeness of middle-class opinions in the nineteenth century. They were not concerned, however, with freedom of thought; they contributed, in fact, to its modern decline. De Tocqueville, however, clearly saw that in "ages of equality" the liberation of the people from ignorance and prejudice by enlightenment may be purchased at the price of equalizing thought.

> There is, and I cannot repeat it too often, there is here matter for profound reflection to those who look upon freedom of thought as a holy thing and who hate not only the despot, but despotism. For myself, when I feel the hand of power lie heavy on my brow, I care but little to know who oppresses me; and I am not the more disposed to pass beneath the yoke because it is held out to me by the arms of millions of men.[48]

Perhaps the most wrathful condemnation of public opinion and its architects, the journalists, was advanced by Sören Kierkegaard. It shocked him deeply that a single person should be able every week or every day to get forty thousand or fifty thousand readers to speak or think like him.[49] His shock might have been cushioned, had he known that the ways men act – to judge by political elections in nineteenth-century Europe as well as twentieth-century America – do not necessarily reflect the preferences of the press they read.

Notes

1. Thomas Hobbes, *Leviathan*.
2. Hobbes, *Leviathan*.
3. For a discussion of secrecy in international negotiations versus secrecy of international agreements see, Harold Nicolson, *Diplomacy*

(London, 1939), and *Peacemaking 1919*, New York, 1939, pp. 123ff.

4. John Locke, "The Epistle to the Reader," in *An Essay Concerning Human Understanding*, ed. by A. C. Fraser, Oxford, 1894, vol. 1, p. 18. The italics are Locke's.

5. Ibid., book 2, chap. 28, section 12. My emphasis.

6. Montaigne, *Essays*, book 3, chap. 8.

7. *The Works of Sir William Temple: A New Edition*, London; 1814, vol. 1, pp. 6–7.

8. Ibid., vol. 3, p. 39.

9. Ibid., p. 44.

10. Rousseau regarded public opinion as "the standard of free society," but as questionable from a "transpolitical point of view." See Leo Strauss, "On the Intention of Rousseau," *Social Research* 14 (December 1947): 473.

11. J. Necker, *A Treatise on the Administration of the Finances of France*, 3rd ed., London, 1787, vol. 1, p. 17. The two best expositions of the treatment of "opinion" and "public opinion" by political theorists are Paul A. Palmer, "The Concept of Public Opinion in Political Theory," in *Essays in History and Political Theory in Honor of Charles H. McIlwain*, Cambridge, Mass., 1936, and Hermann Oncken, "Politik, Geschichtsschreibung und öffentliche Meinung," in *Historisch–politische Aufsätze und Reden*, Berlin and Munich, 1914, vol. 1, pp. 203–44. See also Wilhelm Hennis, "Zum Begriff der öffentlichen Meinung," in *Politik als praktische Wissenschaft*, Munich, 1968, pp. 36–48.

12. Cited from Soulavie's *Mémoires historiques*, in Ferdinand Tönnies, *Kritik der öffentlichen Meinung*, Berlin, 1922, p. 385.

13. Thomas Paine, *Rights of Man*, Modern Library edition, p. 141.

14. Lord Acton, "The Background of the French Revolution," reprinted in *Essays on Freedom and Power*, ed. by Gertrude Himmelfarb, Boston, 1948, p. 267.

15. Gaston Jèze, "Public Debt," in *Encyclopaedia of the Social Sciences*, vol. 12, p. 602. Cf. Thomas Paine's remark: "The French nation, in effect, endeavored to render the late government insolvent for the purpose of taking government into its own hands; and it reversed its means for the support of the new government." Paine, p. 175.

16. Necker, p. 54.

17. Ibid., p. 73.

18. August Wilhelm Rehberg, *Über die Staatsverwaltung deutscher Länder*, Hanover, 1809, p. 58.

19. Sören Kierkegaard, *Die Tagebücher*, selected and translated by Theodor Haecker, Innsbruck, 1923, vol. 2, p. 340.

20. See Charlotte E. Morgan, *The Rise of the English Novel of Manners*, New York, 1911; Leo Lowenthal, *Literature, Popular Culture and Society*, Englewood Cliffs, N.J., 1961; Martin Greiner, *Die Entstehung der modernen Unterhaltungsliteratur; Studien zum Trivialroman des 18. Jahrhunderts*, Hamburg, 1964.

21. Walter Götze, *Die Begründung der Volksbildung in der Aufklärungsbewegung*, Berlin and Leipzig, 1932, p. 64.

22. On the history of coffeehouses in England, see E. F. Robinson, *The Early History of Coffee Houses in England*, London, 1893; Ralph Nevill, *London Clubs: Their History and Treasures*, London, 1911; Hermann Westerfrölke, *Englishe Kaffeehäuser als Sammelpunkte der literarischen Welt im Zeitalter von Dryden und Addison*, Jena, 1924.

23. See Helen Clergue, *The Salon: A Story of French Society and Personalities in the Eighteenth Century*, New York and London, 1907; Erich Auerbach, *Das französische Publikum des XVII. Jahrhunderts*, Munich, 1933; Chauncey B. Tinker, *The Salon and English Letters*, New York, 1915; Conférences du Musée Carnavalet, *Les grands salons littéraires*, Paris, 1928.

24. Jean d'Alembert, *Miscellaneous Pieces in Literature, History and Philosophy*, London, 1764, p. 149.

25. As Aulard has pointed out, "It was by the political song, sung in the theatre, in the cafés and in the street, that the Royalists and Republicans succeeded, principally at Paris, in influencing the people," during the French Revolution. Quoted by Cornwall B. Rogers, *The Spirit of Revolution in 1789*, Princeton, N.J., 1949, p. 26. This book is a monographic study of the propagandistic importance of oral communication, especially lyrics, during the French Revolution.

26. Quoted by Howard Robinson, *The British Post Office*, Princeton, N.J., 1948, p. 302.

27. In chapter 13, Thomasius discussed the origin of error, distinguishing between the "prejudice of human authority" and "the prejudice of precipitation." See the reprint of this chapter as well as the equally relevant chap. 1 of Thomasius' *Ausübung der Sittenlehre* (1696), in F. Brüggemann, ed., *Aus der Frühzeit der deutschen Aufklärung*, Deutsche Literatur, Sammlung literarischer Kunst-und Kulturdenkmäler, Reihe Aufklärung, vol. 1, Berlin and Leipzig, 1928. For the relation between preducice and the demand for enlightening education, cf. especially Thomas Hobbes, *Elements of Law*, ed. by Ferdinand Tönnies, London, 1889: "The immediate cause ... of indocibility is prejudice, false opinion of our own knowledge" (I, 10, section 8), and *Leviathan*, chaps. 13 and 15.

28. Götze, p. 20

29. For a convenient summary of Condorcet's views on education contained in his "Report on Education," presented to the Legislative Assembly on April 20–21, 1792, see Salwyn Schapiro, *Condorcet*, New York, 1934, chap. 11, pp. 196–214. On the educational views of leading writers in the eighteenth century, see F. de la Fontainerie, ed., *French Liberalism and Education in the Eighteenth Century*, New York, 1932.

30. Sieyés, *The Third Estate*, chap. 6

31. According to Alexis de Tocqueville, the revolution "a considéré le citoyen d'une façon abstraite, en dehors de toutes les sociétés particulières, de même que les réligions considérent l'homme en général indépendamment du pays et du temps." *L'Ancien Régime et la Révolution*, 8th ed., Paris, 1877, p. 18.

32. Albert Mathiez, *The French Revolution*, New York, 1928, p. 217.
33. Corneliu S. Blaga, *L'Évolution de la technique diplomatique au dixbuitième siècle*, Paris, 1937, p. 421.
34. Edmund Burke, "Thoughts on French Affairs," in *Reflections on the French Revolution and Other Essays*, Everyman's Library edition, p. 289.
35. Quoted in Shelby C. Davis, *The French War Machine*, p. 100.
36. Max Lehmann, *Scharnhorst*, Leipzig, 1886, vol. 1, p. 323.
37. Hans Delbrück, *Geschichte der Kriegskunst*, Berlin, 1920, vol. 4, p. 469.
38. Ibid., p. 461.
39. Ibid., p. 479.
40. Quoted in W. Allison Hillet and Arthur H. Reede, *Neutrality*, vol. 2: *The Napoleonic Period*, New York, 1936, p. 8.
41. *British Historical and Political Orations from the 12th to the 20th Century*, Everyman's Library edition, pp. 146–48.
42. Nicolson, p. 73.
43. Bismarck, *Memoirs*, vol. 3, p. 157.
44. The Benthamites did not share the belief in natural rights. Bentham had deplored the Declaration of Rights in France because he regarded them as metaphysical and did not believe that political science was far enough advanced for such declarations. Cf. A. V. Dicey, *Law and Opinion in England*, New York, 1930, p. 145, n. 1.
45. Lord Bryce, *The American Commonwealth*, New York, 1919, vol. 2, p. 260.
46. Ibid., p. 257.
47. Thus Bluntschli in his *Staatswörterbuch* (1862), said of public opinion that "it is predominantly the opinion of the large middle class." This notion was predicated upon the conviction that public opinion was a matter of free judgment. "Without training of the reasoning power and the capacity to judge there is, therefore, no public opinion." For the same reason, Bluntschli observed that public opinion is possible in political matters but alien to religious piety (*Ergriffenheit*). Cf. Oncken, pp. 229ff.
48. Alexis de Tocqueville, *Democracy in America*, New York, 1948, vol. 2, pp. 11–12.
49. *Kierkegaard in 1849*; cf. *Kierkegaard*, vol. 2, p. 37.

3 The Phantom Public*
Walter Lippmann

The private citizen today has come to feel rather like a deaf spectator in the back row, who ought to keep his mind on the mystery off there [on the stage], but cannot quite manage to keep awake. He knows he is somehow affected by what is going on. Rules and regulations continually, taxes annually and wars occasionally remind him that he is being swept along by great drifts of circumstance.

Yet these public affairs are in no convincing way his affairs. They are for the most part invisible. They are managed, if they are managed at all, at distant centers, from behind the scenes, by unnamed powers. As a private person he does not know for certain what is going on, or who is doing it, or where he is being carried. No newspaper reports his environment so that he can grasp it; no school has taught him how to imagine it; his ideals, often, do not fit with it; listening to speeches, uttering opinions and voting do not, he finds, enable him to govern it. He lives in a world he cannot see, does not understand and is unable to direct.

In the cold light of experience he knows that his sovereignty is a fiction. He reigns in theory, but in fact he does not govern. When, during an agitation of some sort, say a political campaign, he hears himself and some thirty million others described as the source of all wisdom and power and righteousness, the prime mover and the ultimate goal, the remnants of sanity in him protest. He cannot all the time play Chanticleer who was so dazzled and delighted because he himself had caused the sun to rise.

For when the private man has lived through the romantic age in politics and is no longer moved by the stale echoes of its hot cries, when he is sober and unimpressed, his own part in public affairs appears to him a pretentious

* Reprinted from Walter Lippmann, *The Phantom Public* (London: Macmillan, 1925).

thing, a second rate, an inconsequential. You cannot move him then with a good straight talk about service and civic duty, nor by waving a flag in his face, nor by sending a boy scout after him to make him vote. He is a man back home from a crusade to make the world something or other it did not become; he has been tantalized too often by the foam of events, [and] has seen the gas go out of it . . . .

[B]y their occasional mobilizations as a majority, people support or oppose the individuals who actually govern. We must say that the popular will does not direct continuously but that it intervenes occasionally.

The action of a public . . . is principally confined to an occasional intervention in affairs by means of an alignment of the force a dominant section of that public can wield. We must assume, then, that the members of a public will not possess an insider's knowledge of events or share his point of view. They cannot, therefore, construe intent, or appraise the exact circumstances, enter intimately into the minds of the actors or into the details of the argument. They can watch only for coarse signs indicating where their sympathies ought to turn.

We must assume that the members of a public will not anticipate a problem much before its crisis has become obvious, nor stay with the problem long after its crisis is past. They will not know the antecedent events, will not have seen the issue as it developed, will not have thought out or willed a program, and will not be able to predict the consequences of acting on that program. We must assume as a theoretically fixed premise of popular government that normally men as members of a public will not be well informed, continuously interested, nonpartisan, creative or executive. We must assume that a public is inexpert in its curiosity, intermittent, that it discerns only gross distinctions, is slow to be aroused and quickly diverted; that, since it acts by aligning itself, it personalizes whatever it considers, and is interested only when events have been melodramatized as a conflict.

The public will arrive in the middle of the third act and will leave before the last curtain, having stayed just long enough perhaps to decide who is the hero and who the villain of the piece. Yet usually that judgment will necessarily be made apart from the intrinsic merits, on the basis of a sample of behavior, an aspect of a situation, by very rough external evidence.

We cannot, then, think of public opinion as a conserving or creating force directing society to clearly conceived ends, making deliberately toward socialism or away from it, toward nationalism, an empire, a league of nations or any other doctrinal goal. For men do not agree as to their aims, and it is precisely the lack of agreement that creates the problems that excite public attention. It is idle, then, to argue that though men evidently have conflicting purposes, mankind has some all-embracing purpose of which you or I happen to be the authorized spokesman. We merely should have moved in a circle were we to conclude that the public is in some deep way a messianic force.

The work of the world goes on continually without conscious direction from public opinion. At certain junctures problems arise. It is only with the crises of some of these problems that public opinion is concerned. And its object in dealing with a crisis is to help allay that crisis.

I think this conclusion is unescapable. For though we may prefer to believe that the aim of popular action should be to do justice or promote the true, the beautiful and the good, the belief will not maintain itself in the face of plain experience. The public does not know in most crises what specifically is the truth or the justice of the case, and men are not agreed on what is beautiful and good. Nor does the public rouse itself normally at the existence of evil. It is aroused at evil made manifest by the interruption of a habitual process of life. And finally, a problem ceases to occupy attention not when justice, as we happen to define it, has been done but when a workable adjustment that overcomes the crisis has been made. If all this were not the necessary manner of public opinion, if it had seriously to crusade for justice in every issue it touches, the public would have to be dealing with all situations all the time. That is impossible. It is also undesirable. For did justice, truth, goodness and beauty depend on the spasmodic and crude interventions of public opinion there would be little hope for them in this world.

Thus we strip public opinion of any implied duty to deal with the substance of a problem, to make technical decisions, to attempt justice or impose a moral precept. And instead we say that the ideal of public opinion is to align men during the crisis of a problem in such a way as to favor the action of those individuals who may be able to compose the crisis. The power to discern those individuals is the end of the effort to educate public opinion. The aim of research designed to facilitate public action is the discovery of clear signs by which these individuals may be discerned.

The signs are relevant when they reveal by coarse, simple and objective tests which side in a controversy upholds a workable social rule, or which is attacking an unworkable rule, or which proposes a promising new rule. By following such signs the public might know where to align itself. In such an alignment it does not, let us remember, pass judgment on the intrinsic merits. It merely places its force at the disposal of the side that, according to objective signs, seems to be standing for human adjustments according to a clear rule of behavior and against the side that appears to stand for settlement in accordance with its own unaccountable will.

Public opinion, in this theory, is a reserve of force brought into action during a crisis in public affairs. Though it is itself an irrational force, under favorable institutions, sound leadership and decent training the power of public opinion might be placed at the disposal of those who stood for workable law as against brute assertion. In this theory, public opinion does not make the law. But by canceling lawless power it may establish the condition under which law can be made. It does not reason, investigate, invent, persuade, bargain or settle. But, by holding the aggressive party in check, it may liberate intelligence. Public opinion in its highest ideal will defend those who are prepared to act on their reason against the interrupting force of those who merely assert their will.

The action of public opinion at its best would not, let it be noted, be a continual crusade on behalf of reason. When power, however absolute and unaccountable, reigns without provoking a crisis, public opinion does not challenge it. Somebody must challenge arbitrary power first. The public can only come to his assistance.

That, I think, is the utmost that public opinion can effectively do. With the substance of the problem it can do nothing usually but meddle ignorantly or tyrannically. It has no need to meddle with it. Men in their active relation to affairs have to deal with the substance, but in that indirect relationship when they can act only through uttering praise or blame, making black crosses on white paper, they have done enough, they have done all they can do if they help to make it possible for the reason of other men to assert itself.

For when public opinion attempts to govern directly it is either a failure or a tyranny. It is not able to master the problem intellectually, nor to deal with it except by wholesale impact. The theory of democracy has not recognized this truth because it has identified the functioning of government with the will of the people. This is a fiction. The intricate business of framing laws and of administering them through several hundred thousand public officials is in no sense the act of the voters nor a translation of their will.

But although the acts of government are not a translation of public opinion, the principal function of government is to do specifically, in greater detail, and more continually what public opinion does crudely, by wholesale, and spasmodically. It enforces some of the working rules of society. It interprets them. It detects and punishes certain kinds of aggression. It presides over the framing of new rules. It has organized force that is used to counteract irregular force.

It is also subject to the same corruption as public opinion. For when government attempts to impose the will of its officials, instead of intervening so as to steady adjustments by consent among the parties directly interested, it becomes heavy-handed, stupid, imperious, even predatory. For the public official, though he is better placed to understand the problem than a reader of newspapers, and though he is much better able to act, is still fundamentally external to the real problems in which he intervenes. Being external, his point of view is indirect, and so his action is most appropriate when it is confined to rendering indirect assistance to those who are directly responsible.

Therefore, instead of describing government as an expression of the people's will, it would seem better to say that government consists of a body of officials, some elected, some appointed, who handle professionally, and in the first instance, problems that come to public opinion spasmodically and on appeal. Where the parties directly responsible do not work out an adjustment, public officials intervene. When the officials fail, public opinion is brought to bear on the issue.

This, then, is the ideal of public action that our inquiry suggests. Those who happen in any question to constitute the public should attempt only to create an equilibrium in which settlements can be reached directly and by consent. The burden of carrying on the work of the world, of inventing, creating, executing, of attempting justice, formulating laws and moral codes, of dealing with the technic and the substance, lies not upon public opinion and not upon government but on those who are responsibly concerned as agents in the affair. Where problems arise, the ideal is a settlement by the particular interests involved. They alone know what the trouble really is. No decision by public officials or by commuters reading headlines in the train can usually and in the long run be so good as settlement by consent among the parties at interest. No moral code, no political theory can usually and in the long run be imposed from the heights of public opinion, which will fit a case so well as direct agreement reached where arbitrary power has been disarmed.

It is the function of public opinion to check the use of force in a crisis, so that men, driven to make terms, may live and let live.

Democracy... has never developed an education for the public. It has merely given it a smattering of the kind of knowledge the responsible man requires. It has, in fact, aimed not at making good citizens but at making a mass of amateur executives. It has not taught the child how to act as a member of the public. It has merely given him a hasty, incomplete taste of what he might have to know if he meddled in everything. The result is a bewildered public and a mass of insufficiently trained officials. The responsible men have obtained their training not from the courses in "civics" but in the law schools and law offices and in business. The public at large, which includes everybody outside the field of his own responsible knowledge, has had no coherent political training of any kind. Our civic education does not even begin to tell the voter how he can reduce the maze of public affairs to some intelligible form.

Critics have not been lacking, of course, who pointed out what a hash democracy was making of its pretensions to government. These critics have seen that the important decisions were taken by individuals, and that public opinion was uninformed, irrelevant and meddlesome. They have usually concluded that there was a congenital difference between the masterful few and the ignorant many. They are the victims of a superficial analysis of the evils they see so clearly.

The fundamental difference that matters is that between insiders and outsiders. Their relations to a problem are radically different. Only the insider can make decisions, not because he is inherently a better man but because he is so placed that he can understand and can act. The outsider is necessarily ignorant, usually irrelevant and often meddlesome, because he is trying to navigate the ship from dry land. That is why excellent automobile manufacturers, literary critics and scientists often talk such nonsense about politics. Their congenital excellence, if it exists, reveals itself only in their own activity. The aristocratic theorists work from the fallacy of supposing that a sufficiently excellent square peg will also fit a round hole. In short, like the democratic theorists, they miss the essence of the matter, which is, that competence exists only in relation to function; that men are not good, but good for something; that men cannot be educated, but only educated for something.

Education for citizenship, for membership in the public, ought, therefore, to be distinct from education for public office. Citizenship involves a radically different relation to affairs, requires different intellectual habits and different methods of action. The force of public opinion is partisan, spasmodic, simple-minded and external.

4 Towards a Sociology of Expertness[*]

Israel Gerver and Joseph Bensman

In all societies the quality of expertness (virtuosity in the application of institutionalized skills) is highly valued and eagerly sought. Objectively, expertness is the quality of those who possess highly developed skills and techniques in any given field of activity. Such skills and techniques are consciously known and can be transmitted to others. As a social phenomenon this objective aspect of expertness is only a point of departure for the sociological analysis of expertness and experts. Objective expertness is given social recognition which takes the forms of prestige and esteem valuations and income possibilities. In part the social rewards for expertness are related to the operations of social institutions and in part these rewards are related to the claims to expertness put forth by diverse groups.

The relationship between *objective* and *socially recognized* expertness are not simple ones. For example, groups receiving high status may retain such status even in periods where the institutional bases for their skills have disappeared.[1] Conversely groups of experts may have objectively ascertainable skills but lack social recognition. To further complicate the picture, spurious expertness, e.g., groups lacking skills but claiming social recognition, is another possibility.[2]

Expert status is granted or denied by public acceptance or rejection of claims. In a society where ascriptive criteria are emphasized, the public designation of experts is fairly easy. In an open class society, the public selection of experts and the criteria of expertness are more difficult. The difficulties arise because vast segments of the population are unfamiliar with objective expert skills, unfamiliar with

---

[*] Reprinted from *Social Forces*, vol. 32 (March 1954).

the operations of major social institutions, and therefore unable to evaluate and select experts and criteria of expertness with reference to the requirements of institutional operations.

Thus in complex societies the term "expert" includes a range of real experts, pseudo experts, socially recognized and unrecognized experts, and various combinations of these. Such a heterogeneous mixture implies confusion by the public between the objective and socially recognized expertness. It is this public confusion which provides the basis for the following analysis. That is to say, it is, on the "common-sense" level, paradoxical that as knowledge is ordered and reduced to objectively known techniques, these techniques become more developed and inaccessible to the public at large.

ELABORATION OF CONCEPTS

Historically, the rise of the expert as someone tending to monopolize skills is associated with the development of intricate techniques in a society within which experts have demonstrated socially valuable results of their efforts.[3] Experts do not arrive in a society spontaneously, but are the result of a complex process of institutional development, claims for recognition as experts, and the granting of social recognition by strategic groups.

A significant element in this granting of recognition is the *social visibility* of those claiming expertness and the *social distance* of the conferring groups from the alleged experts.[4] The more distant groups, i.e., those least technically qualified, grant recognition which is based not on a knowledge of expert procedures, methods and information, but instead upon the imputed consequences of expert action. Thus, recognition of expertness carries with it the conferring of prestige.

The procedures and methods of the expert are viewed by the distant lay person as a form of magic. The imputed results of expert action are the results which *appear* to be observable to the distant lay person. The results *actually* observed at a more intimate level, i.e., by other experts,

Towards a Sociology of Expertness

Table 1. Aspects of Expertness

Conferring groups	Criteria of recognition	
	Technical knowledge	*Non-technical knowledge*
In-group	Substantive	Administrative
Out-group	Interpretive	Symbolic

would be assigned to other factors by the particular experts in question. Among peers the expert is granted recognition as expert, less because of results but more with reference to scientific, technical, and procedural competence. Such esteem is not, of course, necessarily congruent with the prestige accruing from out-group evaluation.

The recognition of expertise, then, will vary with the social distance of conferring groups, and their criteria of recognition.[5] When these elements are analyzed, it can be seen that experts are socially recognized in terms of four different possibilities which can be viewed as aspects of expertness found in large scale organizations.[6] (See Table 1.)

Substantive aspects. This aspect, deriving from the dual relationship of a relevant in-group and their criteria of judging expert peers, implies technical virtuosity per se. This means that the substantive aspect of the expert is known fully only to those who possess the requisite knowledge, and thus are in a sufficiently close position to evaluate the operations of others with reference to their possession of techniques, theoretical and empirical knowledge for any given specialized field.

Administrative aspect. This refers to the judgments of the in-group with reference to their selection and evaluation of others who are not practising as substantive experts. However, those viewed under this aspect can communicate with substantive experts, possibly because the administrator may have been trained as a substantive expert. A typical example of what we have in mind in distinguishing the administrative and substantive aspects would be the hospital administrator who is also an M.D. The administrative aspect refers to those experts who coordinate, facilitate, recruit, and arrange the activities of other experts in a formal association in order to execute agreed-upon policies.

Interpretive Aspect. The expert viewed in this manner performs the procedures of negotiating, communicating, translating, and making comprehensible the mysteries of substantive knowledge to the distant and lay public. His expert stature is granted by the laymen, whereas the substantive experts devalue him as a popularizer at best and a vulgarizer at worst. He may be attached to an organization, or he may be in a semi-autonomous position. He is usually not a practising substantive expert for reasons that will be apparent in a later section of this paper.[7]

Symbolic Aspect. Here we deal with those individuals or groups who personify and symbolize expertness in any given complex field for the uninitiated public. However, symbolic experts may personify complexities not only for the distant public, but also for insiders under conditions which are sufficiently complex so that these complexities cannot be understood exclusively and immediately in terms of direct participant experience. For example, an Einstein will symbolize the expert physicist to all in- and out-group members, except perhaps to those who are his peers. However, Einstein is not merely a *self-selected* symbol of expertise; he is a practising substantive expert. In many fields of endeavor the symbolic expert is not actually a substantive expert but appears to be one. The symbolic expert is not necessarily a particular living person but may be a complex of traditional evaluations and definitions which become personified. The history of artistic taste provides numerous examples, such as the evaluations at later times of Rembrandt, Beethoven, Bach, Van Gogh. In science the names of Copernicus and Galileo exemplify the strength of non-living symbols.

These four aspects represent a formulation of the ever-present dilemma of all mass organizations: namely, the problem of simultaneously presenting a favorable image to the public in response to its demands and maintaining the integrity and coherency of the organization. The successful large-scale organization expresses both objectives by orienting the substantive and administrative aspects towards the internal organizational structure, while the symbolic and interpretive aspects are directed towards the rest of the society.

PERSPECTIVES OF EXPERTS

In large-scale organizations these aspects of expertness become recognized and embodied in tables of formal organization.[8] One result of this formal recognition is the segmentation of expert aspects and a tendency towards polarization into expert role types, e.g., *the administrator, the researcher.* While polarization is never actually complete, the assumption that it is complete becomes an heuristic device for the analysis of tensions resulting from differential perspectives of the corresponding expert types. These tensions affect not only particular experts within a given organization but also have consequences for the total organization.

This means that different expert types become preoccupied with different types of problems, e.g., pure research, dealing with the outside public, coordinating formal divisions within an organization, etc. Out of these different problems, each type of expert develops different perspectives corresponding to the peculiarities of his preoccupations. The discussion at this point will concentrate on divergencies of other types from the perspectives of the substantive expert.

The substantive expert is interested most typically in increasing and enlarging the scope of the available knowledge in his field. This means that he is also interested in developing techniques, procedures, and means of making his conceptual schemes more explicit and verifiable.[9] In the role of substantive expert his strategic public consists of other substantive experts and his communications are directed to them. He is not primarily interested in communicating with the general public, and indeed may become increasingly removed from non-experts. Thus, his field of substantive knowledge will appear to distant lay persons increasingly mysterious and incomprehensible as he pursues his demons.[10]

Costs and organizational arrangements interest the substantive expert only insofar as they impinge upon or interfere with his major preoccupations. He is only peripherally interested in the consequences of his results for non-experts, and for the administrative, symbolic, and interpretive types of experts within his own organization. The results expected by others from the practise of his expertness in his job do, however, provide an opportunity for him to develop basic substantive additions to his knowledge.

In contradistinction, the administrative expert aims for efficient means of obtaining organizationally defined practical results. He is interested in minimizing costs, stabilizing and routinizing the flow of operations, and coordinating diverse types of substantive expert activity with the activities of non-experts. The primary concerns of the administrative type are of secondary concern and even irritations to the substantive expert, and vice versa. However, the administrative type may provide a favorable protective strata for the substantive expert and relieve him of extraneous problems of organizational routine. From the viewpoint of the substantive expert, the best administrator is one who takes organizational tasks off his hands, e.g., equipment, supplies, budgetary appropriations, and does not press him for "results" or interfere in his major activities.

Similarly the interpretive and symbolic experts focus on results, i.e., "visible results." The *pure* symbolic type, one who is not a substantive expert as well, is interested in the results but not primarily in the procedures for obtaining them. He symbolizes these results in his role of public representative of a large-scale organization. The interpretive expert who is attached to the organization publicizes the results and creates and maintains the symbolic expert. Both emphasize the magic of scientific technique to the public at large. Both are likely to pressure the substantive experts for publicly demonstrable results, and both are more likely to announce these results before the substantive expert would do so.[11] Such a tendency may be checked by the administrative and substantive experts. The substantive experts tend to be ambivalent towards the symbolic and interpretive types. They can raise the prestige level of expert fields, but may do so by means which are viewed as unwarranted and occasionally reprehensible. Generally the substantive expert views the symbolic and interpretive group as amateurs in the grossest sense.

Typically one can find divisions and conflicts within organizations on the bases of these differing perspectives; but, given these differences, some degree of conflict is intrinsic to complex organization. To the uninitiated this situation is viewed with surprise and alarm. However, conflicts do become real problems when they threaten the effective operation of the organization or imperil the status holders within it.

These differences in perspective not only can account for periodic organizational disruptions but can lead to interesting consequences for the substantive expert as he incorporates the views of others into his own perspective.[12]

No *actual* substantive expert *completely* corresponds to the model previously drawn. As an individual dealing with non-experts, he becomes a symbol of the field for them and is expected to act as a symbol of his profession. In his relationships with administrators, institutionalized symbols, and communicators, the substantive expert is expected to respond to their definitions of his role. To complicate matters further, he also may act in terms of a prior self-image of scientist, professional, and scholar.

Given this plurality of expectations of others and his own occupational standards, the substantive expert may view these expectations as a series of alternative choices. Actually his responses are further limited by his set of personal value preferences which makes the rewards of alternative choices meaningful.[13] In his responses to non-scientific expectations, he may (1) reject behavior which is inconsistent with his image of the scientist; (2) compartmentalize his behavioral responses into work and non-work spheres or public and private patterns, thereby rendering unto Caesar what is Caesar's; or (3) define the situation in its immediacy and act accordingly, thereby responding to the strongest pressures. In this case his behavior does not reflect any particular perspective. Psychologically the long run cost of such segmental behavior is very great. In this case he ceases to be exclusively a substantive expert and acts as if he were a calculating opportunist. He may even become an unwitting instrumentality for achieving the goals of others. In order to minimize conflicts resulting from divergencies between his perspective and external demands, the substantive expert has to respond in the long run to that set of external demands which is most consistent with his own core values and occupational ethos. The rewards for such selective behavior partially determine the pattern of his mobility.

DIVERGENT PERSPECTIVES AND CAREER MOBILITY

In modern large-scale industry, expertise becomes the basis of mobility for the substantive expert into non-substantive positions. Expertise can be an entry point or a necessary requirement for a large number of status positions. Mobility involves the possession of skills of high order and shifts in type of expert perspectives. If these changes are either great or rapid, psychological tensions may result.[14] Tensions among those who shift perspectives or who simultaneously adhere to different perspectives are normal psychological concomitants of institutionalized mobility patterns.[15]

Keeping in mind the roughly drawn differences in perspectives of our four types of expert, we can now focus on the consequences of shifting career, i.e., what can and does occur when, for example, the substantive expert in his mobile career turns into one of the other types?

The substantive expert, when he moves to another position in an organization, is forced to some extent to abandon his original perspective. The requirements of an administrative position, for example, demand a re-focusing and re-orientation of the canons of the disinterested seeker after truth.[16] At the same time the substantive expert retains in part a perspective which has been basic to his professional training and development. There exists in such situations a potential conflict within the mobile expert. Mobility is made difficult by the existence within an expert of these divergent perspectives. If the mobile expert persists in retaining completely the initial substantive ethos, he will be hampered in his administrative duties. If he adopts the administrative experts' perspective, he may feel guilty of abandoning what to him and his formerly significant public is a primary ethos. This can further result in insecurity in his relationships with those experts who still practise their professions. This is especially true, because substantive experts viewing the organization from their special standards are apt to see other expert types as derivative incompetents or restrictive agents, who take credit for substantive work which they both hinder and misunderstand. Thus in all bureaucracies there is a myth that incompetence leads to advancement, e.g., the usage of terms like "kicked upstairs," and other terms in common usage, but usually unprintable.

Similarly such conflicts may arise within the substantive expert who becomes a symbolic or interpretive expert by his own choice. To justify his new symbolic position, the self-selected symbolic expert must increasingly abandon his old ethos and replace it with a symbolic perspective which is congruent with the public's image of his new role. This does not apply of course to the *other-selected* symbolic expert who still is a practising substantive expert—e.g., Einstein, Toscanini, or, in his own time, Darwin. Conspicuous examples of self-selected symbolic experts who abandoned their substantive roles are numerous. Hindenburg and Petain might be conceived of in this way; or in music, Giacomo Rossini; in literature, Alexander Dumas *père*; in painting, Salvador Dali. In the latter instance Dali, while still producing, has selected himself to symbolize surrealism. He secures his expert stature not only by virtue of his accumulated technical perfection but also by behavior which is admitted charlatanry. Dali exemplifies a case of charlatanry which has become a field of expertness. Thus Dali is also a self-selected and self-admitted symbol of charlatanry.[17] Contemporary examples of the self-selected symbolic expert moving from substantive stature can be found in almost all large-scale business, educational, and political institutions.

In order to appeal to the public image, the symbolic expert as head of an operating organization continuously demands "visible results" from substantive experts and claims these results easily in order to legitimize securely his new position. The substantive expert who becomes an interpretive expert may experience similar tensions if he relinquishes his substantive role entirely.

INSTITUTIONAL DETERMINANTS OF EXPERTNESS

The responses to mobility situations, the discrepancies between public and self-images of experts and expertise, the proliferation and divergency of expert perspectives, are not only significant in and of themselves; they attain a broader meaning when viewed in a context of institutional changes. Indeed the dynamics of expertness can also be fruitfully viewed as indicators of changes in the larger society.

The following institutional elements are postulated as conditions for the existence of differentiated expertise: (1) the development of scientific technology with a history of demonstrable results requiring (2) an ever-increasing social division of labor and (3) an ever-increasing segmentation of work tasks occurring as part of (4) the rise of bureaucratic organization based on a rational and "firmly ordered system of super- and subordination," resulting in (5) the physical and social alienation of individuals from others in organizations and from organizations as entities.[18]

The significance of points 1–5 rests upon the technical superiority of bureaucratic organization over other forms and from the resultant absorption of the working force and the rest of society into bureaucratic procedures.[19]

This dominance of society by bureaucracies is not a smooth process and produces resistance; when *scientific technology* (i.e., substantive expertise) becomes ordered by *scientific organization* (i.e., administrative expertise), conflicts between the two become the basis for ideological conflicts. This "silent warfare" of opposing myths has not the spectacular pyrotechnic of "the class struggle," but it is probably as basic in bureaucratic societies. This is not a case of ideology and utopia but rather the frequently overlooked conflict between two conservative vested interest groups.[20]

EXPERTNESS AND LEGITIMACY

Historically, substantive experts have received and taken credit for additions to knowledge and demonstrated practical results. They have also received a high degree of prestige resulting, as previously noted, from achievements not thoroughly understood by the out-group but nevertheless recognized as valuable achievements. Thus substantive experts in our society, especially in fields of work clearly recognized as part of science, are traditionally legitimized. Other groups aspiring to the heights of expertise borrow the halo of science, e.g., scientific salesmanship, advertising, social welfare, scientifically designed toothpaste, breakfast cereals; indeed the whole paraphernalia of science–terminology, equipment, and furnishings–are all used to capitalize on the prestige of scientific expertness. This is apparent even in fields where scientific concepts and techniques are either primitive or nonexistent.[21]

Given this halo of science, the administrative expert who controls the organizational structures employing the substantive expert is in an anomalous position. He is confronted with the stupendous monopolization of accrued legitimacy by science and at the same time is forced to pay homage to science. The administrator's problem in view of his *dominant* position as an official of a bureaucracy is to achieve legitimacy for his position. His problem is especially complicated because the established legitimacy of his subordinates is a barrier to his own. Three possibilities exist, the first of which–the rejection of science–can be usually ruled out.

An outright rejection of science would be tantamount to occupational suicide by the administrator. Non-administrative groups, e.g. the *literati*, may in effect reject science by a romantic affirmation of a nonexistent past. The administrator can, however, attack a particular version of science as being an erroneous distortion of true science. If he is successful, he can substitute his preferred version of science.

The second possibility is to borrow the halo of science and confer it on administration. One way of doing this and gaining public consent is to equate scientific and administrative aspects of an organization and present the total organization to the public as a *scientific organization*.[22] Administrative aspects are easily concealed from the public because of social distance and the complexity of the phenomena. The bureaucratic ethos and ethic[23] is one of concealing internal administration and political arrangements from the public.[24] Both symbolic and attached interpretive experts are instruments for his transvaluation of an organization.[25]

The third method of achieving legitimacy is to create and present administration as a science in its own right—thus the vogues of scientific management, business, and public administration found in contemporary university curricula and in some of the intellectually oriented business organizations. The literature on the application of science to all types of administration has reached monumental proportions and constitutes a growing portion of the behavior sciences. A quasi-scientific undergraduate education is assumed to be a requirement for those aspiring to administrative positions. This development has been fostered by the schools and supported by both businessmen and public administrators.

Both the development of administration as a science and the equating of science and administration within organizations are neither mutually exclusive nor contradictory. The latter is practised by the hard-boiled and non-theoretical working administrator, while the former is the concern of university business schools and intellectuals in business and politics.

EXPERTNESS AND ORGANIZATIONAL POWER[26]

Through time, experts increasingly develop prestige and legitimacy. However, the power and prestige of an individual expert worker (apart from the symbolic personalities) decrease. As any substantive field of expertise increases in prestige, larger numbers of workers are attracted to the field. This growth of an occupational population decreases the indispensability of any *particular* member of that segment of the labor force, making the individual worker more replaceable and interchangeable.[27]

The consequences of the inconsistency between the legitimacy and power of administrators in bureaucratic societies are equally important for the substantive experts. As the substantive field expands in knowledge, concepts, and techniques, specialized fields emerge. As specialists flood into these newer branches, the generalized type of substantive expert tends to disappear from the occupation and can possibly remain as a symbol of the general field. At the work level, only a bureaucracy has the apparatus to handle rationally this proliferation of substantive expertise. The specialists develop narrower perspectives which hamper them in attaining positions within the substantive framework which would permit them to comprehend the larger field of knowledge, work, and organizational context as a totality.[28]

The specialized substantive expert confronted with the omnipresence of bureaucracy is not in a position to deal with it as a totality. Only the higher administrative expert and some of the self-selected symbolic experts can approach such comprehension. Since the substantive specialist cannot deal with organizations as a totality, he is relatively powerless.[29]

The affiliation of the specialized expert with a substantive field which has publicly recognized legitimacy intensifies this quixotic position. The attainment of power for the individual specialist in a bureaucratic setting is made difficult because he is now a specialist and more isolated than the older style substantive expert; he is devalued because he is more subject to manipulation by non-substantive experts; his vulnerability to manipulation is therefore a dual function of his overspecialization and his interchangeability.[30]

Viewed then in the larger historical sense, expertise increasingly develops prestige and legitimacy, but the power and prestige of the individual working expert decrease.

In a bureaucracy the substantive "specialist" expert consequently becomes resentful because his power position is not consistent with his traditional legitimacy. When in addition administrative and symbolic experts borrow his prestige halo and identify it with the organization generally and themselves in particular, moral indignation then achieves its highest level. All the frustrations and resentments developing in fragmented perspectives, isolation, mobility, and powerlessness reach their zenith.

THE INDEPENDENT PROFESSIONAL[31]

The major trends in the development of bureaucratized expertise become pointed in the contemporary difference between the employed and free professional. The special characteristic of the substantive expert who is not employed in a bureaucracy is that he is simultaneously a substantive expert, an administrative expert, and a symbolic figure. Because he is in direct and continuous contact with large numbers of clients, he is viewed as a symbol of the profession and is likely to accept this role and adopt a symbolic perspective. This means that he might exaggerate and emphasize the mystery and magic of his expertness before the uninitiated. As an interpreter he is likely to mix this aspect with his symbolic role. He is also an administrator though relatively little administration is required.

In contradistinction to the bureaucratized expert, the free professional is therefore not oriented towards administrative goals, is not isolated from the public, and is not merely a functionnaire. Instead, all of the separate aspects of the bureaucratized types of experts are integrated into a series of interlocking roles expressed by one person.[32]

What is central to the development of bureaucratized expertness is the separation of roles. Hierarchical and functional integration is emphasized at an organizational level rather than at a personal one. Complexity in social relations is introduced. The public becomes increasingly distant from the administrative and substantive aspects of work and is presented with symbols of organization especially manufactured by interpretive and symbolic experts. Thus a halo of science, efficiency, service, and results is associated with bureaucratic organization for the purposes of those who control it. In common parlance this is known as "public relations" both in its broadest and narrowest sense.

THE COLLAPSE OF SOCIALLY OBJECTIVE REALITY

Because of the alienation of all groups from the actual technical workings of bureaucracy, no single group can judge it from firsthand experience.[33] This is especially true of the distant public. Given increasing role-segmentation, any particular person's experience is relatively valueless as a guide to the comprehension of the experiences of a differentiated complex society. In other words, personal experience does not provide sufficient reference points for the understanding of public affairs.[34] Publicly recognized symbolic systems become increasingly devoid of content and more and more become synthetic substitutes for genuine expressions of experience.

In addition, these synthetic substitutes have little coherency. One reason is the existence of pluralities of vested interest groups and concomitantly a plurality of competing symbol manufacturers. Thus there is no single, integrated, coherent symbolic system which can organize experience. One consequence of this situation is public apathy.[35] Apathy, however, alternates with a rejection of one's own personal experience and a romanticizing of either the past or some not too far distant utopia.[36]

The fragmentation of expertise represents the fragmentation of social experience in an incomprehensible society.[37]

The social scientist is in a unique position in confronting the problems posed here. The very nature of his expertness enables him to go beyond the symbols and analyze the experiential basis of social existence. At the same time his technical virtuosity enables him, if he wishes, to assist in the manufacture and manipulation of symbols or in preparing the ground for symbol manufacturers and manipulators.[38] In a bureaucratic world, power holders can grant him prestige, employability, income, illusion of power and authority if he can demonstrate results. If the latter course is followed, social science can assist in the collapse of reality and the devaluation of experience.[39]

CONCLUSIONS

One relationship between objectively defined expertness and socially claimed and recognized expertness is generally understood by expert groups. In a society where symbolic expressions of reality are emphasized and the underlying experiential reality is devalued, the achievements of experts who manipulate symbols–i.e., the interpretive type and the achievements of those who personify and symbolize a field–transcend the objective skills and techniques associated with an occupation. The attainment of expert status thereby becomes equated with successful public relations. The measure of expertness then is increasingly the extent to which publicizing "leads" to social acceptance.

In bureaucratic settings experts can rarely publicize themselves. As already noted, substantive expertness is often co-opted and publicly presented as an organizational attribute. The net effect, though not necessarily the intention, is that the individual substantive expert in such a situation can usually only publicize the bureaucracy.[40]
Immediately perceivable social reality becomes a chaos of opposing myths and symbolic systems, and the experiential basis of this chaos is relatively inaccessible. As a result the *"real"* world is a public relations world, that is, one of claims and counterclaims by different types of experts and different organizations. Only a few are able to confront this public relations world with their limited experience. The majority cannot find expression for their immediate experience in publicly accessible symbolic systems. They therefore must either retreat into a fantasy or personalized world and reject the public affairs world, or–as is more commonly the case–they passively accept or compulsively affirm particular authoritative pronouncements on the mysterious, incomprehensible world about them.

Notes

1. A. Vidich, "Social Structure of Palau" (unpublished doctoral dissertation, Harvard University, 1952).
2. G. De Francesco, *The Power of the Charlatan* (New Haven: Yale University Press, 1939).
3. T. Parsons, *Essays in Sociological Theory Pure and Applied* (Glencoe, Illinois: The Free Press, 1949), chap. VIII, "The Professions and Social Structure": "This professional authority has a peculiar sociological structure. It is not as such based on generally superior status . . . . It is rather based on the superior 'technical competence' of the professional man . . . A professional man is held to be 'an authority' only in his own field." (p. 189)
4. W. Lippmann, *The Phantom Public* (New York: Harcourt, Brace and Company, 1925): "Modern society is not visible to anybody, nor intelligible continuously and as a whole. One section is visible to another section, one series of acts is intelligible to this group and another to that." (p. 42)
5. Ibid.: "The specific, technical, intimate criteria required in the handling of a question are not for the public. The public's criteria are generalized for many problems; they turn essentially on procedure and the overt, external forms of behavior." (p. 144)

6. Ibid.: "The fundamental difference which matters is that between insiders and outsiders. Their relations to a problem are radically different. Only the insider can make decisions, not because he is inherently a better man, but because he is so placed that he can understand and can act. The outsider is necessarily ignorant, usually irrelevant and often meddlesome, because he is trying to navigate the ship from dry land." (p. 150)

7. A. M. Lee, "Public Relations Counseling as Institutional Psychiatry," *Psychiatry*, vol. VI (August 1943), p. 272 (quoting J. P. Jones and D. McL. Church, *At the Bar of Public Opinion: A Brief for Public Relations* [New York: Inter-River Press, 1939]); also see the article for Lee's analysis of public relations counselors as scientific reformers and psychiatrists catering to institutional problems. For an analysis of the composition and ideology of the interpretive expert, see Leila A. Sussman, "The Personnel and Ideology of Public Relations," *Public Opinion Quarterly*, vol. XII (Winter 1948–49), pp. 697–708. For the most recent appraisal of the role of public relations see William H. Whyte, Jr., *Is Anybody Listening?* (New York: Simon and Schuster, 1952).

8. Robin M. Williams, Jr., 'Application of Research to Practice: Sociological Research and Intergroup Relations', (paper presented before the American Sociological Society, September 3, 1952), pp. 3–6.

9. Max Weber, *From Max Weber: Essays in Sociology*, trans. by H. H. Gerth and C. W. Mills (New York: Oxford University Press, 1946), p. 138.

10. The substantive type is deliberately overdrawn. No persons who are practising experts exclusively adopt this role in *all* their social behavior. The consequences of multiple role involvements are discussed below.

11. Robin M. Williams, Jr., *op. cit.*: "The social scientist is confronted with the further fact that the practitioners tend to be heavily committed to 'action rather than talk': there is a pragmatic emphasis upon 'getting things done,' either because of intense value-commitments and ideological convictions, or because of pressures (from relevant publics, sponsors, administrative superiors, and so forth) to 'show results'." (p. 6)

12. R. K. Merton, *Social Theory and Social Structure* (Glencoe: The Free Press, 1949), chap, VI, "Role of the Intellectual in Public Bureaucracy," pp. 168–172.

13. See Max Weber, *The Theory of Social and Economic Organization*, trans. by Talcott Parsons (New York: Oxford University Press, 1947), pp. 88–124, for a discussion of social action as action involving subjective meanings to actor. See also T. Parsons and E. A. Shils (eds), *Toward a General Theory of Action* (Cambridge: Harvard University Press, 1951), p. 309, for Tolman's statement on the importance of including the actor himself as part of the action situation.

14. William Miller, *Men in Business* (Cambridge: Harvard University Press, 1952), p. 293.

15. R. K. Merton, *op. cit.*, pp. 177–178. See list of frustrations from conflicts of values between intellectuals and policy-makers and from the bureaucratic type of organization itself.

16. William Miller, *op. cit.*, pp. 298–299 (quoting Chester Barnard, *The Functions of the Executive* [Cambridge: Harvard University Press, 1938], p. 224; "The Thirty Thousand Managers," *Fortune*, February 1940, p. 52; and David Riesman, "The Saving Remnant: A Study of Character," in John W. Chase [ed.], *Years of the Modern* [New York: Longmans, Green and Co., 1949], p. 31). See also Merton, *op. cit.*, p. 168.

17. G. De Francesco, *op. cit.*; and S. Dali, *The Private Life of Salvador Dali* (New York: Dial Press, 1942).

18. William Miller, *op. cit.*, pp. 291–292.

19. S. M. Lipset and R. Bendix, "Social Mobility and Occupational Career Patterns, II: Social Mobility," *American Journal of Sociology*, vol. LVII (March 1952), p. 497; and K. Eby, "The Expert in the Labor Movement," *American Journal of Sociology*, vol. LVII (July 1951), Part I, p. 32.

20. Max Weber, *From Max Weber: Essays in Sociology*: "Behind all present discussions of the foundations of the educational system, the struggle of the 'specialist type of man' against the older type of 'cultivated man' is hidden at some decisive point. This fight is determined by the irresistibly expanding bureaucratization of all public and private relations of authority and by the ever-increasing importance of expert and specialized knowledge. This fight intrudes into all intimate cultural questions." (p. 243)

21. William H. Whyte, Jr., *op. cit.*

22. R. Bendix and L. R. Fisher, "The Perspectives of Elton Mayo," *Review of Economics and Statistics*, vol. 31, (November 1945), pp. 312–319, especially pp. 316–319.

23. Ethos refers to a universal principle of bureaucracy, while ethic refers to a personal code of honor, i.e., an internalization of the ethos.

24. Max Weber, *From Max Weber: Essays in Sociology*: "Every bureaucracy seeks to increase the superiority of the professionally informed by keeping their knowledge and intentions secret. Bureaucratic administration always tends to be an administration of 'secret sessions': insofar as it can, it hides its knowledge and action from criticism." (p. 233)

25. William Miller, *op. cit.*, p. 288.

26. Max Weber, *From Max Weber: Essays in Sociology*, pp. 232–239.

27. Karl Mannheim, *Man and Society in an Age of Reconstruction* (New York: Harcourt, Brace and Company, 1940): "The glut of intellectuals decreases the value of the intellectuals and of intellectual culture itself." (p. 100)

28. At a non-occupational level, learned societies attempt to provide a forum for such comprehension.

29. Karl Mannheim, *op. cit.*, p. 47.

30. Shepard Mead, *How to Succeed in Business Without Really Trying* (New York: Simon and Schuster, 1952): "*Don't Be a Specialist.* If you have

a special knack, such as drawing or writing, forget it. You may receive more at the very start for special abilities, but don't forget the *long haul.* you don't want to wind up behind a filing case or writing! It is the ability to Get Along, to Make Decisions, and to Get Contacts that will drive you ahead. Be an 'all around' man of no special ability and you will rise to the top" (pp. 4–5). See also Wilbert Moore, *Industrial Relations and the Social Order* (New York: Macmillan, 1947): "The higher the position a person occupies in a line of authority, the more general must his abilities be." (p. 124).

31. The independent professional is not here regarded as, for example, Laski, Carr-Saunders, Wilson, and Parsons regard him. The emphasis here is rather on those aspects of "free professions" which point up the phenomenon of bureaucratized expertness. Thus such aspects of professionalism as fees, ethical codes, professional societies, journals, etc., are not treated here.

32. A. M. Lee, "The Social Dynamics of the Physician's Status," *Psychiatry*, vol. VII (November 1944), pp. 317–337.

33. Karl Mannheim, *op. cit.*, p. 59.

34. C. W. Mills, *White Collar* (New York: Oxford University Press, 1953): "The issues of politics, it is often said, are now so technical and intricate that the individual cannot be expected to understand them or be alert to their consequences. . . . The idea that the issues are too intricate for a people's decision is a curious blend of bureaucratic perspectives (which transform political issues into administrative problems) and a simplistic notion of democracy (which would equate the public with the executive organs of the government, rather than with effective intervention in general decisions of general consequence)." (pp. 347–348) See also Walter Lippmann, *op. cit.*: "Yet these public affairs are in no convincing way his affairs. They are for the most part invisible. They are managed, if they are managed at all, at distant centers, from behind the scenes, by unnamed powers. As a private person he does not know for certain what is going on, or who is doing it, or where is being carried. No newspaper reports his environment so that he can grasp it; no school has taught him how to imagine it; his ideals, often, do not fit with it; listening to speeches, uttering opinions, do not, he finds, enable him to govern it. He lives in a world which he cannot see, does not understand and is unable to direct." (pp. 13–14)

35. C. W. Mills, *op. cit.*, p. 339.

36. Karl Mannheim, *Ideology and Utopia* (New York: Harcourt, Brace and Company, 1936), *passim.*

37. Max Weber, *From Max Weber: Essays in Sociology*: "Viewed in this way, all 'culture' appears as man's emancipation from the organically prescribed life cycle of natural life. For this very reason culture's every step forward seems condemned to lead to an ever more devastating senselessness. The advancement of cultural values, however, seems to become a senseless hustle in the service of worthless, moreover self-contradictory, and mutually antagonistic ends." (pp. 356–357)

38. R. K. Merton, *op. cit.*, p. 171.
39. Ibid., chap. XIII, especially pp. 323–324 on "Specialization and the Professional Ethic."
40. One exception to this may be found in the occupational society which cuts across specific organizations employing experts. In the professional and learned societies, the expert may achieve recognition as an individual apart from recognition deriving from his bureaucratic membership. This can work in two ways. Individual recognition may be limited to recognition by peer experts. Concomitantly professional and learned societies can function to cut across specifically bureaucratically oriented jobs and permit substantive experts to play out their substantive expert roles apart from their occupationally derived role patterns. Even here, however, the substantive contribution of a particular expert results in the conferring of his peer-granted prestige to the organization which employs him. In university life, as Logan Wilson has searchingly noted, this becomes an important element in institutions' rating of staff.

5 The Mass Society[*]
C. Wright Mills

In the standard image of power and decision, no force is held to be as important as The Great American Public. More than merely another check and balance, this public is thought to be the seat of all legitimate power. In official life as in popular folklore, it is held to be the very balance wheel of democratic power. In the end, all liberal theorists rest their notions of the power system upon the political role of this public; all official decisions, as well as private decisions of consequences, are justified as in the public's welfare; all formal proclamations are in its name.

Let us therefore consider the classic public of democratic theory in the generous spirit in which Rousseau once cried, 'Opinion, Queen of the World, is not subject to the power of kings; they are themselves its first slaves.'

The most important feature of the public of opinion, which the rise of the democratic middle class initiates, is the free ebb and flow of discussion. The possibilities of answering back, of organizing autonomous organs of public opinion, of realizing opinion in action, are held to be established by democratic institutions. The opinion that results from the public discussion is understood to be a resolution that is then carried out by public action; it is, in one version, the 'general will' of the people, which the legislative organ enacts into law, thus lending to it legal force. Congress, or Parliament, as an institution, crowns all the scattered publics; it is the archetype for each of the little circles of face-to-face citizens discussing their public business.

This eighteenth-century idea of the public of public opinion parallels the economic idea of the market of the free economy. Here is the market composed of freely competing entrepreneurs; there is the public composed of discus-

[*] Reprinted from C. Wright Mills, *The Power Elite* (New York: Oxford University Press, 1956).

sion circles of opinion peers. As price is the result of anonymous, equally weighted, bargaining individuals, so public opinion is the result of each man's having thought things out for himself and contributing his voice to the great chorus. To be sure, some might have more influence on the state of opinion than others, but no one group monopolizes the discussion, or by itself determines the opinions that prevail.

Innumerable discussion circles are knit together by mobile people who carry opinions from one to another, and struggle for the power of larger command. The public is thus organized into associations and parties, each representing a set of viewpoints, each trying to acquire a place in the Congress, where the discussion continues. Out of the little circles of people talking with one another, the larger forces of social movements and political parties develop; and the discussion of opinion is the important phase in a total act by which public affairs are conducted.

The autonomy of these discussions is an important element in the idea of public opinion as a democratic legitimation. The opinions formed are actively realized within the prevailing institutions of power; all authoritative agents are made or broken by the prevailing opinions of these publics. And, in so far as the public is frustrated in realizing its demands, its members may go beyond criticism of specific policies; they may question the very legitimations of legal authority. That is one meaning of Jefferson's comment on the need for an occasional 'revolution.'

The public, so conceived, is the loom of classic, eighteenth-century democracy; discussion is at once the threads and the shuttle tying the discussion circles together. It lies at the root of the conception of authority by discussion, and it is based upon the hope that truth and justice will somehow come out of society as a great apparatus of free discussion. The people are presented with problems. They discuss them. They decide on them. They formulate viewpoints. These viewpoints are organized, and they compete. One viewpoint 'wins out.' Then the people act out this view, or their representatives are instructed to act it out, and this they promptly do.

Such are the images of the public of classic democracy which are still used as the working justifications of power in American society. But now we must recognize this description as a set of images out of a fairy tale: they are not adequate even as an approximate model of how the American system of power works. The issues that now shape man's fate are neither raised nor decided by the public at large. The idea of the community of publics is not a description of fact, but an assertion of an ideal, an assertion of a legitimation masquerading – as legitimations are now apt to do – as fact. For now the public of public opinion is recognized by all those who have considered it carefully as something less than it once was.

These doubts are asserted positively in the statement that the classic community of publics is being transformed into a society of masses. This transformation, in fact, is one of the keys to the social and psychological meaning of modern life in America.

In the democratic society of publics it was assumed, with John Locke, that the individual conscience was the ultimate seat of judgment and hence the final court of appeal. But this principle was challenged – as E. H. Carr has put it – when Rousseau 'for the first time thought in terms of the sovereignty of the whole people, and faced the issue of mass democracy.'[1]

In the democratic society of publics it was assumed that among the individuals who composed it there was a natural and peaceful harmony of interests. But this essentially conservative doctrine gave way to the Utilitarian doctrine that such a harmony of interests had first to be created by reform before it could work, and later to the Marxian doctrine of class struggle, which surely was then, and certainly is now, closer to reality than any assumed harmony of interests.

In the democratic society of publics it was assumed that before public action would be taken, there would be rational discussion between individuals which would determine the action, and that, accordingly, the public opinion that resulted would be the infallible voice of reason. But this has been challenged not only (1) by the assumed need for experts to decide delicate and intricate issues, but (2) by the discovery – as by Freud – of the irrationality of the man in the street, and (3) by the discovery – as by Marx –

of the socially conditioned nature of what was once assumed to be autonomous reason.

In the democratic society of publics it was assumed that after determining what is true and right and just, the public would act accordingly or see that its representatives did so. In the long run, public opinion will not only be right, but public opinion will prevail. This assumption has been upset by the great gap now existing between the underlying population and those who make decisions in its name, decisions of enormous consequence which the public often does not even know are being made until well after the fact.

Given these assumptions, it is not difficult to understand the articulate optimism of many nineteenth-century thinkers, for the theory of the public is, in many ways, a projection upon the community at large of the intellectual's ideal of the supremacy of intellect. The 'evolution of the intellect,' Comte asserted, 'determines the main course of social evolution.' If looking about them, nineteenth-century thinkers still saw irrationality and ignorance and apathy, all that was merely an intellectual lag, to which the spread of education would soon put an end.

How much the cogency of the classic view of the public rested upon a restriction of this public to the carefully educated is revealed by the fact that by 1859 even John Stuart Mill was writing of 'the tyranny of the majority,' and both Tocqueville and Burckhardt anticipated the view popularized in the recent past by such political moralists as Ortega y Gasset. In a word, the transformation of public into mass – and all that this implies – has been at once one of the major trends of modern societies and one of the major factors in the collapse of that liberal optimism which determined so much of the intellectual mood of the nineteenth century.

By the middle of that century: individualism had begun to be replaced by collective forms of economic and political life; harmony of interests by inharmonious struggle of classes and organized pressures; rational discussions undermined by expert decisions on complicated issues, by recognition of the interested bias of argument by vested position; and by the discovery of the effectiveness of irrational appeal to the citizen. Moreover, certain structural changes of modern society, which we shall presently consider, had begun to cut off the public from the power of active decision.

The transformation of public into mass is of particular concern to us, for it provides an important clue to the meaning of the power elite. If that elite is truly responsible to, or even exists in connection with, a community of publics, it carries a very different meaning than if such a public is being transformed into a society of masses.

The United States today is not altogether a mass society, and it has never been altogether a community of publics. These phrases are names for extreme types; they point to certain features of reality, but they are themselves constructions; social reality is always some sort of mixture of the two. Yet we cannot readily understand just how much of which is mixed into our situation if we do not first understand, in terms of explicit dimensions, the clear-cut and extreme types:

At least four dimensions must be attended to if we are to grasp the differences between public and mass.

There is first, the ratio of the givers of opinion to the receivers, which is the simplest way to state the social meaning of the formal media of mass communication. More than anything else, it is the shift in this ratio which is central to the problems of the public and of public opinion in latter-day phases of democracy. At one extreme on the scale of communication, two people talk personally with each other; at the opposite extreme, one spokesman talks impersonally through a network of communications to millions of listeners and viewers. In between these extremes there are assemblages and political rallies, parliamentary sessions, lawcourt debates, small discussion circles dominated by one man, open discussion circles with talk moving freely back and forth among fifty people, and so on.

The second dimension to which we must pay attention is the possibility of answering back an opinion without internal or external reprisals being taken. Technical conditions of the means of communication, in imposing a lower ratio of speakers to listeners, may obviate the possibility of freely answering back. Informal rules, resting upon conventional sanction and upon the informal structure of opinion leadership, may govern who can speak, when, and for how long. Such rules may or may not be in congruence with formal rules and with institutional sanctions which govern the process of communication. In the extreme case, we may conceive of an absolute monopoly of communication to pacified media groups whose members cannot answer back even 'in private.' At the opposite extreme, the conditions may allow and the rules may uphold the wide and symmetrical formation of opinion.

We must also consider the relation of the formation of opinion to its realization in social action, the ease with which opinion is effective in the shaping of decisions of powerful consequence. This opportunity for people to act out their opinions collectively is of course limited by their position in the structure of power. This structure may be such as to limit decisively this capacity, or it may allow or even invite such action. It may confine social action to local areas or it may enlarge the area of opportunity; it may make action intermittent or more or less continuous.

There is, finally, the degree to which institutional authority, with its sanctions and controls, penetrates the public. Here the problem is the degree to which the public has genuine autonomy form instituted authority. At one extreme, no agent of formal authority moves among the autonomous public. At the opposite extreme, the public is terrorized into uniformity by the infiltration of informers and the universalization of suspicion. One thinks of the late Nazi street-and-block-system, the eighteenth-century Japanese kumi, the Soviet cell structure. In the extreme, the formal structure of power coincides, as it were, with the informal ebb and flow of influence by discussion, which is thus killed off.

By combining these several points, we can construct little models or diagrams of several types of societies. Since 'the problem of public opinion' as we know it is set by the eclipse of the classic bourgeois public, we are here concerned with only two types: public and mass.

In a *public*, as we may understand the term, (1) virtually as many people express opinions as receive them. (2) Public communications are so organized that there is a chance immediately and effectively to answer back any opinion expressed in public. Opinion formed by such discussion (3) readily finds an outlet in effective action, even against – if necessary – the prevailing system of authority. And (4) authoritative institutions do not penetrate the public, which is thus more or less autonomous in its operations. When these conditions prevail, we have the working model of a community of publics, and this model fits closely the several assumptions of classic democratic theory.

At the opposite extreme, in a *mass*, (1) far fewer people express opinions than receive them; for the community of publics becomes an abstract collection of individuals who receive impressions from the mass media. (2) The communications that prevail are so organized that it is difficult or impossible for the individual to answer back immediately or with any effect. (3) The realization of opinion in action is controlled by authorities who organize and control the channels of such action. (4) The mass has no autonomy from institutions; on the contrary, agents of authorized institutions penetrate this mass, reducing any autonomy it may have in the formation of opinion by discussion.

The public and the mass may be most readily distinguished by their dominant modes of communication: in a community of publics, discussion is the ascendant means of communication, and the mass media, if they exist, simply enlarge and animate discussion, linking one *primary public* with the discussions of another. In a mass society, the dominant type of communication is the formal media, and the publics become mere *media markets*: all those exposed to the contents of given mass media.

From almost any angle of vision that we might assume, when we look upon the public, we realize that we have moved a considerable distance along the road to the mass society. At the end of that road is totalitarianism, as in Nazi Germany or in Communist Russia. We are not yet at that end. In the United States today, media markets are not entirely ascendant over primary publics. But surely we can see that many aspects of the public life of our times are more the features of a mass society than of a community of publics.

What is happening might again be stated in terms of the historical parallel between the economic market and the public of public opinion. In brief, there is a movement from widely scattered little powers to concentrated powers and the attempt at monopoly control from powerful centers, which, being partially hidden, are centers of manipulation as well as of authority. The small shop serving the neighborhood is replaced by the anonymity of the national corporation: mass advertisement replaces the personal influence of opinion between merchant and customer. The political leader hooks up his speech to a national network and speaks, with appropriate personal touches, to a million people he never saw and never will see. Entire brackets of professions and industries are in the 'opinion business,' impersonally manipulating the public for hire.

In the primary public the competition of opinions goes on between people holding views in the service of their interests and their reasoning. But in the mass society of media markets, competition, if any, goes on between the manipulators with their mass media on the one hand, and the people receiving their propaganda on the other.

Under such conditions, it is not surprising that there should arise a conception of public opinion as a mere reaction – we cannot say 'response' – to the content of the mass media. In this view, the public is merely the collectivity of individuals each rather passively exposed to the mass media and rather helplessly opened up to the suggestions and manipulations that flow from these media. The fact of manipulation from centralized points of control constitutes, as it were, an expropriation of the old multitude of little opinion producers and consumers operating in a free and balanced market.

In official circles, the very term itself, 'the public' – as Walter Lippmann noted thirty years ago – has come to have a phantom meaning, which dramatically reveals its eclipse. From the standpoint of the deciding elite, some of those who clamor publicly can be identified as 'Labor,' others as 'Business,' still others as 'Farmer.' Those who can *not* readily be so identified make up 'The Public.' In this usage, the public is composed of the unidentified and the non-partisan in a world of defined and partisan interests. It is socially composed of well-educated salaried professionals, especially college professors; of non-unionized employees, especially white-collar people, along with self-employed professionals and small businessmen.

In this faint echo of the classic notion, the public consists of those remnants of the middle classes, old and new, whose interests are not explicitly defined, organized, or clamorous. In a curious adaptation, 'the public' often becomes, in fact, 'the unattached expert,' who, although well informed, has never taken a clear-cut, public stand on controversial issues which are brought to a focus by organized interests. These are the 'public' members of the board, the commission, the committee. What the public stands for, accordingly, is often a vagueness of policy (called open-mindedness), a lack of involvement in public affairs (known as reasonableness), and a professional disinterest (known as tolerance).

Some such official members of the public, as in the field of labor-management mediation, start out very young and make a career out of being careful to be informed but never taking a strong position; and there are many others, quite unofficial, who take such professionals as a sort of model. The only trouble is that they are acting as if they were disinterested judges but they do not have the power of judges; hence their reasonableness, their tolerance, and their open-mindedness do not often count for much in the shaping of human affairs.

All those trends that make for the decline of the politician and of his balancing society bear decisively upon the transformation of public into mass. One of the most important of the structural transformations involved is the decline of the voluntary association as a genuine instrument of the public. As we have already seen, the executive ascendancy in economic, military, and political institutions has lowered the effective use of all those voluntary associations which operate between the state and the economy on the one hand, and the family and the individual in the primary group on the other. It is not only that institutions of power have become large-scale and inaccessibly centralized; they have at the same time become less political and more administrative, and it is within this great change of framework that the organized public has waned.

In terms of *scale*, the transformation of public into mass has been underpinned by the shift from a political public decisively restricted in size (by property and education, as well as by sex and age) to a greatly enlarged mass having only the qualifications of citizenship and age.

In terms of *organization*, the transformation has been underpinned by the shift from the individual and his primary community to the voluntary association and the mass party as the major units of organized power.

Voluntary associations have become larger to the extent that they have become effective; and to just that extent they have become inaccessible to the individual who would shape by discussion the policies of the organization to which he belongs. Accordingly, along with older institutions, these voluntary associations have lost their grip on the individual. As more people are drawn into the political arena, these associations become mass in scale; and as the power of the individual becomes more dependent upon such mass associations, they are less accessible to the individual's influence.

Mass democracy means the struggle of powerful and large-scale interest groups and associations, which stand between the big decisions that are made by state, corporation, army, and the will of the individual citizen as a member of the public. Since these middle-level associations are the citizen's major link with decision, his relation to them is of decisive importance. For it is only through them that he exercises such power as he may have.

The gap between the members and the leaders of the mass association is becoming increasingly wider. As soon as a man gets to be a leader of an association large enough to count he readily becomes lost as an instrument of that association. He does so (1) in the interests of maintaining his leading position in, or rather over, his mass association, and he does so (2) because he comes to see himself not as a mere delegate, instructed or not, of the mass association he represents, but as a member of 'an elite' composed of such men as himself. These facts, in turn, lead to (3) the big gap between the terms in which issues are debated and resolved among members of this elite, and the terms in which they are presented to the members of the various mass associations. For the decisions that are made must *take into account* those who are important – other elites – but they must be *sold* to the mass memberships.

The gap between speaker and listener, between power and public, leads less to any iron law of oligarchy than to the law of spokesmanship: as the pressure group expands, its leaders come to organize the opinions they 'represent.' So elections, as we have seen, become contests between two giant and unwieldy parties, neither of which the invidual can truly feel that he influences, and neither of which is capable of winning psychologically impressive or politically decisive majorities. And, in all this, the parties are of the same general form as other mass associations.[2]

When we say that man in the mass is without any sense of political belonging, we have in mind a political fact rather than merely a style of feeling. We have in mind (I.) a certain way of belonging (II.) to a certain kind of organization.

I. The way of belonging here implied rests upon a belief in the purposes and in the leaders of an organization, and thus enables men and women freely to be at home within it. To belong in this way is to make the human association a psychological center of one's self, to take into our conscience, deliberately and freely, its rules of conduct and its purposes, which we thus shape and which in turn shape us. We do not have this kind of belonging to any political organization.

II. The kind of organization we have in mind is a voluntary association which has three decisive characteristics: first, it is a context in which reasonable opinions may be formulated; second, it is an agency by which reasonable activities may be undertaken; and third, it is a powerful enough unit, in comparison with other organizations of power, to make a difference.

It is because they do not find available associations at once psychologically meaningful and historically effective that men often feel uneasy in their political and economic loyalties. The effective units of power are now the huge corporation, the inaccessible government, the grim military establishment. Between these, on the one hand, and the family and the small community on the other, we find no intermediate associations in which men feel secure and with which they feel powerful. There is little live political struggle.

Instead, there is administration from above, and the political vacuum below. The primary publics are now either so small as to be swamped, and hence give up; or so large as to be merely another feature of the generally distant structure of power, and hence inaccessible.

Public opinion exists when people who are not in the government of a country claim the right to express political opinions freely and publicly, and the right that these opinions should influence or determine the policies, personnel, and actions of their government.[3] In this formal sense there has been and there is a definite public opinion in the United States. And yet, with modern developments this formal right – when it does still exist as a right – does not mean what it once did. The older world of voluntary organization was as different from the world of the mass organization, as was Tom Paine's world of pamphleteering from the world of the mass media.

Since the French Revolution, conservative thinkers have Viewed With Alarm the rise of the public, which they called the masses, or something to that effect. 'The populace is sovereign, and the tide of barbarism mounts,' wrote Gustave Le Bon. 'The divine right of the masses is about to replace the divine right of kings,' and already 'the destinies of nations are elaborated at present in the heart of the masses, and no longer in the councils of princes.'[4] During the twentieth century, liberal and even socialist thinkers have followed suit, with more explicit reference to what we have called the society of masses. From Le Bon to Emil Lederer and Ortega y Gasset, they have held that the influence of the mass is unfortunately increasing.

But surely those who have supposed the masses to be all powerful, or at least well on their way to triumph, are wrong. In our time, as Chakhotin knew, the influence of autonomous collectivities within political life is in fact diminishing.[5] Furthermore, such influence as they do have is guided; they must now be seen not as publics acting autonomously, but as masses manipulated at focal points into crowds of demonstrators. For as publics become masses, masses sometimes become crowds; and, in crowds, the psychical rape by the mass media is supplemented up close by the harsh and sudden harangue. Then the people in the crowd disperse again – as atomized and submissive masses.

In all modern societies, the autonomous associations standing between the various classes and the state tend to lose their effectiveness as vehicles of reasoned opinion and instruments for the rational exertion of political will. Such associations can be deliberately broken up and thus turned into passive instruments of rule, or they can more slowly wither away from lack of use in the face of centralized means of power. But whether they are destroyed in a week, or wither in a generation, such associations are replaced in virtually every sphere of life by centralized organizations, and it is such organizations with all their new means of power that take charge of the terrorized or – as the case may be – merely intimidated, society of masses.

The institutional trends that make for a society of masses are to a considerable extent a matter of impersonal drift, but the remnants of the public are also exposed to more 'personal' and intentional forces. With the broadening of the base of politics within the context of a folk-lore of democratic decision-making, and with the increased means of mass persuasion that are available, the public of public opinion has become the object of intensive efforts to control, manage, manipulate, and increasingly intimidate.

In political, military, economic realms, power becomes, in varying degrees, uneasy before the suspected opinions of masses, and, accordingly, opinion-making becomes an accepted technique of power-holding and power-getting. The minority electorate of the propertied and the educated is replaced by the total suffrage – and intensive campaigns for the vote. The small eighteenth-century professional army is replaced by the mass army of conscripts – and by the problems of nationalist morale. The small shop is replaced by the mass-production industry – and the national advertisement.

As the scale of institutions has become larger and more centralized, so has the range and intensity of the opinion-makers' efforts. The means of opinion-making, in fact, have paralleled in range and efficiency the other institutions of greater scale that cradle the modern society of masses. Accordingly, in addition to their enlarged and centralized means of administration, exploitation, and violence, the

modern elite have had placed within their grasp historically unique instruments of psychic management and manipulation, which include universal compulsory education
as well as the media of mass communication.

Early observers believed that the increase in the range
and volume of the formal means of communication would
enlarge and animate the primary public. In such optimistic views – written before radio and television and movies –
the formal media are understood as simply multiplying the
scope and pace of personal discussion. Modern conditions,
Charles Cooley wrote, 'enlarge indefinitely the competition
of ideas, and whatever has owed its persistence merely to
lack of comparison is likely to go, for that which is really
congenial to the choosing mind will be all the more cherished and increased.'[6] Still excited by the break-up of the
conventional consensus of the local community, he saw the
new means of communication as furthering the conversational
dynamic of classic democracy, and with it the growth of
rational and free individuality.

No one really knows all the functions of the mass media,
for in their entirety these functions are probably so pervasive and so subtle that they cannot be caught by the means
of social research now available. But we do now have reason
to believe that these media have helped less to enlarge and
animate the discussions of primary publics than to transform them into a set of media markets in mass-like society.
I do not refer merely to the higher ratio of deliverers of
opinion to receivers and to the decreased chance to answer
back; nor do I refer merely to the violent banalization and
stereotyping of our very sense organs in terms of which these
media now compete for 'attention.' I have in mind a sort
of psychological illiteracy that is facilitated by the media,
and that is expressed in several ways:

I. Very little of what we think we know of the social realities of the world have we found out first-hand. Most of
'the pictures in our heads' we have gained from these media
– even to the point where we often do not really believe
what we see before us until we read about it in the paper
or hear about it on the radio.[7] The media not only give us
information; they guide our very experiences. Our standards of credulity, our standards of reality, tend to be set

by these media rather than by our own fragmentary experience.

Accordingly, even if the individual has direct, personal experience of events, it is not really direct and primary: it is organized in stereotypes. It takes long and skillful training to so uproot such stereotypes that an individual sees things freshly, in an unstereotyped manner. One might suppose, for example, that if all the people went through a depression they would all 'experience it,' and in terms of this experience, that they would all debunk or reject or at least refract what the media say about it. But experience of such a *structural* shift has to be organized and interpreted if it is to count in the making of opinion.

The kind of experience, in short, that might serve as a basis for resistance to mass media is not an experience of raw events, but the experience of meanings. The fleck of interpretation must be there in the experience if we are to use the word experience seriously. And the capacity for such experience is socially implanted. The individual does not trust his own experience, as I have said, until it is confirmed by others or by the media. Usually such direct exposure is not accepted if it disturbs loyalties and beliefs that the individual already holds. To be accepted, it must relieve or justify the feelings that often lie in the back of his mind as key features of his ideological loyalties.

Stereotypes of loyalty underlie beliefs and feelings about given symbols and emblems; they are the very ways in which men see the social world and in terms of which men make up their specific opinions and views of events. They are the results of previous experience, which affect present and future experience. It goes without saying that men are often unaware of these loyalties, that often they could not formulate them explicitly. Yet such general stereotypes make for the acceptance or the rejection of specific opinions not so much by the force of logical consistency as by their emotional affinity and by the way in which they relieve anxieties. To accept opinions in their terms is to gain the good solid feeling of being correct without having to think. When ideological stereotypes and specific opinions are linked in this way, there is a lowering of the kind of anxiety which arises when loyalty and belief are not in accord. Such ideologies lead to a willingness to accept a given line of belief; then there is no need, emotionally or rationally, to overcome resistance to given items in that line; cumulative selections of specific opinions and feelings become the pre-organized attitudes and emotions that shape the opinion-life of the person.

These deeper beliefs and feelings are a sort of lens through which men experience their worlds, they strongly condition acceptance or rejection of specific opinions, and they set men's orientation toward prevailing authorities. Three decades ago, Walter Lippmann saw such prior convictions as biases: they kept men from defining reality in an adequate way. They are still biases. But today they can often be seen as 'good biases'; inadequate and misleading as they often are, they are less so than the crackpot realism of the higher authorities and opinion-makers. They are the lower common sense and as such a factor of resistance. But we must recognize, especially when the pace of change is so deep and fast, that common sense is more often common than sense. And, above all, we must recognize that 'the common sense' of our children is going to be less the result of any firm social tradition than of the stereotypes carried by the mass media to which they are now so fully exposed. They are the first generation to be so exposed.

II. So long as the media are not entirely monopolized, the individual can play one medium off against another; he can compare them, and hence resist what any one of them puts out. The more genuine competition there is among the media, the more resistance the individual might be able to command. But how much is this now the case? *Do* people compare reports on public events or policies, playing one medium's content off against another's?

The answer is: generally no, very few do: (1) We know that people tend strongly to select those media which carry contents with which they already agree. There is a kind of selection of new opinions on the basis of prior opinions. No one seems to search out such counter-statements as may be found in alternative media offerings. Given radio programs and magazines and newspapers often get a rather consistent public, and thus reinforce their messages in the minds of that public. (2) This idea of playing one medium off against another assumes that the media really have varying contents. It assumes genuine competition, which is not widely true. The media display an apparent variety and competition, but on closer view they seem to compete more in terms of variations on a few standardized themes than of clashing issues. The freedom to raise issues effectively seems more and more to be confined to those few interests that have ready and continual access to these media.

III. The media have not only filtered into our experience of external realities, they have also entered into our very experience of our own selves. They have provided us with new identities and new aspirations of what we should like to be, and what we should like to appear to be. They have provided in the models of conduct they hold out to us a new and larger and more flexible set of appraisals of our very selves. In terms of the modern theory of the self,[8] we may say that the media bring the reader, listener, viewer into the sight of larger, higher reference groups – groups, real or imagined, up-close or vicarious, personally known or distractedly glimpsed – which are looking glasses for his self-image. They have multiplied the groups to which we look for confirmation of our self-image.

More than that: (1) the media tell the man in the mass who he is – they give him identity; (2) they tell him what he wants to be – they give him aspirations; (3) they tell him how to get that way – they give him technique; and (4) they tell him how to feel that he is that way even when he is not – they give him escape. The gaps between the identity and aspiration lead to technique and/or to escape. That is probably the basic psychological formula of the mass media today. But, as a formula, it is not attuned to the development of the human being. It is the formula of a pseudo-world which the media invent and sustain.

IV. As they now generally prevail, the mass media, especially television, often encroach upon the small-scale discussion, and destroy the chance for the reasonable and leisurely and human interchange of opinion. They are an important cause of the destruction of privacy in its full human meaning. That is an important reason why they not only fail as an educational force, but are a malign force:

they do not articulate for the viewer or listener the broader sources of his private tensions and anxieties, his inarticulate resentments and half-formed hopes. They neither enable the individual to transcend his narrow milieu nor clarify its private meaning.

The media provide much information and news about what is happening in the world, but they do not often enable the listener or the viewer truly to connect his daily life with these larger realities. They do not connect the information they provide on public issues with the troubles felt by the individual. They do not increase rational insight into tensions, either those in the individual or those of the society which are reflected in the individual. On the contrary, they distract him and obscure his chance to understand himself or his world, by fastening his attention upon artificial frenzies that are resolved within the program framework, usually by violent action or by what is called humor. In short, for the viewer they are not really resolved at all. The chief distracting tension of the media is between the wanting and the not having of commodities or of women held to be good looking. There is almost always the general tone of animated distraction, of suspended agitation, but it is going nowhere and it has nowhere to go.

But the media, as now organized and operated, are even more than a major cause of the transformation of America into a mass society. They are also among the most important of those increased means of power now at the disposal of elites of wealth and power; moreover, some of the higher agents of these media are themselves either among the elites or very important among their servants.

Alongside or just below the elite, there is the propagandist, the publicity expert, the public-relations man, who would control the very formation of public opinion in order to be able to include it as one more pacified item in calculations of effective power, increased prestige, more secure wealth. Over the last quarter of a century, the attitudes of these manipulators toward their task have gone through a sort of dialectic.

In the beginning, there is great faith in what the mass media can do. Words win wars or sell soap; they move people, they restrain people. 'Only cost,' the advertising man of the 'twenties proclaims, 'limits the delivery of public opinion in any direction on any topic.'[9] The opinion-maker's belief in the media as mass persuaders almost amounts to magic – but he can believe mass communications omnipotent only so long as the public is trustful. It does not remain trustful. The mass media say so very many and such competitively exaggerated things; they banalize their message and they cancel one another out. The 'propaganda phobia,' in reaction to wartime lies and postwar disenchantment, does not help matters, even though memory is both short and subject to official distortion. This distrust of the magic of media is translated into a slogan among the opinion managers. Across their banners they write: 'Mass Persuasion Is Not Enough.'

Frustrated, they reason; and reasoning, they come to accept the principle of social context. To change opinion and activity, they say to one another, we must pay close attention to the full context and lives of the people to be managed. Along with mass persuasion, we must somehow use personal influence; we must reach people in their life context and *through* other people, their daily associates, those whom they trust: we must get at them by some kind of 'personal' persuasion. We must not show our hand directly; rather than merely advise or command, we must manipulate.

Now this live and immediate social context in which people live and which exerts a steady expectation upon them is of course what we have called the primary public. Anyone who has seen the inside of an advertising agency or public-relations office knows that the primary public is still the great unsolved problem of the opinion-makers. Negatively, their recognition of the influence of social context upon opinion and public activity implies that the articulate public resists and refracts the communications of the mass media. Positively, this recognition implies that the public is not composed of isolated individuals, but rather of persons who not only have prior opinions that must be reckoned with, but who continually influence each other in complex and intimate, in direct and continual ways.

In their attempts to neutralize or to turn to their own use the articulate public, the opinion-makers try to make it a relay network for their views. If the opinion-makers have so much power that they can act directly and openly upon the primary publics, they may become authoritative; but, if they do not have such power and hence have to operate indirectly and without visibility, they will assume the stance of manipulators.

Authority is power that is explicit and more or less 'voluntarily' obeyed; manipulation is the 'secret' exercise of power, unknown to those who are influenced. In the model of the classic democratic society, manipulation is not a problem, because formal authority resides in the public itself and in its representatives who are made or broken by the public. In the completely authoritarian society, manipulation is not a problem, because authority is openly identified with the ruling institutions and their agents, who may use authority explicitly and nakedly. They do not, in the extreme case, have to gain or retain power by hiding its exercise.

Manipulation becomes a problem wherever men have power that is concentrated and willful but do not have authority, or when, for any reason, they do not wish to use their power openly. Then the powerful seek to rule without showing their powerfulness. They want to rule, as it were, secretly, without publicized legitimation. It is in this mixed case – as in the intermediate reality of the American today – that manipulation is a prime way of exercising power. Small circles of men are making decisions which they need to have at least authorized by indifferent or recalcitrant people over whom they do not exercise explicit authority. So the small circle tries to manipulate these people into willing acceptance or cheerful support of their decisions or opinions – or at least to the rejection of possible counter-opinions.

Authority *formally* resides 'in the people,' but the power of initiation is in fact held by small circles of men. That is why the standard strategy of manipulation is to make it appear that the people, or at least a large group of them, 'really made the decision.' That is why even when the authority is available, men with access to it may still prefer the secret, quieter ways of manipulation.

But are not the people now more educated? Why not emphasize the spread of education rather than the increased effects of the mass media? The answer, in brief, is that mass education, in many respects, has become – another mass medium.

The prime task of public education, as it came widely to be understood in this country, was political: to make the citizen more knowledgeable and thus better able to think and to judge of public affairs. In time, the function of education shifted from the political to the economic: to train people for better-paying jobs and thus to get ahead. This is especially true of the high-school movement, which has met the business demands for white-collar skills at the public's expense. In large part education has become merely vocational; in so far as its political task is concerned, in many schools, that has been reduced to a routine training of nationalist loyalties.

The training of skills that are of more or less direct use in the vocational life is an important task to perform, but ought not to be mistaken for liberal education: job advancement, no matter on what levels, is not the same as self-development, although the two are now systematically confused.[10] Among 'skills,' some are more and some are less relevant to the aims of liberal – that is to say, liberating – education. Skills and values cannot be so easily separated as the academic search for supposedly neutral skills causes us to assume. And especially not when we speak seriously of liberal education. Of course, there is a scale, with skills at one end and values at the other, but it is the middle range of this scale, which one might call sensibilities, that are of most relevance to the classic public.

To train someone to operate a lathe or to read and write is pretty much education of skill; to evoke from people an understanding of what they really want out of their lives or to debate with them stoic, Christian and humanist ways of living, is pretty much a clear-cut education of values. But to assist in the birth among a group of people of those cultural and political and technical sensibilities which would make them genuine members of a genuinely liberal public, this is at once a training in skills and an education of values. It includes a sort of therapy in the ancient sense of clarifying one's knowledge of one's self; it includes the imparting of all those skills of controversy with one's self, which we call thinking; and with others, which we call debate. And the end product of such liberal education of sensibilities is simply the self-educating, self-cultivating man or woman.

The knowledgeable man in the genuine public is able to turn his personal troubles into social issues, to see their relevance for his community and his community's relevance for them. He understands that what he thinks and feels as personal troubles are very often not only that but problems shared by others and indeed not subject to solution by any one individual but only by modifications of the structure of the groups in which he lives and sometimes the structure of the entire society.

Men in masses are gripped by personal troubles, but they are not aware of their true meaning and source. Men in public confront issues, and they are aware of their terms. It is the task of the liberal institution, as of the liberally educated man, continually to translate troubles into issues and issues into the terms of their human meaning for the individual. In the absence of deep and wide political debate, schools for adults and adolescents could perhaps become hospitable frameworks for just such debate. In a community of publics the task of liberal education would be: to keep the public from being overwhelmed; to help produce the disciplined and informed mind that cannot be overwhelmed; to help develop the bold and sensible individual that cannot be sunk by the burdens of mass life. But educational practice has not made knowledge directly relevant to the human need of the troubled person of the twentieth century or to the social practices of the citizen. This citizen cannot now see the roots of his own biases and frustrations, nor think clearly about himself, nor for that matter about anything else. He does not see the frustration of idea, of intellect, by the present organization of society, and he is not able to meet the tasks now confronting 'the intelligent citizen.'

Educational institutions have not done these things and, except in rare instances, they are not doing them. They have become mere elevators of occupational and social ascent, and, on all levels, they have become politically timid. Moreover, in the hands of 'professional educators,' many

The Mass Society

schools have come to operate on an ideology of 'life adjustment' that encourages happy acceptance of mass ways of life rather than the struggle for individual and public transcendence.

There is not much doubt that modern regressive educators have adapted their notions of educational content and practice to the idea of the mass. They do not effectively proclaim standards of cultural level and intellectual rigor; rather they often deal in the trivia of vocational tricks and 'adjustment to life' – meaning the slack life of masses. 'Democratic schools' often mean the furtherance of intellectual mediocrity, vocational training, nationalistic loyalties, and little else.

The structural trends of modern society and the manipulative character of its communication technique come to a point of coincidence in the mass society, which is largely a metropolitan society. The growth of the metropolis, segregating men and women into narrowed routines and environments, causes them to lose any firm sense of their integrity as a public. The members of publics in smaller communities know each other more or less fully, because they meet in the several aspects of the total life routine. The members of masses in a metropolitan society know one another only as fractions in specialized milieux: the man who fixes the car, the girl who serves your lunch, the saleslady, the women who take care of your child at school during the day. Prejudgment and stereotype flourish when people meet in such ways. The human reality of others does not, cannot, come through.

People, we know, tend to select those formal media which confirm what they already believe and enjoy. In a parallel way, they tend in the metropolitan segregation to come into live touch with those whose opinions are similar to theirs. Others they tend to treat unseriously. In the metropolitan society they develop, in their defense, a blasé manner that reaches deeper than a manner. They do not, accordingly, experience genuine clashes of viewpoint, genuine issues. And when they do, they tend to consider it mere rudeness.

Sunk in their routines, they do not transcend, even by discussion, much less by action, their more or less narrow lives. They do not gain a view of the structure of their society and of their role as a public within it. The city is a structure composed of such little environments, and the people in them tend to be detached from one another. The 'stimulating variety' of the city does not stimulate the men and women of 'the bedroom belt,' the one-class suburbs, who can go through life knowing only their own kind. If they do reach for one another, they do so only through stereotypes and prejudiced images of the creatures of other milieux. Each is trapped by his confining circle; each is cut off from easily identifiable groups. It is for people in such narrow milieux that the mass media can create a pseudo-world beyond, and a pseudo-world within themselves as well.

Publics live in milieux but they can transcend them – individually by intellectual effort; socially by public action. By reflection and debate and by organized action, a community of publics comes to feel itself and comes in fact to be active at points of structural relevance.

But members of a mass exist in milieux and cannot get out of them, either by mind or by activity, except – in the extreme case – under 'the organized spontaneity' of the bureaucrat on a motorcycle. We have not yet reached the extreme case, but observing metropolitan man in the American mass we can surely see the psychological preparations for it.

We may think of it in this way: When a handful of men do not have jobs, and do not seek work, we look for the causes in their immediate situation and character. But when twelve million men are unemployed, then we cannot believe that all of them suddenly 'got lazy' and turned out to be 'no good.' Economists call this 'structural unemployment' – meaning, for one thing, that the men involved cannot themselves control their job chances. Structural unemployment does not originate in one factory or in one town, nor is it due to anything that one factory or one town does or fails to do. Moreover, there is little or nothing that one ordinary man in one factory in one town can do about it when it sweeps over his personal milieu.

Now, this distinction, between social structure and personal milieu, is one of the most important available in the sociological studies. It offers us a ready understanding of the position of 'the public' in America today. In every major area of life, the loss of a sense of structure and the submergence into powerless milieux is the cardinal fact. In the military it is most obvious, for here the roles men play are strictly confining; only the command posts at the top afford a view of the structure of the whole, and moreover, this view is a closely guarded official secret. In the division of labor too, the jobs men enact in the economic hierarchies are also more or less narrow milieux and the positions from which a view of the production process as a whole can be had are centralized, as men are alienated not only from the product and the tools of their labor, but from any understanding of the structure and the processes of production. In the political order, in the fragmentation of the lower and in the distracting proliferation of the middle-level organization, men cannot see the whole, cannot see the top, and cannot state the issues that will in fact determine the whole structure in which they live and their place within it.

This loss of any structural view or position is the decisive meaning of the lament over the loss of community. In the great city, the division of milieux and of segregating routines reaches the point of closest contact with the individual and the family, for, although the city is not the unit of prime decision, even the city cannot be seen as a total structure by most of its citizens.

On the one hand, there is the increased scale and centralization of the structure of decision; and, on the other, the increasingly narrow sorting out of men into milieux. From both sides, there is the increased dependence upon the formal media of communication, including those of education itself. But the man in the mass does not gain a transcending view from these media; instead he gets his experience stereotyped, and then he gets sunk further by that experience. He cannot detach himself in order to observe, much less to evaluate, what he is experiencing, much less what he is not experiencing. Rather than that internal discussion we call reflection, he is accompanied through his life-expereince with a sort of unconscious, echoing monologue. He has no projects of his own: he fulfills the routines that exist. He does not transcend whatever he is at any moment, because he does not, he cannot, transcend his daily milieux. He is not truly aware of his own daily experience and of its actual standards: he drifts, he fulfills habits, his behavior a result of a planless mixture of the confused standards and the uncriticized expectations that he has taken over from others whom he no longer really knows or trusts, if indeed he ever really did.

He takes things for granted, he makes the best of them, he tries to look ahead – a year or two perhaps, or even longer if he has children or a mortgage – but he does not seriously ask, What do I want? How can I get it? A vague optimism suffuses and sustains him, broken occasionally by little miseries and disappointments that are soon buried. He is smug, from the standpoint of those who think something might be the matter with the mass style of life in the metropolitan frenzy where self-making is an externally busy branch of industry. By what standards does he judge himself and his efforts? What is really important to him? Where are the models of excellence for this man?

He loses his independence, and more importantly, he loses the desire to be independent: in fact, he does not have hold of the idea of being an independent individual with his own mind and his own worked-out way of life. It is not that he likes or does not like this life; it is that the question does not come up sharp and clear so he is not bitter and he is not sweet about conditions and events. He thinks he wants merely to get his share of what is around with as little trouble as he can and with as much fun as possible.

Such order and movement as his life possesses is in conformity with external routines; otherwise his day-to-day experience is a vague chaos – although he often does not know it because, strictly speaking, he does not truly possess or observe his own experience. He does not formulate his desires; they are insinuated into him. And, in the mass, he loses the self-confidence of the human being – if indeed he has ever had it. For life in a society of masses implants insecurity and furthers impotence; it makes men uneasy and vaguely anxious; it isolates the individual from the solid group; it destroys firm group standards. Acting without goals, the man in the mass just feels pointless.

The idea of a mass society suggests the idea of an elite of power. The idea of the public, in contrast, suggests the liberal tradition of a society without any power elite, or at any rate with shifting elites of no sovereign consequence. For, if a genuine public is sovereign, it needs no master; but the masses, in their full development, are sovereign only in some plebiscitarian moment of adulation to an elite as authoritative celebrity. The political structure of a democratic state requires the public; and, the democratic man, in his rhetoric, must assert that this public is the very seat of sovereignty.

But now, given all those forces that have enlarged and centralized the political order and made modern societies less political and more administrative; given the transformation of the old middle classes into something which perhaps should not even be called middle class; given all the mass communications that do not truly communicate; given all the metropolitan segregation that is not community; given the absence of voluntary associations that really connect the public at large with the centers of power – what is happening is the decline of a set of publics that is sovereign only in the most formal and rhetorical sense. Moreover, in many countries the remnants of such publics as remain are now being frightened out of existence. They lose their will for rationally considered decision and action because they do not possess the instruments for such decision and action; they lose their sense of political belonging because they do not belong; they lose their political will because they see no way to realize it.

The top of modern American society is increasingly unified, and often seems willfully co-ordinated: at the top there has emerged an elite of power. The middle levels are a drifting set of stalemated, balancing forces: the middle does not link the bottom with the top. The bottom of this society is politically fragmented, and even as a passive fact, increasingly powerless: at the bottom there is emerging a mass society.

Notes

1. See E. H. Carr, *The New Society* (London: Macmillan, 1951), pp. 63–6, on whom I lean heavily in this and the following paragraphs.
2. On elections in modern formal democracies, E. H. Carr has concluded: 'To speak today of the defence of democracy as if we were defending something which we knew and had possessed for many decades or many centuries is self-deception and sham – mass democracy is a new phenomenon – a creation of the last half-century – which it is inappropriate and misleading to consider in terms of the philosophy of Locke or of the liberal democracy of the nineteenth century. We should be nearer the mark, and should have a far more convincing slogan, if we spoke of the need, not to defend democracy, but to create it.' (ibid. pp. 75–6).
3. Cf. Hans Speier, *Social Order and The Risks of War* (New York: George Stewart, 1952), pp. 323–39.
4. Gustave Le Bon, *The Crowd* (London: Ernest Benn Ltd., 1952 – first English edition, 1896), pp. 207. Cf. also pp. 6, 23, 30, 187.
5. Sergei Chakhotin, *The Rape of the Masses* (New York: Alliance, 1940), pp. 289–91.
6. Charles Horton Cooley, *Social Organization* (New York: Scribner's, 1909), p. 93. Cf. also Chapter IX.
7. See Walter Lippmann, *Public Opinion* (New York: Macmillan, 1922), which is still the best account of this aspect of the media. Cf. especially pp. 1–25 and 59–121.
8. Cf. Gerth and Mills, *Character and Social Structure* (New York: Harcourt Brace, 1953), pp. 84ff.
9. J. Truslow Adams, *The Epic of America* (Boston: Little, Brown, 1931), p. 360.
10. Cf. Mills, 'Work Milieu and Social Structure,' a speech to 'The Asilomar Conference' of the Mental Health Society of Northern California, March 1954, reprinted in their bulletin, *People At Work: A Symposium*, pp. 20ff.

Part II

The Axial Age of Propaganda: From the Great War to the Cold War

6 The Machinery of Propaganda*
Cate Haste

> Propaganda is the task of creating and directing public opinion. In other wars this work has not been the function of government ... but ... in a struggle which was not of armies but of nations, and which tended to affect every people on the globe, this aloofness could not be maintained. Since strength for the purposes of war was the total strength of each belligerent nation, public opinion was as significant as fleets and armies...
>
> *The Organisation and Functions of the Ministry of Information*, Cmnd 9161, 1918.

That was said after four years of war. At the beginning, however, the government had an imperfect grasp of the significance of manipulating public opinion. In a nation converted to the idea of war but seeking articulation of its cause, the government relied on the speeches of politicians to explain the duty to accept and fight the war.

Establishing control of public opinion was a gradual process brought about by *ad hoc* methods. The government did not have a conscious policy for propaganda until later in the war, when it appeared to them that a small section of the population who dissented from the war aims were gaining influence among a war-weary population. For the most part, until then, they relied on the propaganda acitivities of the press, which amplified their call for national unity, and on the activities of a large number of voluntary patriotic organizations, mostly in private hands, who responded to the call to duty by propagating support for the war. Control of public opinion came about through a gradual adaptation to the new circumstances of total war.

---

* Reprinted from Cate Haste, *Keep the Home Fires Burning* (London: Allen Lane, 1977).

It was part of a wider recognition of the new wartime role of government, which entailed the extension of state control into all aspects of national life. Liberal laissez-faire doctrines that prevailed at the outset were eroded under the pressure of war. The principle of voluntaryism, which was equated with individual liberty, died hard. State control was anathema to the Liberals. Yet by the end of the war, the wartime administration, headed by two successive Liberal Prime Ministers, Asquith and Lloyd George, had centralized control of manpower, recruitment and munitions production, and was well on the way to controlling food supplies – and public opinion.

With the country on its side, the government had no need to establish formal propaganda machinery to the home front. No national newspaper opposed the war. In parliament on 6 August, nobody voted against the government, though a few, like Philip Snowden and Ramsay MacDonald, abstained and later formed the nucleus of pacifist opinion. Dissent in the Liberal Party dwindled rapidly. Five Cabinet ministers threatened resignation, but only Lord Morley and John Burns carried out the threat. The others, John Simon, Jack Pease and Lewis Harcourt, espoused the widely held Liberal view that the best way to support the country was to fight for an early victory.

Those groups that had been the focus of pre-war discontent and civil conflict: the official trades union movement, the Labour Party and the women's movement, notably Mrs Pankhurst's Women's Social and Political Union and Mrs Fawcett's National Union of Women's Suffrage Societies, rallied to the call for national unity and actively supported the war. Only a small group of socialists, Liberal backbenchers and trades unionists continued their opposition, working with small support in the Independent Labour Party, the Union for Democratic Control and, later, in the No Conscription Fellowship and in Workers' Committees.

Government propaganda was necessary, however, to justify the war and encourage recruitment. Justification of the war was the corollary of the call for volunteers. The appeal to sacrifice was inseparable from the image of a just war – the crusade which, it was claimed, Britain was fighting in the name of civilization.

Britain's justification for the war lay in the cause of 'Little Belgium'. Until the invasion of Belgium, the government and the press were divided about Britain's moral obligation to support France in the event of German attack. Only a handful of people were, in any case, aware of the exact terms of Britain's obligation to support France under the Entente Cordiale of 1904, because diplomacy had been shrouded in secrecy. Germany's violation of Belgian neutrality provided the moral argument necessary to unite the Liberal Party and the nation.

The government took the lead in defining the terms of an idealistic war. They were formulated by Asquith, the Prime Minister, on 6 August 1914 with the words: 'We are fighting to vindicate the principle that small nationalities are not to be crushed in defiance of international good faith, by the arbitrary will of a strong and overmastering power.' Britain was fighting in a moral crusade for righteousness – 'not for the maintenance of its own selfish interests, but . . . for principles the maintenance of which is vital to the civilized world.' He emphasized Germany's war guilt and Britain's conscientious attempts to keep the peace. 'The war,' he said, 'has been forced upon us', and 'it was only when we were confronted with the choice between . . . the discharge of a binding trust and a shameless subservience to naked force that we threw away the scabbard.'[1]

Lloyd George, Chancellor of the Exchequer, justified the war as a matter of national honour. His conversion from neutrality was typical of the change of attitude of many Liberals. His record with the Pro Boer Liberal Group, and his consistent opposition throughout the previous decade to increases in naval and military expenditure led many to anticipate his support for neutrality. The outbreak of war forced his hand. At the Queen's Hall in September he argued:

There is no man in this room who has always regarded the prospect of engaging in a great war with greater reluctance, with greater repugnance than I have during the whole of my political career. . . . There is no man either inside or outside of this room, more convinced that we could not have avoided it without national dishonour. . . . If we had stood by when two little nations were being

crushed and broken by the brutal hands of barbarism
our shame would have rung down by everlasting ages.

Further vindication of the government's action was provided
by rumours of German atrocities in Belgium and France.
Newspapers gave wide coverage to these, and Asquith exploited them in October:

> We could not stand by and watch the terrible unrolling
> of events – public faith shamelessly broken, the freedom of
> small peoples trodden to the dust, the wanton invasion of
> Belgium and then of France, by hordes who leave be-
> hind them at every stage of their progress a dismal trail
> of savagery, of devastation and of desecration worthy of
> the blackest annals of the history of barbarism.[2]

The lead given by the government was taken up by private
and voluntary organizations. An unquestioning acceptance
of the terms of Britain's justification was echoed in the
speeches and writings of numerous individuals and by patriotic organizations that sprouted daily to spread propaganda
about the war. It was amplified by the patriotic press which
instantly rallied to the call to justify the war and aid the
recruiting campaign.

Literary men were to have an important impact in formulating opinion. An extraordinarily large number of eminent literary figures succumbed to the prevailing mood. One
voice, that of George Bernard Shaw, was all the more conspicuous for withholding wholehearted support for the war.
In a pamphlet 'Commonsense and the War', he argued that
the government used Belgium as a pretext, and that the
real reason was to destroy a dangerous rival. His behav-
iour was so unusual that a question was asked about the
possible suppression of the pamphlet, though no action was
taken against it.

Others publicized their patriotism. On 18 September 1914,
fifty-three writers signed a public statement in *The Times*
supporting a war in which 'destiny and duty . . . call upon
us to defend the rights of small nations and to maintain
the necessary law-abiding ideals of Western Europe against
the rule of "Blood and Iron" and the domination of the
whole Continent by a military caste'. Signatories included

H. G. Wells, Thomas Hardy, Arthur Quiller-Couch, John Masefield, Arnold Bennett, Gilbert Murray, Rudyard Kipling and Arthur Conan Doyle. Conan Doyle also wrote a recruitment pamphlet 'To Arms' which was widely advertised in *The Times*.

Another group of writers, including Edmund Gosse, John Buchan, Thomas Hardy, Henry Newbolt and Gilbert Murray joined the 'Fight for Right Movement', founded by Sir Francis Younghusband, which had as its slogan 'To Fight for Right till Right be Won'. Their manifesto, evangelical in tone, demonstrates the flight from reason to which even leaders of the literary world succumbed when dealing with war:

> The spirit of the Movement is essentially the spirit of Faith: Faith in the good of man; Faith therefore in ourselves, Faith in the righteousness of our Cause, Faith in the ultimate triumph of Right; but with this Faith the understanding that Right will only win through the purification, the efforts and the sacrifices of men and women who mean to *make* it prevail.[3]

Their talents were later used by the government when it set up official propaganda, at first only to neutral and allied countries, later to the enemy and the home front. Gilbert Parker headed propaganda to America at the Secret War Propaganda Bureau. H. G. Wells worked with novelist Colonel John Buchan at the Department of Information formed in 1917, and later with Lord Northcliffe on propaganda to enemy countries at the Ministry of Information formed in 1918. Rudyard Kipling directed propaganda to colonial countries at the Ministry, and Hugh Walpole was responsible for propaganda to Russia at the War Propaganda Bureau and later at the Ministry. Arnold Bennett conducted propaganda to France at the Ministry and eventually became acting Head when Lord Beaverbrook, the Minister, resigned in October 1918.

It was not without a struggle that some writers came round to total support for the war and its aims, and then lent their pens to furthering the cause. Gilbert Murray, a distinguished classical scholar, expressed the dilemma of a number of Liberal intellectuals in his pamphlet, 'How Can

War Ever Be Right?'. He had signed a plea for neutrality published in the *Daily News* on 5 August 1914, and was a member of the Neutrality Committee. In the pamphlet, written in August 1914, he argued that, in war 'you are simply condemning innocent men, by thousands and thousands to death, or even to mutilation and torture', but he also had to agree that 'honour and dishonour are real things'. The Belgian issue had convinced him and he believed that 'the government, in deciding to keep its word at the cost of war, has rightly interpreted the feelings of the average citizen'. Despite his personal hatred of war, he found some comfort in the thought that 'War is not all evil. It is a true tragedy, which must have nobleness and triumph in it as well as disaster', and, though war is painful and horrific, yet 'to have something before you, clearly seen, which you know you must do, and can do, and will spend your utmost strength and perhaps your life in doing, is one form at least of a very high happiness, and one that appeals – the facts prove it – not only to saints and heroes, but to average men'.

Other pamphlets came from equally distinguished pens. H. G. Wells, whose support for the war aims waned later, expressed the belief, in his pamphlet 'The War that will End War', that war would eradicate Prussian militarism. In the *Daily News*, he wrote: 'We are, I believe, assisting at the end of a vast intolerable oppression upon civilization. We are fighting to release Germany and all the world from the superstition that brutality and cynicism are the methods of success, that Imperialism is better than free citizenship.'[4]

From six members of the Oxford Faculty of Modern History came the pamphlet 'Why We Are At War: Great Britain's Case' (10 October 1914) which used historical argument to prove that Germany was the aggressor. Even reasoned argument, it appeared, could only assess the situation in propagandist terms. Chapter six summed up the war as 'a struggle between two nations, one of which claims a prerogative to act outside and above the public law of Europe in order to secure the "safety" of its own State, while the other stands for the rule of public law'. The 'Oxford Pamphlets' on the war followed. A. D. Lindsay contributed one on 'The War to End War', a title that became something of a catch phrase. Sir Edward Cook, later head of the Press Bureau, contributed 'How Britain Strove for Peace', which again set out to prove Germany's war guilt.

Poets played an important part in propaganda. Patriotic verse was published in daily newspapers and in small anthologies and was widely read at the time. For instance, the National Relief Fund produced an anthology sold for charity that included work by John Masefield, Rudyard Kipling, William Watson, Alfred Noyes, Henry Newbolt and Robert Bridges. Most of the poems comprised a clarion call to arms, like Kipling's bellicose piece 'Hymn Before Action':

> The earth is full of anger
> The seas are dark with wrath
> The nations in their harness
> Go up against our path;
> Ere yet we loose the regions –
> Ere yet we draw the blade
> Jehovah of the Thunders
> Lord God of Battles, aid.

The most influential of the voluntary patriotic organizations, which sponsored and distributed these pamphlets, was the Central Committee for National Patriotic Organizations. It was set up in August 1914 as a coordinating body for patriotic activities with Asquith as president and Balfour and the Earl of Rosebery as vice-presidents, and it was run by H. C. Cust and G. W. Prothero. Their aims were described as educational, but the line between education and propaganda in wartime is a fine one. They drew on respectable academic talent – the Oxford pamphlets were commissioned by them – and encouraged support from educational institutions at home and abroad. In the belief that knowledge breeds commitment, their aim, through literature and meetings, was to establish 'such an abiding foundation of reasoned knowledge among all classes by emphasizing the righteousness, the necessity and the life and death character of the struggle, as shall sustain the wills and sacrifices of the British people through the blackest days of weariness and discouragement'.[5]

In addition there were the relief organizations and charities that fed on the wartime mania for sacrifice and added their voice to the cause, while providing both a practical outlet for patriotic energies and a method of filling up leisure time and giving the satisfaction of 'doing one's duty'. Many were concerned with relief of Belgian refugees. One such was the Belgian Relief Fund, formed in August 1914 by Lady Lugard, the Hon. Mrs Alfred Lyttleton, Lord Hugh Cecil and H. E. Morgan, with a view to 'extending hospitality to destitute women and children'. Another was the National Relief Committee in Belgium, formed in early 1915, and chaired by the Lord Mayor of London. During its first year it received £160,000 in contributions and was involved in the distribution of nearly a million Belgian flags, 185,000 posters and 200,000 medallions of King Albert of the Belgians. The posters were commissioned from established artists like the Dutch cartoonist Louis Raemaekers, John Hassall and Frank Brangwyn.

Yet another was the National Relief Fund, started by the Prince of Wales on 6 August in anticipation of unemployment and food shortages. Within two weeks the fund accumulated one and a quarter million pounds.[6]

Charities were getting out of hand. People were asked to contribute right, left and centre – not only money, but every type of comfort for the soldiers. Tobacco Funds, Food Funds and Clothes Funds mushroomed. Queen Alexandra issued a special appeal to women to help relieve the distress of war amongst the families of soldiers and sailors. Queen Mary's Needlework Guild provided patriotic work for women at home. People set about knitting and sewing, making and mending and donating money for every conceivable eventuality. (It was typical of the spirit of voluntaryism that the volunteer patriots failed to notice how unemployment among women in the garment trade was rising and creating new destitution among some former employees.) *The Times* ran a daily column of 'Practical Patriotism – How to be useful in Wartime' which listed home defence organizations and an expanding number of charities to which gifts could be sent. Voluntaryism had run riot, and in March 1916 the situation became so impossible that a group of established charities sent a deputation to the Home Office demanding that a licence should be given before charities could collect money.

The politicians noted these activities with relish. Lloyd George exploited the wartime mania in September at a recruiting meeting, when he appealed to

> something infinitely greater and more enduring which is emerging already out of this great conflict – a new patriotism, richer, nobler, and more exalted than the old. . . . It is bringing a new outlook to all classes. The great flood of luxury and sloth which had submerged the land is receding, and a new Britain is appearing. We can see for the first time the fundamental things that matter in life . . .[7]

Lloyd George's message to civilians was that the spirit of sacrifice was not confined to soldiers. The war was being fought on the home front too. His appeal to the nation to become better people in the just cause of war was part of that fostering of self-righteousness and hatred, based in fear, which overtook the civilian sensibility.

Voluntary patriotic activity had some impact on public opinion, but it was the press that had the greatest influence in moulding attitudes towards the war. The influence of the press was to be greater in this war than in any previous one. For one thing, there were more newspapers. In 1870, there were six London daily papers, four evening papers, and four Sunday papers. By 1900, the number of London dailies had risen to thirteen, evening papers to nine, and Sundays to ten, while by 1914, there was a total of sixteen London dailies, five of which had been established since 1900. They had bigger circulations. There was now a mass reading public, the product of the 1871 Education Act, which influenced the sales not only of the newer papers, but of old established ones as well. In 1886, *The Times* sold 45,754 copies, whereas in 1914 the circulation was 183,196. The new *Daily Mail* was selling at just under a million copies in both 1900 and 1914, while the *Daily Mirror*'s first edition in 1903 sold 276,000.

The introduction of mechanical typesetting and the fall in wood pulp prices had resulted in a considerable reduction in the cost of printing, which made large circulation newspapers an economic possibility.

The man who exploited this possibility was Lord Northcliffe, who had been primarily responsible for establishing popular journalism. He appealed to the tastes of ordinary people, and changed the appearance of newspapers by using bolder typeface and two-column headlines, a tactic that paid off in circulation figures, especially in wartime. He moved away from the traditional party allegiance of the press to take on the role of political commentator independent of party, thus giving himself a political freedom that he used extensively in the war. By 1914 Northcliffe was the most powerful man in Fleet Street, controlling, in addition to his popular journals, *The Times*, which he had acquired from the Walter family in 1908 – thereby realizing his greatest ambition. The *Daily Mail* and *The Times* worked as a balancing act: *The Times* retained a respectable degree of objectivity and serious political comment, while the *Daily Mail* was not only a platform for Northcliffe's views, but provided a more sensational presentation of news and comment.

The press was controlled through censorship, and the government's relationship with the press was not always a happy one. In this war of novelties, one novelty the government had to come to terms with was the extent to which it was dependent on public opinion, and it was some time before it recognized this dependence.

Meanwhile, censorship worked as a form of 'negative propaganda', because, by restricting access to information about the war, a false picture was built up and disseminated among the civilian population. Although all newspapers supported the national cause once war was declared, their patriotism was not rewarded with the confidence of either the government or the military leaders.

Government control of information was established through the Press Bureau, announced on 6 August by Winston Churchill as a machine to ensure that 'a steady stream of trustworthy information supplied both by the War Office and the Admiralty can be given to the Press'.[8] The government had no clear policy on how to do this. The Press Bureau was hurriedly improvised – 'It was never constituted at all – "it growed"', commented Sir Edward Cook, its director from 1915, and the officials were left to work out its scope and methods as experience might suggest.[9]

'Experience' suggested a twofold function for the Bureau – to provide information and to exercise censorship. An issuing department channelled information from the War Office and the Admiralty, and supplied Allied news bulletins, communiqués from the front, and, later, communiqués from all other departments. (The navy had a separate branch and a separate navy censor.) Press articles were surveyed by the Censorship Department. Censorship was compulsory for cables, including press cables, but otherwise press censorship was voluntary, that is, editors were given the freedom to decide which articles to submit to the censor. The Defence of the Realm Acts provided the basis for editorial decisions. DORA, as she was known, was introduced at the beginning of the war to give the government wide powers of control over aspects of national security. The omnibus regulations affecting the press stated that 'No person shall without lawful authority collect, record, publish or communicate, or attempt to elicit any information . . . of such a nature as is calculated to be or might be directly or indirectly useful to the enemy' (Regulation 18 [12]). Further clauses prohibited information on movements of troops, ships and aircraft, or location or description of war material, and there were regulations prohibiting false statements, statements 'likely to cause disaffection to' the success of His Majesty's Forces or those of his Allies, or his relations with foreign powers, and statements 'likely to prejudice recruiting' or undermine public confidence in bank notes or government financial measures (Regulation 27).

The organization of the Press Bureau might have worked in the interests of the civilian population, the government and the press, had it not been for stubbornness on the part of the War Office, and indecisiveness on the part of the government with regard to information. Certain indiscretions by the press merely compounded the muddle. What actually happened was that so little information was released that the home front was left in a state of bewilderment about the nature of the war. Much of the information that did get through was exaggerated, distorted and misrepresented. Of the real nature of trench warfare and the horrific effect of modern weapons, the country remained largely in the dark. For the home front the glamour of war stayed untarnished for a long time. Restriction on information about all aspects of the war eventually led to a gap in understanding about what it was being fought for at all. In an attempt to prevent information reaching the enemy, the War Office and the government succeeded in blinkering the public and creating a myopia about the very nature of the war.

Some indication of the extent of restriction of information is given by the instructions issued by the Press Bureau for the guidance of editors. These instructions originated from the service departments or from the ministries, and editors used them as a basis for deciding whether to submit articles for censorship. Altogether 700 such instructions emanated from the Bureau, covering all aspects of security. During 1915, only twelve suggested prosecutions were referred to the Director of Public Prosecutions, but the Press Bureau was asked to admonish individual editors for indiscreet publications as often as three times a week.[10]

Weather reports were stopped because they might have been useful to the enemy, and from April 1916, chess problems were banned 'unless [editors] are absolutely satisfied that the senders are of British nationality and perfectly reliable', the suspicion being that they might have been coded messages to spies. Zeppelin raids, which caused a great stir, were at first freely reported, and news of the damage confirmed prevailing convictions about German 'frightfulness'. But in September 1916, a Press Bureau instruction severely restricted information on the grounds that 'the military damage has been slight, but at the same time, so long as the Germans think that the raids have great effect, they will be continued, and long accounts tend to produce the impression both in England and abroad that they are of greater importance than they are in reality'.[11] Information was confined to brief official communiqués from the Press Bureau.

Dangers from submarine attack after 1915 caused the news of movements of merchant ships to be banned at various times. Later, publication of names of ships was banned, then the number of ships, and finally only the tonnage of ships lost was published. The circulation of Lloyd's Register and all reference books dealing with mercantile tonnage was severely restricted, and no photographs of British ships were allowed to be published unless they had been 'doctored' by the Censor.

News from the front and the movement of troops was the subject of a very large number of instructions. Details of units or battalions were prohibited in the press as they might have given away the order of battle. Advance predictions of troop movements were checked against secret information and censored if they were accurate. If they were wrong, they could get passed – the Press Bureau never guaranteed the accuracy of the reports it approved, and was not averse to creating mischief for German intelligence.

The War Office, which took the traditional view that wars were the prerogative of the military establishment, acted as the main obstruction to the gathering of information. At the outbreak of war, all newspapers appointed accredited correspondents, but these were not allowed anywhere near the front, and those of them who went to France were so controlled in their movements and deprived of facilities that they had all returned by the end of 1914. Despite a campaign by Lord Riddell, Chairman of the Newspaper Proprietors' Association, and Lord Northcliffe, correspondents were not allowed at the front until May 1915. The government acquiesced in this policy of obstruction. As a concession to the press, an 'Eye Witness' was appointed in September to report on the war as part of his military duty. He was attached to the staff of the Commander-in-Chief, and his reports, after censorship at G.H.Q., were passed on to Lord Kitchener for his personal approval. 'Eye Witness' was Lt Col. Sir Ernest Swinton, whose personal guidelines for his reports for the home front were 'to tell as much of the truth as was compatible with safety, to guard against depression and pessimism, and to check unjustified optimism which might lead to a relaxation of effort'.[12] Not much truth got through those barriers.

Kitchener's policy, as stated in November 1914 in the House of Lords, was that 'it is not always easy to decide what information may or may not be dangerous, and whenever there is any doubt, we do not hesitate to prevent publication'. He alleged that General Joffre, as Commander-in-Chief of the Allied armies, was responsible for this attitude, but Basil Clarke, one of the last correspondents to leave France, believed that 'the persistence of the British government in putting difficulties in the way of newspaper correspondents, while other allied countries were but lukewarm in the matter, tends to confirm the view that the British were leaders in this crusade'.[13] Asquith attributed Kitchener's indifference to the demands of the press to an 'undisguised contempt for the "public" in all its moods & manifestations'.[14]

The explosive dispatch from Amiens in *The Times* of 31 August 1914 highlights some aspects of the relationship between press and government. A *Times* correspondent, Arthur Moore, had managed to make contact with British troops on their retreat from their first engagement in France at Mons. The report he sent back was published under the sensational headlines: FIERCEST BATTLE IN HISTORY. HEAVY LOSSES OF BRITISH TROOPS. BROKEN BRITISH REGIMENTS. The text described how 'the broken British Army fought its way desperately with many stands, forced backwards and ever backwards by the sheer inconquerable mass of numbers', and it was coloured by interviews with soldiers in disarray. It convinced Northcliffe, who published it, of the urgent need for more recruits. F. E. Smith, Head of the Press Bureau, who could have been expected to tone it down, was also convinced. He revealed later that he had not only passed it, but recommended an additional paragraph emphasizing the need for 'men, men and yet more men'. It was an extraordinary thing for the Head of the Press Bureau to admit.

The report was considered a bombshell to national morale. But when, on 5 September, Churchill wrote to Lord Northcliffe: 'I think you ought to realise the harm that has been done. . . . I never saw such panic-stricken stuff written by any war correspondent before; and this served up on the authority of *The Times* can be made, and has been made, a weapon against us in every doubtful state', Northcliffe pointed out that in view of the additions made by the official head of the Press Bureau, 'There was no other possible conclusion except that this was the government's deliberate wish.'[15]

There was an outcry at home. The *Morning Post* came out in defence of a Press Law, the *Daily Sketch* advocated stronger censorship on the grounds that 'it is the view of the mothers of the soldiers' and the *Daily Telegraph* protested against 'highly alarmist stories . . . not justified by the facts'. A Press Bureau statement was issued, associated with Kitchener but written by Churchill, which did what Asquith described as 'dish up for [the public] with all his best journalistic condiments the military history of the week'.[16] It stated that a battle had indeed taken place in which the troops had 'offered a superb and most stubborn resistance', and warned that reports from unauthorized correspondents should be treated 'with extreme caution'. The government was consolidating its forces and bringing down the veil again.

The next day, Asquith gave a vague assurance that arrangements were being made about the supply of news, referring to the appointment of 'Eye Witness'. *The Times*, undeterred by criticism, launched an attack against

the lack of comprehension in high places of the right use of the Press in wartime. . . . The idea prevails apparently, that the Press wants news solely for its own purposes. No conception could be more foolish or obsolete. In a time of great crisis the Press has a great and patriotic duty to perform. It has to stimulate deeper public interest in a struggle which is bound to last a very long time and on which the fate of the Empire depends. It cannot do so if it is kept in the dark.

Some indication of Asquith's attitude to the press is provided in his correspondence about this issue. He wrote to Churchill on 5 September 1914:

My dear Winston,

The papers are complaining, not without reason, that we keep them on a starvation diet.

I think the time has come for you to repeat last Sunday's feat, & let them have thro' the Bureau an 'appreciation' of the events of the week; with such a seasoning of condiments as your well-skilled hand can supply.

For all that the public know, they might as well be living in the days of the prophet Isaiah, whose idea of battle was 'confused noise & garments rolled in blood'.

A number of points emerge from this episode. Firstly, the government's answer to press discontent was not to increase information, but to season what information there was already to make it palatable, that is, filter it beyond any connection with reality. Secondly, it reveals a complete lack of concern about informing the public of the course of a war that was to involve civilians on an unprecedented scale. Lastly, it throws light on the way disasters were treated, namely, as far as possible preventing news of them from being published.

Churchill was a master in this last respect. During the Dardanelles campaign he exercised his art with particular care. Churchill was primarily responsible for this campaign which provoked considerable opposition from his own staff at the Admiralty and from some Cabinet members. When it was abandoned, the government abandoned Churchill. Churchill's concern for public morale, and indeed for his own career led him to take certain liberties with information. Douglas Brownrigg, his Chief Naval Censor, described how he worked:

> He was, of course, a master of language and had a *flair* for framing communiqués. . . . He was also a bit of gambler, that is, he would hold on to a bit of bad news for a time on the chance of getting a bit of good news to publish as an offset, and I must say that it not infrequently came off! On the other hand there were days when it did not, and then there was a sort of 'Black Monday' atmosphere about – a bad 'settling day' sort of look on all our faces.[17]

Secrecy in military and naval matters was, however, excessive. Some thought the danger of too much secrecy was that public confidence in the truth-telling capacity of the government would be damaged. Douglas Brownrigg argued that the issue of public confidence sometimes outweighed military considerations, citing one particular episode as an example. On 27 October 1914 the battleship *Audacious* was sunk by a mine off the Irish coast in full view of the liner *Olympic*, which was carrying a number of American passengers who took photographs of the sinking ship. Lord Jellicoe immediately cautioned Churchill at the Admiralty that the loss of the ship should be kept secret for as long as possible, because the information would be very valuable to the enemy at a time when the margin of British naval supremacy was small. Elaborate plans were formulated under Churchill to keep the *Olympic* at Lough Swilly until another ship could be kitted out at Belfast as an exact replica of the *Audacious*. Publicity was given to her 'repair', and then her rejoining the Fleet. *The Times* criticized the Admiralty for refusing to reveal the facts. No official confirmation appeared until after the war, on 13 November 1918. Brownrigg was in no doubt that 'the continued suppression of the loss of that ship cost us the confidence of the public both here and abroad, and gave the Germans a useful bit of propaganda to use against us'.[18]

Concern about suppression of information was taken up by the Opposition in November 1914. Bonar Law, Leader of the Opposition, challenged the government that 'the Press is more muzzled than is necessary for military reasons and consequently, if that be so, it is disadvantageous from the point of view of every other interest in this country'. He demanded assurance that military considerations were the sole reason for withholding information. Asquith reiterated that information was only withheld 'lest it should give the enemy an advantage he would not otherwise have had'.[19]

Agitation continued in the press. Northcliffe believed that absence of information about the stirring episodes of war was not only damaging to recruitment but detrimental to a proper appreciation at home and abroad of the efforts of the British troops. This constant pressure had its effect, but not until April 1915, when the government finally came to an agreement with Lord Riddell permitting war correspondents to go to the front. The first correspondents reached the front in May. The tense relationship created by the government's attitude to the press inevitably influenced the press attitude to the government, and Northcliffe became more conspicuous in his outspoken criticism of the Asquith government's lack of forcefulness in running the war.

Greater freedom in war reporting lifted the veil a little bit, but censorship was still severe. The home population had very little real idea of the nature of the war. This ignorance facilitated the task of propaganda, since information on which to base real assessment was limited, which made exploitation of fear and patriotism easier.

The government had taken ten months to come to terms with the responsibilities of controlling information. They were even slower in real coordination of propaganda. There was no coordinated propaganda to the home front until 1917. The only government propaganda agency, the Secret War Propaganda Bureau, was established in September 1914 to counter German propaganda and gain neutral countries' support for the Allied cause. A certain amount of material produced by the Bureau was distributed to the home front. It also worked out principles of influencing public opinion that were later developed and used on the civilian population.

The Bureau's first director was Charles Masterman, a Liberal Christian Socialist, former literary editor of the *Daily News* and first director of the National Insurance Commission. He and his colleagues lacked either the Lloyd George flair for rhetoric or the journalistic flair for sensation. For instance, Masterman insisted that atrocity stories should be authenticated to avoid the possibility of being proved wrong. He objected to 'the demand that his department should lose all integrity or sense as a condition of the work they were doing'.[20] Masterman's guiding principle was 'to present facts and arguments based on these facts'. His dilemma was that in wartime facts were not always readily available, and were often unpalatable. His policy paid off. The publication of the Bryce Report was the supreme propaganda achievement of the department. Its apparent authenticity succeeded in eradicating doubts about the truth of German atrocity stories.

The Bureau produced pamphlets commissioned from well-known writers and published politicians' speeches and articles and interviews from the press; these were translated into seventeen different languages and distributed mainly through personal contacts throughout the world. The Bureau started illustrated newspapers, including the *Illustrated War News*, and propaganda newspapers for specific areas: *El Espelho* for Portugal and Brazil, *America Latina*, for Spanish-speaking South America, and *Hesperia* for Greece. They supported the clandestine Belgian paper *L'Indépendance Belge* by providing picture blocks, and generally distributed pictorial matter, posters, films and lectures, while providing resources for the press of neutral countries to put across a favourable view of Britain.

Propaganda to the Allies emphasized the British role in the war, in particular to counteract 'an undercurrent of uneasiness found manifesting itself in France and, to a lesser extent, Russia, as to whether the efforts and sacrifices being made by England were comparable with those of the Allies, or commensurate with the importance of the struggle'.[21] In America, Gilbert Parker, who headed the American section, operated a policy of stealth, in contrast to the bombardment tactics of German propaganda there. He used only personal contacts and personally authenticated documents for distribution in America. American visitors had the Allied point of view put to them in strong terms, and British representatives in America persuaded influential Americans to publicize their case. Opinion in America was by no means entirely pro-Allies. There was a strong group of pro-German propagandists and a large German population. Opposition to the Allies intensified when the British blockade policy seriously affected neutral, especially American, shipping. In 1916, President Wilson was re-elected as the man who would keep America out of the war, and he saw his role as peace-maker between belligerent nations. His equivocations led fervent patriots in Britain to conclude that he was in the pay of the Germans. The propaganda effort built a nucleus of favourable opinion in the country, though America did not actually enter the war until 1917.

German propaganda to neutrals was, in general, less efficient than that of the British. The Germans were not so effective at simplifying the issues of the war into right against wrong, and failed to establish any coordinated machine for propaganda. They were also put at a particular disadvantage when, on 15 August 1914, the Allies cut the transatlantic cable, thus cutting off Germany's main line of communication to America. Germany's main propaganda effort was through press conferences organized by the army and a press service that reported military operations and was responsible for censorship and control of information from the front. Like Britain, Germany failed to realize that in a long war enthusiasm for fighting would wane, but she failed to seize the initiative, not only in counteracting Allied propaganda to neutrals about German war guilt, but also in exploiting in the simplest terms, using simple images, those events that could denigrate the enemy.

The English Secret War Propaganda Bureau was doing exactly this. But there was considerable overlap with other government departments which began to realize the value of propaganda. The Foreign Office was distributing news to neutral countries, and the Foreign Office, Admiralty and War Office had intelligence departments monitoring public opinion abroad. It was an uneasy alliance which, in 1917, was partly resolved with the formation of the Department of Information.

By 1917, the conditions of war had changed. Morale in all countries was deteriorating. The naïve patriotism that fed the early war fever had abated. Three years of attrition produced only stalemate. The toll on human life was undermining civilian morale.

The government had increased its control of most crucial aspects of national life, abandoning laissez-faire methods under the pressure of war. Conscription, introduced in 1916, rationalized recruitment procedures and facilitated control over industrial manpower. Control of munitions production was established under the Ministry of Munitions in 1915. A Food Controller was appointed in January 1917 to cope with food shortages and rising prices, which had produced allegations of profiteering. Rationing was finally introduced, on a restricted basis, in July 1918. Control of public opinion was the next area for government attention.

In reaction to the mood of discontent and war weariness, the government, under Lloyd George (who replaced Asquith in December 1916), began to organize propaganda as an official government activity. A Department of Information, headed by the novelist John Buchan, was set up in February 1917 on an official basis. Sir Edward Carson, a minister in the War Cabinet, was given responsibility for propaganda activities, though he was not altogether a success at the job. The Department took over the work of Wellington House (The Secret War Propaganda Bureau) and helped to coordinate some of the intelligence activities of the service ministries. Its work was primarily concerned with propaganda to Allied and neutral countries.

The Department of Information had sections dealing with the origination and distribution of literature, with monitoring foreign news (in conjunction with the Foreign Office, the Admiralty and War Office Intelligence), with providing news and press articles at home and abroad, and with the production and distribution of film. For the first time journalists were officially involved in propaganda – through an Advisory Committee that included Robert Donald, editor of the *News Chronicle*, C. P. Scott, editor of the *Manchester Guardian*, and Lord Northcliffe. Sir George Riddell, proprietor of the *News of the World*, joined later, and Lord Beaverbrook, who later headed the Ministry of Information, replaced Northcliffe when he went to America to set up the British War Mission, a propaganda agency for America.

On the home front, a new organization came into being, the National War Aims Committee (NWAC), to direct the first propaganda aimed specifically at the home front. Its main function was directly to counteract pacifist propaganda, which the government believed to be exploiting unrest and causing strikes that could jeopardize the whole running of the war.

The NWAC was formed in June 1917 under an all-party executive with Asquith as president, Bonar Law and G. N. Barnes as vice-presidents and the two Chief Whips, Lt Col R. A. Sanders and F. E. Guest, as joint chairmen. This all-party arrangement was designed to allay fears that a propagandist body on the home front could be used for party political gain, fears that were at the root of opposition to the unfamiliar activity of home front propaganda.

From the start, the Committee had a slightly amateurish air about it. It was dependent on voluntary donations and contributions from party funds until November 1917, when £240,000 was voted out of public funds, the largest sum ever spent on home front propaganda. In July 1917 the Committee took over the Central Committee for National Patriotic Organizations (CCNPO), and used their branches for propaganda. The educational spirit of the CCNPO survived within the National War Aims Committee.

The two main aims of the Committee were to 'counteract and, if possible, render nugatory the insidious and specious propaganda of pacifist publications' and to exhort the population to 'inflexible determination to continue to a victorious end the struggle in maintenance of those ideals of Liberty and Justice which are the common and sacred cause of the Allies'.[22] The Committee's general aim was to 'strengthen the national morale and consolidate the national war aims as outlined by the executive government'. Support for these objectives was by no means unanimous. It was precisely the *lack* of clear government war aims that was the focus for discontent, suspicion and criticism of the government. Thus in October 1917 the Brighton and District Trades Council not only turned down a request for cooperation, but voted to burn the Committee's documents and return the ashes. The government's lack of war aims prompted the Labour Party, at its special Conference in August 1917, to draw up a separate Labour Memorandum on War Aims; this memorandum provided the basis for Lloyd George's first major speech on the subject, delivered to a trades union audience at Caxton Hall in January 1918, which was itself a propaganda exercise designed to deflect further criticism.

To counteract pacifist propaganda on the industrial front, the NWAC collected specimens of all types of pacifist literature for analysis, and resolved

> to dwell on the democratic development and improvement of the lot of the working classes which State control and other war changes have already secured; to suggest the prospect of further improvement and greater freedom when the war is over ... [and] to inspire all workers at home with ... a living sense of their responsibility and share in the great task; to give them tangible proof of the government's appreciation; so to brace and hearten them that, however long the war may last, its crusading character may be their dominating thought.[23]

To this end, the Committee concentrated operations in areas of unrest. For example, when a drop in iron ore production was reported in Cumberland, the Committee mounted a special campaign there. Other spheres of operation were Wigan, described by an investigator as 'the worst place for pacifists that I have ever had any experience of, the common allegation being that the war was a capitalist quarrel',[24] and Hull, where it was reported that the men were prepared to 'down tools' on any trifling excuse. NWAC speakers in dockyard areas were advised to hold their meetings away from the dock, and 'to limit themselves to war aims not trade disputes'.[25] When it was observed that women were particularly prone to war-weariness special meetings were set up for them.

The NWAC used the constituency party organizations and local committees of patriotic organizations to arrange meetings and distribute literature. Local meetings and large patriotic rallies were held in industrial areas like one in Birmingham, called 'Win the War Day' (21 Sept. 1918), in which a tank led a procession through the town, while the whole area was bombarded with leaflets and pamphlets: distributed from stalls, handed out by boy scouts, and in the case of 250,000 leaflets, showered from an aeroplane. Between September 1917 and October 1918, 899 meetings were recorded and full-scale campaigns were carried out in 345 out of a total of 468 constituencies. The NWAC headquarters provided speakers, arranged visits to the front, and engaged music hall artists to lighten the proceedings with patriotic songs, and eye-witnesses from the front to recount their experiences. A travelling cinema even toured the country. Speakers at NWAC meetings included politicians, authors and volunteers who were paid a nominal fee, while writers were commissioned to compose some of the fifty pamphlets and articles for the press that emanated from the Committee. Other products included posters, like one entitled 'Huns Ancient and Modern', picture postcards, cigarette cards, banners, cartoons, Christmas cards and twenty-five sketches that were sold at £10 each.

The aim was to persuade the population to continue fighting the war by warning against the dangers of a negotiated peace with Germany, usually by reiterating the horrors of German frightfulness. This was the main theme of the lantern lectures set by the Committee, and the subject of one of their more specious products 'The German Crimes Calendar', which summarized the war in terms of German barbarities. Activities like these did a great deal to fan anti-Germanism, and incurred the hostility of H. G. Wells, at least, who was working on enemy propaganda at Crewe House, and who complained that the Committee was doing nothing except 'antagonizing our people against anything and everything German', while being 'totally unconstructive about the war aims or what was to happen after the war'.[26]

The government was also engaged in propaganda in more specific areas connected with the national interest. Various government departments set up committees to publicize their work and encourage public participation in the government's aims. The propaganda of these bodies was as pervasive as recruitment propaganda had been before conscription. A Ministry of National Service was set up which spent most of its time appealing for National Service Volunteers especially women, to take on civilian jobs and release men for active service. A War Saving Committee was also created to encourage support for National Savings Schemes and the various government War Loan Schemes. It used a nation-wide network of 1,530 local committees, who devoted their energies to promoting thrift.[27] In December 1917, a tank bank was set up in Trafalgar Square that earned £319,640 in one week by selling War Bonds and War Savings Certificates. The first ten customers were girls who had lost their sweethearts in the war.[28]

In this new appeal to sacrifice, the various government committees employed imagery that highlighted the idealistic aims of the war and denigrated the enemy. In January 1917 subscription to the War Loan Scheme was equated with a personal contribution towards the fight for 'mankind's right to march forward towards the dawn of a new life on earth'.[29] Film was used later, including one animated sketch with the slogan 'Every Child Can Help to Stamp out the Hun', showing National Savings stamps obliterating the face of a German soldier, and another with the slogan, 'It's the Last Shilling Which Will Break the Kaiser's Back' with an appropriate simple illustration.

Campaigns to save food in the absence of compulsory rationing prompted a great deal of voluntary propaganda. The government took the lead, with the Director-General of Food Economy, Kennedy Jones, asserting that the public should

> look well at the loaf on your breakfast table and treat it as if it were real gold, because the British loaf is going to beat the German. . . . Women have done nobly in the war, but they must do still more . . . today the kitchen is the key

to victory and is in the fighting line alongside our undying heroes of the trenches and our brave men of the sea.[30]

Altogether 30,000 associations and 1,200 committees were working on propaganda to promote food economy. London was plastered with posters claiming 'Eat less Bread and Victory is Secure'.[31] Rationing, on the basis of 'loose voluntarism', was introduced by the end of 1917. An SOS League was formed which pledged not to exceed the rations laid down by the Food Controller, Lord Rhondda. Three million people joined.

Equally popular was the demand to turn over all available land to cultivation. The King contributed the symbolic gesture of turning over the flower beds round the Queen Victoria memorial to vegetables, and dividing the Royal Parks up into allotments. 'Idle Land for Food' was the slogan. Rowland Prothero, Minister of Agriculture, observed solemnly that 'It is my sincere conviction that it may be on the cornfields and potato lands of Great Britain that victory in the Great War may be lost or won.'[32]

The main government propaganda effort was still, however, directed at neutrals, allies, and the enemy. In February 1918, the Ministry of Information was set up under Lord Beaverbrook. It replaced the failing organization of the Department of Information which, under Sir Edward Carson, had been suffering from inter-departmental squabbles and had lost much of its dynamism. Carson, according to Beaverbrook, was 'hostile to the Prime Minister, critical of the government and nursing a grievance. His enthusiasm for the cause of propaganda was not apparent.'[33] Lord Beaverbrook's enthusiasm, on the other hand, had already been proved by his success at organizing Canadian propaganda during the war.

His appointment sparked off a row in parliament about the ethics of newspapermen becoming members of the government – which became more strident when it was learned that Northcliffe, then a friend of Lloyd George, was to be appointed Director of Propaganda to enemy countries, and was to have direct access to the Cabinet. Austen Chamberlain, of the Unionist War Committee, led the attack, arguing that the presence of newspapermen in government administration made the government responsible for what appeared in the press; at the same time, with uncharacteristic concern for the press, it was argued that newspapers would lose their freedom if proprietors lost the right to comment on government actions. Spencer Hughes observed that journalists were in an ideal position to conduct propaganda, since 'they are not hampered by what Dr Johnson termed "needless scrupulosity."' This hostility petered out when the government became involved in other activities.

Though most of the Ministry's work was with foreign propaganda, it did explore new methods of propaganda for the home front. The use of war artists, started under Masterman's Wellington House operation, and also used by Beaverbrook during his Canadian propaganda experience, was expanded. Official war artists had been allowed to the front in 1916, the first being Muirhead Bone. More were commissioned, and regular exhibitions were held of the work of Bone, Paul Nash, Nevinson, and others.

The most important development was in film, which was used for the first time as a medium for propaganda. At the beginning of the war, although cinema audiences for Charlie Chaplin and D. W. Griffith films totalled twenty million, the official view of film was of 'an instrument for the amusement of the masses: the educated classes thought of "the pictures" as responsible for turning romantic shop boys into juvenile highwaymen, as a sort of moving edition of the 'Penny Dreadful.'"[34] In the course of the war, and particularly under the Ministry of Information, the role of 'the pictures' changed from an instrument for the amusement of the masses into an instrument for the manipulation of the masses. Northcliffe observed in September 1918: 'Speaking as a newspaperman, I hate to confess it, but the motion picture is doing more for the Allied cause than any other means of thought transmission. Not everyone reads the newspapers, and those who do forget what they have read, but no one can forget what he has seen happen on the screen.'[35]

The government took some time to appreciate the power of film. Like war correspondents, cameramen were not allowed to the front until autumn 1915. Masterman pioneered the use of film when, despite resistance from the service departments, he managed to get film of the Grand Fleet, the New Armies in training, and the army in Flanders. With film lent by Vickers Maxim, he put together the propaganda film *Britain Prepared*, which was shown in neutral countries in December 1915. Wellington House released the first major actuality film of the war, *The Battle of the Somme*, in August 1916. It had 2000 bookings in the first two months and raised about £30,000 for military charities.[36]

Earlier on, independent film companies, as anxious to prove their patriotism as anyone else, had made up for the absence of factual film with old travelogues of Belgium and hurriedly-produced patriotic dramas like the Hepworth film fantasy titled *Unfit* (or *The Strength of the Weak*) which opened in October 1914 with the billing: 'Both brothers wish to enlist, only the older is accepted. The younger is "unfit". He goes to the front as a war correspondent and in the end gives his life to save his brother for the sake of a girl they both love.'[37] Recruiting films like *England's Call* were shown accompanied by military bands and girls in khaki singing patriotic songs.

The music hall lightning cartoon sketch was transposed successfully on to film by independent film companies like Neptune Films. Lancelot Steed produced numerous witty and patriotic long cartoons that glorified Britain's war effort and encouraged "Hun-hating" through the simple and prevalent method of ridiculing the enemy.

The first cooperation between the government and the film industry came with the establishment of the War Office Cinematograph Committee in 1916. It took over the Trade Committee which had already been showing actuality film taken at the front by such cameramen as Geoffrey Mallins and Lt J. B. McDowell. The Committee was chaired by Beaverbrook, with William Jury representing the trade, Reginald Brade from the War Office, and later Sir Graham Greene from the Admiralty. They cooperated with the Department of Information's cinema division, which made films for distribution in neutral countries. Regular biweekly news films were started in British cinemas in 1917.

The Ministry of Information officially adopted film, and set up its own studios staffed by professional film-makers in order to produce short propaganda films. These films were made for other government departments, using actresses like Ellen Terry to dramatize a message that aimed, for instance, to recruit women into munitions factories or the land army, or to encourage food economy by providing hints on alternative menus or how to grow your own food. Frequently, the dramatizations were intended to show how moral censure would fall on people who failed to do their duty. After the success of the French film, *Mothers of France*, starring Sarah Bernhardt, film-makers stressed the stirring human angle rather than the purely military aspects of the war. In 1917, the War Office partly sponsored D. W. Griffith's, spectacle, *Hearts of the World*, which was released in 1918.

The Ministry also invented the 'film tag', a short film of about two minutes embodying in story form some useful moral such as 'Save Coal' or 'Buy War Loans'. It was attached at the end of the newsreels and often took the form of a witty lightning sketch cartoon by Lancelot Steed and others. By 1918 film had arrived as a medium of propaganda.

Most of the Ministry's work was with foreign propaganda, however, Northcliffe headed propaganda to enemy countries, Rudyard Kipling directed colonial propaganda, and Lord Rothermere, Northcliffe's brother, directed propaganda to neutral countries. Despite a great deal of hostility from the Foreign Office, which had its own propaganda machine and intelligence branches, the Ministry set up a structure for acquiring information and disseminating propaganda. Propaganda in enemy countries worked to undermine morale and foment revolution amongst dissident groups in the Balkans and the Habsburg Empire. Devices were perfected for dropping leaflets behind enemy lines and generally destroying morale amongst German troops by emphasizing the magnitude and strength of the Allies and the effects of the blockade on Germany. General Ludendorff, after searching around for an excuse for the German defeat, found the answer in the effectiveness of British propaganda. This was also an admission of the failure of German propaganda, especially in neutral countries, where, Ludendorff wrote, 'We were subject to a moral blockade', as a result of Allied propaganda there.

Meanwhile the French conducted their propaganda through the Maison de la Presse, set up under the Ministry of Foreign Affairs in 1916, which dealt with intelligence, provided news, information and literature for propaganda in neutral countries, and laid particular stress on the religious nature of the war, on an appeal to avenge the humiliation of 1871, and on the fight for justice and freedom from oppression. This organization produced propaganda about atrocities in France in order to influence neutral opinion. France, too, had been slow to coordinate propaganda, since the main effort was concentrated at the beginning on the military offensive against the enemy, and it was the military that took over control of the press. There was a great deal of voluntary propaganda, and by March 1917, 30,000 societies with more than eleven million members in France and overseas had banded together in the Union des Grandes Associations Contre La Propagande Ennemie, which worked in neutral countries and at home. After a more or less abortive attempt by Northcliffe to coordinate Allied propaganda in March 1918, the French reorganized their various propaganda agencies under the Centre d'Action de Propagande Contre L'Ennemie which utilized the organization and agents in neutral countries, and assisted in undermining morale behind the German lines with its own leaflets and pamphlets.

When America entered the war in 1917, the whole propaganda effort was immediately made official under George Creel's Committee on Public Information, which consisted of the Secretaries of State and the Secretaries for the Army and Navy. In its overseas propaganda effort aimed at destroying German morale the Committee emphasized the strength the addition of American troops had given to the Allied forces. In particular, it portrayed President Wilson as a man who embodied the ideals of freedom and democracy, an image that was particularly useful in the Committee's appeal to the ordinary German to detach himself from the power of the Prussian Junker class, which had brought so much misery to the world. At home, recruitment propaganda stressed in particularly vivid posters the barbarity of the Germans and their 'frightfulness'.

By 1918, British propaganda to the home front, no less than propaganda abroad, was established as an essential aspect of modern warfare. The realization, slow to dawn, that efficiency at the front was dependent on efficiency and morale at home was crucial to the development of government propaganda machinery to manipulate the civilian response to war. By 1918, the home front was fighting its own war: against the 'enemy in our midst' and against the phantom fears roused by war and exploited by propagandists in order to inflame hatred against enemy aliens and pacifists, as much as against Germans. Wartime propaganda generated fear, hatred and illusion, and confused more than clarified the issue for a nation that was undergoing one of the greatest tragedies of modern history.

Soldiers returning from the war found an England they did not recognize:

> England was beastly in 1918; it was in the hands of the dismal and incompetent. Pessimism raged among those who knew nothing of the war; *défaitisme*, the desire to stop the war at all costs, even by the admission of defeat, broke out among the fainthearts; while those at home who still had the will to fight preferred to use the most disgusting means – to fight by lying propaganda, and by imitating the bad tradition of the German Army which consistently made war against civilians. No wonder that a genuine and silent pacifism was rising in the breast of the war-weary populations. Envy, hatred, malice and all uncharitableness, fear and cruelty born of fear, seemed the dominant passions of the leaders of the nations in those days. Only in the trenches (on both sides of No Man's Land) were chivalry and sweet reasonableness to be found.[38]

Notes

1. Asquith in the House of Commons, 27 August 1914.
2. Asquith in Cardiff, 2 October 1914.
3. Imperial War Museum pamphlet, *The Fight for Right Movement*, p. 5.
4. *Daily News*, 14 August 1914.
5. *Annual Report*, Central Committee for National Patriotic Organizations, 1916. Located in the Reference Library of the Imperial War Museum.
6. *Report*, National Relief Committee in Belgium, May 1916.
7. *The Times*, 20 September 1914.

8. House of Commons, 6 August 1914.
9. Sir Edward Cook, *The Press in Wartime* (London: Macmillan, 1920), p. 42.
10. Public Records Office, Ministry of Information files 4/1B Secret Report, Military Press Control. *A History of the Work of M.I. 7 1914–1919*, p. 9. M.I. refers to Ministry of Information.
11. Quoted in R. D. Blumenfield, *All in a Lifetime* (London: Ernest Benn, 1931), p. 130.
12. Major General Sir Ernest D. Swinton, *Eye Witness* (London: Hodder & Stoughton, 1932), p. 53.
13. Basil Clarke, *How the Progress of the War was Chronicled by Pen and Camera*, quoted in John Terraine, *Impacts of War* (London: Hutchinson, 1970), p. 95.
14. Asquith to Venetia Stanley, 5 September 1914, quoted in Martin Gilbert, *Winston S. Churchill*, vol. III: 1914–1916 (London: Heinemann, 1971), p. 71.
15. Gilbert, op. cit., p. 70.
16. Gilbert, op. cit., p. 71.
17. Rear Admiral Sir Douglas Brownrigg, *Indiscretions of a Naval Censor* (London: Cassell, 1920), p. 13.
18. Brownrigg, op. cit., p. 33.
19. 68 House of Commons, 11 November 1914, col. 19.
20. L. Masterman, *C. F. G. Masterman* (London: Nicholson & Watson, 1939), p. 275.
21. Public Records Office, Ministry of Information Files 4/5, Second Report of the Work Conducted for the Government at Wellington House, C. F. G. Masterman, February 1916. As noted in the text, Wellington House was The Secret War Propaganda Bureau.
22. Resolution passed at the Inaugural meeting of the National War Aims Committee, 4 August 1914, Queen's Hall.
23. Public Records Office, Ministry of Information Files 4/4A. All quotes from Report (Secret) NWAC, *Home Publicity during the Great War*, National War Aims Committee, p. 2.
24. Ibid.
25. NWAC, op. cit., pp. 5, 6.
26. Reginald Pound and Geoffrey Harmsworth, *Northcliffe* (London: Cassell, 1959), p. 648.
27. Caroline Playne, *Britain Holds On, 1917–1918* (London: George Allen & Unwin, 1931), p. 171.
28. Playne, p. 173.
29. Hartley Withers in the *Economist*, 10 January 1917.
30. Kennedy Jones in Edinburgh, 19 May 1917, quoted in Playne, op. cit., p. 66.
31. Playne, p. 65.
32. Michael MacDonagh, *In London During the Great War* (London: Eyre & Spottiswoode, 1935), p. 164. Prothero made the remark on 26 December 1916.
33. Lord Beaverbrook, *Men and Power, in 1917–1918* (London: Oldbourne, 1959), p. 266.

34. Public Records Office, Ministry of Information Files 4/6, *Report: War Cabinet Committee on Overlapping and Production and Distribution of Propaganda*, Minute on the Cinema Industry and its Relation to the Government, John Boon, 8 June 1918.
35. Ibid.
36. *The Bioscope*, 12 October 1916.
37. *The Bioscope*, 10 September 1914.
38. Charles Edmonds, *A Subaltern's War* (London: Peter Davies Ltd, 1929), p. 188.

7 America's First Propaganda Ministry: The Committee on Public Information During the Great War[1]*

Robert Jackall and Janice M. Hirota

Within a week of the congressional declaration of war on Germany on 6 April 1917, President Woodrow Wilson established the Committee on Public Information (CPI) by executive fiat. The CPI brought together, under one organizational roof, leading journalists, publicists, and advertising men, along with novelists, academic intellectuals, moral crusaders, and muckrakers of every sort from the entire land. A whole generation of what might be called experts with symbols – opinion-shapers, image-makers, interpretive geniuses, and storytellers of every sort – honed their already sharp skills to sell America's Crusade to the American public and the idea of America to the world. This essay examines the CPI in some detail. By looking at one key organization in the infancy of mass communications, the essay tries to discern the essential problems faced by men and women in organizations dedicated to mass persuasion, the organizing techniques they characteristically adopt to solve those problems, and the habits of mind that their work typically generates.

Wilson appointed George Creel as chairman of the Committee on Public Information. Creel was a former muckraking journalist from Kansas City by way of Denver and Greenwich Village. At various times during his tumultuous career he was a crusader against government and police corruption, prostitution and other vice, and John D.

---

* Published for the first time in this volume.

Rockefeller's private industrial army. He also fought for child-labor laws, women's rights, and electoral reform. Creel was also a long-time booster of Wilson and had worked assiduously for the President's re-election in 1916, organizing among other things a "blue-ribbon" committee of publicists and writers to produce pamphlets on the President's behalf. In fact, as America's entrance into the European war seemed inevitable in the spring of 1917, Creel himself, reflecting somewhat arcane knowledge gained perhaps from his Roman Catholic father, had urged Wilson to create a government agency to coordinate "[n]ot propaganda as the Germans defined it, but propaganda in the true sense of the word, meaning the 'propagation of faith'".[2] As Creel saw matters, such an agency was imperative both to ensure newspapers' voluntary self-censorship on military matters and especially to develop and sell the powerful motivating ideas that alone could galvanize behind the war effort the energies of a society splintered into warring factions by years of ambivalent neutrality.[3] Even more to the point, such an effort had to contend with incipient social splits of various sorts. America of 1917 evinced in embryo many of the social characteristics typical of our contemporary brawling social order: a melting pot of ethnic, racial, and language groups that never melted; a large foreign-born population that did not read English, or for that matter speak it effectively, and an equally large sector of native-born citizens who were illiterate or semiliterate; a battlefield of class conflicts, some naked, some mediated by bureaucratic structures, all largely obscured by intensive status scrambling within classes; an urbanizing social order clinging to rural myths; and a hodgepodge of clanging political and cultural ideologies.

Both in order to "hold fast the inner lines" on the domestic front and to "Carry the Gospel of Americanism to Every Corner of the Globe," all in a "fight for the *minds* of men," Creel created a free-wheeling, vast, sprawling organization that, by the war's end, utilized every available means of shaping public opinion.[4] Here we focus only on those divisions of the CPI most directly concerned with shaping opinion through symbol manipulation and management.[5]

As a newspaperman, Creel's immediate instinct was to commandeer the written word. He established a News

Division that produced a daily newspaper, the *Official Bulletin*, with a circulation of 100 000 for the duration of the war, as well as regular bulletins, the forerunner of today's "news handouts," sometimes complete with editorials, for distribution to the nation's newspapers. Later the CPI's Publication Division, headed by Guy Stanton Ford, professor of history at the University of Minnesota, engaged historical scholars at all of the nation's leading universities to produce 10 publications in a *Red, White, and Blue Series* with titles such as "How the War Came to America," "The President's Flag Day Address, with Evidence of Germany's Plans," "Conquest and Kultur," and the "War Cyclopedia: A Handbook for Ready Reference on the Great War." The division also produced 21 pamphlets in the *War Information Series*, including "American Loyalty," "Lieber and Schurz: Two Loyal Americans of German Birth" and "The German–Bolshevik Conspiracy," several *Loyalty Leaflets*; and publications for The Friends of German Democracy and for the American Alliance for Labor and Democracy, a front group created to reach American workers. Millions of copies of these publications, many of them little more than dignified broadsides, were distributed around the world, some translated into several languages. It was, in fact, a bottleneck in the printing of pamphlets cranked out under Ford's leadership that led Creel, at the suggestion of Edward Sisson, to recruit as a troubleshooter Carl Byoir, who had worked for Sisson when the latter was the editor of *Cosmopolitan Magazine*. Byoir was a young man, originally from Iowa, who, at the age of 28, already had sales, advertising, publishing, newspaper reporting and editing experience as well as a Columbia University law degree. When Byoir solved the printing logjam by bypassing the Government Printing Office and making a series of ingenious arrangements with printers in New York City whom he knew from his magazine experience, Creel asked him to stay on as associate chairman of the Executive Division. He became Creel's right-hand man, the center of the vast administrative correspondence that the CPI both generated and received, and the head at various times of several CPI divisions, an indication of Creel's confidence in his abilities.[6]

Creel knew, however, that vast segments of the public

formed their images of the world neither from news nor from pamphlets with scholarly trappings, but rather from stories with a human-interest angle. The Division of Syndicated Features captured the services of some of the most important novelists, short-story writers, and essayists of the day to produce a steady stream of feature stories and articles for the nation's press. Some of the most important figures in this work were Samuel Hopkins Adams, Booth Tarkington, Mary Roberts Rinehart, Walter Lippmann, and Harvey O'Higgins, who also served for a time as an associate chairman of the CPI. Although some intellectuals dissented vigorously against the Great War, they had little impact on national debate. One of the CPI's great triumphs was the extent to which it succeeded in enlisting wordsmiths of every sort to frame the war as a crusade for democratic ideals and traditions threatened by autocracy, parameters that made dissent seem foolish at best.

But the written word had its limits in a society that was, after all, still largely semiliterate. Moreover, only personal persuasive fervor could gain recruits for a moral crusade filled with great visions. Creel gave Chicagoan Donald Ryerson official CPI sanction to go national with a fledgling organization called the Four Minute Men, already speaking in Chicago's movie houses on war topics. Under the later leadership of William McCormick Blair, the Four Minute Men grew into an army of 75 000 men and women who gave 755 190 pointed, orchestrated speeches in movie houses in 5200 communities around the country on topics such as "Why We Are Fighting," "Unmasking German Propaganda," "Where Did You Get Your Facts?" and, of course, on all the Liberty Loan campaigns that financed the war.[7] The Four Minute Men were in effect a national broadcasting outfit years before commercial radio became available, at least for those social groups that regularly flocked to the movie houses.[8] The Speaking Division, headed by Arthur E. Bestor, president of the Chautauqua Institution, complemented the Four Minute Men and later merged with that division, sending hundreds of speakers, men and women, American and Allied, military and civilian, crisscrossing almost every corner of the country to give inspirational talks.

But the CPI made its greatest, and perhaps its most lasting, impact with its use of visual images of the war. Some of these were straightforward exhibitions. For instance the CPI provided war exhibits to a number of state fairs in the spring of 1918, followed by a gigantic War Exposition in Chicago, complete with war paraphernalia of every sort, including huge guns and remnants of U-boats and German planes. The exposition, which featured a mock battle that stirred great crowd enthusiasm, then travelled to more than 20 cities.

Other images, by far the most important, were manufactured outright by separate divisions of the CPI that sometimes worked in concert. The first of these formed was the Division of Pictorial Publicity, headed by Charles Dana Gibson, the president of the Society of Illustrators. Creel tells us in his autobiography that Gibson had wandered into Creel's makeshift office during the first week of the war with a poster that he wanted to contribute to the cause and left with a mandate to organize the artists of America behind the war effort.[9] James Montgomery Flagg, Herbert Paus, N. C. Wyeth, Howard Chandler Christy, Henry Reuterdahl, Joseph Pennell, Charles Buckles Falls, and Edmond Tarbell were only among the most well-known of the scores of artists that flocked to Gibson's call and produced the hundreds of riveting visual images of bayoneted soldiers marching or going "over the top," of submarine victims, of defenseless mothers with clinging children about to be attacked, of coyly seductive Christy girls appealing to men to prove their manhood by joining the service, or of the Spirit of America as a re-embodied Joan of Arc.[10] The clients for the work ranged from the American Red Cross, to the American Library Association, to the Signal Corps, to the YMCA and YWCA, to the U.S. Boys Working Reserve, to the National Committee of Patriotic Societies, to the CPI's Division of Films and many more.[11]

The Division of Cartoons sometimes borrowed material directly from the Division of Pictorial Publicity, but usually generated on its own widely accessible images on virtually every aspect of the war. The division issued a weekly Bulletin for Cartoonists that coordinated the work of the nation's cartoonists.[12] Each bulletin urged the production of cartoons around a number of certain themes, often complete with captions to unify a particular campaign, while leaving the pictorial creative details to the cartoonists themselves.

Among many other suggestions, cartoonists were encouraged to urge boys to work on farms during summers (bulletin no. 1); to urge farmers to feed garbage to hogs (bulletin no. 2); to urge women to take the industrial places of men gone to war (bulletin no. 3); to urge the public to save coal by personally supervising the care of furnaces and to limit each individual's consumption of sugar to three pounds a month (bulletin no. 4); to urge women to become Army or Navy nurses and to encourage people to send to the boys in training camps Smileage Books ("Send him a smile") admitting them to Liberty Theaters (bulletin no. 5); to point out to industrial workers the disastrous results of striking during wartime (bulletin no. 6); to urge the public to root German property interests out of America (bulletin no. 7); to urge women to join the "army of food producers" by picking fruits and berries and to tell the public to beware of German lies (bulletin no. 8); to stimulate greater patriotism by depicting what Americans are doing "over there" in contrast with "over here" and to oppose the lynchings of Negroes and attacks on those suspected of being enemy sympathizers (bulletin no. 9); to urge industrial workers of all sorts to stick to their jobs because of the high costs of labor turnover (bulletin no. 10); to undercut German propaganda at home by supporting the "Where did you get your facts?" campaign, to encourage the public to salvage pencils, old kid gloves, and tin foil, and to call American soldiers "Yanks" instead of "Sammies," a term the soldiers despised (bulletin no. 11); to warn the public of the dangers of overconfidence "even though the boys over there seem to have the Huns on the run" (bulletin no. 12); to stress the importance of making English the universal spoken language in the United States as a means of "patriotizing" foreign-born citizens (bulletin no. 13); to help legitimate the President's order and the Senate's bill prohibiting the making or sale of intoxicating beverages as a war-related necessity (bulletin no. 14); to point out to the public the enormous sacrifices in blood and money France was making in the war as a way of urging the American public to greater sacrifice (bulletin no. 15); to create public censure of soldiers who were AWOL by encouraging fathers, mothers, wives, and sweethearts to send their soldiers back to duty with a smile (bulletin no. 19); to urge resistance to premature "peace propaganda" "until the last vestige of Germany's crime is atoned for" (bulletin no. 19); to keep alive "the tradition of the American mother" by helping the United War Work Campaign organizations that were "mothering our boys" (bulletin no. 20); and, after the 11 November 1918 armistice, to remind the public that the war's end would not bring the boys home until the rebuilding of France and Belgium was well underway (bulletin no. 23).

Some cartoons were syndicated and sent around the country and world. Perhaps the best known were the scathing cartoons of C. R. Macauley, distributed by The Butterfield Syndicate in New York. Macauley specialized in caricatures of "soap-box traitors," that is, anyone who criticized any aspect of war policies; and especially in portraits of the bestial "Hun," usually depicted as a bellowing, fang-toothed, waxed-mustachioed gorilla wearing a *pickelhaube*, the famous Prussian spiked helmet, leaving a trail of ravished young maidens named "Law of God and Man," "Right," "Justice," "Humanity," "Hope," "Faith," "Charity," and "Decency".[13] The cover of one of the last bulletins (no. 25) reflected the estimate that the Division of Cartoons had of its own work in comparison with that of other divisions. The cover pictured a balance held by "Public Opinion". On one side, high in the air, was the side of the scale with heavy tomes labeled pamphlets and editorials, parchment, and quill and inkpot; on the other, tilting the scale sharply downward, was a single sheet of paper labeled "Cartoons". However self-promotional, the judgment was undoubtedly accurate. Harking back to the Elizabethan era of chapbooks and broadsides, mass cartoons in the First World War reduced infinitely complicated matters to single specific images, complete with pointed slogans. They became in effect harbingers of the simplifying interpretive expertise necessary for communicating with mass audiences.

The same kind of immediate, graphic appeal came out of the Division of Films, which produced, promoted, approved, or distributed a flood of films about all aspects of the war.[14] The CPI produced a number of documentaries on the actual machinery of war, such as "Torpedo Boat

Destroyers," "Making of Big Guns," "The Bath of Bullets," and "The Storm of Steel"; others recounted the social dimensions of army life, such as "In a Southern Camp" and "Army and Navy Sports"; still others focused on particular occupational groups essential to the war effort, such as engineers, lumberjacks, and shipbuilders. The Division of Films also produced a handful of feature films, including "America's Answer," "Under Four Flags," and the most famous "Pershing's Crusaders". The handout advertising the latter film for its showing in Chicago's Orchestra Hall suggests the tone of most of the film propaganda of the period:

> Ths first official American War Film shows the grim earnestness of the United States Government in its war activities and its determination to stamp out Kaiserism. Our boys in Khaki are pictured in the very front firing lines. You see Americans taking over the fighting trenches. You see Secretary of War Baker and General Pershing inspecting our preparations in France. You see the first German prisoners captured by our brave boys, – two dozen disheartened, defeated Boches. The last half of the picture is entirely devoted to what our boys are accomplishing 'over there.'
>
> You also see what Uncle Sam's countless civilian army is doing 'over here.' Miles of cantonments grow over-night. You see the raw recruit become the hardened fighter. Fleets of aeroplanes darken the skies. Massive ships of steel, concrete and wood speed down the ways. Mighty guns and projectiles are made before your very eyes. Millions of uniforms are turned out with magic-like rapidity. You realize that every American is doing his best to help win this war. Our great Navy, our huge and growing Army, and all our immense resources of field and mine and forest are in this struggle to the successful end. It is a picture that every soldier's mother, wife, or sweetheart will want to see. YOU MAY SEE YOUR BOY OVER THERE[15] (emphasis in original).

The division also subcontracted the production of several one-reelers, for which it provided the scenarios and all necessary authorization and assistance, including film shorts on women in war work, on both American Indians and Negroes in the military forces and in domestic war-related work, and on the merchant marines. Through an export licensing agreement the division also forced all producers of commercial entertainment films destined to be shown abroad to require their foreign exhibitors to show CPI propaganda films as the price of seeing Charlie Chaplin and other American film heroes. The export agreement also enabled the CPI to stop the export of gangster films, which, key members of the committee felt, portrayed American society in an unfavorable light. Finally, the Division of Film sanctioned the production of many entertainment films that were actually thinly disguised propaganda, such as "Mutt and Jeff at the Front," "To Hell with the Kaiser," and the remarkable "The Kaiser, the Beast of Berlin," a film boosted by several national patriotic societies apparently because of the exuberant animosities that it stirred. It is worth noting in passing that American film stars, notably Theda Bara, Douglas Fairbanks, and Mary Pickford among many others, worked tirelessly in the war effort, particularly in selling Liberty Bonds, thus forging an early link between celebrity and national power.

Perhaps the most important CPI division, and certainly the only one that linked the power of visual images with sharply pointed interpretive texts, was the Division of Advertising. Advertisers and advertising men were involved in war-related work almost from the beginning of America's involvement in the conflict, although the Division of Advertising was not officially established until 20 January 1918. Right after America entered the war and the first Liberty Loan drive was launched, a group of advertising men went to Washington to suggest that the government advertise the campaign by purchasing space in various printed media. The notion was rejected, of course, because the swell of patriotic sentiment at the war's outset demanded voluntary contributions in every area. One of the group, William Rankin, head of a leading advertising agency in Chicago, developed a plan whereby individual advertisers purchased advertising space and donated it to the government. Following Rankin's lead, many publications directly donated space for war advertising, and by the war's end 800 publishers of newspapers, farm papers, college papers, trade publications, magazines, and house organs, among others, had donated space for war-related advertising. The situation seems to have been chaotic for most of 1917 with, on the one hand, offers of donated space pouring in from all over the country as well as from different organizations of advertising groups, and, on the other, government agencies of every sort approaching the CPI with campaigns that they wanted advertised. Finally, after receipt of a formal offer of assistance from William H. Johns, president of both the George Batten Advertising Agency and the American Association of Advertising Agencies (AAAA), representing 115 firms, Creel met with key representatives of the New York advertising community and established the division in December 1917. In a follow-up letter the next day he appointed Johns as chairman of the division and charged him as follows:

> Your work, for the moment, is to be a clearing house for all advertising aid offered to the Government. For the present it will be my own task to secure the cooperation of all other departments of Government. In short, all of the departments of Government will be in a position to let me know what their needs are. You will be in position to let me know what the advertising interests of the country can offer for the fulfillment of these needs. Questions of advertising policy are for you. Questions of government policy are for me. . . .
>
> It seems to me the first work to be done is the completion of the organizations representing advertising interests of the country with which you will come in contact. You are to proceed at once to invite all of the organizations of national advertising, not now represented, to organize themselves on a basis of self-organization for war work in order that they may offer their services to this new National Board.[16]

Creel also appointed Carl Byoir to be the liaison with the new division, with power to act on Creel's behalf, a task that Byoir fulfilled with great relish, not only because he considered himself an advertising man[17] but because it brought him into association with the most prominent and powerful advertising men of the time. In addition to Johns, the rest of the board of directors was a Who's Who of the advertising world. It included William D'Arcy, president of the Associated Advertising Clubs of the World, representing 180 advertising clubs; Herbert S. Houston, former president of the same organization; O. C. Harn, chairman of the National Commission of the same organization; L. B. Jones, president of the Association of National Advertisers; and Jesse H. Neal, secretary of Associated Business Papers, representing 500 trade publications. Thomas Cusack of Chicago, the acknowledged king of outdoor advertising, was later added to the board of directors, though not without some controversy, as we shall describe later. The division was housed in the Metropolitan Tower in New York City, immediately adjacent to, and essentially a part of, the offices of the American Association of Advertising Agencies.[18]

The Division of Advertising worked on several major campaigns during its brief history. These included a campaign to recruit skilled workers for the shipyards; the fourth Liberty Loan drive, featuring for general audiences "Public Opinion" as a young woman in a toga, whom all men fear and who judges not on the basis of declarations of verbal allegiance, nor uncovered head and solemn mien, but by the material aid given to the fighting men, and for college audiences an image of the Kaiser in cap and mortar looming over a college campus in military chaos with a reminder that "in the vicious guttural language of Kultur the degree of A.B. means Bachelor of Atrocities"; the War Savings Stamps drive that, after reflecting that it's a good thing that American soldiers can't hear many people's expressions of self-indulgence, urges the public to "save the thoughtless dollars" and buy Savings Stamps; and campaigns for the Red Cross, the "Greatest Mother in the World," clasping to her breast a battered doughboy on a stretcher. There was also the "Spies and Lies" campaign, urging the public to help suppress groundless rumors and gossip and to turn in anyone spreading pessimistic stories; the Selective Service campaign, which posted advertisements about draft registration in thousands of public buildings, streetcars, subways, railway stations, banks, YMCA branches, and other locales; the "Kill Every Rat" campaign for the Department of Agriculture; the Smileage campaign to provide free entertainment for the boys in training camps; several campaigns advertising the YMCA, which provides comfort and rest for soldiers who come "Out of the Mouth of Hell"; and a series of campaigns urging parents and sweethearts to "be game" and write only cheerful letters to the boys at the front, remembering that "He Will Come Back a Better Man"; and, finally, a campaign urging the public to write to the CPI for its war publications to help thwart "The Hohenzollern Dream," that is, a huge bayoneted German soldier with *pickelhaube* stomping over Manhattan's skyscrapers.

The Division of Advertising was a crossroads for the whole occupational community of advertising during the war. It worked with war advertising committees in more than 80 clubs all over the country that were affiliated with the Associated Advertising Clubs of the World; it worked with the war service committees of two dozen national associations; it employed the services of 39 advertising agencies, 51 artists, and 30 printing houses. It coordinated the contributions of more than 130 advertisers and of hundreds of general monthly, weekly, and semimonthly magazines, farm papers, and technical and trade publications. In the judgment of its chairman, William H. Johns, the division had succeeded in "educating official Washington to the use and value of advertising and of the skillful direction of it".[19] This was apparently true since, right after the war, the Department of Labor asked for and received the AAAA's assistance in helping to minimize labor unrest by persuading advertisers to insert prepared messages into advertising copy. The AAAA received other similar requests, such as one from the United States Shipping Board regarding the future of the merchant marines. In July 1919, after the United States War Department became a national advertiser with an appropriation of $185 000 for recruitment advertising, the AAAA executive board authorized a committee of its own members to present to the Secretary of the Navy the idea of forming a composite advertising agency to respond to the government's advertising needs. The request was approved and the resulting Advertising Agencies Corporation worked with the Army and Navy in recruiting and in the disposal of surplus stores until the organization was disbanded in March 1928.[20] In short, public-service advertising began with the Great War.[21]

In the process of all this work the men and women of the CPI developed, at least *in germine*, the entire vast apparatus of public-opinion formation that we now take for granted, together with its typical occupational worldviews. First, the concentration-fastening event of the Great War, coupled with the CPI's monopoly over the flow of war information and the policy of "voluntary censorship" by newspapers, accelerated a movement toward "placing news," one begun earlier in the century on a much smaller scale by the public relations counsels of magnates and corporations in trouble.[22] Essentially, the war reported in American newspapers was the war that the CPI wanted the American people to see, a moral struggle against cruel tyranny, barbarity, and imperialist expansion with no hint of commercial motivation.[23] After the war large organizations and individuals of every sort became skilled at placing their own news, that is, issuing their own propaganda. In a speech given in 1935, Carl Byoir suggested the extent of this practice:

> You can pick up your morning paper, pick up the papers that most pride themselves on being the finest sources of news and if you read them with the practiced eye of the publicist or propagandist, you will find that perhaps 60 per cent of all the news of that paper, outside of the results of ball games, sporting events and financial items, is propaganda.[24]

Today, public relations practitioners generally estimate the amount of placed news to be 80 percent of all that is printed or appears on the electronic media. Even allowing for professional exaggeration, there is scarcely any doubt that most of what the public reads, sees, or hears is material that promotes some fixed viewpoint.

Second, years before the availability of radio, the CPI developed, at least in a primitive form, the centralized and standardized techniques of truly *mass* communication. Essentially this involved a coordinated promulgation of themes, usually complete with technical advice on how to execute them, but with considerable allowance for local innovative variation and initiative. For instance, one Katherine Ridgeway of Brookline, Massachusetts, wrote to the committee saying: "I am going to speak to more than one hundred thousand people within the next 10 weeks on Chautauqua work in the east New England states and New York. I [shall] fill the entire evening in interpreting stories, plays, and poems and shall devote 30 minutes or more to the vital issues of the war. Now may I ask you to give me the outline of the most needful things to tell these people . . . ."[25] The Speaking Division undoubtedly provided her with a copy of its regular bulletin with its "Hints for Speakers: The Issues of the War at a Glance," which gave a capsule glance at salient issues, complete with rhetorical flourishes that the very experienced Chautauqua speakers could use as they wished.[26]

Again, in January 1918 the United States Shipping Board desparately needed more workers in the shipyards. The Four Minute Men undertook a campaign to recruit skilled workers in all relevant trades and to alert the public to the importance of shipbuilding. The campaign was deemed so important that the director, William McCormick Blair, took the unusual step of presenting in the bulletin the full text of a very long speech entitled "The Man of the Hour – The Shipbuilder," complete with a detailed outline of all the major themes, with asterisks marking the sentences that referred back to bold-typed material in the text for easy reference for speakers preparing their own speeches.[27] But this was only an elaborate version of the kind of systematizing work that always characterized the bulletin. The bulletin normally provided the subject for any given week's speeches, a list of "important points for all speakers," sometimes as many as a dozen "suggestions for outlines" of speeches and a list of "suggestions for opening words and phrases". Bulletins also sometimes provided whole paragraphs that speakers could incorporate into their talks and often two "typical illustrative speeches". But, though provided with uniform material that they could cobble together, speakers were always encouraged to invest themselves in their speeches and to say what was on their minds about a topic. Similarly the weekly Bulletin for Cartoonists provided a steady stream of "cartoon tips" for cartoonists around the country to encourage a certain timely uniformity in the selection of which war theme to treat. For example, a special edition of the bulletin suggested that cartoonists develop their work around the following ideas for the 6 April 1918 "Win-the-

War" day: "A patriot is as a patriot does"; "Do more than your 'bit,' do your best"; and "By buying bonds, help halt the Hun".[28] Cartoonists were encouraged to send into the bureau any cartoons that utilized the ideas of the bulletin. The best of these were then circulated to gain a wider, perhaps national audience.

The CPI's strategy of providing strong centralized guidance in the shaping of public opinion generated some emulators. For instance the National Committee of Patriotic Societies, only one of the innumerable private patriotic organizations spawned by the war, put out a detailed magazine-sized booklet entitled "How to put in Patriotic Posters the stuff that makes people STOP–LOOK–ACT!"[29] Intended as a guide to competitors in the ship poster competition of the United States Shipping Board, the publication details: the steps one must undertake to analyze the composition of one's audience; the crucial importance of emotional rather than intellectual appeals; the necessity of stark simplicity rather than fine detail in design; the fundamental power of visual images conveying action rather than rest; and the desirability of bold colors rather than subtle hues. The Division of Advertising adopted a similar course for organizing all the advertising it generated. Government officials who wanted advertising for some campaign approached the division and worked out with its leaders a detailed statement of purpose and strategy. With such frameworks in hand, the division let out the work to volunteer advertising agencies as well as to members of the Division of Pictorial Publicity, who then returned the finished work for review by a committee composed of division leaders and government officials. The advertisements were then published or displayed in space paid for by contributions from various business and community groups.

By the end of the war CPI leaders, with all of the sprawling organization's divisions in place and operating at full tilt, saw the possibilities of even greater coordination, as illustrated by the proposed campaign to raise money for the war work of the YMCA. The plan reads:

It is proposed that the Committee on Public Information offers the services of its various divisions in the form of an organized and definite plan of campaign each co-operating with the other, and in turn cooperating with the principal unit – the Y.M.C.A. organization. The work the Committee is thus called upon to do is no more than it perhaps would do under any circumstance, but instead of each Division working independently and at different times, the service of the entire Committee is put into one definite message and so told or merchandized to the American Public through the channel of a campaign plan put out over the name of the Y.M.C.A.[30]

The plan goes on to argue that there is "only one story to be told and one way to tell it". To this end, the Division of Advertising was to prepare a series of advertisements for publication in a whole range of journals, from farm magazines, to women's journals, to educational publications, as well as local newspapers. The Division of Pictorial Publicity was to develop a series of posters, coordinated with the illustrations used in the advertising campaign. The Division of Films was to produce a 1000-foot film showing the YMCA's work in France. The Four Minute Men were to speak in 5300 communities telling their audience the same story as that appearing in the advertisements and posters, and "linking very closely with the message carried in the films". The Division of Speakers was to send nationally prominent speakers to all states to reinforce the work of the Four Minute Men. The Division of Pictures was to secure and syndicate throughout the country a complete series of original pictures of YMCA men in service in the war zone. The Division of Syndicated Features was to develop a series of feature articles that combined pictures and written messages "into one dominating feature story". The Division of News was to place in newspapers everywhere the hundreds of items of genuine news value about the YMCA. The Division of Foreign Societies was to help the YMCA prepare its message for 34 different nationalities, that is, ethnic groups that retained strong social and linguistic ties to their native lands. And the Division of Distribution was to deliver all the printed literature effectively and promptly. In short the idea, in the words of the proposal, was to "marshall all these working forces into a dominating and working machine". Parts of

this plan were already in place as a result of earlier CPI
work on behalf of the YMCA, but as things turned out the
armistice obviated any point of fully implementing it. Still,
the proposal suggests early perceptions of the possibilities
of using the apparatus of mass communications to satu-
rate public opinion on a particular issue. An almost iden-
tical plan of wholly coordinated communications activity
was also in the works to "encourage and stimulate labor
production in industries engaged in war work".[31]

Third, this mass-communications apparatus depended for
its effectiveness on the thorough mobilization of crucial targeted publics, by now, of course, commonplace wisdom in
the field of public relations. Admen have always tried to
embed multiple appeals in advertisements in order to reach
out to different groups. For instance, in the first Liberty
Loan drive, the copy appeals were to ". . . the wealthy
through patriotism and the fact that the bonds are non-
taxable . . . to the middle classes . . . through patriotism
and the fact that to purchase a bond will be the beginning
of a beneficial habit of thrift . . . to the poorer classes the
absolute safety of the investment . . . [and] to the foreign
born . . . that here is an opportunity for them to prove . . .
their loyalty".[32] But advertising is always a scattershot blast
into the wind when contrasted with the careful rifleshot
aim of public relations. To mobilize publics, as Carl Byoir
explained in 1935, one has to take two steps: first, to set
up an actual or fictive organization adorned with the names
of respected people who "establish in themselves the sound-
ness of the movement and the integrity of its purpose"; second, to "enlist those organizations already in existence which
can be of assistance in carrying out [a] plan," taking care
to identify the real policy makers of these organizations
rather than the titular heads and "[a]fter you have national
organization . . . go after local organization, by states, by
cities and towns. Then . . . put behind your local leader the
local representatives of all the national forces which you
have previously enlisted. Then . . . drive for the result [one]
is after."[33]

One of the most important publics during the Great War
was, of course, working men. Industrial working conditions
were still abysmal; unions were organized only with the

greatest of difficulty; and, from the perspective of employers, relatively high wages in the shipbuilding and munitions industries were causing disruptive labor mobility. Among the many efforts that the CPI adopted to address the labor question, two in particular illustrate the principles and tactics of local organization. First, after briefly coordinating labor activities through its own Division of Industry, the CPI set up and bankrolled the American Alliance for Labor and Democracy with offices on Chambers Street in New York. The legendary Samuel Gompers, then president of the American Federation of Labor, was named as president of the alliance, with several populists and ex-socialists appointed to its executive committee. In its first six months, according to one of its own publications, the alliance formed 150 branches throughout the country, distributed 1 198 000 pamphlets in all states, held a National Labor Loyalty Week, conducted 200 public mass meetings, placed 10 000 columns of publicity, and mailed a weekly news service to 600 newspapers.[34] Among the alliance's publications were pamphlets by the dean of labor historians, John R. Commons, including "German Socialists and the War" and "Why Workingmen Support the War". The latter was an exhortation to all workers, but particularly to socialists, to back the war because "[n]ever before was a war carried on by workingmen. Never before, in war or in peace, was the voice of labor in government so powerful as it is now in America."[35] At the same time employers of every sort were writing the CPI suggesting ways of stimulating patriotism among workers. These included ideas to distribute posters for bulletin boards in the shipyards to motivate workers there or to point out to workers the many ways they could help the fighting boys, from buying bonds to knitting sweaters.[36]

The CPI approached employers in an exactly parallel manner. In the spring of 1918 one Clarence Howard, president of Commonwealth Steel Company in St Louis, sent a letter to his employees stressing teamwork and emphasizing how important domestic production was to the war effort. The letter attracted Byoir's attention and the two subsequently met in Washington. With Byoir's help and encouragement, Thomas then sent out to heads of companies engaged in government work across the country another letter soliciting opinions about a centralized plan to educate workers by establishing a regular service at every plant. "The plan would go out to every plant including patriotic posters, patriotic booklets or payroll inserts signed by the U.S. Government. *There would be an official button sanctioned by the War and Navy Departments and a Service Flag for the home, to stimulate the pride of the worker and his family in the work he is doing toward winning the war.*" The plan also involved motion pictures about the war to bring the struggle home to workers, as well as to show them quality work being done by other workers at home and abroad. Thomas stressed that he aimed at cooperation between capital and labor and wanted "[h]umanics as well as mechanics". Enthusiastic letters promptly poured back to Thomas, many with additional suggestions; all replies were, of course, forwarded to Byoir. There is scarcely any doubt that Byoir had a large hand in the entire scheme, including the drafting of the second letter.[37] It is worth noting in passing, as James Mock and Cedric Larson point out in their fine treatment of the CPI's dealings with the labor question, that the CPI leaders maintained a remarkably balanced position in industrial disputes. In particular they often pointed out to business interests the unseemliness of calling for sacrifice by workers without reciprocal concessions on profits; and they eschewed ideological positions of either the right or the left and kept their eyes on the main goal of maintaining civilian morale.[38]

The CPI made similarly skillful use of organizational fronts, as well as already existing institutional machinery and leadership, in dealing with other important publics, notably foreign-born Americans through the various "loyalty leagues".[39] Perhaps the CPI's most successful use of the front was Byoir's invention of the "League of Oppressed Nations," an organization that coordinated all the ethnic loyalty groups. On 4 July 1918 Byoir arranged for a pilgrimage by leaders of 33 of these groups to Mount Vernon, Virginia, where President Wilson addressed them; simultaneously Thomas G. Masaryk, then president of the Czechoslovak National Council, promulgated the Czech Declaration of Independence at Independence Hall in Philadelphia. And on the same day, in 800 American cities, ethnic groups of all sorts staged loyalty demonstrations. Byoir later arranged a fete for Masaryk in Carnegie Hall entitled "The Will of the Peoples of Austria–Hungary: Victory Meeting for the Oppressed Nationalities of Central Europe," complete with an honorary committee with some of New York's most luminous names to help strengthen Masaryk's claim of leadership of free Czechoslovakia.[40]

Fourth, by inventively exploiting the possibilities of every available medium, the CPI tried to give a pointed direction and a common vocabulary – slogans, rallying cries, pictorial symbols, as well as the requisite loathsome images of the enemy – to the frenzy of patriotic fervor that swept the nation during the "war to end all wars". One can get a glimpse of the range and depth of this fervor by looking at only a few of the suggestions that poured into CPI headquarters at 10 Jackson Place in Washington or found their way there by referral from other government officials. There were innumerable ideas for propaganda themes and strategies, some of which were adopted outright or in altered form, although most were politely declined. For instance, a letter to Creel warning of the dangers of gossip and rumor-mongering and suggesting an ad campaign cautioning the public "to keep their mouths shut" led to the famous "Spies and Lies," the "Gossip That Costs Human Lives!" and the "Have You Met this Kaiserite?" campaigns run by the Division of Advertising.[41] There were also letters suggesting that "in order to more perfectly stimulate the home spirit for victory, you ask all Americans to sign all their business and personal correspondence with the phrase 'yours for victory and liberty'";[42] that the CPI sanction the formation of a nationwide "How Do You Know It Club," the members of which would be "furnished with a button asking this question and whenever anyone makes a remark about the army, navy, or government, it will be the duty of said member to flash this button and ask how do they know it to be true";[43] that the CPI sanction a national movement to encourage Americans "in every hall where people meet" to "Sing the [National] Anthem Every Day";[44] that the CPI sanction "The Society of the Lusitania," with the insignia the "coat of arms of the Imperial German Empire with a clot of blood across with the slogan 'the blot that won't come off,'" each member of which would "boycott everything German, [and] have nothing to do with anything German, goods, language, music or sentiment";[45] that German be suppressed in all schools, in addition to shutting down all German newspapers;[46] that, through local Councils of Defense, every man be presented with a pledge card to "protect [the soldier's] home from the enemy within," which one either signed or went on record as having refused to sign;[47] and that the CPI give more extensive publicity to German atrocities to convince American farmers about the dangers of the war.[48]

The CPI also heard about actions already taken by different groups or individuals in a spirit of patriotism, such as the "On Your Guard" poster and card campaign by the Worchester (Massachusetts) Chamber of Commerce, urging the suppression of any remarks that might "give aid or comfort to our enemies," or the speech "Over Here," given to any audience that Earl Derr Biggers could find, about young Jimmy Gerson about to go off to war and explaining to his old German grandfather how the war was saving America from becoming a nation of "softies".[49] The CPI was also sometimes asked to act as a moral arbiter of patriotism to prevent the misconstruction of wholly well-meaning actions, such as when the Basking Ridge Fire Company, No. I, wrote to the CPI, as a federal authority, asking whether the CPI thought the fire company's annual fundraising carnival displayed an "unpatriotic spirit". Byoir responded: "I do not see how anyone could construe as unpatriotic an event designed to support the fire company," adding that the organization might wish to incorporate "some purely patriotic features" in its affair.[50]

In short, any notion that the CPI manufactured the stridently moralistic, deeply resentful, xenophobic, highly emotional wash of public sentiments about the war that engulfed the entire nation gains little support from a close reading of the CPI files. A significant portion of the American citizenry has always listened closely to nativist, primitive appeals, and the First World War helped the flowering of chauvinistic groups such as the National Security League and the American Defense Society. Moreover, for two years preceding the CPI's establishment, in an effort to get America involved in the war British propagandists had bombarded the American public with largely fabricated images of the rape of "little Belgium," the outraging of nuns, and the massacre of women and children.[51] If anything, as Byoir noted later, the real issue was discarding the "tens of thousands of impractical suggestions and unworkable plans with which every war-time organization is promptly flooded . . . the great danger [of which] is that they do not all, by any means, come from the cracked-pots and half-wits of the nation but most of the worst of them come from people whose very eminence and success in other fields make their theories dangerous because they catch you off-guard".[52]

Given such public sentiment, the task of the CPI was not to create opinion about the war, but to mold it. Seen from this perspective, of course, the very name of the committee was disingenuous, indeed a front of sorts for its principal mission, although the name seems to have confused some people. For instance, a W. Ray Lewis wrote to the CPI offering a chart of nations at war, which he thought might be useful in the committee's educational work. Byoir responded: "This generally informative matter is not part of our task. As I conceive it, we are here to interpret, as far as we are able, to the people of America the high ideals for which America fights, the justice of our cause, and the autocratic aims of our enemies." He wrote somewhat more pointedly to Bruce Bliven of *Printer's Ink*: "[I]n a sense the whole work of the Committee is in the last analysis simply a tremendous world advertising job."[53] Advertising and public relations both take the dough of existing sentiment, the world as it is, and work it into forms that tell people what to think and especially to get them to act in a certain way. In this sense the CPI was America's first propaganda ministry, a term that most of the leaders of the organization used without embarrassment, at least in private.

Fifth, the CPI was also a modern workplace, peopled by men and women of great talent and sizable egos, a cockpit of personal ambition and competition. Undoubtedly, genuinely felt patriotic sentiments fueled the organization's fantastic range of activities. But, as happens in any large organization, the CPI's leaders were also beseiged with requests for patronage and favors of all sorts, from letters of recommendation to secure admission to an officers' training program, to requests to sanction an application for a post as a noncommissioned regimental sergeant major.[54] Moreover there were hundreds of people seeking a post with the CPI itself, often men deferred from the draft, such as William Magill who wrote: "I chafe that at fifty I am a mere spectator where I should be an active participant, partaking of the dangers of the conflict," or from applicants who felt "[I]t is every man's duty to do everything in his power to help win the war."[55] Even when such men were willing to work for nothing, there were so many applicants that names were simply kept on file; those who asked for remuneration were usually told that nothing was or would be available, although there were some important exceptions to this.[56] At the higher levels of the organization the scramble for prestige that is typical of all bureaucracies, with the upward-looking stance they inevitably engender, was particularly intense. The prestige of doing war-related work and, most especially, the social access to important peers that such work afforded were, after all, the principal rewards that the CPI offered businessmen, most of whom worked for the CPI while still engaged in their own affairs.

The struggle for ascendancy in the Division of Advertising between the New York men and the Chicago men suggests the kinds of tensions at issue. The tight circle of New York advertising men who were grouped around the newly formed American Association of Advertising Agencies dominated the Division of Advertising from its informal start in December 1917, when Creel gave the nod to the AAAA over the several other groups that had offered help. All of the original appointees to the board of the Division of Advertising were part of that inner circle, including William D'Arcy, who, though he hailed from St Louis, was considered an "Eastern man". Nonetheless D'Arcy pushed for the appointment to the board of Thomas Cusak of Chicago, whose outdoor advertising firm was the largest in the country. The Chicago advertising men resented the New York crowd's influence; D'Arcy saw Cusak's appointment as one way to mollify that anger. Cusak wrote to Creel on 1 December

1917, formally offering his services. But Creel delayed in making a formal appointment. There was opposition to Cusak's appointment from industrial plant owners, and this was the reason eventually cited for the delay. However correspondence going on at the same time between William Rankin of Chicago and Byoir suggests that matters were more complicated. Byoir greatly admired Rankin's energetic work on the first Liberty Loan drive, mentioned earlier, and the two regularly corresponded, exchanged humorous notes, and saw one another frequently, either in New York or Chicago. Rankin's letters burn with the Chicago man's resentment of New York dominance in the CPI and it is abundantly clear that Rankin expected a place on the board of directors of the Division of Advertising, although he also desired an even bigger job, indeed an entire division of which he would be chairman.[57]

In the meantime Cusak engineered a barrage of wires and letters to Washington from third parties on his own behalf, indicating that he would accept the appointment to the board when it was offered, although other evidence suggests that his friends were warning him away from the position. Creel was under pressure on a number of fronts: the New York men wanted to maintain their dominance; Chicago wanted in; both Cusak and Rankin wanted the Chicago slot, and in fact Rankin, who was personally backed by Creel's right-hand man, wanted more than one spot for the west. Creel told Byoir to meet with Cusak and straighten things out. There was a comical missed meeting in New York between Byoir and Cusak, followed by indignant wires and letters from Cusak to Creel. In the end Creel gave the nod to Cusak to represent Chicago. Rankin was never appointed to the board, nor to the big job with the CPI that he dreamed of.[58]

All large organizations breed these sorts of struggles for prestige. The ferocity of the struggles indicates the importance that men and women in a particular occupational community attach to the social networks, circles, cliques, and personal associations of their worlds in making and breaking reputations and careers. Those who already were and especially those who wanted to be big-time propagandists saw the CPI and the Great War as the chance of a lifetime.

Finally, the CPI helped shape among emerging experts with symbols what are now in advertising and public relations occupationally characteristic notions of the power of mass persuasion, together with accompanying images of a malleable public. A profound disillusionment followed the Great War among former soldiers, intellectuals and artists, among the general public in all belligerent countries, and even among some former propagandists.[59] When the full extent of the war's human carnage became evident and the enormous social dislocation that it created in Europe began to produce the early harbingers of political fanaticism, some of the leading participants in the CPI wondered about the mass irrationalities that they had helped fan, such as the cartoonlike stereotypes of bestial, bloodthirsty Germans, the unbridled moral fervor sanctified by images of the cross and motherhood, or the suspicions about the loyalties of dissenters of any sort.[60] President Wilson himself, according to George Creel, was especially afraid of the disillusionment that would follow the inevitable dashing of expectations about America as the world's savior, created to a great extent by CPI propaganda.[61] But instead of producing searching questions about the implications of the techniques of mass persuasion, such reflections typically took a practical turn. Struck by the gullibility of the public, experts with mass symbols wondered whether propaganda might work as well in peacetime as it had during the Great War.[62]

Notes

1. The archival research for this paper was supported by a grant from the National Endowment for the Humanities, Division of Research, Interpretive Research Grant #RO-21493–87, "Experts with Symbols: Advertising, Public Relations, and the Culture of Advocacy".
2. See George Creel, *Rebel at Large: Recollections of Fifty Crowded Years* (New York: G. P. Putnam's Sons, 1947), p. 158. Though not explicit, the reference is to the Sacred Congregation *de Propaganda Fide* established by Pope Gregory XV (1621–3) to train priests for work in the Counter Reformation in Europe and for missionary work in foreign lands.

3. In Creel's view, the social divisiveness had many sources. Years later, he wrote:

> During the three and a half years of our neutrality the United States had been torn by a thousand divisive prejudices, with public opinion stunned and muddled by the pull and haul of Allied and German propaganda. The sentiment of the West was still isolationist; the Northwest buzzed with talk of a 'rich man's war,' waged to salvage Wall Street loans; men and women of Irish stock were 'neutral,' not caring who whipped England, and in every state demogogues raved against 'warmongers,' although the Du Ponts and other so-called 'merchants of death' did not have enough powder on hand to arm squirrel hunters (Creel, *Rebel at Large*, p. 157).

4. "Holding fast the inner lines" was a widespread war slogan of the time. The title of Creel's informal history of the Committee on Public Information is *How We Advertised America: The First Telling of the Amazing Story of the Committee on Public Information that Carried the Gospel of Americanism to Every Corner of the Globe* (New York and London: Harper and Brothers Publishers, 1920).

5. The CPI had many divisions not mentioned here. Among the most important were the Division of Women's War-Work, the Foreign Language Newspaper Division, and the Division of Work Among the Foreign-born.

6. Byoir's CPI papers are voluminous and cover virtually every aspect of the organization. See National Archives, Judicial and Fiscal Branch, *Records of the Committee on Public Information*, Record Group 63, CPI 1 A-4, A-5, A-6, and A-7. The record of Byoir's career before 1917 and his long career as a central figure in public relations after the CPI experience is less well documented. See, however, Robert James Bennett, *Carl Byoir: Public Relations Pioneer* (Madison: University of Wisconsin, MA Thesis, School of Journalism, 1968). In addition to other papers, Bennett had access to Byoir's incomplete, unpublished autobiography, a document that now is missing. Byoir's firm, Carl Byoir and Associates, was absorbed in 1986 by Hill and Knowlton, another large public relations firm. Apparently a lot of Byoir's papers, including the autobiography, were lost in the transition, not an uncommon occurrence. Fortunately for other scholars Bennett provides large segments of the autobiography.

7. See National Archives, Judicial and Fiscal Branch, *Records of the Committee on Public Information*, Record Group 63, CPI 11A-A1, B1, B3, C2; 11B-A1, A2, A3, A6, B2, and B3 for the original materials on the Four Minute Men. The most comprehensive and best treatment of this organization is Alfred E. Cornebise, *War As Advertised: The Four Minute Men and America's Crusade 1917–1918* (Philadelphia: The American Philosophical Society, 1984).

8. Many students of the mass media have argued that the main

frequenters of the movies in the early years of the century were working-class immigrants and their offspring. Recent work suggests that the class composition of moviegoers was always very diverse, with middle-class attendance at least equalling that of the working class. See Larry May, *Screening Out the Past* (New York: Oxford University Press, 1980). In any event, a lot of people went to the movie houses. A contemporary account estimated that between 10 and 13 million people went to the movies every day in the United States, an astonishing figure considering that the nation's population in 1917 was 100 000 000. See "The War Work of the Four-Minute Men: With An Introductory Letter by President Wilson," *The Touchstone*, vol. 3, no. 6 (September, 1918).

9. See George Creel, *Rebel At Large: Recollections of Fifty Crowded Years* (New York: G. P. Putnam's Sons, 1947), p. 162. James R. Mock and Cedric Larson tell a different story about Gibson's involvement in *Words That Won the War: The Story of the Committee on Public Information 1917–1919* (Princeton, N. J.: Princeton University Press, 1939), p. 101. In their account, Creel sent Gibson a telegram, while Gibson was involved in a meeting of the Society of Illustrators, asking him to arrange a committee of artists to help with the war effort. Gibson later went to Washington to launch the Division of Pictorial Publicity. Creel's more dramatic account is typical of his generally flamboyant presentation; in this instance it served his purpose of emphasizing the spontaneity of the CPI's early growth.

10. There are several collections of First-World-War posters. See, in particular, Joseph Darracott and Belinda Loftus, *First World War Posters* (London: Imperial War Museum, 1972); Joseph Darracott, *The First World War in Posters* (New York: Dover Publications, 1974); and Maurice Rickards, *Posters of the First World War* (New York: Walker & Company, 1968).

11. See, for instance, the interim "Report of the Work Accomplished by the Division of Pictorial Publicity" from 1 October 1917 to 1 March 1918, CPI 1 A-5, Box 35, Folder 12.

12. National Archives, Judicial and Fiscal Branch, *Records of the Committee on Public Information*, Record Group 63, CPI 1 C-5, Box 47 for the whole series of the Bulletin for Cartoonists.

13. See in particular The Butterfield Syndicate's collection of Macauley's work "America's Spirit in the War". National Archives, Judicial and Fiscal Branch, *Records of the Committee on Public Information*, Record Group 63, CPI 1 A-5, Box 33, Folder 5.

14. This section draws largely on Creel's account in *How We Advertised America*, pp. 117–32, and on Mock's and Larson's treatment in *Words That Won the War*, pp. 131–53.

15. See National Archives, Judicial and Fiscal Branch, *Records of the Committee on Public Information*, Record Group 63, CPI A-5, Box 34, Folder 6.

16. Letter to Creel from W. H. Johns, 22 November 1917. Letter from Creel to W. H. Johns, 21 December 1917, CPI 1 A-4, Box 37, Folder 4. In his letter to Johns, Creel says that the CPI had already had offers of help from seven other advertising associations.

17. Byoir wrote a letter to W. C. Freeman, the general manager of *Advertising News*, complaining about an editorial attack on George Creel that had appeared in Freeman's weekly. Apparently the editorial had charged Creel with putting himself forward, as usual, at the expense of the advertising profession. After indicating that he had read the editorial "with a feeling closely akin to nausea," Byoir writes:

> If there is one group of men in America in relation to whose work Mr. Creel has demonstrated not alone competence, but a broad visioned comprehension of the possibilities of their profession in helping to win the war, it is the advertising men. If there is one group of men in America who ought to be appreciative of the work of the Committee on Public Information, it is the advertising men. . . . In organizing his Division of Advertising, [Creel] displayed an absolute lack of that desire to thrust himself forward with which your editor charges him, and instead of appointing men toward whom he might have personal leanings, he democratically deferred to the opinion of the advertising profession and appointed men whom they themselves had chosen as their leaders. . . .As an advertising man I do feel very deeply that the editor of a magazine reflecting the thought and opinion of that great profession, has done a very mean and bitter thing in writing such an editorial without one word of acknowledgement of Mr. Creel's unselfish aid to advertising men in war-time (National Archives, Judicial and Fiscal Branch, *Records of the Committee on Public Information*, Record Group 63, CPI 1 A-4, Box 30, Folder 10).

The letter is uncharacteristically sharp for Byoir, whose correspondence is generally marked with a remarkable evenness. The letter is perhaps best read not just as Byoir's defense of Creel, but as Byoir's self-defense vis-à-vis an important occupational reference group.

18. The American Association of Advertising Agencies (AAAA) had itself just been formed on 4 June 1917. According to Richard Turnbull, a senior vice president of the AAAA, the organization was the final product of at least six efforts to organize the advertising business on a national basis. Turnbull's paper is "Genesis of the American Association of Advertising Agencies" (New York: AAAA, 1969), unpublished manuscript in the AAAA's library. The national efforts were: 1873, the Advertising Agents Convention; 1885, The Association of General Newspaper Agents; 1896, the Association of Advertising Agents; 1900, the American Advertising Agents Association; 1912, the National Association of General Advertising Agents; and 1916, the Affiliated Association of Advertising Agents. The last, Turnbull tells us in his introduction, "resulted in a loose amalgamation of regional or local groups, which led directly to [the] creation of the AAAA a year later". The key local group, of course, was that in New York, the Association of New York Advertising Agents, which had its first recorded meeting on 16 March 1911. It was this group that established a committee to work toward a

national association, a committee that included among its members Frank Presbrey, who later wrote an important book on advertising, and W. H. Johns. Only a few weeks after the New York Association began, Johns was elected chairman of the organization. Turnbull's account is based on surviving AAAA records. He also utilized the careful work of Roger H. Clapp, *Prelude to the Four A's: The Development of Advertising Agency Associations in the United States 1865–1917* (Amherst, Mass: Amherst College, BA Thesis in American Studies, 1954).

19. Johns made the remark in a report to the executive board of the American Association of Advertising Agencies, of which, of course, he was also president. The remark is cited in an unpublished report by Richard Turnbull, "Marshalling the Forces of Advertising in the National Interest 1917–1920" (New York: AAAA, June 1969).

20. Richard Turnbull, who, as mentioned earlier, later became a senior vice president of the AAAA and a student of the organization's history, was the very young assistant treasurer of the Advertising Agencies Corporation. He was present at its demise and undoubtedly heard all extant stories about the Division of Advertising from his senior colleagues. He seems to be the only advertising insider to link the CPI's First-World-War advertising efforts explicitly with the parallel developments during the Second World War.

21. See Turnbull, "Marshalling the Forces of Advertising in the National Interest". Turnbull says: "In its purpose and functioning, the Division of Advertising was the World War I counterpart of the War Advertising Council (later renamed the Advertising Council) of the Second World War." It is important to note that James W. Young of J. Walter Thompson, the man usually credited with inventing the idea for the Advertising Council, exchanged letters with Carl Byoir during the Great War. Byoir had invited Young to join the CPI, a proposition that greatly interested Young. Byoir wanted him to go to France, but they also discussed the possibility of Young going to Washington to work for the CPI without severing his business connections. As it happened, Young withdrew owing to business pressures.

22. The early master of placing news was Ivy Lee, whom the Rockefellers hired away from the troubled Pennsylvania Railroad after the massacre of striking workers and families at Ludlow, Colorado in 1914. See the biography of Lee by Ray Eldon Hiebert, *Courtier to the Crowd* (Ames, Iowa: University of Iowa Press, 1966). Lee knew that public prominence always commands newspaper ink and he always encouraged his clients to be frank and direct. See Ivy Lee, Occasional Paper No. 3, *The Problem of International Propaganda*, An Address by Ivy Lee Before a Private Group of Persons Concerned With International Affairs, in London, 3 July 1934 (New York: 1934).

23. Consider, for instance, the uproar that ensued when a visiting Englishman named H. Val Fisher gave an address to the American Association of Advertising Agencies, later published as a full-page advertisement in the leading newspapers of 16 cities and circulated in one of the house newsletters of the William H. Rankin Co. In

his published talk, Fisher gave the brief, but frank, appraisal: "No nation stands to gain so much commercially from the war as does America." The executive board of the CPI's Division of Advertising had approved the text of the advertisement. After it was published, Carl Byoir wrote to Rankin, who was a close professional associate and personal friend, admonishing him for letting the lines get past him. Rankin's response suggests both how taken for granted Fisher's appraisal was among men of affairs and how well Rankin understood the CPI's larger purposes:

> Frankly, the two lines that you quote – 'no nation stands to gain so much commercially from the war as does America' – made no impression on me whatever, and I did not know they were in Mr. Fisher's address. . . . It could have been an easy matter to have cut those two lines out, and, if I had had the same thought regarding those two lines that you have, I would have cut them out. But, frankly, I think those two lines are the truth. . . . [Still] I will take it upon myself to tip Val Fisher off to the fact that it would be a good idea in his future talks not to mention the fact . . . that no nation stands to gain so much commercially from the war as does America. While that is true, yet I agree with you [that] we do not want to advertise the fact.

See William Rankin to Carl Byoir, 21 September 1918. National Archives, Judicial and Fiscal Branch, *Records of the Committee on Public Information*, Record Group 63, CPI 1 A-4, Box 32, Folder 1.
24. See Carl Byoir, "Influencing Public Opinion," lecture delivered at The Army War College, Fort Humphreys, Washington, DC, 7 October 1935 (Carlisle Barracks, PA: Army War College Curricular Archives, U.S. Army Military History Institute), p. 3.
25. CPI 1 A-4, Box 32, Folder 3.
26. CPI 1 A-5, Box 42, Folder 5. The bulletins for the Speaking Division drew on other publications of the CPI, but framed the issues in the florid language to which the Chautauqua audiences were accustomed. Bulletin no. 2, January 1918, for instance, suggests some themes for those speaking on the origins of the war:

> All the world is at war with Germany, since Germany makes war on all the world. Germany defies all the world. Germany would master the world. Germany would sack the whole world. Germany so declares. Germany provoked war – We held our peace. Germany invaded Belgium. We held our peace. . . . Germany slew women and children. We held our peace. . . . Germany murdered our citizens. We choked down our wrath. . . . Germany broke solemn promises – We clung to shattered faith. . . . Germany – at length loosed war on us and on all neutrals. Then we saw the only out was to go through. Beset by war – the United States fights for world peace.

The same bulletin goes on to suggest similar language for other themes, namely, "The Cause at Stake" and "The Onrushing Event."
27. The Four Minute Men, bulletin no. 22 (28 January 1918). National

Archives, Judicial and Fiscal Branch, *Records of the Committee on Public Information*, Record Group 63, CPI 11A, A1, Box 131.
28. National Archives, Judicial and Fiscal Branch, *Records of the Committee on Public Information*, Record Group 63, CPI 1 A-5, Box 33, Folder 5.
29. The booklet was written by Matlack Price, the author of another book on posters, and Horace Brown of the National Committee of Patriotic Societies (Washington, DC: National Committee of Patriotic Societies, 6 June 1918). National Archives, Judicial and Fiscal Branch, *Records of the Committee on Public Information*, Record Group 63, CPI 1 A-5, Box 35, Folder 12.
30. National Archives, Judicial and Fiscal Branch, *Records of the Committee on Public Information*, Record Group 63, CPI 14-A1, Box 232. Carl E. Walberg, the Washington representative of the Division of Advertising, wrote the proposal. The proposal is undated, although an internal reference suggests that it was written in early fall 1918 since the proposal anticipates a full-scale drive in late October.
31. See "Plan to Enlist Employers and Employees, Engaged in Essential War Industries, in a 'Victory Army of Workers' By Stimulating and Encouraging Production." National Archives, Judicial and Fiscal Branch, *Records of the Committee on Public Information*, Record Group 63, CPI 1-A4, Box 31, Folder 31. In the copy in the records the word "Workers" is crossed out and the word "Industry" handwritten in. The document is undated but accompanied by two sets of handwritten notes to Byoir from "Hanahan," whose identity is unknown. One of the notes is dated 23 May 1918. The document proposes a scheme to "bring home to the worker himself the direct connection of the work he performs at home with the man on the firing line. . . ." It envisions the cooperation of all the divisions of the CPI to be engaged in the YMCA effort noted in the text, except the Division of News.
32. The National Advertising Agency Board, Advertising and Selling Plan, *The Liberty War Loan*, 3 May 1917.
33. Byoir, "Influencing Public Opinion," pp. 10–11.
34. "What Can Your Local Branch Do?" (New York: American Alliance for Labor and Democracy, n.d.), CPI 1 A-5 Box 33, Folder 2.
35. Ibid. Loyalty Leaflet No. 2 (New York: American Alliance for Labor and Democracy, n.d.), p. 5.
36. See, for instance, the correspondence to the CPI from Houstus L. Gaddis, service director of the Great Lakes Engineering Works in Detroit, of 31 January 1918, CPI 1-A4, Box 30, Folder 5. See also the article "When the War Will End! A Prediction Based on Incontrovertible Facts" in the *Brooklyn Eagle*, 27 June 1918, by Eugene V. Brewster, the managing editor of the *Motion Picture Magazine* and *Motion Picture Classic*, and the letter of praise to him from Byoir on 3 July 1918, CPI 1-A4, Box 30, Folder 13. Brewster predicted that the war would end in six years or six months, depending on the extent to which the American public became involved in the war effort.
37. The Howard letter to Commonwealth employees is in CPI 1-A4,

Box 30, Folder 7. Howard's later letter to other companies and the correspondence with Byoir about the responses he received may be found in CPI 1-A4, Box 31, Folder 11. At one point H. C. Belville, Thomas's assistant president, got into the act as the recipient of replies to Howard's letter. Some of these suggest that the men at Commonwealth did not know quite how to proceed with the flow of ideas from fellow businessmen that their letter had stimulated. The 11 July 1918 correspondence from L. M. Fessenden of Valley Falls, RI, to Belville illustrates the point. Fessenden asks where is the CPI response to the idea of initiating a Campaign of Education of Employees Along Patriotic Lines. CPI 1-A-4, Box 30, Folder 7.

38. Mock and Larson, *Words That Won The War*, pp. 187–212.
39. The CPI helped establish loyalty leagues with every group of foreign-born nationals of European extraction. So Swedish-Americans formed the John Ericsson League of Patriotic Service; Danish-Americans established the Jacob A. Riis League of Patriotic Service; Finnish-Americans began the Lincoln Loyalty League; Italian-Americans started the Roman Legion; Hungarian-Americans had the American–Hungarian Loyalty League; and so on. The most important group, of course, was the American Friends of German Democracy, the target of a great deal of controversy, which the CPI backed after extensive investigation. In May 1918 the CPI established the Division of Work Among the Foreign-born in order to work more directly with these important publics. See George Creel's account in *How We Advertised America*, pp. 184–99.
40. For a brief account of Byoir's work with the League of Oppressed Nations, see Robert James Bennett, *Carl Byoir: Public Relations Pioneer*, pp. 55–6. Bennett's account is based on an interview with Elsie Sobotka, Byoir's long-time secretary. Robert Jackall heard essentially the same account from George Hammond, Byoir's long-time business associate, in an interview on 15 August 1991 in Mystic, Connecticut. Hammond also provided the original program for the fete at Carnegie Hall. Wilson's speech at Mount Vernon is reported in *The New York Times*, 5 July 1918.
41. See letter from F. Carey of *The Daily States* of New Orleans to George Creel on 1 July 1918. Byoir responded favorably to Carey on 19 July. Carey had also suggested "organizing a league to be on a lookout for these 'mongers' and report them so they may be sent a personal letter warning them of the harm they are doing." (National Archives, Judicial and Fiscal Branch, *Records of the Committee on Public Information*, Record Group 63, CPI 1-A4, Box 30, Folder 17).
42. Letter from Private Harry Rubinstein of the 11th Company, 3rd Battalion, Camp Upton, of 3 June 1918. CPI 1 A-4, Box 32, Folder 3.
43. Letter to the CPI from George M. Rittelmeyer of Jackson, Mississippi, CPI 1-A-4, Box 32, Folder 3.
44. Newspaper article by Charles D. Isaacson, "Giving the National Anthem a New Meaning," in *The Globe and Commercial Advertiser*, n.d., sent to the CPI with a letter suggesting national adoption. Byoir wrote back on 8 April 1918 commending him on the idea.
45. Letter to Creel from an official of the United Service Selling Company

of Cleveland, Ohio, identity of author unknown, 28 June 1918, CPI
1-A4, Box 32, Folder 6.

46. Letter to Charles W. Henke, publicity director of the Commission
of Public Safety in St Paul, Minnesota, from Jno. S. Tolverson,
president of the First National Bank in Fulda, Minnesota, 17 April
1918. Henke's organization was apparently one of the many dis-
tributors of the CPI's published material; Tolverson wrote to him
about getting more copies of pamphlets on German propaganda:
CPI 1 A-4, Box 32, Folder 7. Henke sent a copy of the letter to
the CPI.

47. Letter from O. F. Frisbie of Yukon, Oklahoma, to Newton Baker,
U.S. Secretary of War, 18 April 1918. Baker responded with a polite
acknowledgement of the suggestion. The correspondence was then
sent privately to the CPI, probably because Frisbie's letter to Baker
was accompanied by a copy of a letter that Frisbie had written to
W. I. Thomas, the sociologist at the University of Chicago. Thomas
had written an article for a newspaper questioning aspects of the
war. Part of Frisbie's letter reads:

> We have had so far to contend with the dynamiter, the fire-bug,
> the poisoner – but just now is the beginning [sic] to come to
> light the class of traitor more awful than the worst Pro-German,
> if you please, the worst Hun, including the Kaiser himself, if
> such is possible. A miscarriage of nature, in the form of a man,
> who fails to hold even more sacred, than the honor of his own
> mother, and his own sister; the sanctity of a soldier's home and
> the honor of his dependents. . . . To my mind there could only
> be one punishment sufficient for this crime, and it falls far short
> of what you have deserved. To take your life in retribution for
> the wrong you have done, would be entirely inadequate. Every
> traitor of your class should be by a National Law brought under
> a surgeon's knife, and in addition your face adequately marked
> to identify you for all time to every eye that is cast upon you. If you
> miss this punishment, it will be through a miscarriage of justice.

Such primitive nativism was fairly widespread.

48. Letter to the CPI from officials of the Citizens Patriotic League of
Covington, Kentucky, 1 April 1918, CPI 1 A-4, Box 30, Folder 6.

49. Both the Worchester Chamber of Commerce poster and its accompanying correspondence and the text of Biggers's speech may be
found in CPI 1 A-4, Box 30, Folder 18. The sentiments in Biggers's
speech bear some reflection since they suggest in popular form
fundamental tensions in our society echoed throughout this century. "Young Jimmy Gerson" says to his grandfather:

> I tell you, we need this war. If we'd stood aside and not got into
> it, we'd have become the greatest nation of softies that ever sat
> down to a hearty meal. We were heading that way. Who reads
> books any way? Nobody – we crowded into movie theaters and
> dulled our wits with the childish stuff. Who stayed at home and

talked things over? Nobody – we piled into the car and hit the high spots. Who had time to think about life? Not a soul – we were due for a fox trot at a road house. We were pleasure mad. We'd forgot how to live.

50. Ibid.
51. For a general overview of propaganda in Britain during the First World War, see Cate Haste, *Keep the Home Fires Burning* (London: Allen Lane, 1977). The most important documentary source for British propaganda was the notorious *Bryce Report of Alleged German Atrocities*, commissioned by Lord Asquith in December 1914.
52. Byoir, "Influencing Public Opinion," p. 6.
53. Lewis was assistant superintendant of the documents room at the House of Representatives. Byoir's letter to him is dated 17 April 1918, CPI 1 A-4, Box 31, Folder 31. Byoir wrote to Bliven on other CPI business on 9 July 1918 and enclosed a copy of a speech that he had given to the New Washington Advertising Club. Byoir made the remark cited in the text in reference to that talk.
54. See the correspondence between Byoir and Raymond Ahearn, 18th Co., 1st Officer Regiment, Camp Johnson, Florida, 14 July 1918 and Byoir's subsequent letter to the commanding officer of Camp Johnson: CPI 1 A-4, Box 30, Folder 4. Also the correspondence between Byoir and John Cavanaugh of Iowa, about one Don Shaw and the latter's application for work in the Judge Advocate's Office.
55. Letter from William Magill to the CPI, 8 May 1918, CPI 1 A-5, Box 32, Folder 5. See the letter to Byoir from P.(?) L. Atkinson of 6 June 1918. Atkinson was then working at *Cosmopolitan Magazine*, Byoir's former employer: CPI 1 A-4, Box 30, Folder 4.
56. The correspondence of H. D. Cullen of Atlanta to Creel illustrates the point. On 7 April 1918 Cullen wrote asking for a job at expenses, citing his seven years of advertising experience. Byoir wrote back on 3 May 1918 saying:

> We have had to make it a rule not to employ any salaried men. . . . [We are] already in a situation where we have dozens of applications on file from those who are in the fortunate position where they can offer their services to the government without remuneration.

The story had a happy ending. Cullen wrote back to Byoir on 13 May 1918, telling him that he had just been made state secretary of the Four Minute Men: CPI 1 A-4, Box 30, Folder 23.
57. The correspondence between Byoir and Rankin may be found in CPI 1 A-4, Box 32, Folder 1. Rankin was the leading advocate of Chicago advertising. On 20 December 1917 he wired Byoir: ". . . Board as now constituted entirely New York and you know Chicago is advertising center for newspapers of country while New York is magazine center. . . ." On 21 December he wrote:

> However, the one big thing – and I can see that you have it in mind too – is not to have the Chicago men feel that New York

men dominate in Washington advertising. As a matter of fact, the Chicago men have led the way in every movement and in nearly every plan where advertising has been used to benefit the Government.

On 23 December in a handwritten note, he says:

Have me appointed on the Board – before 31st if you can. Then also have me appointed Special Advisory Counsel, Bureau of Public Information, Chicago – on all subjects – you know that is what I have [wanted] ever since you & I met.

On 7 January he writes again, suggesting the composition of the board and also urging Byoir to establish a new division, called the Board of Federal Co-operation, with Rankin as chair. This organization would act as a liaison between the government and the media. At this point Rankin's ambitions seem to be focused on both goals. On 8 January Rankin writes suggesting that Cusak might not take a position on the board even if one is offered since Cusak's Washington friends in outdoor advertising were pushing for a separate organization. Rankin also suggests Alfred Mace of the National Biscuit Company as an alternative to Cusak. On 14 February, in a handwritten note, Rankin returns to this theme, once again pushing Mace. He says:

Another thing – Mace, Adv Mgr of the National Biscuit Company is the man for the place – instead of Dobbs of Atlanta. If Mace will not take it, then get a Chicago man. The Chicago Adv. Club feels it is directed at 'Chicago' by NY men when they do not have an advertiser from Chicago on the Board – It so happens that Johns, Jones, Harn, Houston are all considered Eastern men [and] that's the way the Asso[ciated] Ad Clubs have been run by Dobbs-Houston-D'Arcy-Harn.

He goes on to say:

I wish you could also take the trouble to write C. H. Burlingame that I was not *purposely* left off the Board – but you had a bigger job in mind for me which was offered but I could not accept. It will help the Chicago *spirit*. . . .

But that week, Jesse Neal's appointment to the board was announced and Rankin wrote to Byoir on 23 February with evident disappointment:

You know I have been patient and have awaited many Wednesdays and other days, also Thos. Cusack, et al, but when the papers came out this week with Neal's appointment and not mine, I thought, well, after all, is it worth while? I know you will have a good excuse, but it does seem to me that you should have sent my name out first.

Were it not for the fact that some of my friends feel that the New York men have been given preference over Chicago men, who really had the ability and did the work, I would not bother you at all. The Chicago Advertising Club too feels that Chicago has been overlooked.

You know I have made good every promise I have made to you and I want you now to make good on your promises to me. I know you want to make an offer to me that is better than just a member of the Division of Advertising, but let's forget that for the present – that can come later.

But, as it happens, it never did, nor did the big job that Rankin desired ever come about. Despite his disappointment, Rankin seems to have been irrepressible. He did a great deal of work to make the War Exposition in Chicago the huge success it was and Byoir wrote him on 12 July 1918:

I want to thank you for all you have done in connection with the Allied War Exposition. You put me under obligation so often that I do not know how I will ever be able to repay you.

Byoir's note may be the main clue to understanding Rankin's character and the reason why he was shut out of the inner circle of advertising men in the CPI during the war. He was a man of great energy, drive and vitality, who obligated others to himself with sheer virtuosity and relentlessness. Not everyone appreciates such habits of mind.

58. The whole correspondence between Creel and Cusak, Byoir and Cusak, and various third parties and Creel may be found in CPI 1 A-4, Box 30, Folder 24. Of particular interest is the incident of the missed meeting between Byoir and Cusak. On 13 February 1918 Creel had wired Cusak asking him to meet Byoir in New York on the Friday of that week. (Byoir went to New York every Friday, stayed at the Vanderbilt Hotel, and conducted CPI business there.) Cusak wrote back to Creel on 25 February describing what happened:

I received a wire from you on the 13th of this month, asking if it would be possible for me to meet Mr. Carl Byoir in New York on Friday. I wired you that I would be in New York all week, and afterwards wired you that you could inform me at what time Mr. Byoir desired to see me.

On receipt of the latter wire, you wired me that Mr. Byoir would be at the Vanderbilt Hotel. As I stop there when in New York, I left my card in Mr. Byoir's box a week ago last Friday. The next day Mr. Byoir left his card in my box. I called up Mr. Byoir's room but he was not in.

I cannot understand this action. I only left the Vanderbilt Hotel last Friday afternoon. I have been there, and at my office at the Flat Iron Building, which has not been visited by Mr. Byoir. I do not know what you wished Mr. Byoir to see me about. On the whole the action is, to my mind, rather odd. . . .

I have been asked by you to serve on the committee on Advertising for the Government, and acquiesced in this after urgent solicitation by Mr D'Arcy and others.

For some reason the Committee appointment was then immediately held up until Mr. Byoir could interview me. Mr. Byoir evidently thought it was not important enough to interview me about.

Will you be kind enough to explain what this all means. I have not sought the position on this Committee, and acquiesced to it only after urgent solicitation of members of our committee, and by those interested in the Government work.

There followed a flurry of wires and letters until the matter was resolved with Cusak's formal appointment on 22 March 1918.

59. The record of disillusionment in the aftermath of the war is vast. To take only a few examples, see Robert Graves, *Good-bye to All That* (Garden City, NY: Doubleday Anchor Books, 1957), a revised edition of his 1929 autobiography, C. E. Montague, *Disenchantment* (London: Chatto & Windus, 1922) and Walter Lippmann, *The Phantom Public* (New York: Harcourt, Brace and Company, 1925). Although it is not entirely accurate to speak of disillusionment in the case of Arthur Ponsonby since he was a dissenter during the war, his *Falsehood in Wartime* (London: G. Allen & Unwin, Ltd, 1931) was an important document exposing the flimsiness of many wartime distortions. Disillusionment among the Germans was, if anything, even more profound. For only one graphic example, see, in particular, the work of Otto Dix, Museum of Modern Art, New York City.

60. See, for example, Harry Reichenbach, *Phantom Fame* (New York: Simon and Schuster, 1931), p. 240.

61. Creel reports the following conversation with Wilson while they were crossing the Atlantic to the Paris conference. Wilson is quoted as saying:

It is a great thing that you have done, but I am wondering if you have not unconsciously spun a net for me from which there is no escape. It is to America that the whole world turns today, not only with its wrongs, but with its hopes and grievances. The hungry expect us to feed them, the roofless look to us for shelter, the sick of heart and body depend upon us for cure. All of these expectations have in them the quality of terrible urgency. There must be no delay. It has been so always. People will endure their tyrants for years, but they tear their deliverers to pieces if a millennium is not created immediately.... What I seem to see – with all my heart I hope that I am wrong – is a tragedy of disappointment (Creel, *Rebel at Large*, p. 206).

62. See, for instance, Edward Bernays's book *Propaganda* (New York: Liveright, 1928), especially pp. 27–8.

8 The State and Propaganda*
Z. A. B. Zeman

'It is like a dream. Wilhelmstrasse belongs to us. The Führer is already working in the Chancellery. We are standing upstairs at the window, and hundreds of thousands of people are passing by in the flaming light of torches before the grey president and the young Chancellor, and they are gratefully acclaiming them. . . .'[1] When Goebbels recorded the events of 30 January he was no less surprised than moved. The young man who had come to the hostile city six years before was now witnessing its final conversion to the true faith: at long last, Germany had awakened. The future promised unlimited possibilities.

The first foundations for the management of the German people by the state had been laid down some time before the day of Goebbels's exultation. He had become the *Reichspropagandaleiter* of the party on 9 January 1929; his chance to strengthen his own position and to extend the powers of his office came in 1932. Its activities overlapped to a great extent with those of the *Reichsorganisationsleitung* – the department of party organization – headed by Gregor Strasser. And when the ever-present problem of Gregor Strasser's position inside the party flared up again in the autumn of 1932, Goebbels seized this chance to reorganize and strengthen the administration of propaganda. He was convinced that Hitler was getting ready to take over power in Germany, and he carried out the reorganization of the propaganda apparatus with this end firmly in his mind. Its main function had been, until then, the efficient transmission of directives down the hierarchy of local organizations; now, Goebbels's main concern was the broadening of the

*Reprinted from Z. A. B. Zeman, *Nazi Propaganda*, (London: Oxford University Press, 1964).

central organization and the dividing of it into specialized sections that could look after every aspect of propaganda.

The section dealing with 'active propaganda' (*Amt I*) formed the core of the organization: it dealt with the execution of political agitation, from the monster meetings with their problems of architectural design, accommodation, transport and so on (there was a special subsection for *Grossveranstaltungen*: the organization of the party rallies was run, however, by an independent permanent office in Nürnberg, which came under the direct supervision of the *Reichspropagandaleiter*) to the small meetings in the countryside. The main subsection, which had a comparatively long history behind it, was concerned with *Rednerwesen*, the direction of public speaking. The office of 'active propaganda' also distributed its own newspaper, *Unser Wille und Weg*, which had been founded in 1931.

Then there were sections dealing with 'culture' – including architecture, Hitler's special sphere of interest – with radio, film and 'liaison with offices of the state'. These sections were expanded after January 1933; until then they existed only in a rudimentary form. The same division was perpetuated on the lower levels of party organization: the *Gaupropagandaleiter* was responsible for five sections corresponding to those in the central office on the provincial level; lower down in the hierarchy, there were the *Kreispropagandaleiter* – the district director of propaganda – the *Ortsgruppenpropagandaleiter*, who worked on the level of local party organization, and finally the *Stützpunktpropagandaleiter* – the cell-leader. All these ranks led a separate existence from the rest of the party organization; the hierarchy was used for transmitting orders downward, and passing information – situation reports, 'audience research' and so on – upwards. Regular monthly situation reports were passed on from the lowest level through the same hierarchy. By 1934, the party propaganda apparatus employed some 14,000 people.[2]

Nevertheless the machinery that controlled Nazi propaganda activities was carefully concealed from public view. The marionettes were there for all to see, but the strings, and the string pullers, would have spoilt the illusion. On one occasion, Goebbels had a fit of blinding fury because an illustrated magazine published a picture of a man putting on a record of a triumphal bell chime after a special announcement; at a press conference in Berlin selected journalists were informed that 'problems of stage management [*Regiefragen*] should not on principle come before the public. All that goes on behind the backcloth belongs to stage management.'[3]

Although the internal structure of party propaganda apparatus was often reshaped, and although its functions frequently overlapped with those of other party or, after 1933, state departments, it gave Goebbels a unique position of power. It was further strengthened when he became, in March 1933, the first Nazi Minister of Popular Enlightenment and Propaganda.

The possibility of backing up propaganda by the full weight of the machinery of the state was exploited to the full by the Nazis shortly after Hitler's appointment as Chancellor. Coercion could be substituted, when necessary, for persuasion; the terror that had been inflicted on the Germans by the storm-troopers before 1933 could now be meted out by the state. On the evening of 27 February, fire raged inside the *Reichstag*. It is immaterial whether it was started by a demented Dutch Communist pyromaniac or by the Nazis themselves, or independently by both; the fact remains that the Nazi action against their political opponents was swift and ruthless. By no means partisans of parliamentary institutions, the Nazis used the *Reichstag* fire as a pretext for their first move towards large-scale political repression. They declared it to be a Communist plot, the beginning of a Communist revolution. On the day after the fire, Hindenburg was made, by Hitler, to sign a decree for the protection of 'the People and the State', which suppressed those sections of the constitution relating to civil liberties, and authorized the central government to assume, whenever necessary, complete power in the federal states.

The SA troopers now appeared in the role of the defenders of the state. They were used as a supplementary police force for arresting thousands of their fellow-countrymen; the first concentration camps were set up. The Communists suffered first and foremost; the Social Democrats, and the leaders of the liberal parties, soon joined them in the camps.

The last semi-democratic elections took place in an atmosphere of terror. The Nazis had suppressed most of the newspapers run by their political enemies; they now had the broadcasting system at their disposal. Despite these advantages and their attempt to extract the full propaganda value from the threat of a Communist revolution, the Nazis did not gain a clear majority. They polled 43.9 per cent of the total vote. Only when the fifty-two deputies of Hugenberg's German National Party were added to the 288 National Socialist deputies did Hitler's government achieve a marginal majority in the *Reichstag*.

But this was only a minor obstacle. A few days after the elections Goebbels was appointed, on 13 March, the Minister of Popular Enlightenment and Propaganda. A stream of letters and well-wishers began to pour into the office of the new Minister: this was not a routine appointment, as no such office had existed before. A week later, Hitler saw the Enabling Law through the *Reichstag*; it gave his government dictatorial powers. In these circumstances, the main aim of Nazi propaganda was to achieve the identification of the party with the state. The opening of the new *Reichstag*, on 21 March, served this purpose admirably. It was stage-managed by Goebbels, and the garrison church at Potsdam provided a suitable setting. The place had powerful historical associations: Frederick the Great was buried here, it was a reminder of Prussia's past. Among such memories there was no place for democratic, parliamentary ideals; the tradition was authoritarian, underscored by past military glory. The Nazis turned up in force, and so did the living relics of the Empire in their splendid uniforms of a bygone age. Hindenburg made a speech to the deputies assembled in the garrison church; he was followed by Hitler. Again, the same image as on 30 January occurred to Goebbels.[4] The grey, old President with the young Chancellor: the past and the future of Germany were united in the present moment; Germany's honour was restored, and the shameful recent memories were safely buried.

Goebbels was a busy man in the first months after the formation of Hitler's government. The Nazi leaders no longer saw their party as one of the competitors in the political arena; the point now was to eliminate all competition, while completing a watertight *Gleichschaltung* of every aspect of political activity. And not only that: every facet of national life had to be inspired from a single source and directed by a central authority. In their own view, the Nazis possessed the only infallible panacea.

Propaganda occupied, as we have observed, a focal position in the Nazi scheme of things when the party was still on the road to power; after 1933 Goebbels's Ministry was placed in a corresponding key position. According to Hitler's decree, published in June, the Minister was responsible for 'all tasks of spiritual direction of the nation'.[5] This vague directive gave Goebbels's Ministry a wide scope. Other departments of state had to give up a variety of their former functions in its favour. The Ministry of the Interior handed over to Goebbels the supervision of radio, films, press, and theatre; the protection of works of art and memorials, and the regulation of state celebrations and holidays; the Foreign Ministry had to give up – at any rate in theory – the control of the whole range of propaganda abroad. (The organization of the Ministry and the division of tasks inside it corresponded closely to that of the party department of propaganda, *Reichspropagandaleitung*). Apart from the sections for active propaganda, radio, films, press, there were sections dealing with theatre, creative arts, music, and writing. (In the *Reichspropagandaleitung*, all these latter activities came under the direction of the *Kulturamt*.) There were also special sections dealing with propaganda abroad, foreign press, and the *Fremdenverkehrsabteilung*. The last section looked after tourist traffic; for a National Socialist this did not simply mean going abroad for holidays, or foreigners coming to Germany for the same purpose. Although the Nazis erected no 'iron curtain' around Germany, tourism became a political exercise that was closely linked with the overall propaganda effort.

Most of the top positions in the Ministry and in the *Reichspropagandaleitung* were held by the same men; the two institutions in fact merged, at many points, into one apparatus. The key *Abteilung II* acted as the general staff of the Ministry; policy was formulated here, ideas were discussed and worked out in detail; it also included sections dealing with specific tasks, such as the fight against Marxism, the

Versailles peace treaties, anti-semitic propaganda, eastern and borderland problems. The head of the whole department was Wilhelm Haegert, who also managed the liaison section of the *Reichspropagandaleitung*; Leopold Gutterer, who looked after the section which dealt with large meetings (*Grossveranstaltungen*) inside the party propaganda organization, also acted as a principal (*Referent*) in the *Abteilung II* in the Ministry; Hans Kriegler was head of the departments of broadcasting both in the Ministry and in the *Reichspropagandaleitung*, as well as acting as the President of the *Reichsrundfunkkammer*. Division of labour between the two organizations was purely functional, and it did not affect questions of general policy. The Ministry was, for instance, responsible for the organization of state visits and state celebrations, whereas the *Reichspropagandaleitung* carried out the celebrations of the various party anniversaries.

Centralization of all propaganda activities implied, for Goebbels, the elimination of every alternative source of information. In this respect, his most difficult task lay in the *Gleichschaltung* – the achievement of uniformity – of the press. When Hitler became the Chancellor of the Republic there existed over 4,703 newspapers in Germany; their political make-up was highly differentiated, they had a long tradition behind them, and some of them had acquired, in the course of the years, a nation-wide reputation. They all made heavy demands on the pool of skilled journalists: Hitler and Goebbels had not been very successful in the competition for their services. The Nazis ran only a small section of the very diverse press; at the beginning of 1933 they had 121 dailies and periodicals – most of them with low circulation – at their disposal. By the end of 1934 the situation had drastically changed. The party then controlled some 430 newspapers directly, and indirectly all the German press.

But the uniformity achieved in those years was by no means obvious at a first glance. Only the extremists in the movement advocated a radical suppression of all the former democratic press, which would put the party, at once, into a monopoly position.[6] Goebbels was well aware of the difficulties involved in replacing the variegated press of

Germany. He maintained that the monopoly of direction
behind the scenes should continue to flow through the traditional variety of channels.[7] Goebbels chose to advance along
the line of least resistance. In this way the readers' habits
would not be suddenly broken, and the Nazi journalists would
not be faced with a task beyond their powers. The long-
term views on the development of the German press –
Goebbels very likely shared them with Max Amann, the party
publisher, and with Rudolf Hess – were that the *NSDAP*
press would eventually come to dominate the field, not so
much because of its intrinsic value and merits, but because
of the help the party authorities could render it.[8] The Germans could be educated, or perhaps even compelled, to
read Nazi newspapers and periodicals.

The slow erosion of the independence of the German press
was carried out in a variety of ways. The *Reichstag* fire served
as a pretext for the suppression of all Communist newspapers, and a ban on those run by the Social Democrat
Party. The ruthless suppression of hundreds of newspapers
was followed by a more oblique step. The *Wolff
Telegraphenbüro*, was transformed into the *Deutsches
Nachrichtenbüro*, and the other agencies were also brought
into line. As well as regulating the flow of news at its very
source, Goebbels tackled the problem from the other end,
on the editorial level. Official press conferences had been
introduced in Germany during the First World War, and in
1919 they became a regular feature of journalists' activities in Berlin. They were run by the *Reichspressechef* or his
deputy, and their main purpose was to explain the official
attitude of the government on the most important issues of
the day to the editors of the national newspapers, and to
answer their questions. Soon after Goebbels became the
Minister of Propaganda, the conduct of the conferences
passed into the hands of the press department of his Ministry. It controlled the admission of journalists to these
meetings, as well as the information that was dispensed to
them. And under Goebbels's régime, the conference gradually
lost its original function – to inform the journalists. This
was taken over by the *Deutsches Nachrichtenbüro*, the official
news agency, which issued material suitable to serve as the
basis for commentaries and leaders. The agency also pro-

vided a small circle of Nazi journalists and party functionaries with strictly confidential material intended for their
personal use. The press conference then issued only orders:
they came from Goebbels, and he had the whole apparatus of the state behind him if he wished to enforce them.

The Nazis attempted to create their own image of an
ideal editor: a man who was not a mere technician, but a
fighter for their ideals. They had a romantic picture of
such a person, which they derived from the 'period of
struggle' before 1933; Weiss, the editor of the *Völkischer
Beobachter*, described him in the following manner: 'A National
Socialist editor never was a journalist exclusively but always
and foremost a propagandist, very often a newspaperman,
a speaker, and an SA trooper in one person. We want editors who will support their Führer and the new Reich not
because they have to do so, but because they want to.'[9] In
the meantime, however, Goebbels could not rely on cynical
journalists being willing to accept his 'ideals'. In the autumn of 1933, the Nazis reinforced their press policy by
legislation. The *Schriftleitergesetz* – the law of 4 October –
followed the lines that Hitler had first expounded in the
party programme some thirteen years earlier. The law declared the office of an editor to be an official position, which
could not be held by a person without German citizenship,
or who had been deprived of his rights as a citizen, who
was a Jew, or who was married to one. When discharging
their functions, editors were placed under a variety of restrictions. They were bound by law not to confuse their
'private [good] with the general good in a manner misleading to the public';[10] they were not to print anything
that might harm Germany's ability to defend herself, her
economy or culture or indeed anything that broke the rules
of 'good conduct'. The paragraphs of the law, especially
those concerning the functions of the editor, entirely ruled
out any possibility of editorial independence; the right to
express a personal view of the government was entirely denied to the German journalists. The law gave the Ministry
of Propaganda an instrument for the achievement of a complete uniformity of the press: there was no need for censorship because the editor's most important function was that
of a censor.

Goebbels defended the press law in a speech to the journalists on the day of its publication. He argued that the free expression of opinion could seriously threaten the state, and that personal liberty depended on the degree of freedom that 'can be enjoyed by the nation, and the freedom of the individual will be the narrower the greater the dangers are that temporarily threaten the state'. Only much later – in 1942 – did Goebbels explain what he meant by temporary danger: he said that freedom of opinion could be established only when the German nation reached the 'maturity' of the English people, a process that would take at least a century.[11] At the conference on 4 October Goebbels further argued that the state was not able to give up the means of controlling the press, because of the tendency, among the Germans, to take the printed word much more seriously than the spoken word. He talked to the assembled journalists as one of them; he attempted to make the law palatable to them by pointing out that it raised their professional status, and that it strengthened their position in relation to the publisher.

Nevertheless, even in this respect – the relation between the editor and the publisher – the freedom of the journalist to choose his own employer was being gradually whittled down. The operations of Max Amann constituted another line of attack on the independence of the press. He may have disapproved of those clauses of the law that downgraded the relation between the publisher and the editor to a purely contractual basis: nevertheless, by the autumn of 1933, Amann knew that he was well on the way to becoming a dictator of German publishing. In the early years of the party's activity in Bavaria, Max Amann had been its business manager as well as the director of the Franz Eher Verlag, the official Nazi publishing house. As Hitler's personal friend, the proprietor of the Eher Verlag, the chairman of the Union of German Newspaper Publishers, and as the Secretary of the Press Chamber (*Reichspressekammer*), Amann was, by 1933, in a unique position of power. He used it to bring, gradually, a large part of German publishing under his control. His first opportunity came when all the Communist and Social Democrat press was banned after the *Reichstag* fire: by the end of the year, some 1,500 publishers were robbed of their business. The decrees issued in April 1935 for the 'preservation of newspaper publishing', for the 'extirpation of newspapers dealing in scandal' and so on offered Amann further opportunities for the reorganization of publishing. Before Amann started building his empire under Hitler's patronage, some 80 per cent of all publishing houses were run as family businesses; their number decreased rapidly, constantly harassed and decimated by the government and by Amann. Even most of the newspapers run by the Scherl Verlag – it was controlled by Hitler's former ally Hugenberg – were gradually swallowed up by Amann's organization. If in 1933 the Nazis ran only 2.5 per cent of all German newspapers, by 1944 82 per cent of the remaining 977 newspapers were controlled, directly or indirectly, by Amann.[12] In 1939 the Amann concern employed 600 editors-in-chief of publishing houses and 3,000 journalists, apart from many thousands of administrative employees.

Although in 1941, on the occasion of Max Amann's fiftieth birthday, Hitler could congratulate his friend on the superlative work he had done for the Nazi idea, the *Gleichschaltung* of the German press had been a slow, costly, and laborious process. By comparison, the control of the film industry and of broadcasting was easier of achievement, and it produced, from the Nazi point of view, more impressive results. For this, there were a number of reasons. Both the privately owned film industry and the state-run broadcasting system were only recently developed as the means of mass communication; they possessed neither the set traditions nor the wide diversity of the press. Although the Nazis had gained little first-hand experience of these media before 1933, Goebbels understood their importance, and he had begun plotting their capture some time before the Nazis came to power.

It has been suggested that the productions of the German film industry in the Weimar Republic prepared the ground for the establishment of the Nazi régime. Mr. Siegfried Kracauer, for instance, concluded his study of the German film *From Caligari to Hitler* with this perceptive paragraph:

Irretrievably sunk into retrogression, the bulk of the German people could not help submitting to Hitler. Since

Germany thus carried out what had been anticipated by her cinema from its very beginning, conspicuous screen characters now came true in life itself. Personified day-dreams of minds to whom freedom meant a fatal shock, and adolescence a permanent temptation, these figures filled the arena of Nazi Germany. Homunculus walked about in the flesh. Self-appointed Caligaris hypnotized innumerable Cesares into murder. Raving Mabuses committed fantastic crimes with impunity, and mad Ivans devised unheard-of tortures. Along with this unholy procession, many motifs known from the screen turned into actual events. In Nürnberg, the ornamental pattern of Nibelungen appeared on a gigantic scale: an ocean of flags and people artistically arranged. Souls were thoroughly manipulated so as to create the impression that the heart mediated between brain and hand. By day and night, millions of feet were marching over city streets and along highways. The blare of military bugles sounded unremittingly, and the philistines from the plush parlours felt very elated. Battles roared and victory followed victory. It all was as it had been on the screen. The dark premonitions of a final doom were also fulfilled.[13]

Although it is true to say that some films reflected various Nazi tendencies in German life in the pre-Hitler era, and that many of the people connected with the making of films gladly accepted the patronage of Goebbels, German cinemas had largely been showing commercial films, free from any political tendency. High production costs had to be covered by adequate box-office returns: Goebbels attacked precisely these films in a speech to the representatives of the industry in February 1934. He sharply criticized the manner in which German film-making was 'debased' by the dictates of capital, and the low level of the routine film produced purely for the sake of box-office returns; he said that German film-makers must learn to regard their profession as a service, and not as a source of profit.

Some time before this speech, the law for the establishment of a 'Provisional Film Chamber' was published:[14] it was mainly concerned with bringing the film industry into the 'general economic framework' of the state. The film companies began to be heavily subsidized from official funds, and then one after the other were taken over by the state; the largest of them – Hugenberg's UFA company – was acquired in 1937. In less than five years the film department of the Ministry of Propaganda acquired a monopoly in film production; this policy was accompanied by the gradual elimination of foreign competition for the favours of the German filmgoers. No one could compete with Goebbels as an independent producer.

The Minister rated the value of films as a weapon of propaganda very high indeed; he also had a liking for the world of film, and he gave it a good deal of personal attention. Even well-known directors had to tolerate Goebbels's interference with their business; they often had to make changes in their casts and re-shoot whole scenes at the Minister's bidding. Apart from the propaganda documentaries – films of party rallies, of the Berlin Olympic Games and the heavily slanted newsreels – a number of films with strong political tendencies were made. *Jud Süss* put across the antisemitic message; *Hitlerjunge Quex* glorified the party and its youth; *Friesennot* underlined the trials of the Germans living outside the frontiers of Hitler's state. Indeed, in this *genre*, the Nazis scored some popular successes, which they attempted to match on the stages of the German theatres. The achievement and the technique of film-producing collectives could not however be employed in traditional theatre; individual authors could be neither discovered nor coerced as easily. In theatre, the Nazis had to be content to rely on the old repertoire, and to select from it the plays that suited them best.

Goebbels was attracted to films because they were easier to make and mould and because they reached much wider audiences than live theatre. Nevertheless, their limitations as an instrument of propaganda soon became apparent. Although box-office considerations were done away with, not all the films made in Germany could carry a high charge of Nazi propaganda. A large sector of the industry went on producing entirely apolitical films: indeed, the initial enthusiasm of the Nazi film-makers to put across their message gradually cooled off. Although the Hitler Youth Quex had mercifully perished at the hands of Communist thugs, he was revived during the war. Now a fully grown man, he appeared as Pilot Quex, a figure of comedy rather than of high-minded drama. In this respect, Goebbels failed: the kind of films he criticized in February 1934 continued to be made; the German public had to be amused.

When Goebbels became the Minister of Propaganda, the newspaper and film industries were privately owned: the broadcasting system was, on the other hand, state-run. It had some ten years' history behind it; although it had eluded the grasp of the Nazis before 1933, the imposition on it afterwards of centrally directed uniformity proved comparatively simple. For the Nazi propagandists, the control of broadcasting was the most coveted prize. Indeed, in June 1932 Hitler made his support of von Papen's government conditional on the grant to his party of broadcasting facilities; after that, numerous pronouncements by high party functionaries bore witness to their interest in the medium. At the opening of the radio exhibition in Berlin in August 1933, Goebbels quoted Napoleon, who had described the press as the 'seventh Great Power', and he continued: 'What the press was for the nineteenth century, wireless will be for the twentieth. One could alter the words of Napoleon, and call it the eighth Great Power.'[15]

In Germany, as in many other European countries, the two powers clashed. Mass-circulation press and broadcasting catered for the same public, and their functions – especially as far as the dissemination of news was concerned – were similar. Their rivalry had by no means been resolved before Hitler became Chancellor: the Nazi propagandists later favoured broadcasting at the expense of the press; Goebbels regarded it as a much more effective means of influencing the masses. In a small circle of his collaborators, he expressed the view that the press was an 'exponent of the liberal spirit, the product and instrument of the French revolution', whereas broadcasting was 'essentially authoritarian', and, therefore, a suitable 'spiritual weapon of the totalitarian state'.[16] Since Hitler hardly ever listened to wireless, Goebbels had a greater freedom of action in this than in any other field of propaganda; he also valued the fact that the spoken word disappeared without trace. He often allowed his broadcasters to exploit this liberty.

Yet though broadcasting was the pampered child of Nazi propagandists, the principle by which it had to give way to the claims of the press to bring important news first – this had been established in the Weimar Republic – was continued. In this respect, Max Amann's influence was decisive: until the outbreak of war speed in the dissemination of news was sacrificed in favour of the established prerogatives of the press.[17]

The new masters of the German broadcasting system laid special stress on the development of 'political broadcasts' – from dramatic poems set to music, composed to glorify the past of the party, to Hitler's speeches. Indeed, the latter were the focal point of Nazi radio programming; as many as fifty speeches by Hitler were transmitted in 1933. But in this respect the Nazi broadcasters had a lot to learn. Hitler's first radio message was followed by a flood of complaints from all parts of Germany; another recording had to be made, this time slower and less slurred, and it was broadcast the following day with better results. The Nazi propagandists learned their lesson; from October 1933, when the Führer announced Germany's departure from the League of Nations, until late in the war, Hitler made no studio broadcast. The contact with the 'masses' was the essential stimulus of his speaking, and its effect was further strengthened by the 'acoustic backcloth': the applause, the rhythmic chant of *Sieg Heil*, the off-stage noises of the large meeting. Without the direct *rapport* with his audience, and without the background it provided, Hitler was a failure as a speaker. He was unable to learn the technique – President Roosevelt in his 'fireside chats' was its master – which confined the speaker in the studio and left him to address a mass audience, but one composed of individuals in the privacy of their homes.

The most impressive achievement of the Nazi broadcasters lay, however, in the creation of this mass audience. In May 1933, German radio manufacturers undertook to produce a cheap, uniform set, the *Volksempfünger*. A few months later, the first 100,000 of these sets reached the market, and in 1934 the power of the transmitters was increased by 30 per cent. When the war broke out, some 3,500,000 sets had been sold.[18] In 1939, 70 per cent of all German households owned a wireless set: the highest precentage anywhere in the world. But the Nazi policy-makers were not quite satisfied with this situation: they did not regard the housewife and her family as a safe enough audience. Compulsory listening was developed alongside the compulsory attendance of meetings and the purchase of Nazi newspapers. Loudspeakers were introduced into factories, and production stopped when an important party or state broadcast was being transmitted; the completion of the plan for the installation of 6,000 'loudspeaker pillars' in the streets (here the Nazis imitated the practices introduced by the rulers of Soviet Russia early in the nineteen twenties) was interrupted by the war.

Indeed, during the six years of peace they allowed themselves, the Nazis interfered in every aspect of public and private life to an extent unknown in Germany's history. The work of the Germans, their holidays, the new buildings in their towns, the education of their children, the newspapers they read, the films they saw, and the radio programmes they listened to bore the Nazi stamp. By 1935, however, behind the propaganda façade, there loomed three solid actualities of Nazi achievement. While other European governments were still struggling with the aftermath of the economic crisis, the Nazis had solved it in Germany; by the Nürnberg laws, the Jews had been deprived of German citizenship; in the background, there were the means of coercion, the Gestapo and the concentration camps. Many of the original aims of the National Socialists had been achieved: power and success were now living realities, and not merely the objects of veneration from afar. This of course strengthened the hand of the propagandists: the citizens of the Nazi state were trapped, and they had to listen to incessant sermons on the excellence of their capture. Nevertheless, the actual value of propaganda changed, and even declined, after the National Socialists had reached their goal. Before 1933, it had served as the main instrument in the drive for capturing the masses, for laying the foundations for the capture of power in the state. But once he achieved this power the state rather than the party, became Hitler's main object of interest. The creation of Goebbels's Ministry of course bore witness to the continued prominence of propaganda in the Nazi system; its main task, however, was to win popular support for the National Socialist state. Violence – the reverse side of the propaganda coin – received, as it were, official sanction. From a private army that had operated on the fringes of legality, the SA became an executive organ of the state. And soon other agencies of repression became available. At the same time, outside Germany, new horizons opened before Nazi propaganda.

Notes

1. Joseph Goebbels, *Vom Kaiserhof zur Reichskanzlei* (Berlin, 1934), entry on 30 January 1933, p. 251.
2. Karlheinz Schmeer, *Die Regie des öffentlichen Lebens in Dritten Reich* (Munich, 1956), p. 32.
3. Karlheinz Schmeer, p. 28.
4. Joseph Goebbels, *Vom Kaiserhof zur Reichskanzlei*, p. 285.
5. Karlheinz Schmeer, p. 38.
6. Walter Hagemann, *Publizistik im Dritten Reich. Ein Beitrag zur Methodik der Massenführung* (Hamburg, 1948), p. 34.
7. Walter Hagemann, p. 35.
8. Confer National Archives, Washington, D.C., Record Group No. T. 81, documents pertaining to Nazi press policy, especially document 28539.
9. Weiss, editor of the *Völkischer Beobachter*, in a speech to the journalists' conference at Cologne in November 1935, quoted by Walter Hagemann, op. cit., p. 39.
10. *Reichsgesetzblatt*, 1933, Part I, p. 714.
11. Walter Hagemann, op. cit., p. 37.
12. Walter Hagemann, op. cit., p. 40.
13. Siegfried Kracauer, *From Caligari to Hitler* (Princeton: Princeton University Press, 1947), p. 272.
14. *Reichsgesetzblatt*, 1933, Part I, p. 483.
15. Joseph Goebbels, as quoted by Walter Hagemann, op. cit., p. 45.
16. Heinz Pohle, *Der Rundfunk als Instrument der Politik. Zur Geschichte des dt. Rundfunks 1923–38* (Hamburg, 1955), p. 241.
17. Heinz Pohle, op. cit., pp. 239–40.
18. Heinz Pohle, op. cit., p. 257.

9 Goebbels' Principles of Propaganda*

Leonard W. Doob

Among the Nazi documents salvaged by American authorities in Berlin in 1945 are close to 6,800 pages of a manuscript ostensibly dictated by Propaganda Minister Goebbels as a diary that covers, with many gaps, the period from January 21, 1942 to December 9, 1943. The material was typed triple-spaced in large German-Gothic script and with wide margins upon heavy watermarked paper, with the result that the average page contained less than 100 words. About 30 per cent of this manuscript – the most interesting and generally the most important parts – has been very accurately and idiomatically translated by Louis P. Lochner.[1] The analysis in the present article is based upon careful examination of the entire document which is now in the Hoover Institute and Library on War, Peace, and Revolution at Stanford University.[2]

The material undoubtedly was dictated by Goebbels, but it is not necessarily an intimate or truthful account of his life as an individual or propagandist. He was too crafty to pour forth his soul to a secretary. What he said must have been motivated by whatever public audience he imagined would eventually see his words; or – as Speier has pointed out[3] – the document may possibly represent parts of an authentic diary that were selected by him or someone else for some specific purpose. A section called "Yesterday – Military Situation," with which each day's entry began and which Lochner has sensibly omitted altogether, was definitely not written by Goebbels: the writing was most objective; often the same events mentioned therein were reported again and commented upon in other parts of the same day's entry; and infrequently a blank page appeared under the same

---

* Reprinted from *Public Opinion Quarterly*, vol. 14 (1950).

heading with the notation "to be inserted later." In the manuscript we have, there are few personal details. Instead it appears that Goebbels wished to demonstrate an unswerving loyalty to Hitler; to expose the ineptitudes of the German military staffs; to boast about his own accomplishments, his respectability, and his devotion to the Nazi cause; and to place on the record criticism of rival Nazis like Goering and Rosenberg.

The nature of the document would be a problem most germane to an examination of Goebbels' personality or the history of Nazidom, but these topics are not being discussed here. Attention has been focused only on the principles that appear to underlie the propaganda plans and decisions described in the manuscript. Spot checks suggest but do not prove that the words of the diary actually correspond to the activities of Goebbels' propaganda machine. One typical example of the correspondence must suffice. The entry in the diary for November 11, 1943, contained this observation: "There is no longer any talk in the English press of the possibility of a moral collapse of the Reich. On the contrary, we are credited with much greater military prowess than we enjoy at the moment. . . ." On the same day, the *Berliner Illustrierte Nachtausgabe* carried an editorial that asserted that the "jubilant illusions" of the British regarding a German collapse have "suddenly changed to deep pessimism; the enemy's strongest hopes are crushed." Two days later the headline of the leading article in the *Voelkischer Beobachter* was "War of Nerves Departs." On November 13 the diary stated that the English "have been imagining that exactly on this day [November 11] there would be in the Reich a morale breakdown which, however, has now been pushed by them into the invisible future." A day later a Nazi official spoke over the domestic radio: "The key-dates chosen by the enemy are now passed: our people have repulsed this general attack. . . ."

All that is being assumed, in short, is that the manuscript more or less faithfully reflects Goebbels' propaganda strategy and tactics: it is a convenient guide to his bulky propaganda materials. He always magnified the importance of his work, no doubt to indicate his own significance. The truth of what he dictated in this respect is also irrelevant, inasmuch as the effects of his efforts are not being scrutinized.

The analysis that follows, it must constantly be remembered, is based on a very limited period of Goebbels' stewardship, a period in which on the whole Germany was suffering military and political defeats such as the winter campaigns in Russia, the withdrawal from North Africa, and the capitulation of Italy. From time to time, nevertheless, events such as temporary military advances and the triumphs of Japan in Asia occurred; hence there are also suggestions as to how Goebbels functioned as a winner. The writer has checked primary and secondary sources from 1925 through 1941 and after 1943, and is therefore at least privately confident that the principles are not limited to the diary.

In this analysis a principle is adduced – in an admittedly but unavoidably subjective manner – from the diary when a minimum of six scattered references therein suggests that Goebbels would have had to believe, consciously or unconsciously, in that generalization before he could dictate or behave as he did. To save space, however, only a few illustrations are given under each principle. Whenever possible, an illustration has been selected from the portion published by Lochner: the reader has readier access to that volume than to the manuscript at Stanford. The same procedure has been employed regarding references. A quoted phrase or sentence is followed by the number of the page being cited, either from the Lochner book (in which case just the number is given in parentheses), or from the Stanford manuscript (in which case the number is preceded by the letter "M," and represents the Library's pagination). The concluding sentence of each paragraph, moreover, contains the one reference considered to be either the best or the most typical for the entire paragraph, again preferably from the Lochner book.

These principles purport to summarize what made Goebbels tick or fail to tick. They may be thought of as his intellectual legacy. Whether the legacy has been reliably deduced is a methodological question. Whether it is valid is a psychological matter. Whether or when parts of it should be utilized in a democratic society are profound and disturbing problems of a political and ethical nature.

PRINCIPLE 1: PROPAGANDISTS MUST HAVE ACCESS TO INTELLIGENCE CONCERNING EVENTS AND PUBLIC OPINION

In theory, Goebbels maintained that he and his associates could plan and execute propaganda only by constantly referring to existing intelligence. Otherwise the communication would not be adapted either to the event or the audience. As Germany's situation worsened, he permitted fewer and fewer officials to have access to all relevant intelligence. By May of 1943 he persuaded Himmler to supply unexpurgated reports only to himself (p. 373).

The basic intelligence during a war concerns military events. Each day's entry began with a separate description of the current military situation. There is every indication that Goebbels was kept acquainted with Germany's own military plans (p. 162).

Information about Germans was obtained most frequently from the reports of the *Sicherheits-Dienst* (SD) of the secret police. In addition, Goebbels depended upon his own Reich Propaganda Offices, German officials, and written or face-to-face contacts with individual German civilians or soldiers. As has been shown elsewhere,[4] little or none of this intelligence was ever gathered or analyzed systematically. Once Goebbels stated that the SD had conducted "a statistical investigation . . . in the manner of the Gallup Institute," but he said he did "not value such investigations because they are always undertaken with a deliberate purpose in mind" (M p. 827). Goebbels, moreover, tended to trust his own common sense, intuition, or experience more than formal reports. He listened to his mother because, he said, "she knows the sentiments of the people better than most experts who judge from the ivory tower of scientific inquiry, as in her case the voice of people itself speaks" (p. 56).

The SD as well as German officials supplied intelligence concerning occupied countries. Information about enemy, allied, and neutral nations was gathered from spies, monitored telephone conversations, and other classified sources; from the interrogation of prisoners as well as from the letters they received and sent; and from statements in or deductions from those nations' mass media of communication. Here, too, Goebbels often relied upon his own intuitive judgment, and he seldom hesitated to make far-reaching deductions from a thread of evidence. A direct reply by the enemy, for example, he unequivocally interpreted as a sign of his own effectiveness: "a wild attack on my last article" by the Russian news agency "shows that our anti-Bolshevik propaganda is slowly getting on Soviet nerves" (p. 271).

PRINCIPLE 2: PROPAGANDA MUST BE PLANNED AND EXECUTED BY ONLY ONE AUTHORITY

This principle was in line with the Nazi theory of centralizing authority and with Goebbels' own craving for power. In the diary he stressed the efficiency and consistency that could result from such a policy (M p. 383). He felt that a single authority – himself – must perform three functions.

First *it must issue all the propaganda directives.* Every bit of propaganda had to implement policy, and policy was made clear in directives. These directives referred to all phases of the war and to all events occurring inside and outside of Germany. They indicated when specific propaganda campaigns should be begun, augmented, diminished, and terminated. They suggested how an item should be interpreted and featured, or whether it should be ignored completely. Goebbels willingly yielded his authority for issuing directives only to Hitler, whose approval on very important matters was always sought. Sometimes gratification was expressed concerning the ways in which directives were implemented; but often there were complaints concerning how Goebbels' own people or others were executing a campaign. The Nazi propaganda machine, therefore, was constantly being reorganized (p. 341).

Second, *it must explain propaganda directives to important officials and maintain their morale.* Unless these officials who either formally or informally implemented directives were provided with an explanation of propaganda policy, they could not be expected to function effectively and willingly. Through his organizational machinery and also through personal contact, Goebbels sought to reveal the rationale of his propaganda to these subordinates and to improve their morale by taking them, ostensibly, into his confidence. The groups he met varied in size from an intimate gathering in his home to what must have been a mass meeting in the Kroll Opera House in Berlin (p. 484).

Third, *it must oversee other agencies' activities that have propaganda consequences.* "I believe," Goebbels told Hitler, "that when a propaganda ministry is created, all matters affecting propaganda, news, and culture within the Reich and within the occupied areas must be subordinated to it." Although Hitler allegedly "agreed with me absolutely and unreservedly," this high degree of unification was not achieved (p. 476). Conflicts over propaganda plans and materials were recorded with the following German agencies: Ribbentrop's Foreign Office and its representatives in various countries; Rosenberg's Ministry for the Eastern Occupied Areas; the German Army, even including the officers stationed at Hitler's G.H.Q.; the Ministry of Justice; and Ley's Economic Ministry. Goebbels considered himself and his ministry troubleshooters: whenever and wherever German morale seemed poor – whether among submarine crews or the armies in the East – he attempted to provide the necessary propaganda boost (p. 204).

Goebbels' failure to achieve the goal of this principle and its corollaries is noteworthy. Apparently his self-proclaimed competency was not universally recognized: people whom he considered amateurs believed they could execute propaganda as effectively as he. In addition, even a totalitarian regime could not wipe out personal rivalries and animosities in the interests of efficiency (M p. 3945).

PRINCIPLE 3: THE PROPAGANDA CONSEQUENCES OF AN ACTION MUST BE CONSIDERED IN PLANNING THAT ACTION

Goebbels demanded that he rather than the German Ministry of Justice be placed in charge of a trial in France so that "everything will be seized and executed correctly from a psychological viewpoint" (M p. 1747). He persuaded Hitler, he wrote, to conduct "air warfare against England . . . according to psychological rather than military principles" (p. 313). It was more important for a propagandist to help plan an event than to rationalize one that had occurred (p. 209).

PRINCIPLE 4: PROPAGANDA MUST AFFECT THE ENEMY'S POLICY AND ACTION

Propaganda was considered an arm of warfare, although Goebbels never employed the phrase "psychological warfare" or "political warfare." Besides damaging enemy morale, he believed that propaganda could affect the policies and actions of enemy leaders in four ways.

First, *by suppressing propagandistically desirable material that could provide the enemy with useful intelligence.* Often Goebbels claimed that he refused to deny or refute enemy claims concerning air damage: "it is better," he said in April of 1942, "for the English to think that they have had great successes in the air war than for them actually to have achieved such victories" (M p. 2057). For similar reasons he regretfully censored items concerning the poor quality of Soviet weapons, Germany's plans to employ secret weapons, and even favorable military news (p. 272).

Second, *by openly disseminating propaganda whose content or tone caused the enemy to draw the desired conclusions.* "I am also convinced," Goebbels stated in the spring of 1943, "that a firm attitude on our part [in propaganda] will somewhat spoil the appetite of the English for an invasion" (p. 302). As the Battle of Tunisia drew to a close, therefore, the resistance of German troops there was used as an illustration of what would happen if the European continent were invaded. Perhaps, Goebbels must have reasoned, General Eisenhower's plans might be thus directly affected; British or American public opinion might exert influence upon SHAEF; or the morale of the armies in training for the invasion might be crippled (M p. 4638).

Third, *by goading the enemy into revealing vital information about itself.* At the end of the Battle of the Coral Sea Goebbels believed that the Japanese had scored a complete victory. The silence of American and British authorities was then attacked "with very precise questions: they will not be able to avoid for any length of time the responsibility of answering these questions" (M p. 2743).

Fourth, *by making no reference to a desired enemy activity when any reference would discredit that activity.* Goebbels did not wish to bestow a "kiss of death" on matters that met his approval. No use was made of news indicating unfriendly relations between two or more of the countries opposing Germany because – in Goebbels' own favorite, trite, and oft repeated words – "controversy between the Allies is a small plant which thrives best when it is left to its own natural growth" (M p. 941). Likewise the Nazi propaganda apparatus was kept aloof from the Chicago *Tribune,* from a coal strike in the United States, and from anti-Communist or pro-fascist groups in England. Quarrels between Germany's enemies, however, were fully exploited when – as in the case of British–American clashes over Darlan – the conflict was both strong and overt (p. 225).

PRINCIPLE 5: DECLASSIFIED, OPERATIONAL INFORMATION MUST BE AVAILABLE TO IMPLEMENT A PROPAGANDA CAMPAIGN

A propaganda goal, regardless of its importance, required operational material that did not conflict with security regulations. The material could not be completely manufactured: it had to have some factual basis, no matter how slight. It was difficult to begin an anti-semitic campaign after the fall of Tunis because German journalists had been failing to collect anti-Jewish literature. Lack of material, however, never seems to have hindered a campaign for any length of time, since evidently some amount of digging could produce the necessary implementation. Journalists were dispatched to a crucial area to write feature stories; steps were taken to insure a supply of "authentic news from the United States" (p. 92); a change in personnel was contemplated "to inject fresh blood into German journalism" and hence better writing (p. 500); or, when necessary, the Protocols of Zions were resurrected (p. 376).

Like any publicity agent, Goebbels also created "news" through action. To demonstrate Germany's friendship for

Finland, for example, a group of ailing Finnish children was invited to Germany on a "health-restoring vacation" (M p. 91). The funerals of prominent Nazis were made into news-worthy pageants; the same technique was applied to the French and Belgian victims of British air attacks. German and Nazi anniversaries were celebrated so routinely that the anniversary of the founding of the Three Power Pact was observed even after the downfall of the Italian member (M p. 5859).

PRINCIPLE 6: TO BE PERCEIVED, PROPAGANDA MUST EVOKE THE INTEREST OF AN AUDIENCE AND MUST BE TRANSMITTED THROUGH AN ATTENTION-GETTING COMMUNICATIONS MEDIUM

Much energy was devoted to establishing and maintaining communications media. Motion picture theaters and newspapers were controlled or purchased in neutral and occupied countries. "It's a pity that we cannot reach the people of the Soviet Union by radio propaganda," Goebbels stated, since "the Kremlin has been clever enough to exclude the Russian people from receiving the great world broadcasts and to limit them to their local stations" (p. 453). The schedule of many German radio programs was adjusted when the British introduced "double summer time." A dilemma existed regarding receiving sets in occupied countries: if they were confiscated, people would be cut off from Nazi as well as enemy propaganda; if they were not, both brands could be heard. Inside the Reich, machinery was created to reopen motion picture theaters as quickly as possible after heavy air raids (M p. 5621).

Some kind of bait was devised to attract and hold an audience. What Goebbels called "propaganda" over the radio, he believed, tended after a while to repel an audience. By 1942 he had concluded that Germans wanted their radio to provide "not only instruction but also entertainment and relaxation" (M p. 383), and that likewise straight news rather than "talks" were more effective with foreign audiences. Like any propagandist in war time, he recognized that a radio program could draw enemy listeners by providing them with the names of war prisoners. The best form of newspaper propaganda was not "propaganda" (i.e., editorials and exhortation), but slanted news that appeared to be straight (M p. 4677).

Goebbels was especially attached to the motion picture. At least three evenings a week he previewed a feature film or newsreel not only to seek relaxation and the company of film people but also to offer what he considered to be expert criticisms. Feature pictures, he stated, should provide entertaining and absorbing plots that might evoke and then resolve tension; simultaneously they should subtly affect the attentive audience not through particular passages but by the general atmosphere. Evidence for Goebbels' belief in the supreme importance of newsreels comes from the fact that he immediately provided his newsreel company with emergency headquarters after one of the heaviest air raids Berlin experienced toward the end of 1943. "It costs much trouble to assemble the newsreel correctly each week and to make it into an effective propaganda weapon," he observed on another occasion, "but the work is worthwhile: millions of people draw from the newsreel their best insight into the war, its causes, and its effects." He also believed that newsreels provided "proof" for many of his major propaganda contentions: visual images – no matter how he himself manipulated them before they were released – possessed greater credibility than spoken or written words (M p. 335).

Goebbels never stated explicitly whether or not in his opinion some media were better suited to present particular propaganda themes than others. Only stray observations were made, such as that leaflets were ineffective when "opinions are too rigid and viewpoints too firm" (M 2065). His one basic assumption appears to have been that all media must be employed simultaneously, since one never knew what type of bait would catch the variety of fish who were Nazi targets (M p. 828).

PRINCIPLE 7: CREDIBILITY ALONE MUST DETERMINE WHETHER PROPAGANDA OUTPUT SHOULD BE TRUE OR FALSE

Goebbels' moral position in the diary was straightforward: he told the truth, his enemies told lies. Actually the question for him was one of expediency and not morality. Truth, he thought, should be used as frequently as possible; otherwise the enemy or the facts themselves might expose falsehood, and the credibility of his own output would suffer. Germans, he also stated, had grown more sophisticated since 1914: they could "read between the lines" and hence could not be easily deceived (M p. 1808).

Lies, consequently, were useful when they could not be disproved. To induce Italians to leave the areas occupied by English and American forces and then to shanghai them into Germany as workers, Goebbels broadcast the claim that "the English and Americans will compel all men of draft age to enlist" (p. 462). Even truth, however, might damage credibility. In the first place, some apparently true statements could later turn out to be false, such as specific claims concerning the damage inflicted by planes against enemy targets. Then, secondly, truth itself might appear untrue. Goebbels was afraid to inform the Germans that General Rommel had not been in Africa during the closing days of the campaign there: "everybody thinks he is in Africa; if we now come out with the truth when the catastrophe is so near, nobody will believe us" (p. 352).

Similarly, every feature and device had to maintain its own credibility. A special communiqué or bulletin was employed, for example, to announce important events. Goebbels was afraid to resort to this device too frequently, lest it lose its unusual character, and hence he released some significant news through routine channels (M p. 5799).

PRINCIPLE 8: THE PURPOSE, CONTENT, AND EFFECTIVENESS OF ENEMY PROPAGANDA, THE STRENGTH AND EFFECTS OF AN EXPOSÉ, AND THE NATURE OF CURRENT PROPAGANDA CAMPAIGNS DETERMINE WHETHER ENEMY PROPAGANDA SHOULD BE IGNORED OR REFUTED

Most of the time Goebbels seemed mortally afraid of enemy propaganda. Even though he had controlled all the mass media in Germany since 1933, he must have been convinced that Germans had not been completely converted to the Nazi cause, or at least that they might be corrupted by enemy efforts. He admitted in January of 1942 that "foreign broadcasts are again being listened to more extensively" even though death could be the penalty for doing so (p. 44). Fourteen months later he noted with dismay that "the English and Americans have greatly expanded their radio broadcasts to the Axis countries and intend to step them up even more" (p. 312).

Goebbels' first impulse was to reply to enemy propaganda. He wrote as though he were a member of a great International Debating Society and as if silence on his part would mean the loss of the argument and of his own prestige. Actually, however, he judiciously balanced a number of factors before he decided to ignore or refute enemy claims (M p. 2593).

In the first place, he analyzed enemy propaganda. If it seemed that the goal of the propaganda was to elicit a reply, he was silent. "The English," he stated on February 6, 1942, "are now employing a new mode of propaganda: they commit General Rommel to objectives which at the moment he certainly cannot have, in order to be able to declare perhaps in eight or fourteen days that he has not reached these goals" (M p. 423). A direct reply would have been equivalent to selling the German armies short. His practice was to expose such traps to his subordinates and then to have them maintain silence in the mass media (M p. 4606).

On the other hand, a reply was made if it were felt that the enemy was transmitting blatant falsehoods. Since almost any enemy statement was considered false, Goebbels believed that only the blatant ones should be exposed. In this category he included claims that Germans had bombed Vatican City, that there had been "disturbances in Berlin" (M p. 4664), that Stalin was adopting a more lenient policy toward religion, and so on (M p. 4971).

Ineffective enemy claims required no reply, since a refutation would either give them more currency or else be a waste of propaganda energy. Enemy propaganda was very frequently branded as being ineffective, judgments that appear to have been either intuitive or rationalizations of an inability to reply. Effective enemy propaganda, however, demanded immediate action. The enemy, for example, was seldom permitted to acquire prestige; thus Goebbels attacked British boasts concerning a parachute landing at Le Havre, a raid on St. Nazaire, and the occupation of Madagascar. Sometimes it appears as though he instituted counter-proceedings not because the enemy was being successful but simply because he was able to do so. When the enemy was thought to be employing horoscopes and other occult propaganda against Germany, a reply in kind was immediately prepared. If the enemy seemed to be scoring an especially important propaganda triumph in its "war of nerves" – specifically at the beginning of the heavy British raids on German cities, after the downfall of Mussolini, or in the midst of strong pressure on Turkey by Britain in the late fall of 1943 – the only really adequate reply was considered to be a speech by Hitler himself (p. 251).

Then, secondly, Goebbels examined his own propaganda arsenal before he assayed a reply. He kept silent if he believed that his case, in the absence of facts or arguments, would appear too weak. He was so afraid of the German National Committee which the Russians formed in Moscow that he carried on no counter-propaganda against this group. Sometimes an enemy claim was disregarded and a counter-claim advanced. As Germany was attacked for her treatment of Jews, the policy of "complete silence" seemed unwise: "it is best to seize the offensive and to say something about English cruelty in India or the Near East" (M p. 3064) and also to "intensify . . . our anti-Bolshevik propaganda" (M p. 3225).

Goebbels tried, too, to estimate in advance the effectiveness of a rebuttal. If his own case as well as the enemy's appeared strong but if the enemy's might look stronger because of his attempts to refute it, he withheld his fire. It always seemed better to concentrate on the dissemination of a Hitler speech rather than to reply to foreign critics. Often, however, he believed that an exposé could protect Germans or help immunize foreigners from an enemy campaign that was either about to be or actually had been launched. Peace appeals by the three allies were therefore anticipated, and his reply to the communiqué from the Teheran Conference was "biting and insolent; we empty buckets of irony and derision over the Conference" (p. 545).

In the third place, Goebbels believed that his current propaganda had to be surveyed before enemy propaganda could be ignored or refuted. He attempted no reply when that reply might divert attention away from, or when it ran counter to more important propaganda themes. "There's no point in concerning oneself daily with new themes and rumors disseminated by the enemy," he stated, since it was essential to concentrate on the "central theme" of anti-Semitism (M p. 4602). In March of 1943 he permitted "Bolshevik reports of victories... to go into the world unchallenged": he wanted Europe to "get the creeps," so that "all the sooner it will become sensible" and cooperate against the Russians (p. 284).

PRINCIPLE 9: CREDIBILITY, INTELLIGENCE, AND THE POSSIBLE EFFECTS OF COMMUNICATING DETERMINE WHETHER PROPAGANDA MATERIALS SHOULD BE CENSORED

Goebbels had no scruples whatsoever concerning the use of censorship. "News policy," he stated, "is a weapon of war; its purpose is to wage war and not to give out information" (p. 210). His decision rested upon three pragmatic considerations (p. 299).

Goebbels recognized, first, that often credibility might be impaired if an item were censored: "in excited and strained times the hunger for news must somehow be satisfied" (p. 40). When the Foreign Office censored news that he considered important, he complained that "by that sort of policy we are fairly compelling the German public to listen to foreign and enemy broadcasts" (p. 164). Again and again, therefore, he felt that he had to speak up, although he would have preferred to be silent. Toward the end of 1943, for example, he stated that the problem of evacuating people from the bombed areas "has become so serious that it must be discussed with the clarity it deserves" (M p. 6435).

The usual policy was to suppress material that was deemed undesirable for German consumption, but simultaneously to employ it in foreign propaganda if it were suited thereto. Tales concerning alleged cannibalism by the Soviets were spread in foreign countries, but such material was banned inside Germany lest it terrify Germans whose relatives were fighting the Russians. Sometimes, however, undesirable material was not censored domestically in order to maintain its credibility abroad (M p. 2699).

Censorship was invoked, in the second place, when intelligence concerning the outcome of a development was insufficient. Here Goebbels wished either to preserve credibility or to have more facts before formulating a directive. Military forecasts he considered especially risky, but he also avoided comments on political events outside the Reich until he could fairly definitely anticipate their effects upon Germany (M p. 5036).

Then, finally, Goebbels estimated the possible effects of communicating the information. Censorship was pursued when it was thought that knowledge of the event would produce a reaction that was undesirable in itself or which, though desirable under some circumstances, was not in line with a current directive. Judged by the kind of news he suppressed, Goebbels was afraid that the following might damage German morale: discussions about religion; statements by officials in neutral or occupied countries that were hostile to Germany or by enemy officials that might evoke sympathy for them; enemy warnings that there would be raids before heavy ones began and – later – the extent of the damage inflicted by enemy planes; dangerous acts which included the assassination of officials, sabotage, and desertion; the unfortunate decisions or deeds of German officials; the belittling of German strength by an occurrence such as the escape of General Giraud from a German prison; an unnecessarily large increase in Germans' anxiety; and hints that Germany did not approve completely of her Axis partners (p. 249).

PRINCIPLE 10: MATERIAL FROM ENEMY PROPAGANDA MAY BE UTILIZED IN OPERATIONS WHEN IT HELPS DIMINISH THAT ENEMY'S PRESTIGE OR LENDS SUPPORT TO THE PROPAGANDIST'S OWN OBJECTIVE

Although his basic attitude toward enemy propaganda was one of contempt, Goebbels combed enemy broadcasts, newspapers, and official statements for operational items. Here he was not motivated by the somewhat defensive desire to reply to the enemy, but by offensive considerations: words of the enemy (Cf. Principle 8) could help him reach his propaganda goals. "In the morning we published in the German press a collection of previous Churchill lies and featured ten points; this collection is making a deep impression on the neutral press and shows Churchill to be, as it were, the Admiral of Incapability" (M p. 202). In particular the enemy provided a basis for Goebbels' "strength-through-fear" campaign as indicated below in Principle 16. "This fellow Vansittart is really worth his weight in gold to our propaganda" (p. 342), he wrote, and likewise he felt that any discussion in England or Russia concerning reparations or boundary questions after Germany's defeat "contributes significantly to the maintenance and strengthening of morale" inside the Reich (M p. 765).

PRINCIPLE 11: BLACK RATHER THAN WHITE PROPAGANDA MUST BE EMPLOYED WHEN THE LATTER IS LESS CREDIBLE OR PRODUCES UNDESIRABLE EFFECTS

By "black" propaganda is meant material whose source is concealed from the audience. Goebbels disguised his identity when he was convinced that the association of a white medium with himself or his machine would damage its credibility. At one time, for example, he wanted to induce the English to stop bombing Berlin by convincing them that they were wasting their bombs. He claimed that he used rumor-mongers to spread the idea there that the city "for all practical purposes is no longer capable of supporting life, *i.e.*, no longer exists" (M p. 6654). Presumably the tale had a better chance of being believed if German authorities were not connected with it. A most elaborate plan was concocted to try to deceive the Russians regarding the section of the front at which the Germans in the summer of 1942 had planned their offensive. A German journalist, who had first been sent deliberately to the Eastern front, was then dispatched to Lisbon where he was to commit, ostensibly under the influence of liquor, what would appear to be indiscretions but which actually were deceptions. In addition, it was planned to plant "a camouflaged article... through middlemen either in the Turkish or the Portuguese press" (p. 226), and the *Frankfurter Zeitung* was made to print an "unauthorized" article which was later "officially suppressed and denounced in press conference" (p. 221). Goebbels sought to increase the number of Soviet deserters by improving the prisoner-of-war camps in which they would be kept – this ancient psychological warfare device rested on the hope that news of the improvement would reach Soviet soldiers through informal channels. Otherwise, except for a security-conscious hint from time to time, the diary made no reference to black operations inside enemy countries (M p. 4235).

Goebbels also utilized black means to combat undesirable rumors inside the Reich. An official denial through a white medium, he thought, might only give currency to the rumors, whereas what he called "word-of-mouth" propaganda against them could achieve the desired effects. This method was employed to offset German fears that "in case more serious raids were to occur, the government would be the first to run away" from Berlin (p. 421). At all times "citizens who are faithful to the state must be furnished with the necessary arguments for combatting defeatism during discussions at their places of work and on the streets" (p. 401). Sometimes, however, rumors were officially attacked when, in Goebbels' opinions, all the facts were completely and unequivocally on his side (p. 518).

PRINCIPLE 12: PROPAGANDA MAY BE FACILITATED BY LEADERS WITH PRESTIGE

Such a principle is to be expected from Goebbels, whose Nazi ideology stressed the importance of leadership. Germans, it was hoped, would feel submissive toward propaganda containing the name of a prestigious leader. Ostensibly Goebbels always anticipated momentous results from a Hitler statement especially during a crisis; he noted routinely that the communication had been received by Germans with complete enthusiasm or that it "has simply amazed the enemy" (p. 506).

Leaders were useful only when they had prestige. Goebbels utilized propaganda to make heroes out of men such as Field Marshal Rommel. In the privacy of his diary he savagely attacked German leaders whose public behavior was not exemplary, since they thus disrupted propaganda that urged ordinary Germans to make greater sacrifices and to have unswerving faith in their government. An incompetent Nazi official was not openly dismissed from office, lest his incompetence reflect upon "the National Socialist regime"; instead it was announced that he had been temporarily replaced because of illness (p. 224).

PRINCIPLE 13: PROPAGANDA MUST BE CAREFULLY TIMED

Goebbels always faced the tactical problem of timing his propaganda most effectively. Agility and plasticity were necessary, he thought, and propagandists must possess at all times the faculty of "calculating psychological effects in advance" (p. 204). Three principles seemed to be operating:

First, *the communication must reach the audience ahead of competing propaganda.* "Whoever speaks the first word to the world is always right," Goebbels stated flatly (p. 183). He sought constantly to speed up the release of news by his own organization. The loss of Kiev was admitted as quickly as possible "so that we would not limp behind the enemy announcement" (M p. 6061).

Second, *a propaganda campaign must begin at the optimum moment.* Goebbels never indicated explicitly or implicitly how he reached the decision that the time to begin a campaign or make an announcement was either ripe or right. He made statements such as "we have held back for a very long time" when using an Indian leader, who as a German puppet committed his country to a war against England, "for the simple reason that things had not advanced far enough as yet in India" (p. 107). At one point he stated that counter-propaganda against enemy claims should not be too long delayed: "one should not let such lying reports sink in too deeply" (M p. 2430).

Third, *a propaganda theme must be repeated, but not beyond some point of diminishing effectiveness.* On the one hand, Goebbels believed that propaganda must be repeated until it was thoroughly learned and that thereafter more repetition was necessary to reinforce the learning. Such repetition took place over time – the same theme was mentioned day after day – as well as in the output of a single day. An anti-Semitic campaign, for example, continued for weeks, during which time "about 70 to 80 per cent of our broadcasts are devoted to it" (p. 366). On the other hand, repetition could be unnecessary or even undesirable. It was unnecessary when "the material thus far published has completely convinced the public" (p. 386). It was undesirable when the theme became boring or unimpressive, as occurred in connection with announcements concerning German submarine successes. Sometimes, moreover, booming guns at the start of a campaign, though desirable psychologically, could make the propaganda too "striking" and consequently result in a loss of credibility (M p. 6343).

PRINCIPLE 14: PROPAGANDA MUST LABEL EVENTS AND PEOPLE WITH DISTINCTIVE PHRASES OR SLOGANS

Again and again Goebbels placed great stress upon phrases and slogans to characterize events. At the beginning of 1942, for example, he began a campaign whose purpose was to indicate economic, social, and political unrest in England. He very quickly adopted the phrase "*schleichende Krise*" – creeping crisis – to describe this state of affairs and then employed it "as widely as possible in German propaganda" both domestically and abroad (M p. 762). His thinking was dominated by word-hunts: privately – or semi-privately – in his diary he summarized his own or enemy propaganda with a verbal cliché, even when he did not intend to employ the phrase in his output. He admitted that the experiencing of an event was likely to be more effective than a verbal description of it, but he also recognized that words could stand between people and events, and that their reaction to the latter could be potently affected by the former (M p. 1385). To achieve such effects, phrases and slogans should possess the following characteristics.

First, *they must evoke desired responses that the audience previously possesses.* If the words could elicit such responses, then Goebbels' propaganda task consisted simply of linking those words to the event which thereafter would acquire their flavor. When the British raid on St. Nazaire in March 1942 was aborted, Goebbels decided to claim that it had been made to appease the Russians who had been demanding that their ally engage in military action. The raid was dubbed the "Maisky Offensive," after the Soviet envoy in London. Sometimes news could speak for itself in the sense that it elicited desired responses without the addition of a verbal label. A military victory was not interpreted for Germans when Goebbels wished them to feel gratified. Most news, however, was not self-explanatory: Goebbels had to attach thereto the responses he desired through the use of verbal symbols. The most regulated news and commentary, nevertheless, could produce undesirable and unintended actions; even a speech by Hitler was misinterpreted (M p. 4677).

Second, *they must be capable of being easily learned.* "It must make use of painting in black-and-white, since otherwise it cannot be convincing to people," Goebbels stated with reference to a film he was criticizing (M p. 271). This principle of simplification he applied to all media in order to facilitate learning. The masses were important, not the intellectuals. All enemy "lies" were not beaten down, rather it was better to confine the counter-attack to a single "school example" (M p. 2084). Propaganda could be aided, moreover, by a will to learn. Cripps' appeal to European workers under German domination to slow down on the job, for example, was ignored: "it is difficult to pose a counter-slogan to such a slogan, for the slogan of 'go slow' is always much more effective than that of 'work fast'" (p. 107).

Third, *they must be utilized again and again, but only in appropriate situations.* Here Goebbels wished to exploit learning that had occurred: the reactions people learned to verbal symbols he wished to transfer easily and efficiently to new events. He criticized English propaganda because "its slogans are changed on every occasion and hence it lacks real punch" (M p. 1812). The context in which people's reactions occurred was also important. "I forbid using the word *'Fuehrer'* in the German press when applied to Quisling," Goebbels declared, "I don't consider it right that the term *Fuehrer* be applied to any other person than the *Fuehrer* himself. There are certain terms that we must absolutely reserve for ourselves, among them also the word 'Reich'" (p. 66).

Fourth, *they must be boomerang-proof.* Goebbels became furious when he thought of the expression "Baedeker raids, which one of our people so stupidly coined during a foreign press conference" (M p. 2435): it interfered with his own effort to call British raids wanton attacks on "cultural monuments and institutions of public welfare" (M p. 2301). "There are certain words," he added, "from which we should shrink as the devil does from Holy Water; among these are, for instance, the words 'sabotage' and 'assassination'" (p. 93).

PRINCIPLE 15: PROPAGANDA TO THE HOME FRONT MUST PREVENT THE RAISING OF FALSE HOPES WHICH CAN BE BLASTED BY FUTURE EVENTS

It was clear to Goebbels that the anticipation of a German success along military or political lines could have certain immediate beneficial effects from his viewpoint. The confidence of Germans and the anxiety of the enemy could be increased. Such tactics, however, were much too risky: if the success turned out to be a failure, then Germans would feel deflated and the enemy elated. His own credibility, moreover, would suffer. For this reason he was wildly indignant when, after the German army withdrew, the enemy ascribed to him "premature reports of victories" at Salerno. Actually, he claimed, the announcements had come from German Generals (p. 457).

Often the false hopes seemed to spring from the Germans themselves, a form of wishful thinking that occurred spontaneously as they contemplated the possibility of an offensive by the German armies, as they received news of a single victory, or as they imagined that the enemy could be defeated by political events. Goebbels, therefore, frequently issued warnings about "false illusions" and he prevented particular victories from being trumpeted too loudly. At other times enemy propaganda strategy was thought to be committing the German armies to military goals that they could not be expected to achieve (p. 118).

PRINCIPLE 16: PROPAGANDA TO THE HOME FRONT MUST CREATE AN OPTIMUM ANXIETY LEVEL

For Goebbels, anxiety was a double-edged sword: too much anxiety could produce panic and demoralization, too little could lead to complacency and inactivity. An attempt was constantly made, therefore, to achieve a balance between the two extremes. The strategy can be reduced to two principles (M p. 6162).

First, *propaganda must reinforce anxiety concerning the consequences of defeat.* Enemy war aims were the principal material employed to keep German anxiety at a high pitch. "The German people must remain convinced – as indeed the facts warrant – that this war strikes at their very lives and their national possibilities of development, and they must fight it with their entire strength" (p. 147). Lest the campaign of "strength-through-fear" falter, no opportunity was missed to attack enemy peace terms that might appear mild. Anti-Bolshevik campaigns attempted not only to stiffen German resistance but also to enlist the cooperation of all neutral and occupied countries. On the one hand, Goebbels tried to convince himself in the diary that Germans would not be misled again – as they had been, according to his view, in the First World War – by enemy peace terms: they "are quite accurately acquainted with their enemies and know what to expect if they were to give themselves up" (M p. 6684). On the other hand, he felt very strongly that Germans were most vulnerable to peace propaganda. He feared, for example, that American propaganda might be directed "not . . . against the German people but against Nazism" (p. 147) and "we can surely congratulate ourselves that our enemies have no Wilson Fourteen Points" (p. 47).

Occasionally it became necessary to increase the anxiety level of Germans concerning a specific event. On February 24, 1942, after the first disastrous winter campaign in Russia, Goebbels "issued orders to the German press to handle the situation in the East favorably, but not too optimistically." He did not wish to raise false hopes but, perhaps more importantly, he did not want Germans to "cease to worry at all about the situation in the East" (p. 99).

Second, *propaganda must diminish anxiety (other than that concerning the consequences of defeat) that is too high and that cannot be reduced by people themselves.* Air raids obviously raised German anxiety much too high, but they were a situation over which Goebbels could not exercise propaganda control. In other situations involving a demoralizing amount of anxiety he could be more active. "To see things in a realistic light" when the military situation in Tunisia became hopeless, German losses were portrayed as being "not of such a nature that as a result our chances for [ultimate] victory have been damaged" (M p. 4542). In contrast, he attempted to use the same principle in reverse – the so-called "strategy of terror" – against his enemies. Leaflets were dropped on English cities "with pictures of the damage done by the English in Luebeck and Rostock, and under them the Fuehrer's announcement of his Reichstag speech that reprisal raids are coming" (p. 193).

PRINCIPLE 17: PROPAGANDA TO THE HOME FRONT MUST DIMINISH THE IMPACT OF FRUSTRATION

It was most important to prevent Germans from being frustrated, for example, by immunizing them against false hopes. If a frustration could not be avoided, Goebbels sought to diminish its impact by following two principles:

First, *inevitable frustrations must be anticipated.* Goebbels' reasoning seems to have been that a frustration would be less frustrating if the element of surprise or shock were eliminated. A present loss was thus endured for the sake of a future gain. The German people were gradually given "some intimation that the end is in sight" as the fighting in Tunisia drew to a close (p. 352). They likewise received advance hints whenever a reduction in food rations was contemplated; the actual announcement, nevertheless, always disturbed them (M p. 1484).

Second, *inevitable frustrations must be placed in perspective.* Goebbels considered one of his principal functions to be that of giving the Germans what he called a *Kriegsüberblick,* a general survey of the war. Otherwise, he felt, they would lose confidence in their régime and in himself, and they would fail to appreciate why they were being compelled to make so many sacrifices (M p. 4975).

PRINCIPLE 18: PROPAGANDA MUST FACILITATE THE DISPLACEMENT OF AGGRESSION BY SPECIFYING THE TARGETS FOR HATRED

Goebbels had few positive gratifications to offer Germans during the period of adversity covered by the diary. He featured enemy losses, quite naturally, whenever he could and whenever Germans were not over-confident. Only once did he praise Germans for withstanding the enemy as long as they had. By and large, the principal technique seems to have been that of displacing German aggression on to some out-group (M p. 6220).

Favorite hate objects were "Bolsheviks" and Jews. Goebbels was disturbed by reports that indicated that "the fear of Bolshevism by the broad masses of European peoples has become somewhat weaker" (M p. 4572) or that "certain groups of Germans, especially the intellectuals, express the idea that Bolshevism is not so bad as the Nazis represent it to be" (p. 335). Anti-Semitic propaganda was usually combined with active measures against Jews in Germany or the occupied countries. German aggression was also directed against American and British pilots, but on the whole the United States and Great Britain did not stir Goebbels' wrath, at least in the diary (p. 147).

In enemy countries Goebbels had a strong penchant for engaging in "wedge-driving": he sought to foment suspicion, distrust, and hatred between his enemies and between groups within a particular country. He thus assumed that the foundation for hostility between nations or within a nation already existed for historical reasons or as a result of the frustrations of war. His task was to direct the aggression along disruptive channels (p. 46).

PRINCIPLE 19: PROPAGANDA CANNOT IMMEDIATELY AFFECT STRONG COUNTER-TENDENCIES; INSTEAD IT MUST OFFER SOME FORM OF ACTION OR DIVERSION, OR BOTH

In almost all of his thinking about propaganda strategy and objectives, Goebbels adopted the distinction between what were called *Haltung* (bearing, conduct, observable behavior) and *Stimmung* (feeling; spirit, mood).[5] After a heavy raid on a German city, he generally claimed that the *Haltung* of the people was excellent but that their *Stimmung* was poor. He wished to have both of these components of morale as favorable as possible. *Stimmung* he considered much more volatile: it could easily be affected by propaganda and events; it might be improved simply by offering people some form of entertainment and relaxation. *Haltung* had to be maintained at all costs, for otherwise the Nazi régime would lose its support and people would be ready to surrender. Germans, in short, were compelled to preserve external appearances and to cooperate with the war effort, regardless of their internal feelings. As more and more defeats and raids were experienced, Goebbels became convinced that *Stimmung* had to be almost completely ignored (M p. 6452).

Goebbels clearly recognized his own propaganda impotency in six situations. The basic drives of sex and hunger were not appreciably affected by propaganda. Air raids brought problems ranging from discomfort to death which could not be gainsaid. Propaganda could not significantly increase industrial production. The religious impulses of many Germans could not be altered, at least during the war. Overt opposition by individual Germans and by peoples in the occupied countries required forceful action, not clever words. Finally, Germany's unfavorable military situation became an undeniable fact. When propaganda and censorship could not be effective, Goebbels advocated action or, in one of his official positions (for example, as Gauleiter of Berlin), he himself produced the action. Diversionary propaganda he considered second-best (M p. 3508).

Consider his propaganda with reference to military defeats. For a while he could describe them as "successful evacuations" (p. 461). For a while he could even conceal their implications. Eventually, however, they were too apparent, especially after the heavy air raids began and the difficulties of fighting a two-front war increased. Then he was reduced not quite to silence but certainly to despair. At the end of the fighting in Tunisia he was forced to conclude that the following propaganda themes were not proving impressive: "our soldiers there have written a hymn of heroism that will be graven eternally on the pages of German history; they retarded developments for half a year, thereby enabling us to complete the construction of the Atlantic Wall and to prepare ourselves all over Europe so that an invasion is out of the question" (p. 360). He tried to divert Germans through another anti-Bolshevik campaign, but this too was insufficient. What Germans really needed were "some victories in the East to publicize" (M p. 4433). German losses in Russia, moreover, plagued Goebbels. Whenever possible, he tried to offset news of defeat in one section with reports of victories in others, but by 1943 he simply had no favorable news to employ as a distraction. *Stimmung* was doomed, and even *Haltung* worried him: "at the moment we cannot change very much through propaganda; we must once again gain a big victory somewhere" (M p. 3253). Most fortunately, that victory and ultimate triumph never came.

Notes

1. Lochner, Louis P. [Editor]. *The Goebbels Diaries*. New York: Doubleday & Company, 1948.
2. The writer wishes to express his gratitude to Mr. Philip T. McLean of the Library for making arrangements to have the manuscript microfilmed; to the Yale Attitude Change Project for paying the costs of the microfilm; and to Professor Carl F. Schreiber of Yale University for aid in translating some of the more difficult words and phrases.
3. Speier, Hans. Review of Lochner, *op. cit.*, *Public Opinion Quarterly*, Fall, 1948, pp. 500–505.
4. United States Strategic Bombing Survey. *The Effects of Bombing on German Morale*, vol. I Washington, D.C.: U.S. Government Printing Office, 1947, p. 42.
5. Lochner has ignored the distinction and has generally translated both as "morale," a term Goebbels likewise occasionally employed in an equally ambiguous manner.

10 How to Detect Propaganda*
Institute for Propaganda Analysis[1]

We are fooled by propaganda chiefly because we don't recognize it when we see it. It may be fun to be fooled but, as the cigarette ads used to say, it is more fun to know. We can more easily recognize propaganda when we see it if we are familiar with the seven common propaganda devices. These are:

1. The name-calling device.
2. The glittering-generalities device.
3. The transfer device.
4. The testimonial device.
5. The plain-folks device.
6. The card-stacking device.
7. The band-wagon device.

Why are we fooled by these devices? Because they appeal to our emotions rather than to our reason. They make us believe and do something we would not believe or do if we thought about it calmly, dispassionately. In examining these devices, note that they work most effectively at those times when we are too lazy to think for ourselves; also, they tie into emotions that sway us to be "for" or "against" nations, races, religions, ideals, economic and political policies and practices, and so on through automobiles, cigarettes, radios, toothpastes, presidents, and wars. With our emotions stirred, it may be fun to be fooled by these propaganda devices, but it is more fun and infinitely more in our own interests to know how they work.

* Reprinted from *Propaganda Analysis*, vol. i, no. 2 (1937).

NAME CALLING

"Name calling" is a device to make us form a judgment without examining the evidence upon which it should be based. Here the propagandist appeals to our hate and fear. He does this by giving "bad names" to those individuals, groups, nations, races, policies, practices, beliefs, and ideals that he would have us condemn and reject. For centuries the name "heretic" was bad. Thousands were oppressed, tortured, or put to death as heretics. Anybody who dissented from popular or group belief or practice was in danger of being called a heretic. In the light of today's knowledge, some heresies were bad and some were good. Many of the pioneers of modern science were called heretics; witness the cases of Copernicus, Galileo, Bruno. Today's bad names includes: fascist, demagogue, dictator, red, financial oligarchy, communist, muck-raker, alien, outside agitator, economic royalist, utopian, rabble-rouser, trouble-maker, Tory, constitution wrecker.

"Al" Smith called Roosevelt a communist by implication when he said in his Liberty League speech, "There can be only one capital, Washington or Moscow." When Smith was running for the presidency many called him a tool of the pope, saying in effect, "We must choose between Washington and Rome." That implied that Smith, if elected president, would take his orders from the pope. Recently Justice Hugo Black has been associated with a bad name – Ku Klux Klan. In these cases some propagandists have tried to make us form judgments without examining essential evidence and implications. "Al Smith is a Catholic. He must never be president." "Roosevelt is a red. Defeat his program." "Hugo Black is or was a Klansman. Take him out of the Supreme Court."

Use of bad names without presentation of their essential meaning, without all their pertinent implications, comprises perhaps the most common of all propaganda devices. Those who want to maintain the status quo apply bad names to those who would change it. For example, the Hearst press applies bad names to communists and socialists. Those who want to change the status quo apply bad names to those who would maintain it. For example, the *Daily Worker* and the *American Guardian* apply bad names to conservative Republicans and Democrats.

GLITTERING GENERALITIES

"Glittering generalities" is a device by which the propagandist identifies his program with virtue by use of "virtue words." Here he appeals to our emotions of love, generosity, and brotherhood. He uses words such as truth, freedom, honor, liberty, social justice, public service, the right to work, loyalty, progress, democracy, the American way, constitution defender. These words suggest shining ideals. All persons of good will believe in these ideals. Hence the propagandist, by identifying his individual group, nation, race, policy, practice, or belief with such ideals, seeks to win us to his cause. As name-calling is a device to make us form a judgment to reject and condemn, without examining the evidence, glittering generalities is a device to make us accept and approve, without examining the evidence.

For example, use of the phrases, "the right to work" and "social justice" may be a device to make us accept programs for meeting the labor–capital problem which, if we examined them critically, we would not accept at all.

In the name-calling and glittering-generalities devices, words are used to stir up our emotions and to befog our thinking. In one device "bad words" are used to make us mad; in the other "good words" are used to make us glad.

The propagandist is most effective in the use of these devices when his words make us create devils to fight or gods to adore. By his use of the bad words, we personify as a "devil" some nation, race, group, individual, policy, practice, or ideal; we are made fighting mad to destroy it. By use of good words, we personify as a god-like idol some nation, race, group and so on. Words that are bad to some are good to others, or may be made so. Thus, to some the New Deal is "a prophecy of social salvation" while to others it is "an omen of social disaster."

From consideration of names, "bad" and "good," we pass to institutions and symbols, also "bad" and "good." We see these in the next device.

TRANSFER

"Transfer" is a device by which the propagandist carries over the authority, sanction, and prestige of something we respect and revere to something he would have us accept. For example, most of us respect and revere our church and our nation. If the propagandist succeeds in getting church or nation to approve a campaign on behalf of some program, he thereby transfers its authority, sanction, and prestige to that program. Thus we may accept something that otherwise we might reject.

In the transfer device symbols are constantly used. The cross represents the Christian Church. The flag represents the nation. Cartoons such as Uncle Sam represent a consensus of public opinion. Those symbols stir emotions. At their very sight, with the speed of light, is aroused the whole complex of feelings we have with respect to church or nation. A cartoonist, by having Uncle Sam disapprove a budget for unemployment relief, would have us feel that the whole United States disapproves relief costs. By drawing an Uncle Sam who approves the same budget, the cartoonist would have us feel that the American people approve it. Thus, the transfer device is used both for and against causes and ideas.

TESTIMONIAL

The "testimonial" is a device to make us accept anything from a patent medicine or a cigarette to a program of national policy. In this device the propagandist makes use of testimonials. "When I feel tired, I smoke a Camel and get the grandest 'lift'." "We believe the John Lewis plan of labor organization is splendid; C. I. O. should be supported." This device works in reverse also; counter-testimonials may be employed. Seldom are these used against commercial products such as patent medicines and cigarettes, but they are constantly employed in social, economic, and political issues. "We believe that the John Lewis plan of labor organization is bad; C. I. O. should not be supported."

PLAIN FOLKS

"Plain folks" is a device used by politicians, labor leaders, business men, and even by ministers and educators to win our confidence by appearing to be people just like ourselves – "just plain folks among the neighbors." In election years especially candidates show their devotion to little children and the common, homey things of life. They have front-porch campaigns. For the newspaper men they raid the kitchen cupboard, finding there some of the good wife's apple pie. They go to country picnics; they attend service at the old frame church; they pitch hay and go fishing; they show their belief in home and mother. In short, they would win our votes by showing that they're just as ordinary as the rest of us – "just plain folks," – and, therefore, wise and good. Business men are often "plain folks" with the factory hands. Even distillers use the device. "It's our family's whiskey, neighbor; and neighbor, it's your price."

CARD-STACKING

"Card-stacking" is a device in which the propagandist employs all the arts of deception to win our support for himself, his group, nation, race, policy, practice, belief or ideal. He stacks the cards against the truth. He uses under-emphasis and over-emphasis to dodge issues and evade facts. He resorts to lies, censorship, and distortion. He omits facts. He offers false testimony. He creates a smoke-screen of clamor by raising a new issue when he wants an embarrassing matter forgotten. He draws a red herring across the trail to confuse and divert those in quest of facts he does not want revealed. He makes the unreal appear real and the real appear unreal. He lets half-truth masquerade as truth. By the card-stacking device, a mediocre candidate, through the "build-up," is made to appear an intellectual titan; an ordinary prize fighter a probable world champion; a worthless patent medicine a beneficent cure. By means of this device propagandists would convince us that a ruthless war of aggression is a crusade for righteousness. Some member nations of the Non-Intervention Committee send their troops to intervene in Spain. Card-stacking employs sham, hypocrisy, effrontery.

THE BAND WAGON

The "band wagon" is a device to make us follow the crowd, to accept the propagandist's program en masse. Here his theme is: "Everybody's doing it." His techniques range from those of medicine show to dramatic spectacle. He hires a hall, fills a great stadium, marches a million men in parade. He employs symbols, colors, music, movement, all the dramatic arts. He appeals to the desire, common to most of us, to "follow the crowd." Because he wants us to follow the crowd in masses, he directs his appeal to groups held together by common ties of nationality, religion, race, environment, sex, vocation. Thus propagandists campaigning for or against a program will appeal to us as Catholics. Protestants, or Jews: as members of the Nordic race or as Negroes; as farmers or as school teachers; as housewives or as miners. All the artifices of flattery are used to harness the fears and hatreds, prejudices and biases, convictions and ideals common to the group; thus emotion is made to push and pull the group on to the band wagon. In newspaper articles and in the spoken word this device is also found. "Don't throw your vote away. Vote for our candidate. He's sure to win." Nearly every candidate wins in every election – before the votes are in.

PROPAGANDA AND EMOTION

Observe that in all these devices our emotion is the stuff with which propagandists work. Without it they are helpless; with it, harnessing it to their purposes, they can make us glow with pride or burn with hatred, they can make us zealots in behalf of the program they espouse. Propaganda as generally understood is expression of opinion or action by individuals or groups with reference to predetermined ends. Without the appeal to our emotion – to our fears and to our courage, to our selfishness and unselfishness, to our loves and to our hates – propagandists would influence few opinions and few actions.

To say this is not to condemn emotion, an essential part of life, or to assert that all predetermined ends of propagandists are "bad." What we mean is that the intelligent citizen does not want propagandists to utilize his emotions, even to the attainment of "good" ends, without knowing what is going on. He does not want to be "used" in the attainment of ends he may later consider "bad." He does not want to be gullible. He does not want to be fooled. He does not want to be duped, even in a "good" cause. He wants to know the facts and among these is included the fact of the utilization of his emotions.

Keeping in mind the seven common propaganda devices, turn to today's newspapers and almost immediately you can spot examples of them all. At election time or during any campaign, "plain folks" and "band wagon" are common. "Card-stacking" is hardest to detect because it is adroitly executed or because we lack the information necessary to nail the lie. A little practice with the daily newspapers in detecting these propaganda devices soon enables us to detect them elsewhere – in radio, newsreel, books, magazines, and in expressions of labor unions, business groups, churches, schools, political parties.

Note

1. [Editor's Note] The Institute for Propaganda Analysis was established in October 1937 with its original offices at 130 Morningside Drive in New York City. Its aim, as stated in one of its early publications, was "to conduct objective, non-partisan studies in the field of propaganda and public opinion. . . . [I]t seeks to help the intelligent citizen to detect and to analyze propaganda, by revealing the agencies, techniques, and devices used by propagandists." The Institute drew together several leading intellectuals of the day. These included Charles A. Beard, Hadley Cantril of Princeton University, Paul Douglas of the University of Chicago and later United States Senator from Illinois, Robert S. Lynd of Columbia University, and Leonard W. Doob of Yale University, whose essay on Joseph Goebbels is Chapter 9 of this volume. Most of the organizational work seems to have been done by Clyde R. Miller of Columbia University. In its monthly newsletters, one of which is reproduced here, the Institute covered a wide variety of issues relating to propaganda, including analyses of propaganda in the newspapers, movies, radio, in various corporate campaigns, and in textbooks and school curricula. The

Institute's members directed the bulk of their attention, of course, to the role of propaganda in the great struggle between Western democracy and the forces of fascism. In addition to its newsletters, which reached about 5500 subscribers, the Institute published study guides complete with worksheets, suggested activities, and discussion notes on various aspects of propaganda for more than 550 high schools and 3000 adult study groups, including labor unions, professional organizations, and farm groups. The Institute suspended operations after Pearl Harbor; its last newsletter (vol. IV, no. 13) appeared on 9 January 1942. Two books also appeared under the Institute's auspices: *The Fine Art of Propaganda: A Study of Father Coughlin's Speeches*, edited by Alfred McClung Lee and Elizabeth Briant Lee (New York: Harcourt, Brace and Company, 1939) and Harold Lavine and James Wechsler, *War Propaganda and the United States* (New Haven: Yale University Press, 1940).

11 Theater of War: American Propaganda Films During the Second World War*

Jessica A. Meyerson

A GATHERING OF FORCES

The scholar Paul Fussell once wrote that during the Second World War all of "the various outlets of popular culture behaved almost entirely as if they were creatures of their governments. . . . They spoke with one voice."[1] Fussell's comment conjures up the classic image of propaganda production, one in which insidious governments tell their lackeys what to say and are dutifully obeyed. In reality the production of America's wartime propaganda was a much more complex process, one in which individual writers, artists, and film-makers often clashed over the nature and scope of the nation's propaganda campaign. Dissension and discord surrounded most of the country's major propaganda efforts, from the Office of War Information's radio campaigns to the intelligence community's psychological warfare programs; but the greatest conflicts over propaganda production may have arisen out of the United States Army's attempts to become a major center of film production.

During the Second World War Hollywood movie-makers emerged as some of America's most vocal pro-war propagandists. With strong roots in the European immigrant community, Hollywood film-makers were, in general, fierce patriots and strong opponents of the rise of fascism. As early as 1939, Hollywood directors began to produce powerful anti-Nazi works such as Anatole Litvak's "Confessions of a Nazi Spy". Once America actually entered the war they began

---

* Published for the first time in this volume.

their work in earnest, producing literally hundreds of films with prominent anti-Nazi and antifascist themes. Some of the industry's most zealous patriots even abandoned the comfortable world of commercial movie-making and enlisted in the military.

During the first three years of the war the United States armed forces recruited some of Hollywood's finest creative personnel for the production of government propaganda films. Hundreds of patriotic Hollywood directors, producers, editors, and writers answered the nation's call to arms, only to find themselves trapped in the ironic position of defending democracy from within the United States' most authoritarian regime – the military. Often these transplanted Hollywood film-makers (particularly directors) found themselves working in a hierarchical framework that allowed for very little creative autonomy and permitted almost absolute censorship. Nonetheless film-makers such as Frank Capra, John Ford, and George Stevens sought to produce propaganda films that conveyed their own personal perceptions of the war, in addition to the government's preapproved ideological messages. Like previous generations of American propagandists, they fought constantly to produce a political environment in which their own work could flourish, in which a delicate balance between the political correctness of the time and personal autonomy could be struck. Sometimes they were successful. Sometimes they were not. But in the course of their work they created a film empire that rivaled even classical Hollywood in its complexity and creativity.[2]

This military film empire was composed of several different competing divisions, each specializing in a different genre of motion-picture production. During the First World War the United States Signal Corps produced all the armed forces' educational and training films. However their products were mostly unambitious instructional films with limited inspirational value. The introduction of powerful Axis propaganda films in the 1930s, particularly the Nazi work "The Triumph of the Will," quickly revealed the limitations of Signal Corps projects. One of the main tasks of transplanted Hollywood talent in the Second World War was to introduce new and more sophisticated film-making techniques to the military. Three dynamic centers of propaganda-film production emerged in the armed forces between the years 1942 and 1946: John Ford's Field Photographic Branch of the Office of Strategic Services (specializing in daredevil intelligence work), Frank Capra's 834th Signal Corps Detachment of the United States Army (specializing in inspirational orientation films), and various special motion-picture coverage units and combat-photography crews of the armed forces (specializing in documentary footage of combat situations).

The function and style of each of these film-making agencies was determined by a few selected directors who either created their own military divisions or molded already existing institutions to their needs. From 1939 to 1942 John Ford and Frank Capra, two of Hollywood's most famous "auteur" directors, were both engaged in struggles to develop independent military agencies uniquely suited to their own tastes and ideological agendas. Ford's Field Photographic Branch, conceived several years before the war, was a militant spy organization that clearly reflected his own preoccupation with conventions of manly courage and heroism. Similarly Frank Capra's 834th Signal Corps, home of the patriotic "Why We Fight" series, was the logical offspring of a "populist" director whose commercial films were devoted to celebrating the virtues of America's common man. In the last years of the war, embittered combat photographers such as John Huston and George Stevens also created a new genre of field documentaries that expressed their growing ambivalence about the violence of the war. Not even the relentlessly depersonalized regimes of the American armed forces prevented these men and others like them from embracing challenges and creating institutions that reflected their own agendas. They remained auteurs.

JOHN FORD'S ARMY

The earliest of the special film detachments to be developed was the Office of Strategic Services' Field Photographic Branch (colloquially called Field Photo), created entirely by the famous western film-maker John Ford. Ford was one of classical Hollywood's most colorful luminaries. A self-styled fighting Irishman, a swaggering macho bully, and a grand manipulator with a flair for the dramatic, Ford was also depression-era Hollywood's most renowned and respected American director. By 1941 he had garnered an unprecedented four Academy Awards for best director of the year and his work was universally praised in rapturous tones. Years later fellow director Frank Capra dubbed him "the complete director . . . a man to whom the megaphone has been what the chisel was to Michelangelo, his life, his passion."[3]

Ford's extraordinary reputation stemmed from 25 years of unusually exceptional and prolific film-making. He went to Hollywood in 1914 as a brash 19 year old. By the start of the Second World War John Ford had directed 106 films. Most of them were commercial successes and virtually all those produced after 1931 were critical triumphs. Ford's talents as a director were also remarkably diverse. He moved easily from one motion-picture genre to the next. He was well known for his works concerning the Irish lower class, films such as "The Informer" and "Riley the Cop"; his maritime adventures "Salute" and "Seas Beneath" were both box-office hits; and many of his more serious films were among the most acclaimed social dramas of the Depression: "The Grapes of Wrath," "Arrowsmith," and "How Green Was My Valley," to name just a few.

Still, Ford's special province, the genre that made him great, was the American western. No other American director ever did so much to shape the traditions of a whole area of film-making as John Ford did through his 54 western films. It was Ford who discovered John Wayne, the quintessential western hero; it was Ford who produced the archetypal cowboys and Indians drama," Stagecoach," in 1939; and it was Ford who, over four decades, developed a mythic cinematic depiction of the American frontier as a testing ground of men's mettle and the last bastion of rugged individualism.[4]

But for all his success and prestige as a film-maker, John Ford's chief love was not the American cinema. In his own life, as in his films, Ford was notoriously obsessed with rituals of manhood and demonstrations of machismo. From the time of his childhood in a small Irish-American fishing village he nursed dreams of a life of adventure and military heroism on the high seas. As his wife Mary once observed, "the navy was Jack's heart and soul".[5] As a young man living in the seaport town of Cape Elizabeth, Maine, Ford attempted to join the navy and merchant marines during the First World War, but his poor eyesight prevented his enlistment. It was only after this disappointment that he went west to California as a kind of substitute in his quest for adventure.

Still, Ford never abandoned his dreams of a heroic naval career and in the early 1920s he was lucky enough to discover a new means of serving his country and proving his courage; he became a spy. In 1920 Ford married the niece of Admiral Victor Blue, chief of United States Naval Operations, and he used his new family connections to gain entry to some of the navy's most elite circles. In the early 1920s he was introduced to Vice Admiral James T. Wilkinson and Captain Elias Zachiaras, who, along with Dudley Wright Knox and Ralph Van Demen, composed the leadership of a small counterespionage group based in San Diego, California. The members of this group, concerned about the Japanese military escalations in the Pacific Ocean, were attempting to gather intelligence information that could be used to justify a build-up of the US Pacific Fleet. Learning of their intentions, Ford volunteered his services as a reconnaissance photographer. He was awarded a Lt Commander's commission in the Naval Reserve and was sent off on a series of intelligence missions in the South Pacific. In June 1929, under the pretense of scouting locations for his next film, Ford journeyed to Mexico and Hawaii, where he filmed strategic areas of the coastline. In 1934 he was sent on a second similar mission to the Philippines, where he documented America's vulnerable naval installations.[6]

In Ford's opinion, however, such occasional reconnaissance missions represented only a small fraction of film's potential intelligence applications. By the late 1930s it had become obvious to him that American involvement in the Second World War was inevitable. He knew that one of the most valuable resources in wartime situations is a reliable intelligence and information network. To help satisfy this predicted need, the fiercely independent film-maker began a private effort to organize an army of skilled field photographers. The Nazis were just beginning to experiment with field photography in their own military campaigns, but Ford's efforts set a precedent for American film-makers. In late 1939 he hired an ex-marine named Jack Pennick to recruit volunteers from Hollywood motion-picture studios. Together the two men trained over 200 film technicians, writers, editors, cameramen, and even make-up specialists to produce movies in combat situations. These 200 volunteers were divided into tiny production crews, each one capable of filming, editing, and scoring a complete documentary. To prevent possible work stoppages from deaths in combat, all members of Ford's unit were trained to perform every procedure in the film-making process. After two years of intensive training in an old, abandoned film studio in California, Pennick and Ford decided that they were finally ready to unveil their pet project to the armed forces. In 1941, shortly before the bombing of Pearl Harbor, John Ford reported to the Naval High Command that he was prepared to offer them the intelligence services of 210 carefully drilled combat photographers: 15 smoothly functioning camera crews with 35 officers and 175 enlisted men. To make his offer as palatable as possible, Ford even had his crews produce a demonstration documentary for the navy, an infamously graphic training film on venereal disease, entitled "Sex Hygiene".[7]

After some deliberation the navy purchased the demonstration film, but the High Command showed little interest in creating an official home for Ford's special force. Members of the Atlantic Fleet Admiralty, who were unfamiliar with Ford personally but had heard stories of his legendary independence and recalcitrance, were understandably dubious about accepting into their ranks some 200 nonmilitary personnel. In addition, the fact that many of Ford's recruits were past draft age or, like Ford himself, physically impaired, did little to inspire confidence. In the end only the intervention of Colonel "Wild Bill" Donovan, head of America's embryonic national intelligence agency then called the Office of Strategic Services (OSS), saved Ford's unit from an ignoble end.

When Colonel Donovan received word of Ford's recruiting and training activities in Hollywood, he decided that such a group of trained experts could be instrumental in America's intelligence war. In Autumn 1941, following the navy's rebuff of Ford, Donovan asked President Franklin Delano Roosevelt to have Ford's people incorporated into the armed services and placed under the OSS's command. This request prompted the acceptance of Ford's army in the armed forces in September 1941 as "the Field Photographic Branch," under the direct command of Donovan and President Roosevelt. The Army gave the new organization an office and film laboratory in the south Agricultural Building in Washington DC. The branch's mission was "to photograph both for Records and for our intelligence assessment, the work of guerrillas, saboteurs and resistance outfits" in addition to undertaking "special projects".[8]

THE BATTLE OF MIDWAY

The first and most celebrated of Ford's special projects came six months after the bombing of Pearl Harbor. In May 1942 the OSS and Navy Intelligence captured and decoded a secret Japanese communiqué revealing the date and time of a planned attack on Midway Island, a small American naval base in the Pacific. After much heated debate and hard-fought negotiations, the naval brass and Donovan agreed that the course of the battle should be captured on film for propaganda purposes. John Ford volunteered to act as the documentary's "director".[9]

The day before the Japanese attack was scheduled to take place, 3 June 1942, Ford was flown with several assistants to the tranquil island of Midway. For 24 hours the photographers did nothing but collect background footage of the American sailors and soldiers expectantly awaiting the battle. They captured images of confident young men swimming happily in the clear blue ocean; they photographed the comical struts of the birds that populated the desolate sandy island; and in the evening they went from one small group of soldiers to the next, recording the tense, quiet moments of conversation that preceded combat. Then, just before sunrise on the day of the attack, Ford's men dispersed and reported to their field positions: some of the photographers were stationed to film the combat from the decks of battleships, others from the cockpits of helicopters or planes.

Ford, of course, saved the most dangerous assignment for himself. Knowing that electricity generators are among the first targets in any air raid, the film-maker perched himself high atop a tower on the island's power house and awaited the enemy's arrival.[10] Just after dawn, the first wave of Japanese Zeros flew over the horizon and began strafing the American compound. Huge fires and fierce fighting immediately erupted on all sides of the director's exposed position. The concussions from the bombs exploding nearby made the ground shake so severely that many of the images captured on Ford's hand-held 16 mm camera jump wildly like shots in an amateur home movie. However, despite the disruption, Ford remained resolutely focused on his task. According to eyewitnesses stationed just below the energy tower he could be heard shouting throughout the assault – "yelling at the attacking Zeros to turn right or left" so he could capture them on film, "and cursing them out when they disobeyed directions".[11] These spirited shouts only ceased halfway through the battle, when Ford was struck in the arm by a piece of flying shrapnel and knocked unconscious. For several minutes he lay helpless and exposed on the top of the tower, but he eventually managed to rise to his feet, bind up his wound, and stoically finish filming the battle. It was perhaps the most glorious moment of the fighting Irishman's life, for when the battle subsided and the Japanese fleet and air force retreated in defeat, John Ford descended from his perch a recognized hero.

Yet for Ford a new type of battle was just beginning. In order to transform his Midway footage into the kind of documentary feature he wanted, Ford had to enter into combat with the military hierarchy. Almost immediately after Midway, word of Field Photo's feats spread throughout the various branches of the armed forces. Rumors circulated among high-ranking officials that Ford's precious footage was going to be seized and turned over to the interservices newspool, where it would undoubtedly be chopped up for use in routine newsreels. Determined to use his material for a more ambitious project, Ford quickly gathered up all of his unit's exposed footage and fled, absent without leave, to Hollywood. Working in secret in an old, abandoned editing room at Metro Studios, he assembled a rough cut of the unit's film, which he then turned over to his assistant, Robert Parrish, for further editing. While Parrish worked furiously to meet the 24-hour deadline Ford had given him, the film director frantically assembled the rest of his production crew. He recruited two script writers, Dudley Nichols, a liberal Democrat, and James McGuiness, a conservative Republican, to produce a politically "neutral" script for the documentary; he convinced four prominent movie stars – Jane Darwell, Henry Fonda, Donald Crisp, and Irving Pichel – to narrate for him, and Hollywood's finest sound man, Phil Scott, to dub in a score arranged by the prominent film composer Al Newman. The result of this makeshift film crew's efforts was perhaps the best American Second-World-War documentary ever produced, an exciting, emotionally draining 18-minute color film, entitled simply "The Battle of Midway".[12]

As film scholar Tag Gallagher has noted, the strength of "The Battle of Midway" lies in its originality. The film set a formal precedent for American documentary film-making. Previously the public had only glimpsed isolated moments from the theater of war – an image here or there tucked away in a movietone newsreel montage. Such flickering and sanitized images did little to impress on the American public the drama and thrill of combat. But Ford's film presents his audience with a complete, dramatic, first-hand view of war. It tells the viewers an entire, inspiring story of a single battle.

The film begins sentimentally with the close-up shots of the young soldiers awaiting battle. All of the footage that Ford and his crews collected during the 24 hours before the attack is included here: pictures of young men swimming, laughing, talking nervously in small groups. Then a glorious sunrise appears. A ray of golden light pierces through two cloud banks at dawn, and suddenly the first Japanese Zeros come soaring out of the sky. The battle itself is depicted through a series of disorienting, flickering images of conflagration: a hospital is bombed; a fighter plane explodes; flames rise up from the decks of battleships. Most of these scenes evoke a sense of confusion and chaos in the viewer, but Ford is careful to avoid making the experience of combat too confusing or horrific. Instead the general chaos is punctuated with a few well-placed scenes of extraordinary bravery that work to reinforce stereotypical visions of heroism. The most famous of these "warrior-hero" scenes depicts a group of determined marines working to hoist the American flag over the base even as they are surrounded on all sides by fire and destruction. While this image is displayed the national anthem swells over the soundtrack, and Irving Pichel's voice quietly confirms, "Yes, this really happened".

Once Ford gives his viewer a flavor of combat's more inspirational qualities, the fighting suddenly ceases, replaced with stern images of the aftermath of war. Naval rescue squads comb the seas looking for downed fighter pilots; wounded soldiers are rushed to hospitals. A sentimental rendition of taps is sounded when the dead are buried at sea. During this funeral sequence the audience sees the determined faces of the survivors who watch the burial. Their faces, in conjunction with the image of the American flag, still flying high over the Midway Island base, make it clear that the heroic deaths were not in vain. Finally, the film concludes with an optimistic coda: three signs, each bearing a different statistic about the number of Japanese planes and ships destroyed at Midway Island, flash across the screen. This tally is a final reaffirmation of the American soldiers' inspirational achievement. Their courage and bravery have defeated a dangerous enemy, and the battle itself has exposed what is best and brightest in American youth. The upbeat strains of "Over There" soar over the soundtrack and the screen fades to black. In the end the message of "The Battle of Midway" is similar to the message conveyed in many of Ford's early western films. Ford suggests that ritualized forms of violence can expose mankind's most noble qualities, thereby justifying all the pain and suffering of the war.

It is impossible to estimate with any certainty the impact that "The Battle of Midway" had on the American public. However, documented accounts of viewers' reactions suggest that all who saw the film were deeply affected by it. When Ford screened the documentary for President Roosevelt and his family at the White House in late May, Eleanor Roosevelt is said to have burst into tears when watching the funeral sequence. (Ford shrewdly included a shot of the President's own son, James Roosevelt, attending the Midway soldiers' funeral.) And when the film was over Roosevelt made his legendary proclamation, "I want every mother in America to see this picture."[13] The film, originally intended only for a military audience, was duly distributed by Twentieth Century Fox to 500 civilian theaters throughout America. "The Battle of Midway" received an equally spectacular reception at its premiere in Radio City Music Hall. As eyewitness Robert Parrish later described the scene, "It was a stunning, amazing thing to see. Women screamed, people cried, and the ushers had to take them out. The people, they just went crazy...[14] After producing such a passionate public response there was little surprise when the film won Ford his fifth Oscar, for best documentary of the year, at the 1943 Academy Awards.

Still, the war did not stop in May 1942 for Ford and the members of Field Photo. After he had finished production work on the Midway project, Ford joined Air-Force legend James Doolittle on his raids over Tokyo, Marcus Island and Wotje. Then, in November, he and his men were sent to Great Britain, where they received special guerrilla combat training to prepare them to film the North African invasion. Ford and his Field Photo crews embarked on a madcap dash through Casablanca, Oran, and Algiers. As they traced across the continent collecting dramatic footage, their fame spread. When, in January 1943, Ford returned to Washington DC for a briefing he found that volunteers had swelled the membership of his organization to over 600. Jack Ford was now in command of the largest, most celebrated, and most efficient army of field photographers in the allied armies. Nevertheless the film director's reputation could not protect him from criticism and outrage when Field Photo produced its second and last major documentary, "December 7".

FIELD PHOTO AND THE "DECEMBER 7" CONTROVERSY

In early 1943 Ford and one of his most valued assistants, Gregg Toland, became embroiled in a dispute with military authorities over Toland's film on the bombing of Pearl Harbor. In early 1942 Bill Donovan had instructed Ford to have a Field Photo crew prepare a "documentary" on the bombing of the harbor. Ford appointed Toland, the superb cinematographer now known for such classics as "Citizen Kane," "The Little Foxes," and "The Best Years of Our Lives," to supervise the filming. It was a particularly important and treacherous assignment for a variety of reasons.

Producing the film was unusually complicated because no American footage of the actual attack existed.[15] In most wartime documentaries about a particular battle, American film-makers simply spliced together real footage of combat situations to tell a coherent story. The use of authentic material was especially crucial in American "documentaries" since real combat scenes endowed films such as "The Battle of Midway" with a thin veneer of objectivity and often staved off charges of propaganda. Even overtly reconstructed works, such as the films in Frank Capra's "Why We Fight" series relied as much as possible on authentic newsreel footage. However, with no genuine material with which to work, Toland was forced to reconstruct the entire bombing of Pearl Harbor in a dramatic fashion. He spent several months in Hawaii researching the situation and then retreated to Fox Studios in California, where he used rear-screen projection techniques to emulate a convincing battle sequence.[16] The production of combat footage was not the only obstacle Toland's project had to overcome. The four big branches of the armed services – the Army, Navy, Army Air Corps, and Marines – were extremely suspicious of any OSS inquiries or investigations into their activities. The High Admiralty of the Atlantic Fleet was particularly anxious to find any excuse to discredit the new intelligence agency; a trumped-up docudrama (such as "December 7") could provide many opportunities to do that. As a result Donovan ordered Toland to produce a documentary that was as uncontroversial as possible.[17]

Unlike the film's technical challenges this order proved to be beyond Toland's skills and certainly beyond his desires. Toland and many of his Field Photo comrades were enraged by the US military's lack of preparedness at Pearl Harbor. For many years before the catastrophe at Pearl

Harbor John Ford and other Field Photo organizers had argued the merits of encouraging a military build-up in the Pacific. Their frustration at being ignored clearly shaped the editing and construction of "December 7". National leaders and military officials who attended the film's confidential screening in the spring of 1943 saw a searing indictment of the American military's blindness and naïveté. In direct contradiction to Donovan's instructions, Toland's original version of "December 7" contained only a tiny segment that recreated historical events in a dispassionate way. Instead much of the film's "plot" centers around an imagined dispute held between two godlike figures on the day before the bombing. One of the figures is a tall, bearded, Uncle Sam type identified only as "US"; the other is a smaller, white-suited man identified as "Mr C." (short for Mr Conscience). On the afternoon of 6 December US (played by Walter Huston) is sitting around complacently reflecting on the paradise-like qualities of Hawaii. Mr C. (Harry Davenport) approaches US in the midst of this reverie and attempts to convince him that there are hidden dangers in the Pacific region. Mr C. quotes statistics about Hawaii's large Japanese population and cites recent instances of espionage on the islands. However US remains resolutely oblivious to any foreign threat. Then the audience briefly sees Toland's reconstructed scenes of the tragic battle itself before the film resumes its polemics. After the bombing of Pearl Harbor is complete, the camera shows the final consequences of US's stubborn blindness. Row upon row of graves roll across the screen and the voices of the dead describe their pasts. A final damning partisan attack against isolationism is made when one dead soldier's voice predicts America's future: "I'm putting my bets on the Roosevelts and the Churchills," he says, carefully enunciating the names of leaders who demanded early military action against the Axis powers.[18]

The preview of "December 7" in late 1943 triggered a small explosion within the US Navy's High Command and effectively ended Field Photo's reign as the US military's premiere documentary-making body. Virtually all of the politicians and military officials who attended the 85-minute screening of Toland's film were appalled by its ferocity. On the grounds that it was "too outrageous and politically disruptive," Roosevelt ordered that the film be confiscated and withheld from further showings, either public or private. Claiming that further works like "December 7" might endanger national morale, the President also mandated the censorship of all future Field Photo productions. Branded rebels and malcontents by most of the military hierarchy, Ford, Toland, and several other high-ranking Field Photo officers were dispersed to remote outposts in South America and India, where they remained for almost a year filming obscure guerrilla campaigns for intelligence purposes. During this period of exile, other dynamic centers of propaganda-film production sprang up within the military.

FRANK CAPRA AND "WHY WE FIGHT"

The most notable of the new groups was Frank Capra's 834th Signal Corps Detachment, creators of the most famous and successful American propaganda film project of the Second World War, the "Why We Fight" film series. The series was the brainchild of Capra and General George C. Marshall, chief of staff of the United States Armed Forces. Marshall was a major supporter of modernizing the Army's propaganda techniques. He believed strongly that films could be used to inspire and educate American troops in new ways.[19] Shortly after the war began he suggested making a series of films explaining to soldiers why the conflict overseas was so important. Such works could, he believed, play a major role in overcoming the isolationist sentiment that still lingered among many Americans. To oversee the project Marshall selected Hollywood's most famous patriot, the Italian-American film-maker Frank Capra.

Capra was the prototype of the grateful American immigrant. The sixth child of an Italian family that had emigrated to America in 1903, he viewed himself as the hero of a Horatio Alger story. As a young man growing up in Los Angeles's Italian ghetto, he worked hard at summer jobs, studied diligently, and eventually won a scholarship to the Throop Polytechnic Institute (now the California Institute of Technology), where he studied chemical engineering. After graduating in 1918 Capra experimented with a variety of jobs, including a brief stint in the army during the First World War, before eventually finding his way into film-making in the early 1920s. In Hollywood he apprenticed at a variety of writing, producing, and assistant-directing jobs for five years, before finally achieving fame in 1926 as the director of a series of silent comedy shorts starring Harry Langdon. Then, during the Great Depression, he began a precipitous rise to "super-director" status. In 1934 he achieved unparalleled celebrity as the director of "It Happened One Night," America's first screwball comedy (and the first American movie ever to sweep all the major Academy Awards). In 1936, prompted by his success to produce more ambitious and socially meaningful films, he embarked on a series of sentimental political dramas about the rise of America's common man. The films in this political cycle, "Mr. Deeds Goes to Town," "You Can't Take it With You," and "Mr. Smith Goes to Washington," all seemed to strike some resonant chord within the Depression-era American public, and every film that Capra directed in the late 1930s was a box-office smash. In 1941 he crowned his career as the film champion of democracy with the release of "Meet John Doe," a thinly veiled parable about the rise of fascism in Europe that finally won him plaudits from the intelligentsia as well as the public.

But it was not simply Capra's obvious obsession with populist, patriotic themes that attracted General Marshall; it was also the director's reputation as a sly wheeler-dealer who knew how to challenge authority and get things done. Because of his films' commercial success, Capra enjoyed an unusual degree of power and independence within the Hollywood studio system. Using his status as Columbia Pictures' most prestigious film director as a bargaining chip, Capra managed to coerce the studio's tyrannical head, Harry Cohen, into giving him almost complete creative autonomy. In a system where most directors were treated as second-class citizens, Capra gained the right by 1936 not only to direct, but also to produce, write, and edit his own films.[20]

Marshall believed that only a film-maker with Capra's legendary skills as a negotiator and manager could overcome the bureaucratic and financial challenges implicit in producing the "Why We Fight" films. And indeed Capra faced many obstacles to the project's completion. The most important was a dearth of resources. Although General Marshall strongly supported using films to educate American soldiers, several members of Congress were suspicious of the "Why We Fight" series, believing it was the first step in a military propaganda campaign to brainwash American soldiers. As a result, throughout 1942 and 1943 the House Appropriations Committee threatened to deny the Army funding for the "Why We Fight" films. In addition, during the early years of the war (when hundreds of film-makers descended on the nation's capitol) Capra and other government film-makers in Washington confronted a severe shortage of filmstock and equipment. The absence of a clear chain of command to authorize Capra's activities further complicated the lack of resources; throughout the war two competing military divisions, the US Signal Corps, and a newer entity called the US Morale Branch, vied for control of the "Why We Fight" films.[21]

Capra's response to these problems was typical of the decisive, dynamic director; working without authorization, he chose to create a completely autonomous production unit, one funded and staffed in large part by nonmilitary, Hollywood personnel. Within weeks of his enlistment in spring 1942 the director had located a makeshift studio for his productions. In the center of an inner courtyard at the Department of Interior next to the North Interior Building stood a small, square service shed that housed the heating and cooling machinery for the surrounding structures. Most of the edifice was crammed with generator and air-conditioning equipment, but its first two floors also housed the Interior Department's little-used 16 mm film facility. There were editing rooms, projection areas, storage vaults, and several "antique" 35 mm projectors, all of which Capra quickly commandeered.[22]

There, in the isolated rooms of "the cooling tower" – as the building was affectionately known – Capra also began to interview film-makers for his makeshift production crew. Two of the first men he recruited were Edgar "Pete" Peterson, a former employee for the "March of Time" newsreels, who served as Capra's personal assistant and man Friday throughout the war, and Anatole Litvak, a Russian-born Hollywood director known for the 1939 antifascist film "Confessions of a Nazi Spy," mentioned earlier.

In April 1942 these three men journeyed together to New York's Museum of Modern Art to view the museum's extensive collection of Nazi propaganda films. The most famous film they saw was Leni Riefenstahl's celebrated "The Triumph of the Will". Watching Riefenstahl's endless parade of invincible goose-stepping Nazi soldiers, and wave after wave of cheering Nazi crowds, Capra was "scared [as] hell".[23] Yet Riefenstahl's images, suffused as they were with the raw power and frenzied energy of Hitler's mass rallies, also inspired the director with an idea: why not completely bypass the problem of producing original footage for an American film by re-editing and manipulating the enemy's own propaganda works? With a small, gifted crew of writers and editors Capra felt confident that he could rearrange Nazi and Japanese propaganda footage in ways that would emphasize the frightening, mindless, and dehumanizing qualities of fascist regimes. "[I decided to] use the enemies own films to expose their enslaving ends," the director wrote many years later.[24]

Capra, along with a handful of hand-picked assistants, including Peterson, Litvak, another Hollywood director named Tony Vieller, and two prominent screenwriters, Leonard Spiegelglass and Robert Heller, hammered out rough outlines for the seven 57-minute films that would eventually become the "Why We Fight" series. Each of the films provides a narrative and visual history of some major event of the war. The first film, "Prelude to War," tells the story of the rise of totalitarianism in the Axis powers; the second and third, entitled "The Nazi Strike" and "Divide and Conquer," recount Hitler's conquest of most of Europe; the fourth and fifth movies tell of the heroic feats of America's allies in "The Battle of Britain" and "The Battle of Russia"; the sixth depicts Japanese tyranny in the "The Battle of China"; and the seventh and final film, "War Comes to America," describes the "glorious history" of the world's oldest democracy and the nation's courage in confronting the Nazis.

Each film followed Capra's original plan for telling a story through a complex montage of enemy newsreels and motion pictures. For example, in the series' first film, "Prelude to War," a picture of a wounded Chinese man that appeared in the background of a Japanese newsreel on the conquest of Manchuria was blown up and juxtaposed with hundreds of other images of wounded Asians from other films to create an endless chronicle of Japanese oppression and brutality. By contrasting such re-edited, transplanted images with more positive icons from Western society – the Liberty Bell, Abraham Lincoln, the Holy Bible – the films in the "Why We Fight" series introduced an extremely affecting contrast between the benefits and privileges of Western democracy and the terrors of Axis-sponsored fascism. The basic oppositions presented in the films (freedom versus slavery, truth versus lies, courage versus cowardice) were, of course, all obvious oversimplifications of complex ideological issues. However these seemingly thoughtless generalizations only underscored the wisdom of Marshall's decision to recruit Capra for the "Why We Fight" project. Unlike more ambitious and controversial film directors, such as John Huston, Capra understood well the basic principles of effective propaganda: the simpler, more direct, and more readily comprehensible an argument is, the more likely people are to believe it. By the end of the war the thematic conventions and simple didactic approach of Capra's series had come to dominate most Allied propaganda films.

The next task was acquiring the necessary footage from enemy propaganda films, a step complicated by the ongoing feud between the two Army branches in charge of orientation films.[25] Since the beginning of the First World War all Army film production had traditionally been the province of the US Army Signal Corps. For 20 years this branch had competently churned out basic training films on subjects such as avoiding trench foot and cleaning and discharging rifles. Marshall and many others believed that the Signal Corps command lacked the imagination and talent to produce more ambitious projects such as the "Why We Fight" films. So Marshall assigned Capra to work under the Army's newly formed Morale Branch. This branch was composed of a small elite clique of communications experts from the world of radio, journalism, and film; it was conceived as a "propaganda think tank," responsible for brainstorming about bold new ways of educating soldiers and raising their morale. Although the Morale Branch seemed an ideal home for Capra's project, a number of problems developed. The Signal Corps' charter gave its officers absolute authority over most aspects of Army film production, including the distribution of film stock and other photographic materials, and Capra's men in the Morale Branch were frequently denied access to Signal Corps film archives and equipment. The rivalry between the two groups reached a crisis in May 1942, when some Signal Corps commanders, jealous of the Morale Branch's growing importance, refused to allow Capra to use the Army's collection of enemy propaganda films and newsreels for his series. According to his autobiography, Capra attempted to seize the films without approval, but was threatened with court martial after his actions were discovered.[26] For a brief time it seemed that the "Why We Fight" films would have to be abandoned, a victim of bureaucratic infighting. But the project was saved when another of Capra's enthusiastic supporters, Brigadier General Frederick Osborn, arranged a shrewd compromise between the two competing factions. He appointed Capra as head of his own independent production unit. This was placed officially under the auspices of the Signal Corps, thus allowing the film-maker access to all of the Signal Corps' equipment and facilities. Then he placed Capra's unit on temporary assignment to the Morale Branch, giving the director greater creative freedom than a normal Signal Corps unit commander might have. On 2 May 1942 the compromise was made official, and Capra's famed 834th Signal Corps Detachment was born.[27]

With the resolution of these bureaucratic difficulties Capra was able to begin his work in earnest. No one could have anticipated what a monumental undertaking the production of his "reconstructed" montage films would be. First of all, translators had to sort through the thousands of feet of newsreel footage that began to pour into the cooling-tower studio throughout the months of May, June, July, and August. Then, once the enemy's material had been translated and transcribed, a director, editor, composer, and screenwriter were assigned to each of the seven films. Editing such montage collections took months and months. Even when properly edited, Capra and his co-workers found that enemy footage did not always communicate exactly what they wanted. For example, the earlier "Why We Fight" films involving accounts of the Nazi conquest of Europe often attempted to give the viewer a sense of military strategy on a large scale. The value of individual images of particular times and places to illustrate such a global strategy was limited; and it was eventually decided that some kind of animation effect was necessary to complete the films.[28]

Once Capra began production of the seven films he quickly realized that they required all the resources of a major motion-picture studio, and he set about erecting one for himself. First he assembled a professional film-making staff, half of them military personnel working directly for him and half of them friends from the Hollywood community. The most important members of Capra's crew remained constant throughout the war: directors Litvak and Vieller, screenwriter Eric Knight, chief editor William Hornbeck, and the ever-resourceful Edgar Peterson worked on all of the "Why We Fight" movies. The rest of Capra's list of contributors was equally impressive. Expert translators for the project were supplied by the Museum of Modern Art film archives and by the Army's Intelligence Services. Hollywood "super-directors" William Wyler, John Huston, and George Stevens all directed or helped direct projects produced by Capra. Playwright Garson Kanin and novelist James Hilton both wrote screenplays for Capra. Oscar-winning composers Alfred Newman and Dimitri Tiompkin handled all the scoring, and finally, Walt Disney and his finest animators provided free maps and other animated effects for all of Capra's military films.

Within months of beginning work Capra's burgeoning crew became cramped in its makeshift quarters. Capra approached his old friend Darryl Zanuck and asked to use the old, abandoned Western Avenue studios at Twentieth Century Fox. Zanuck agreed and Capra moved his entire project to Hollywood in late summer 1942. The Signal Corps did not authorize the move and it denied Capra's request for adequate furnishings and equipment. But Capra managed to re-outfit the decrepit facility with creaky office equipment "borrowed" from neighboring studios.[29] In addition Capra convinced the sound, music, and dubbing departments at Fox, Paramount, and MGM studios to lend him their facilities when his own proved inadequate. By the end of his first six months in the Army Capra had accomplished something truly remarkable: with little support from the military and with few financial resources the Italian-American film-maker had created one of the nation's most powerful and talented independent film studios. And he had placed himself at its head.

"Prelude to War" was the first product from Capra's studio. It was screened for Marshall and President Roosevelt in October 1942. The two men were extremely impressed by Capra's skillful reweaving of old motion-picture and newsreel film clips, and they wholeheartedly endorsed the film's simple but compelling didactic approach. As with Ford's "The Battle of Midway," Roosevelt suggested that "Prelude to War" be released not just to soldiers but also to civilians.

The film was released to American theatergoers in mid-1943 and met with great acclaim from film critics, who praised both its inspirational qualities and its creative use of montage effects.[30] In addition the film shared the 1943 Academy Award for Best Documentary Film with "The Battle of Midway". By early 1944 all of the various "Why We Fight" movies had been released to either military or civilian audiences, and they also met with widespread praise. Although the series was originally designed for the Army's training program, the Navy, Marine Corps, and Coast Guard all eventually incorporated the series into their boot-camp curricula. In 1944 Joseph Stalin saw Capra's fifth installment, "The Battle of Russia," and requested that the film be translated into Russian so that it could be shown to Soviet troops. Winston Churchill used all seven films for his own country's military training programs. He even recorded his own introduction to the works stating: "I have never seen or read a more powerful statement of our rightful case against the Nazi tyranny than these films portray."[31] The films were eventually translated into French, Spanish, Chinese, Russian, and Portuguese. By the end of the war they were shown to soldiers and civilians in every corner of the globe, from North Africa to New Zealand.

The huge popularity of the series quickly transformed Capra into the darling of the military propaganda establishment. In 1944 the director was named assistant chief of all Army Pictorial Services and his 834th Signal Corps Detachment took charge of producing dozens of full-length propaganda films. Most of America's most famous Second-World-War propaganda films, including the fiercely bigoted "Know Your Enemy Japan" and the groundbreaking "The Negro Soldier," were produced by Capra's group; and today Capra remains the best remembered American propagandist of the Second World War. Much of the success of his films can be attributed to their extremely straightforward and uncomplicated approach to selling the war. While the independent-minded director frequently had to fight military officials about where, when, and how he produced his movies, there was relatively little debate over his films' naïve immigrant vision of America as a land of opportunity and freedom embattled against an evil, oppressive enemy. Other propagandists with less simplistic visions, such as the combat photographer John Huston, encountered much greater opposition to their films. In some cases they were silenced all together.

JOHN HUSTON AND THE SIGNAL-CORPS COMBAT PHOTOGRAPHERS

While John Ford's Field Photographic Branch fought to immortalize the heroic deeds of America's fighting men, and Frank Capra's 834th Signal Corps Detachment preached a simple-minded patriotism, a third group of armed forces film-makers sought to capture the "human side" of war, meticulously recreating the periods of boredom, agony, fear, valor, and occasional triumph that characterized the lives of common combat soldiers.

The combat photographers of the US Signal Corps produced some of the most exciting and complex documentaries of the Second World War. Like the Field Photo photographers, these officers were supposed to capture live footage of soldiers in battle. However, unlike the Field Photo crews, they did not have authority to roam freely throughout Europe, moving from one dramatic confrontation to the next. Instead each Signal Corps crew was assigned to follow a particular army or company for an indefinite period of time, giving the combat photographers a special opportunity to observe and record the minute details of life at the front. William Wyler spent weeks with a single bomber crew, studying their living habits for his thoughtful and carefully detailed documentary "The Memphis Belle".[32] Other film-makers, such as John Huston, were given the time and resources necessary to film not only a moment of pitched battle, but also the month before and after the battle. As a result, films such as Huston's "Report from the Aleutians" often lack the action-packed aura of Field Photo's work, but they possess instead an unusual quality of intimacy and realism that is unparalleled in the work of any other Second-World-War propagandists.

Eventually prolonged exposure to combat conditions led some of these photographers to question the ultimate value of the war effort. The most famous of these "pacifist" directors was the brooding young prodigy John Huston. When the war broke out Huston was only 35 years old. Unlike the veteran film-makers Capra and Ford, he had only two directing credits to his name. Yet he was still widely recognized as one of Hollywood's greatest talents. Part of his renown grew out of his work as an author – between 1932 and 1941 Huston gained a reputation as one of the movie industry's most successful screenwriters. He developed the screenplays and storylines for many prestigious projects, including "Amazing Dr Clitterhouse" and "High Sierra". In an era where sentimentality and escapism seemed to dominate the American cinema, his writing was greatly respected for its hard-edged realistic quality. Huston could write slapstick comedy (as in certain scenes from "Sgt York") or indulge the public's taste for emotional melodrama ("Jezabel"), but in works such as "Juarez" and "Dr Erlich's Magic Bullet" he also revealed an unfashionable capacity to embrace life's darker side. Employing dialogue that was clearly modeled on the bleak, direct style of Ernest Hemingway, Huston wrote many screenplays that dealt with unglorified violence, death, dishonesty, and the abandonment of hope.

These signature qualities certainly prevailed in Huston's directing debut. In 1941 the 35-year-old novice made film history with the release of a dark, gloomy, gangster drama entitled "The Maltese Falcon". The film, with its dim "motivated" lights, rainy streets, dark alleys, and cynical, self-destructive hero, Sam Spade, helped to set many of the conventions for one of America's most important film genres: film noir.[33] Huston followed this auspicious debut with another critical hit, the 1942 tearjerker "In This Our Life." That same year he was in the middle of completing his third picture, a big-budget action story called "Across the Pacific," when his enlistment papers arrived.

Huston was dispatched to the Aleutian Islands to prepare a documentary on the region's unusually high casualty rate. Combat in the Aleutian Islands had begun in spring 1942. By early June the Japanese had managed to seize control of two key islands in the Aleutian chain, Attu and Kiska. American troops fell back to a defensive position on the barren, mountainous island of Adak. During July and August the US forces remained there, constructing an airfield from which to launch bomber attacks on Japanese-held territories some 250 miles away.

Knowing of these events, Huston went to Adak expecting to record heroic deeds and spectacular deaths in heated fire fights over the Pacific. But what neither Huston nor his Signal Corps commanders knew was that most of the American casualties in the Aleutian theater were not combat-related; instead the vast majority of American bomber crews were being ravaged by weather conditions. Hurricane-strength gales and heavy rains constantly assaulted Adak and many of the B-26 bombers used in American raids were disabled when simply trying to take off or land. Once a plane was actually safely aloft, it still ran an exceptionally high risk of being blown off course and lost forever. (B-26 bombers, unlike the famous "Flying Fortresses" developed a few months later, lacked radar technology.) In his autobiography, "*An Open Book*," Huston recalls one particular day when nine out of twelve planes sent out simply disappeared somewhere over the Pacific, never to be seen again.[34]

Such flying conditions made it difficult for Huston and his five-man crew to record combat footage. Although the photographers tried several times to accompany pilots on their missions, most of these ended disastrously. In one especially notorious incident a plane in which Huston was riding suddenly developed brake problems while landing. The bomber slew wildly off course, sheared the wings off two grounded planes, and finally flipped over before coming to a halt. Huston and most of the other members of the crew, miraculously, were uninjured, but the captain and his copilot were trapped inside the dented cockpit. A daring rescue mission eventually extricated the two unconscious men, but the incident helped mark Huston and his camera crew as bad luck ("Hoodoo") passengers.[35] Recognizing that he and his men could not construct a conventional report on combat situations or high casualty rates under these conditions, Huston decided to redefine the emphasis of his film-making. The final version of "Report From the Aleutians" has less to say about the experience of combat than it does about the daily lives and rituals of combat soldiers. Like "The Battle of Midway," "Report from the Aleutians" contains prebattle sequences of soldiers engaged in tense discussions before going into combat. Again there are pictures of young men laughing, praying, or dying together. However Huston lavishes far more detail on the subject of soldiers' lives than does Ford, and his film manages to create a deeper sense of identification and intimacy. Not only do we see the men in especially dramatic moments immediately preceding or following life-threatening encounters, we also share in quieter, more personal scenes. We see soldiers crowding around a mail carrier, anxious for a letter from home. We sense the homesickness that falls over the camp when at sunset some young marine begins to pick out the sad notes of a ballad on his pocket harmonica. The men peel potatoes or wash their hands in their helmets. And precisely through these mundane images the audience comes to empathize with the soldiers.

It took Huston approximately four months to gather the material for "Report From the Aleutians." He returned to the Signal Corps' Astoria film studio to edit his project. After the film was released to military audiences to great acclaim, the director spent several months in the US working with Frank Capra's unit on staged footage and dramatic recreations for the allied documentary "Tunisian Victory." Then, in the fall of 1943, Huston was asked to film US troop movements in war-torn Italy. This assignment profoundly changed the young director's feelings about the war.

Huston had his crew film the heroic activities of the 143rd Infantry Regiment in the Liri Valley some 40 miles outside Rome. The 143rd and other detachments in the Liri Valley area were engaged in a fierce struggle with Germans for control of a small town called San Pietro. The town lay at the head of Highway 6, an important transportation route for German forces.

Like most of the rest of the Liri Valley, San Pietro was still occupied by the German army when Huston and his men arrived on the scene. The Americans were just beginning their assault on the region. Military experts claimed that the German position was impregnable. There were five enemy battalions in the region and the entrance to the valley had been mined. San Pietro itself was surrounded on all sides by booby traps, barbed wire, and enough machine guns to stave off any number of frontal assaults. The fighting promised to be bloody and fierce.

In the first two weeks of filming three Allied attacks were repulsed. Casualties, especially among the group of Texas Rangers that Huston accompanied, were unusually high. Each day after the fighting subsided Huston and his crew wandered over the fields littered with American, British, French, and, occasionally, German corpses. Cameraman Jules Buck took hundreds of pictures of dead and dismembered young men, capturing forever their frozen expressions, their severed arms and hands, and their split-open stomachs. The most horrifying carnage of the battle resulted when the US High Command abandoned conventional infantry attacks on San Pietro and sent in 16 tanks to seize the town. The terrain in the Liri Valley was totally unsuited for tank warfare. While the big machines lumbered over the rocky slopes and hillsides of San Pietro, 12 were destroyed by enemy fire, instantly killing many of the men inside. Years later Huston described the scene: "We could see the tanks burning and exploding, and men running and trying to hide. After it was over we crept forward and photographed the results."[36] The results were gruesome indeed. More than

1100 soldiers in the 143rd Infantry Regiment of the 36th Texas Infantry Division were killed or wounded in the Liri Valley campaign. Huston himself was twice almost killed when mistaken intelligence information led his camera crews into the town of San Pietro before the Germans had actually finished withdrawing.[37]

These events powerfully affected Huston. He returned to America determined to produce a film that captured both the heroism and the horror of the 143rd's ordeal. In many ways the film that he pieced together was quite conventional. It tells the story of an American victory, tracing the battle of San Pietro from the first moments when Allied troops entered the Liri Valley to their final triumph when the townspeople of San Pietro are "given back" their village. But the film's plot and imagery are anything but conventional. The footage dwells on the loss of life, with bloody corpses and dismembered limbs shown littering the battlefields. There are scenes of soldiers from the ill-fated tank assault being packed in body bags. As it happened, Huston and Buck had previously interviewed several of these same soldiers. Now Huston has them speak for themselves on film, describing their hopes and dreams for the future even as the camera records the internment of their corpses.

Even the final sequences of the film, which depict the liberation of San Pietro and the village's return to normality, seem laced with treacherous ironies. We see the women and children of the village descend from the caves and forests in which they have been hiding and return to the streets of San Pietro. But these streets offer little reward for all the blood and anguish that has been spent to win them. When it is finally freed from German tyranny the town is little more than a collection of ruins. The mortar fire and constant fighting in the region have leveled most of the buildings, including the village's beautiful 300-year-old church. The citizens of San Pietro are liberated; but they are only freed to return to nonexistent homes and a future filled with poverty and despair. With ever increasing force the final images of the film remind the viewer that 1100 American lives were lost for these meager laurels of destruction and sorrow.

Armed Forces commanders who saw the preview of Huston's film in August 1944 were even more shocked and disturbed than they had been by "December 7". Many of the audience members walked out in protest midway through the one-hour screening; and as soon as the special screening was over Huston was inundated with phone calls and messages of protest.[38] Every major Signal Corps official called the director to voice disapproval of the film, including one particularly irate War Department liaison officer who berated the director for his "antiwar" drama. (This particular attack provoked Huston's famed ironic response: "Gentlemen, if I ever make anything other than an antiwar film, I hope you take me out and shoot me.")[39]

Within days of the screening Huston's film was declared top secret and the five reels of "The Battle of San Pietro" were spirited away to an unknown military vault. The film might have remained there indefinitely were it not for the intervention of Frank Capra's patron, General Marshall. Still deeply interested in America's propaganda efforts and intrigued by the furor over Huston's film, Marshall arranged for a private screening in late 1944. Unlike other military commanders he was impressed with "San Pietro's" frank depiction of the hardships of war, and instead of condemning the work he stubbornly defended it, arguing that only honest and explicit films such as Huston's could fully prepare American soldiers for combat.[40] At Marshall's urging, in April 1945 a shortened and toned-down version of the film was eventually released to soldiers and the public.

The edited version deleted the body-bags scene, along with some of the more gruesome images of dismembered corpses and strewn limbs. But "The Battle of San Pietro" still remained the most powerful and affecting vision of the horrors of war ever released to American audiences. Upon seeing it James Agee, the film critic for *The Nation*, proclaimed the film the best movie of 1945. "It is as good a war film as I have seen," he wrote in review, "In some ways the best."[41] Those American soldiers who were required to watch it in basic training endorsed the film even more powerfully. The novelist Herbert Gold later wrote that the film helped him "acquire a notion of mortality" and prepare himself for the reality of war. He described it as "a masterpiece of experienced, immediate horror".[42]

But the military was far less interested in masterpieces of horror than it was in upbeat, inspirational films, such as "The Battle of Midway," that boosted soldiers' morale and created an esprit de corps. Huston's third film in his war trilogy, "Let There Be Light," found no saving angel, no General Marshall, to intervene on his behalf. Like "December 7," that film became a casualty of war.

EPILOGUE: THE HUMAN SALVAGE OF WAR

All of the Hollywood film-makers who produced military propaganda films during the Second World War were deeply changed by their experiences. Frank Capra emerged from his tenure with the military bureaucracy with a new sense of the importance of artistic freedom and independence. In 1946 he joined forces with three other "Hollywood Colonels," George Stevens, William Wyler, and producer Samuel Briskin, to form one of the movie industry's first independent production companies, Liberty Films. During its brief lifespan this studio produced two of the American cinema's most beloved classics, Capra's perennial holiday favorite, "It's A Wonderful Life," and Wyler's somber study of postwar America, "The Best Years of Our Lives". The creation of Liberty Films also set a precedent for other creative directors and producers who wished to liberate themselves from the tyrannical studio heads and formulaic "house styles". During the 1950s independent production companies modeled after Capra's helped destroy the old studio system.

However the war shaped other transplanted directors in different ways. George Stevens, the combat photographer who helped to film the liberation of Dachau and other concentration camps, remained haunted forever by his experiences. He later turned from directing the light comedies that had made him famous to serious, brooding dramas such as "The Diary of Anne Frank" and "A Place in the Sun". John Ford, ever the fierce patriot, was so touched by the sacrifices and heroism of his fellow countrymen that he devoted much of his personal time and resources after the war to creating a retirement community for wounded veterans.

No film director clung quite so tenaciously to his remembrances of war as John Huston. After VE day in 1946,

Huston found himself unable to erase from his mind San Pietro's images of carnage and death. He began to suffer from what he identified as a mild form of anxiety neurosis. Every time Huston heard a car backfire he threw himself to the ground. While living in New York City he sometimes found himself walking in Central Park with a loaded pistol tucked firmly into his trousers, feverishly anticipating some cathartic confrontation with a robber or vagrant.

Such symptoms proved to be only temporary, but they galvanized Huston's will to make one last documentary for the armed forces. Instead of resigning his commission he arranged to produce and direct a Signal Corps film study of psychologically disturbed veterans. For six weeks in 1946 he and his men quite literally lived inside the army's psychiatric facility at Mason General Hospital in Long Island. Working around the clock, they filmed the treatment programs of 75 mentally ill combat veterans. The illnesses of the patients varied from simple tics to serious psychoses. Their treatments included everything from electroshock therapy to hypnosis.

From this raw material the army expected Huston to distill a cheerful, optimistic story about renewal and recovery, one that showed "how men who suffered mental damage in the service should not be written off but could be helped by psychiatric treatment".[43] Huston's Mason General project was entitled "Let There Be Light," and it does offer a thin veneer of optimism and hope. The narrative shows the unfolding of a triumphant battle. First we see 75 soldiers arrive in Long Island on a passenger ship. Only their weary, dejected looks mark them as different from any group of fresh-faced recruits disembarking from troop carriers in the Pacific or Europe. The film follows them through psychiatric treatment, an emotionally exhausting process analogous to combat. Most of the patients are victorious and are able to regulate the most severe of their symptoms, either through hypnosis or drug therapy. Finally, the film shows the "soldiers" after the "battle" returning to normal activities such as baseball and talking in group meetings about the jobs they will have and friends they will see when they return home. Like victorious fighting men, they then board the ships and buses that have carried them into combat and resume their lives as normal citizens.

Huston clearly intends this cheerful narrative framework to placate his military sponsors. However the images, substance, and tone of "Let There Be Light" all belie any facile reassurances of quick recovery. Most of the scenes of the treatment process, or "battle," in this film are deliberately selected for their menacing and desperate quality. One young officer cannot even mention the experience of combat without breaking into tears. An even younger sailor speaks with a strange lisp to avoid making the sibilant sound that reminds him of mortar fire. And a marine who suffers from psychosomatic paralysis presents a haunting reminder of the war's lingering effects. Questioned under hypnosis about their combat experiences, these once-healthy and virile young men are transformed into fragile infants, completely at the mercy of their emotions. They scream, they cry, they curl up into the fetal position. Such scenes of regression make it difficult, if not impossible, for the viewer to accept the narrator's benign reassurances that these men will soon recover from their mysterious and hidden wounds. "Let There Be Light" provides the first thorough documentary study of post-traumatic stress syndrome and its devastating effects.

Unfortunately such a study was not exactly what the military wanted. As soon as Signal Corps officials saw what Huston had done with his material, they forbade the film's release. All of the military's copies of "Let There Be Light" were classified and placed in the same vaults that had earlier entombed "The Battle of San Pietro". Even a private showing of the film that Huston had scheduled for critics at the Museum of Modern Art was canceled. In a moment of high drama, military police broke into the Museum seconds before the curtain was scheduled to rise and wrested the five reels of film from an irate projectionist.[44]

Huston vigorously protested the seizure and censorship of his work. "Let There Be Light" was intended as his epilogue on the damaging effects of war and the director was determined to see it released. Since the war was over and military security was no longer an issue, Huston demanded to know why the film was being withheld from the public. Signal Corps officials replied that "Let There Be Light" violated psychiatric patients' rights to privacy. But Huston's crew had obtained personal releases from every one of the patients before the filming began. Huston reminded his commanders of the existence of these forms, only to be told that they had mysteriously disappeared from the files at headquarters.

Years later Huston analyzed the real motivations for the army's censorship of "Let There Be Light". He attributed the Signal Corps' actions to an unwillingness to destroy "the warrior myth". He wrote:

> The film wasn't released because wounds you can see – heroes without legs or arms – are acceptable, because it shows a love of country and patriotism and the right stuff; but with men who were emotionally injured, who'd been destroyed in their spirits, that's a different question. The authorities wanted to maintain the warrior myth which said that our American soldiers went to war and came back stronger for the experience. Only the weaklings fell by the wayside.[45]

Unlike "December 7" and other earlier controversial army films, "Let There Be Light" did not simply critique military strategy in a particular battle or campaign. Instead it questioned the whole military enterprise, suggesting that men were not always strengthened and enriched by testing themselves in battle. Cold War military officials felt so threatened by the film's revelations that they refused to let it be shown for more than 30 years. It was not until 1980, after Vietnam had already effectively destroyed the myth of the warrior hero, that "Let There Be Light" was finally screened for a small audience in Washington, DC.

The army's stubborn refusal to release Huston's film, even after other censored works such as "December 7" became available to the public, stands as an abiding testament to the turbulent nature of propaganda production during the Second World War. Throughout the war cynical realists such as Huston, naïve patriots such as Capra, and military strategists such as Ford all struggled for a voice in the nation's public dialogue about the war. Their behavior was typical of many of the deeply impassioned film-makers, artists, and writers who lent their services to the Roosevelt administration during the war. These volunteer propagandists refused to see themselves as passive agents of the government; instead they worked constantly, and with varying levels of success, to incorporate into their work their own personal ideological visions of the war. The political and administrative battles of men such as Capra, Ford, and Huston, and their counterparts in agencies such as the Office of War Information, make it clear that not all of the nation's wartime propagandists spoke with one voice. They spoke with many voices, but some were heard more clearly than others.

Notes

1. Paul Fussell, *Wartime* (New York: Oxford University Press, 1989), p. 180.
2. There are a number of excellent archival resources available for researching the Army's Second-World-War propaganda films. Most films produced by the Signal Corps or other military branches are available for viewing at the Motion Picture Branch of the National Archives in Washington, DC. Many films are also available at the film archives of the Museum of Modern Art in New York City. MOMA's archives also include production and translation notes from several of the "Why We Fight" films. Military records on motion pictures can be found in the Army Pictorial Division Case Files of the Chief Signal Corps Officer of the US Army. These records are currently located in the National Army Records Center at Suitland, Maryland. Few books have been writen abut the US military's wartime film campaign, but in the early 1970s film scholar William Thomas Murphy published in the *Journal of Popular Culture* several brief articles on the "Why We Fight" films and the propaganda films of John Ford. There are also several biographies of each of the key Army filmmakers currently in print. Particularly outstanding are Tag Gallagher's, *John Ford: The Man and His Films* (Berkeley: University of California Press, 1986), Lawrence Grobel's *The Hustons* (New York: Scribner & Sons, 1989), and Joseph McBride's *Frank Capra: The Catastrophe of Success* (New York: Simon & Schuster, 1992). Capra's and Huston's autobiographies, respectively entitled *The Name Above the Title* (New York: Vintage, 1985) and *An Open Book* (New York: Ballantine Books, 1980), both provide useful and colorful accounts of these directors' military experiences. However one should use these autobiographical texts cautiously, since both authors have been accused of stretching the truth and misremembering events. Readers interested in more general studies of Hollywood's contributions to Second-World-War propaganda should consult Clayton R. Koppes, *Hollywood Goes to War: How Politics, Profits, and Propaganda Shaped World War II Movies.* (New York: Free Press; London: Collin Macmillan, 1987) and Bernard Dick *The Star Spangled*

Screen: The American World War II Film (Lexington, KY: Univ. Press of Kentucky, 1985).

3. Frank Capra, *The Name Above the Title*, p. 246.
4. Tag Gallagher, *John Ford: The Man and His Films*. Gallagher provides the best general overview of Ford's lifetime of work. For a specific discussion of Ford's contributions to the Western genre, see J. A. Place, *The Westerns of John Ford* (New York: Citadel Press, 1979).
5. Andrew Sinclair, *John Ford* (New York: Dial Press, 1979), p. 28.
6. Sinclair, pp. 45–58.
7. Gallagher, *John Ford: The Man and His Films*, p. 202.
8. Ibid.
9. Gallagher, pp. 201–10.
10. Gallagher, p. 208.
11. Gallagher, pp. 205–6.
12. Robert Parrish, *Growing Up in Hollywood* (New York: Harcourt, Brace & Jovanovich, 1976), pp. 141–50.
13. Sinclair, *John Ford*, p. 113.
14. Parrish, *Growing Up in Hollywood*, p. 141.
15. William T. Murphy, "John Ford and The World War II Documentary," *Film and History I* (February 1976), pp. 1–8. Toland was extremely secretive about his work in Hollywood and for many years the footage in his films was believed by most viewer to be authentic. Only Murphy's groundbreaking study in 1976 brought the truth to light.
16. Ibid.
17. Thomas Troy, *Donovan and the CIA* (Maryland: Altheia Press, 1981), pp. 80–108.
18. Gallagher, *John Ford: The Man and His Films*, p. 214.
19. Forrest C. Pogue, *George C. Marshall*, vol. III, *Organizer of Victory 1943–45* (New York: Viking Press, 1973), pp. 91–2.
20. Frank Capra, *The Name Above the Title*, passim. Despite its many self-serving exaggerations and fictions, Capra's colorful autobiography remains the best and most gripping account of the director's rise to success. A less-flattering, more-balanced portrait of the director, arguing that much of his success was based on the work of others, has also recently been published. See Joseph McBride, *Frank Capra: The Catastrophe of Success*.
21. McBride, *Frank Capra: The Catastrophe of Success*, p. 457.
22. Frank Capra, *The Name Above the Title*, pp. 327–43.
23. McBride, *Frank Capra: The Catastrophe of Success*, p. 466.
24. Capra, *The Name Above the Title*, pp. 327–43.
25. McBride, *Frank Capra: The Catastrophe of Success*, p. 457.
26. Capra, *The Name Above the Title*, p. 330.
27. Orders officially establishing Capra's unit can be found at the National Army Records Center in Suitland, Maryland. See "Special Services Case Files" of the Chief Signal Officer of the Army Pictorial Division, US Army Signal Corps.
28. William Thomas Murphy, "The Method of Why We Fight," *Journal of Popular Film I* (summer 1972), pp. 185–96.

29. Capra, *The Name Above the Title*, pp. 321–41.
30. Ibid.
31. McBride, *Frank Capra: The Catastrophe of Success*, pp. 453–70.
32. Axel Madsen, *William Wyler: The Authorized Biography* (New York: Crowell, 1973). In 1990 Wyler's 1943 documentary was remade into a feature film for commercial release, also entitled "The Memphis Belle".
33. J. P. Telotte, *Voices in the Dark: The Narrative Patterns of Film Noir* (Urbana: University of Illinois Press, 1989), pp. 13–18.
34. John Huston, *An Open Book*, p. 89.
35. Ibid.
36. Huston, *An Open Book*, p. 110.
37. Lawrence Grobel, *The Hustons* (New York: Charles Scribner & Sons, 1989), pp. 234–63.
38. Huston, *An Open Book*, p. 119.
39. Grobel, *The Hustons*, p. 262.
40. Grobel, *The Hustons*, p. 263.
41. Ibid.
42. Ibid.
43. Jon Huston, *An Open Book*, p. 126.
44. Ibid.
45. Huston, *An Open Book*, p. 125.

12 Mass Persuasion: A Technical Problem and a Moral Dilemma*
Robert K. Merton

September 21, 1943, was War Bond Day for the Columbia Broadcasting System. During a span of eighteen hours – from eight o'clock that morning until two the next morning – a radio star named Kate Smith [a singer] spoke for a minute or two at repeated intervals. (Stardom implies a mammoth audience: it was estimated that in 1943 some 23,000,000 Americans listened to Smith's daytime programs in a week and some 21,000,000 to her weekly evening program.)

On sixty-five distinct occasions in the course of the day, she begged, cajoled, demanded that her listeners buy war bonds. Within the narrow borders of her brief messages, Smith managed to touch upon a variety of themes enshrined in American culture. She talked of neighbor boys from American towns and villages, now facing danger and death in other lands. And people listened. She told dramatic tales of generosity and sacrifice by soldier and civilian alike. People continued to listen. She invoked themes of love and hate, of large hopes and desperate fears, of honor and shame. Apparently, there was nothing here of a cut-and-dried radio script. This was presented as a personal message, iterated and reiterated in a voice often broken, it seemed, by deep emotion. And people did more than listen.

Before nightfall, Smith could begin to announce large totals of bond pledges. At one climactic moment, she reported that listeners in Los Angeles had that day subscribed several million dollars in response to her appeals. Each succeeding

* Reprinted from Robert K. Merton, *Mass Persuasion: The Social Psychology of a War Bond Drive* (New York and London: Harper & Brothers, 1946).

announcement acclaimed a swelling national sum of pledges. By the end of this, her third all-day drive, Smith had shattered her previous bond-selling records. During her first drive, she had amassed a million dollars in pledges and her second had netted two millions. But this Third War Loan appeal far outstripped her earlier efforts, resulting in thirty-nine million dollars of bond pledges in the course of the one day. Here, apparently, was an extraordinary instance of mass persuasion.

We decided to study the Smith bond drive on the assumption that it would provide a peculiarly instructive case for research into the social psychology of mass persuasion. This is *not* a study of Kate Smith. Her bond drive merely provides the material for an investigation of the structure and dynamics of mass persuasion in our society.[1]

The power of speech, which so fascinates Kate Smith that she threatens to doff the feathers of a songbird for the mantle of an orator, is no simple faculty lodged in the person of a persuasive speaker. This much is clear from our inquiry into a minor episode of mass persuasion. The over-all strategy of persuasion made use of a special social situation in which mass interest and emotions were centered on a national co-operative venture. Varied techniques and devices were employed to move the audience from a state of mind to definite action. But these devices of mass persuasion, primarily *technical* in character though they are, have a *moral* dimension as well. In adopting the standpoint of the technician, we are interested only in questions of what proved effective and how it came to be so. From the standpoint of the citizen, we want to raise questions of a broader social and moral nature. Yet the technical and moral implications are in fact closely interlaced and do not permit us the convenient splitting of our personality into the technician and the citizen selves. The techniques employed in mass persuasion have direct social implications and a code of morals immediately limits the choice of effective techniques.

THE TECHNICAL DIMENSION

Perhaps the most general finding of our inquiry is the configurative or patterned nature of this episode of mass persuasion. The elements that entered into this pattern extend far beyond the gross emotional symbols employed by Smith. This was no simple event in which the use of the "correct appeals" alone served to persuade large numbers of people. To have confined our inquiry to the content of what Smith said would have been to overlook the more general pattern of persuasion. The analysis of this content alone provides only a limited clue to what proved persuasive and it is, at best, inevitably thin, partly misleading and seriously incomplete. "Copy slant," as the phrasings are called by those versed in the arts of commercial persuasion, were an integral but not decisive part of the total event.

The general finding that it was not only what Smith had to say that furthered persuasion led to the observation that other effective components of her campaign had been fashioned before the day of the marathon. The process of persuasion was well under way before she began her daylong exhortations. To ignore this fact by focusing solely on her appeals during the marathon would be to lose sight of integral phases of the campaign.

Likely to be neglected, if only because it is so obvious, is the important role played by the war itself, with the shared sentiments and values that it brought about. Expressing and partly shaping these sentiments was the continuing flow of appeals, pronouncements and facts broadcast through radio, print, film, and word of mouth, all dealing with the central place of war bonds as a civilian contribution to a national effort. To a large extent, of course, Smith rode the crest of this wave. Her appeals were carried along by an upsurge of common motivations and interests. She had, so to speak, a vast emotional capital on which to draw for her own bond drive.

Similarly antedating the marathon were the public images of Smith, themselves the product of years of sedulous attention to the building of a public reputation. The effectiveness of what she had to say cannot be dissociated from these public images. She had long since become identified as a patriot non-pareil, at once a leader and, in words broadcast by ex-Governor Al Smith during the fourth drive, "one of the little people of America." It was this imagery, antedating the bond drive and reinforced by it, that could lead devoted followers to rally round their idol and lay their bond pledges upon the altar of their devotion. It was this imagery, also, that permitted the bond pledge to become simultaneously an expression of their fealty to Smith and to their country. She had long been for many an object of loyalty, a public figure who stood beyond conflicting group interests, who espoused nothing but the undebated virtues and the sacred symbols. The prevalence of these images testifies to the powerful role of publicity in a mass society. (It will be remembered that although fourteen of approximately a thousand New Yorkers had never heard of the ex-presidential candidate Wendell Willkie, only one could not identify the radio singer Kate Smith.) And, as we have seen, the appeals typically expressed by Smith were carefully tailored to her public images.

If the fusion of sentiments brought on by the war and the carefully nurtured reputation of Smith were indispensable preconditions, the technique of the marathon itself contributed further to her effectiveness. For it was not only what she *said* but what she *did* during the marathon that enhanced persuasion. The public sacrifice presumably entailed by a daylong stint at the microphone set Smith apart from others who "only talked but didn't act." Propaganda of the deed proved persuasive among some who rejected propaganda of the word. Listeners who revealed their profound distrust of the "power of speech" were moved by the symbolic act.

It was within this context – a concert of effort motivated by the war, a kaleidoscopic set of public images of Smith and the tactics of the marathon – that Smith's appeals took effect. The context supplied cogency to words which might otherwise have been less than persuasive. But once this context was provided, the choice of appeals and their precise formulation became decisive in affecting the degree of mass persuasion. This seems to be shown by the enormous increase of pledges obtained by Smith in her fourth bond drive which followed by some months the drive we have been examining. The thirty-nine millions of pledges in the third grew to a hundred and ten millions in the fourth all-day drive. A few excerpts from the Smith broadcasts in the latter marathon will show how technicians in the management of public opinion come to develop more "effective" appeals.

TECHNICIANS IN SENTIMENT

At various points in our study we have noted types of audience reaction which indicated that the Smith appeals were
less effective than they might otherwise have been. Some of
her themes elicited a counterreaction. For example, her exclusive appeal to sentiment antagonized some listeners who
defined the purchase of bonds as a "rational investment."
So, too, she failed to quicken the interest of male listeners
who felt that her appeals were directed primarily to women.
In other instances we found that she had not directly appealed to certain prevalent sentiments – e.g., that it would
profane a sacred obligation to accept special premiums for
the purchase of a bond. These technical flaws in the third
bond drive are selected precisely because Smith's script
writers obviously sought to remedy them in her next drive.
They thus permit us to see how technicians apply their
skills to the persuasion of large sectors of the population.

By early evening, when the male folk had presumably
returned home from work, Smith began to address broadcasts explicitly to them. Plainly, she wished to capture the
"rationalists" in the male audience, a sector which had
apparently been largely unmoved by her previous bond drives.
The tactics employed in these broadcasts are revealing. If
she wished to motivate those listeners who looked upon war
bonds primarily as a secure investment, one might suppose
that she would address herself directly to the war-bonds-
as-safe-investments theme, so often used in the national bond
campaigns. But this is precisely what she avoided. For, as
we have seen, a direct financial appeal would be out of
character for Smith. To preserve intact the public image
of Smith-the-moralist and yet to reach the group who here-
tofore had defined bonds in terms of secular investments,
her script writers employed a complex of delicately interlaced techniques. It will be instructive to follow these techniques in detail if we are to understand the careful maneuvers
of these tacticians in public sentiment.

Smith opened the broadcasts to men with a forthright
personal statement of an observation which was disturbing
her, at once allaying any impression that she intended to
criticize her male listeners.

Now, I'd like to talk to the men. Oh, you men have been sending in your orders too. I don't mean that, but I've got something on my mind that concerns the men of this nation and I'd like to talk it over.

Having struck this keynote of candor in which she is about to engage in a heart-to-heart talk, she at once launched into a reported indictment of men who purchase bonds in the spirit of a calculating investor. Her listeners, of course, knew that the morally superior motivation for the purchase of war bonds is that of disinterested moral obligation. They knew that war bonds are primarily sacred rather than secular, that they are symbols of consecrated national purpose rather than merely smart investments. Smith's description of the portrait of the calculating investor presumably set in train feelings of guilt and shame among those who recognized the portrait as something of a self-likeness. Smith etched the portrait in acid:

> *It's been said* that listeners who pride themselves on being rational don't phone in pledges for bonds because they feel such a purchase is the result of emotional pressure. *I've been told* that to men, buying bonds is a form of business, that it's handled like a business deal. *I've been told* that men buy their bonds through banks. Oh yes, *some of these people say,* 'Men like to hear Kate Smith sing songs, but when she tries to play on their emotions and begs them to buy just one more bond, they balk. Because bond-buying is the result of planning ahead, the result of budgeting and bookkeeping. Bond-buying is a careful considered investment, not to be undertaken at the sound of a voice, at the stories of atrocities committed on American boys who are prisoners of the Japanese, American boys lying in hospitals, wounded and maimed. That's emotionalism.'

This juxtaposition of the cold-blooded, utilitarian investor and American boys wounded and maimed presumably provoked acute feelings of guilt, self-blame and unworthiness among those who detected in her description something more than an unfounded caricature of themselves. But throughout, it will be noted, this indictment stemmed not from Smith herself, but from others. ("It's been said..." "I've been told..." "Some of these people say...") She was merely reporting a series of "charges" which impugn the moral character of the American man at home. Only then, having stimulated anew a sense of inner conflict among her listeners, did Smith take up her own position. And, in accord with her public role as a mother figure, she rejected the out-group of "critics" and identified herself with her male listeners:

> Yes, that's what *they* say, *some of these wise people* who know only the world of dollars and cents, profit and loss, the jingle of the cash register, the cold figures in a bank book. That's what they say and gentlemen, I tell you now, *I ... DON'T ... BELIEVE ... IT! I say THEY LIE*, these people who think our American businessmen don't like emotionalism, don't harbor sentiment in their hearts.

This indignant rejection of the implied criticism, this re-affirmation of faith in the American male character, erased the occasion for self-blame. Smith-the-mother-figure provided reassurance. For those who experienced moral conflict, she gave moral succor. She allied herself confidently with American men everywhere, in the market place, the workshop and the office, asserting her conviction that the occasion for conflict was seeming rather than real. These men had it in them to see the right and to do the right. There was no need for guilt, for she had ready proof that they had only lofty motives, immune from attack by themselves or by others. And in all this Smith reinforced the claims of moral obligation. In this battle of motives, she sided with the Superego against the Ego.

> I say they lie, because these businessmen, these factory workers, these office employees, these older men who are doing a job at home are Americans, and coming closer to their homes and their hearts, they're the fathers of these sons for whom I'm working today.

And then, lest complacency set in, she reinforced the dictates of conscience in a crescendo of sacrosanct symbols:

> They are the fathers of these splendid boys who have gone into battle, not because they liked war, not because

they had any inner urge to bomb and kill and destroy, not because they yearned to leave the little town or the big city that was home. They went because of the ideals, and sentiment, and love of country. They went for the highest motives that young men can have, the same motives that sent you, their Dads, to war in 1917: the willingness to give their lives to keep a free America free, and to bring new freedom, new blessed peace to enslaved countries across the sea. They went because little children were being bombed as they recited their lessons in school, or as they sang their hymns in church on Sunday. They went because they felt that burning inner urge to fight for the right.

And having once again activated feelings of guilt and remorse, Smith built an easy road to atonement. The purchase of a war bond, more specifically the purchase of a bond from Smith who rejects out of hand the notion that bonds may also serve one's narrowly defined self-interest, such an act would testify beyond all question to one's moral integrity. An immediate symbolic act would wash away all semblance of guilt and shame.

Nobody can tell me their fathers here at home aren't bursting with pride. Nobody can tell me that they can sit down coolly and separate sentiment, – emotionalism, if you want to call it that – from bond-buying. Nobody can tell me that it's just a matter of bookkeeping or planned investment, when they lay those invasion dollars on the line.... How about you, Mr. America? Are you going to count the cost, and add up careful investments, and do planned bookkeeping when our kids overseas have some accounts of their own to balance – to balance in blood. How about you? Will you listen to your heart – now?

This intricate pattern of Smith's initial reinforcement of inner conflicts and of her confident support of the "higher" motives of disinterested moral obligation followed by the suggestion that the purchase of a bond from Smith would wipe out all sense of self-humiliation – this pattern of appeals, new to her fourth bond drive, presumably served its purpose. For in a later broadcast, Smith could go on to say:

> Just a little while ago, I spoke to the fathers of America, the American Dads who back in 1917 went off to war, just as their fine sons are doing today. I said that some people were saying that our American men didn't buy bonds on the spur of the moment – just like that. They were not ruled by sentiment. And I said – I didn't believe it. *I said my little say, and you American Dads from coast to coast answered, answered from your heart, just as I knew in my heart that you would. You're still answering, your orders are still pouring in.* They're riding across the land in proud procession, adding up the dollars, putting the cash on the line, to make a pathway for your sons to march on to victory, and to come home to peace. Thank you – thank you. We've got not one but two backbones to this nation . . . The Dads of 1917, and the sons of 1944.

The reference to the twin backbones of the nation was not only a peculiar anatomical trope; it was a figure of speech which helped bind together the earlier and later broadcast which made up this marathon. For earlier in the day ex-Governor Smith had made it clear that Kate Smith too was numbered among those who are "the backbone of the nation."

> We don't think of you, Kate, as an impressive personality, or the Queen of the Air, or anything like that. We think of you as plain Kate Smith, as one of the little people of America, and when I say that, I mean one of the average, everyday folks who, incidentally, are the backbone of the nation. It's the plain, average everyday kids from the little towns who are winning this war. It's the average everyday Americans at home who are winning this war. It's the average everyday Americans at home who are piling up these tremendous bond sales. . . . You reach those people because you are those people.

And drawing upon this image of plain Kate Smith, the script writers introduced another theme largely absent from the previous bond drive. We found, it will be remembered, that fully half of a cross section of a thousand New Yorkers experienced a conflict between the secular and the sacred aspects of war bonds and that they viewed special prizes and "bonuses" for the purchase of a bond as virtually profaning a moral obligation. ("You don't sell your patriotism

– that's how I feel...") Still representing the national superego, so to speak, Smith assailed the conscience of those who require special inducements to pledge a bond:

> I'm just a plain simple American, with a plain, simple, straightforward message. I'm no glamour personality who offers you a flower from my hair, who promises you an autograph, or a picture, or a souvenir booklet. This is no Bingo game we're playing. And I don't think you want any of these things. I think you want what I want, what our men overseas want, what one hundred and thirty million Americans want. We want to get this war over.

These few instances from the fourth bond drive are perhaps sufficient to suggest the tactics of the technicians in sentiment. They never lose sight of the prevailing images of Smith. Only those appeals are used which are consistent with these images, thus serving not only to elicit the desired bond pledge but also to reinforce these images anew. The appeal to narrow self-interest, for example, could not be part of Smith's grammar of motives. It would seriously conflict with the public character to which her script writers give studied expression. Within the vocabulary of purpose which is consistent with her public character, however, scriptwriters have a wide range of choice. Typically, they seek out sources of guilt and inner conflict among her listeners and direct their thrusts toward these areas of moral vulnerability. Having reinforced the conflict, they at once suggest a ready solution. To say, therefore, that they appeal to sentiment is to be something less than adequate. Their techniques can be more precisely defined. By utilizing the tensions between disinterested moral obligation and narrow self-interest, they motivate the listener to follow their suggestion. An immediate act promises surcease from moral conflict. And through the generous use of sacred symbols, invulnerable to attack, they ally Smith with national pieties.

THE MORAL DIMENSION

Our primary concern with the social psychology of mass persuasion should not obscure its moral dimension. The technician or practitioner in mass opinion and his academic counterpart, the student of social psychology, cannot escape the moral issues which permeate propaganda as a means of social control. The character of these moral issues differ somewhat for the practitioner and the investigator, but in both cases the issues themselves are inescapable.

The practitioner in propaganda is at once confronted by a dilemma: he must either forego the use of certain techniques of persuasion which will help him obtain the immediate end-in-view or violate prevailing moral codes. He must choose between being a less than fully effective technician and a scrupulous human being or an effective technician and a less than scrupulous human being. The pressure of the immediate objective tends to push him toward the first of these alternatives.[2] For when effective mass persuasion in sought, and when "effectiveness" is measured solely by the number of people who can be brought to the desired action or the desired frame of mind, then the choice of techniques of persuasion will be governed by a narrowly technical and amoral criterion. And this criterion exacts a price of the prevailing morality, for it expresses a manipulative attitude toward man and society. It inevitably pushes toward the use of whatsoever techniques "work."

The sense of power that accrues to manipulators of mass opinion, it would appear, does not always compensate for the correlative sense of guilt. The conflict may lead them to a flight into cynicism. Or it may lead to uneasy efforts to exonerate themselves from moral responsibility for the use of manipulative techniques by helplessly declaring, to themselves and to all who will listen, that "unfortunately, that's the way the world is. People are moved by emotions, by fear and hope and anxiety, and not by information or knowledge." It may be pointed out that complex situations must be simplified for mass publics and, in the course of simplification, much that is relevant must be omitted. Or, to take the concrete case we have been examining, it may be argued that the definition of war bonds as a device for curbing inflation is too cold and too remote and too difficult a conception to be effective in mass persuasion. It is preferable to focus on the sacred and sentimental aspects of war bonds, for this "copy slant" brings "results."

Like most half-truths, the notion that leaders of mass opinion must traffic in sentiment has a specious cogency. Values *are* rooted in sentiment and values *are* ineluctably linked with action. But the whole-truth extends beyond this observation. Appeals to sentiment within the context of relevant information and knowledge are basically different from appeals to sentiment which blur and obscure this knowledge. Mass persuasion is not manipulative when it provides access to the pertinent facts; it is manipulative when the appeal to sentiment is used to the exclusion of pertinent information.

The technician, then, must decide whether or not to use certain techniques which though possibly "effective" violate his own sentiments and moral codes. He must decide whether or not he should devise techniques for exploiting mass anxieties, for using sentimental appeals in place of information, for masking private purpose in the guise of common purpose.[3] He faces the moral problem of choosing not only among social ends but also among propaganda means.

Although less conspicuous and less commonly admitted, a comparable problem confronts the social scientist investigating mass opinion. He may adopt the standpoint of the positivist, proclaim the ethical neutrality of science, insist upon his exclusive concern with the advancement of knowledge, explain that science deals only with the discovery of uniformities and not with ends and assert that in his role as a detached and dispassionate scientist, he has no traffic with values. He may, in short, affirm an occupational philosophy which appears to absolve him of any responsibility for the use to which his discoveries in methods of mass persuasion may be put. With its specious and delusory distinction between "ends" and "means" and its insistence that the intrusion of social values into the work of scientists makes for special pleading, this philosophy fails to note that the investigator's social values do influence his choice and definition of problems. The investigator may naïvely suppose that he is engaged in the value-free activity of research, whereas in fact he may simply have so defined his research problems that the results will be of use to one group in the society, and not to others. His very choice and definition of a problem reflects his tacit values.

To illustrate: the "value-free" investigator of propaganda proceeds to the well-established mode of scientific formulations, and states his findings: "*If* these techniques of persuasion are used, *then* there will be (with a stated degree of probability) a given proportion of people persuaded to take the desired action." Here, then, is a formulation in the honored and successful tradition of science – apparently free of values. The investigator takes no moral stand. He merely reports his findings, and these, if they are valid, can be used by any interested group, liberal or reactionary, democratic or fascistic, idealistic or power-hungry. But this comfortable solution of a moral problem by the abdication of moral responsibility happens to be no solution at all, for it overlooks the crux of the problem: the initial formulation of the scientific investigation has been conditioned by the implied values of the scientist.

Thus, had the investigator been oriented toward such democratic values as respect for the dignity of the individual, he would have framed his scientific problem differently. He would not only have asked which techniques of persuasion produce the *immediate result* of moving a given proportion of people to action, but also, what are the *further, more remote* but not necessarily less significant, *effects* of these techniques upon the individual personality and the society? He would be, in short, sensitized to certain questions stemming from his democratic values which would otherwise be readily overlooked. For example he would ask, Does the unelaborated appeal to sentiment which displaces the information pertinent to assessing this sentiment blunt the critical capacities of listeners? What are the effects upon the personality of being subjected to virtual terrorization by advertisements which threaten the individual with social ostracism unless he uses the advertised defense against halitosis or B.O.? Or, more relevantly, what are the effects, in addition to increasing the sale of bonds, of terrorizing the parents of boys in military service by the threat that only through their purchase of war bonds can they ensure the safety of their sons and their ultimate return home? Do certain types of war bond drives by celebrities do more to pyramid their reputations as patriots than to further the sale of bonds which would otherwise not have been purchased? No single advertising or propaganda campaign may significantly affect the psychological stability of those subject to it. But a society subjected ceaselessly to a flow of "effective" half-truths and the exploitation of mass anxieties may all the sooner lose that mutuality of confidence and reciprocal trust so essential to a stable social structure. A "morally neutral" investigation of propaganda will be less likely than an inquiry stemming from democratic values to address itself to such questions.

The issue has been drawn in its most general terms by John Dewey: "Certainly nothing can justify or condemn means except ends, results. But we have to include consequences impartially. . . . It is wilful folly to fasten upon some single end or consequence which is liked, and permit the view of that to blot from perception all other undesired and undesirable consequences."[4] If this study has one major implication for the understanding of mass persuasion, it consists in this recognition of the intimate interrelation of technique and morality.

Notes

1. [Editor's note] *Mass Persuasion* used both quantitative and qualitative techniques to analyze the propaganda of the Third War Loan drive. Merton and his associates, Marjorie Fiske and Alberta Curtis, did a detailed content analysis of the transcripts of Kate Smith's broadcasts. A team of interviewers did 100 focused, but nondirective, interviews with people who had heard Smith's broadcasts in order to specify what was perceived in Smith's appeals. Finally, the project did a survey of a structured sample of 978 people in the New York area to test specific issues that had emerged in the earlier materials.

2. R. K. Merton, "Social Structure and Anomie," *Amer. Soc. Review*, 1938, 672–82.

3. During the war, imagination triumphed over conscience among advertisers who "ingeniously" related their products to the war effort. Radio commercials were not immune from this technique. A commercial dentist for example, suggests that a victory smile helps boost morale and that we can have that smile by purchasing our dentures from him. So, too, a clothing manufacturer reminds listeners that morale is a precious asset in time of war and that smart clothes, more particularly Selfridge Lane Clothes, given a man confidence and courage. Even ice cream becomes essential to the war effort. "Expecting your boys back from an army camp? Give them JL Ice

Cream. They get good food in the army and it's your job to give them the same at home." And a manufacturer of cosmetics becomes solicitous about the imbalance in the sex ratio resulting from the war. "Fewer men around because of the war? Competition keen? Keep your skin smooth. Keep attractive for the boys in the service when they come marching home." Office of Radio Research, *Broadcasting the War*, Bur. Intelligence, Office of War Information, 1943, p. 37.

4. John Dewey, *Human Nature and Conduct* (New York: Henry Holt & Co., 1922), pp. 228–229. Cf. R. K. Merton, "The Unanticipated Consequences of Purposive Social Action," *American Sociological Review* vol. I, 1936, pp. 894–904.

13 The Cold War System of Emotion Management: Mobilizing the Home Front for the Third World War*

Guy Oakes

NUCLEAR STRATEGY AND NATIONAL MORALE

During the early years of the Cold War, American national security strategists arrived at an interpretation of the probable American reaction to a nuclear attack on the United States. They also developed a program designed to bring this reaction into conformity with American policy for containing Soviet power. The national security establishment read the public response to the possibility of a nuclear attack as an expression of panic or terror. Such a reaction was not consistent with the role that planners had reserved for the American people in implementing the grand strategy for national security in the postwar era. This strategy required the American public to exhibit credible expressions of determination to fight a nuclear war. Such demonstrations of public resolve were part of an effort to deter the Soviet Union from expanding its influence by means that might precipitate just such an event. Acting on their reading of the moral psychology of the American people, civil defense specialists developed a plan for the administration and control of public emotions about nuclear war, and especially about the prospects of a nuclear attack on American cities. This plan constituted a system of emotion management that would suppress an irrational terror of nuclear

* Published for the first time in this volume.

weapons and foster in its stead a more pragmatic nuclear fear. Civil defense organizations would then be in a position to employ nuclear fear in their programs of human resource management. Nuclear fear, properly channeled, would motivate the public to deliver the domestic support that was regarded as essential to the policy of containment.[1]

By the late 1940s the basic objective of American foreign policy was the containment of Soviet power, which would be achieved through collective security arrangements with America's European allies. Collective security was regarded as the foundation of the postwar world order of the "American Century". An economic system of free enterprise and a political system of democratically governed states – laissez faire in the economic sphere and popular sovereignty in the political sphere – would create the new Pax Americana. Collective security rested on nuclear deterrence. If the Soviets threatened war in Europe, the United States would guarantee the peace by a counterthreat of nuclear retaliation against the Soviet homeland. If the armored divisions of the Red Army rolled through the Fulda Gap on their way to the Atlantic, American nuclear bombs would fall on Moscow and Leningrad.[2] Deterrence was based on the assumption that nuclear war, like the Second World War, depended upon an uncertain variable: the resolve of the American people. After September 1949, when American atomic energy experts established that the Soviets had exploded their own atomic bomb, the logic of deterrence assumed that Americans would be willing to risk nuclear war in order to preserve national security. How could the American determination to fight such a war be guaranteed in view of the unprecedented dangers it posed for personal and national survival?

In the words of James A. Forrestal, the first Secretary of Defense and one of the original Cold Warriors, the period framed by the American nuclear monopoly would define the "years of opportunity" for American foreign policy. If the American economy could outproduce the world, if its navy could secure sea lanes for international trade, and if its leaders could threaten enemies of the postwar international order with the atomic bomb, then the United States would be able to adopt an aggressive foreign policy and assume otherwise unacceptable risks in rebuilding the world economy and restoring the balance of power.[3] But what would happen when the years of opportunity ended and the Soviets developed their own arsenal of atomic weapons? Would the American people demonstrate the resolve needed to face the extraordinary dangers of a permanent crisis in national security if these dangers included a nuclear attack on their own cities?

These questions posed the problem of American national will, a matter of considerable apprehension and anguish on the part of national security planners in the early years of the Cold War. The ability of the United States to secure world peace against the expansion of Soviet communism depended upon its capacity to project a credible threat to fight a nuclear war. The plausibility of this threat was held to depend upon the moral resources of the American people. Did they possess the resolution to master the new perils and make the hard sacrifices that a nuclear war would require? American national security planners had grave doubts that their fellow citizens would pass the test for world leadership in the nuclear age. These doubts were grounded in a harsh judgment of the American character. According to this view, Americans were frivolous, superficial, and selfish. Because of their addiction to pleasure, they had become soft, weak, and irresponsible. A life of mindless consumption had produced moral corruption and decadence. As a result Americans lacked the courage needed to oppose a powerful and ruthless enemy in the hazardous world of the Cold War.[4]

These considerations formed the context in which civil defense planners began to reflect on the psychological and moral presuppositions of American nuclear policy. The main concern of these planners was the construction of a domestic consensus that would support the grand strategy for national security, and above all the role of nuclear deterrence in this strategy. An apparently intractable issue in this endeavor was the problem of nuclear terror, an hysterical fear of nuclear weapons that appeared to rule out such a consensus. Nuclear terror, it seemed, would weaken American national will and make it impossible for the United States to assume its position of leadership in the Western struggle against communism.

NUCLEAR TERROR AND THE PROBLEM OF PANIC

The phenomenon of nuclear terror was a persistent theme in the Cold War culture of the 1950s and a crucial issue in strategic thought on civil defense.[5] Early civil defense theory held that the prospect of a nuclear attack on the United States would create an extravagant emotional response. The American people, terrified by weapons that seemed to place at risk not only human life, but an entire way of life, and perhaps even life itself, would take no steps to protect themselves. Nuclear terror involved a complete loss of emotional control. Thus it precluded the cool discipline and confident proficiency that civil defense theorists regarded as appropriate responses to the bomb. Lacking self-control, victims of nuclear terror would become completely egocentric and amoral. Either they would hazard a blind and irrational flight to save themselves, oblivious to their obligations and the needs of others; or they would collapse, equally irrationally, into a state of confused inaction and stupor. In either case nuclear terror would destroy the emotional restraints and moral sanctions that tie individuals to their routine roles and responsibilities. As a result it would break down the norms that underpin the social order.

The psychology of nuclear terror was perhaps best captured by Philip Wylie – prolific novelist and short-story writer, pulp magazine essayist, and author of *Generation of Vipers*, a scathing and intemperate indictment of what he took to be fundamental hypocrisies and illusions of American life. In the early 1950s Wylie worked as a special consultant to the Federal Civil Defense Administration (FCDA).[6] In 1954 he published *Tomorrow!*, a novel that depicts a Soviet nuclear attack on the fictional midwestern twin cities of Green Prairie and River City in the mid-1950s.[7] On the Saturday afternoon before Christmas the Soviet Union launches a nuclear strike against the United States, obliterating its major cities, killing millions, and producing a level of destruction that threatens American national existence. As a result the surviving population is reduced to panic.

When warning of the impending air raid is communicated to the center of the city, unprepared motorists panic and create huge traffic jams. Masses of pedestrians fill the sidewalks and streets, trampling over abandoned vehicles as well as one another. Shoppers in heedless flight crack ribs, break legs, and crush their fellow citizens to death in a futile effort to save themselves. Victims of the attack, driven to a frenzy by the bomb blast and the firestorm it creates, assault one another as well as the police and military units summoned for their protection. Police are forced to fire on crowds of rioting civilians in order to protect themselves and restore order. Drunken members of the underclass – finally unrestrained by the force of law and fear of the police – loot homes in outlying suburbs, murder the owners, and rape their daughters. Waves of refugees from the city ravage the midwestern countryside, burning barns and houses for warmth and robbing stores for food and jewelry. Urban crowds sack and burn villages and strip them of their resources for survival, only to move on to other towns where the pillage is repeated. Control of the marauding civilian population becomes the new front in the post-attack world. In Wylie's vision of Middle America in the 1950s, only the power of the police can prevent social chaos. Nuclear terror, the panic caused by a nuclear attack and its aftermath, overwhelms the institutions of law enforcement. The result is a breakdown of social order: a post-Hobbesian world deprived of a calculating, utilitarian rationality and governed by uncontrolled and violent passions.[8]

The FCDA framed its conception of nuclear terror by reference to what civil defense theorists called "the problem of panic." Certainly the most widely circulated statement of this conception was the article on panic by Frederick "Val" Peterson, President Eisenhower's first administrator of the FCDA: "Panic: The Ultimate Weapon?", published in *Collier's*. On the whole, press coverage of civil defense in the 1950s exhibited a relationship of mutual self-interest between the FCDA and the mass media, acutely perceived and assiduously cultivated by both sides. Newspapers, magazines, radio, and television competed to gain official certification for their publications and broadcasts on civil defense as an official national security seal of approval. Both print and broadcast media submitted prepublication and preproduction drafts of scripts and articles to the FCDA for criticism and approval. The press solicited the FCDA for technical data and information concerning official civil defense policy. They also sought assurances that they had not compromised national security. The public affairs office of the FCDA took advantage of the interest of the press in official inside knowledge. In addition it exploited the enthusiasm of the press for informal self-surveillance and official government censorship, using the media to distribute its own version of nuclear reality.

In his *Collier's* article Peterson confronted readers with what he regarded as a paradoxical fact: although the American people are citizens of the most powerful nation on earth, they are also the most "panic-prone". This consideration led Peterson to pose a series of increasingly hysterical questions.

> What will you do if one day an atomic bomb blasts your town? Will you take calm emergency action – or will you dash screaming into the ruined streets, a victim of your own horror? In a war, the whole country's survival could depend upon your reaction to disaster . . . because mass panic may be far more devastating than the bomb itself . . . What will you do – not later, but right then and there?[9]

Like the atomic bomb, panic is also fissionable: "It can produce a chain reaction more deeply destructive than any explosive known." This means that "if there is an ultimate weapon, it may well be mass panic – not the A-bomb. Mass panic – not the A-bomb – may be the easiest way to win a battle, the cheapest way to win a war."[10] Peterson admitted that a Soviet atomic attack against American cities would produce grave damage. However, the reaction of terror in the surviving population would create even more serious dangers. To illustrate this point he asked readers to envisage the survivors of a nuclear attack on Manhattan: "a hungry pillaging mob – disrupting disaster relief, overwhelming local police and spreading panic in a widening arc." Although New York might present distinctive problems of civil defense that other cities would not be forced to confront, Peterson cautioned readers that comparable perils faced every American city exposed to atomic bombing.[11]

FROM NUCLEAR TERROR TO NUCLEAR FEAR

In response to the problem of panic, civil defense theorists developed an ambitious program of public emotion management.[12] Emotion management may be understood as a strategy for the mobilization, administration, discipline, and control of emotional life. The creation of those who aspire to the status of authorities and guardians of the soul, a system of emotion management conceives the emotional life as framed by three basic parameters: cognitive standards, practical norms, and strategic controls. Emotion management defines the standards that tell us what it is possible to feel, what the scope and limits of emotional experience are, and what our feelings mean. It also defines emotional norms that tell us what is expected of us emotionally, what the limits of acceptable emotional expression are, what we ought to feel in specific circumstances, and how these feelings should be expressed. Finally, it defines a technology of emotional control that tells us not only what we are able to do with our emotions and how we can use them, but also how our emotions and their expression can be deployed to our advantage.

A system of emotion management treats emotions not so much as private inner experiences or states and the inaccessible objects that may be felt in these states, but rather as cultural artifacts – products of knowledge, intelligent planning, and practical endeavors.[13] The practices that form our culture tell us not only what can be done and what we should do, but also what can be felt and what we should feel, what feelings can be expressed and how we should express them. If emotions are cultural artifacts, it follows that they can be intentionally, even self-consciously, formed, molded, manipulated, worked at, and worked upon. This means that emotions are possible objects of intention, attention, and action.

The Cold War system of emotion management was a propaganda endeavor and a marketing effort. Its purpose was to promote and sell civil defense to the American people by means of a public information program that would realize several closely linked objectives. The program would teach Americans what they needed to know about nuclear weapons, spell out norms that specified appropriate responses to a nuclear attack, and elaborate techniques for the control of emotions under attack. The principal strategy employed by the Cold War system of emotion management was to replace the destructive emotion of nuclear terror with a restrained and prudent nuclear fear that could be controlled by the civil defense establishment in accordance with the premises of American national security policy. The purpose of this strategy was to convince the American people that the decisive weapon in the Soviet arsenal was not the atomic bomb, but their own terror of atomic attack. Nuclear terror, not the bomb, was the absolute weapon. Accordingly this strategy represented an attempt to persuade the public that the object of its deepest anxieties should not be the possibility of a Soviet assault on American cities, but their own irrational response to such a possibility. It followed that nuclear terror also displaced the bomb as the ultimate object of anxiety.

A key manoeuvre in the turn from nuclear terror to nuclear fear was the subjectification of the nuclear threat. This process of internalization – transposing the problem posed by nuclear weapons from the domain of politics to that of psychology, from the sphere of public policy to that of private therapy – was essential to the logic of Cold War emotion management. It consisted in shifting the main communist menace from nuclear weapons to the American response to these weapons. The success of this manoeuvre required the American people to identify the ultimate Soviet weapon not as the atomic bomb, but rather as their own emotional instability and weakness in the face of a Soviet atomic attack. Therefore the chief obstacle to the American victory over communism lay within the soul of each individual American citizen. In the final analysis, the inadequacy of the American response to Soviet expansion was not due to errors of public policy, the bad judgment of political or military leaders, or the questionable loyalties of diplomats. On the contrary it could be traced to fundamental defects in the American character. From the standpoint of civil defense planners, the advantages of this manoeuvre are clear. The daunting technological, political, and public relations problem of how to devise plausible strategies for personal and national survival in a nuclear attack is translated into a much more manageable personal, psychological, and therapeutic problem for which the individual citizen is ultimately responsible: how do I make sure that I do not become a communist dupe, a threat to American national security, and the paramount weapon in the Soviet project of world domination? This is a question of emotional self-knowledge and self-control. The main problem it poses is not how to survive a nuclear war, but how to manage oneself so that irrational fears do not produce a breakdown in self-discipline.

By interpreting nuclear terror as the most important element of the nuclear crisis, and thereby psychologizing and depoliticizing the problem of survival under nuclear attack, civil defense planners were trying to effect a fundamental displacement in public consciousness. Such a process involves three steps.

First, the American people are told that they must scrutinize their own psychology, which, they are warned, is the major threat both to their own personal survival and to national security. Anxieties about nuclear attack, which pose technological and political problems that are ultimately irresolvable, are transformed into worries about the reasonableness of these very anxieties. Irrational terror of nuclear weapons becomes the real danger. As a result Americans lose sight of the crucial role of nuclear weapons in national security policy and the status of these weapons as the main threat to survival. Their primary concern is not the possibility of a nuclear attack, but the possibility that the quality of their own performance under attack might be seriously compromised by panic.

Second, Americans are supplied with new norms specifying how nuclear weapons should be experienced. The only intelligent and responsible attitude to take toward the bomb is a healthy and measured fear. As the politically correct response to the bomb, nuclear fear replaces nuclear terror. In the social psychology of Cold War emotion management, nuclear terror produces panic, apathy, or stupefaction. However a robust and prudent fear can serve as a useful stimulus to motivate individual citizens to protect themselves from the dangers of nuclear attack. Most important, the belief that self-protective measures can be effective will mobilize public action on behalf of civil defense programs. These programs, in turn, will provide the domestic support required by national security policy. If the American people, motivated by a rational fear of nuclear attack, can be convinced that careful planning, sound training, and firm moral discipline will enable them to survive such an attack, then the crucial domestic requirement of national will essential to the strategy of deterrence will be met.

Finally, Americans are told that the cure for the contagion of panic is civil defense. It is possible to control the irrational fears that produce panic only by participating in civil defense training. According to this view, civil defense is a social technology of emotion control that teaches the public not only how to manage their new-found anxieties about nuclear terror, but also how to channel their fear of nuclear attack to their own best advantage and – most important – in ways that support national security policy. This final step involved a full-scale national marketing program on behalf of civil defense as emotion management. Civil defense became the therapy of choice in "beating" panic and the most effective weapon the American people could use to defend themselves in the Cold War.

The logic and pragmatics of the shift from nuclear terror to nuclear fear – in the pregnant phrase of the 1950s, "learning to live with the bomb" – are clearly articulated in the *Project East River* report. A study of American civil defense commissioned during the Truman administration and completed in 1952, *Project East River* became "the Bible of civil defense".[14] The authors of the special appendix on panic in the report treat the possibility of panic under nuclear attack as a "working assumption". In their view the prevention and control of panic in the event of such an attack are major objectives of civil defense. A subsection of the appendix, ominously entitled "The Special Problems of Mob Aggression, Rioting, Scape-Goating, Looting, Etc.," interprets the American public as a xenophobic, emotionally inflammatory, and violence-prone mass. Its assessment of whether the public would respond to an attack on American cities by undertaking productive civil defense work or by hunting down scapegoats could not have encouraged

FCDA officials. In considering this question the report cites recent race riots, lynchings, and the "indiscriminate seizure" of Japanese-Americans during the Second World War as evidence that "senseless aggression" and mob action could be expected in the event of a surprise attack.[15]

In light of these considerations *Project East River* outlines a program of emotional re-education designed to instruct the public in the proper response to the bomb.

> Civil defense education must make people aware that a considerable degree of fear under attack is normal and inevitable. As with the development of healthy attitudes among combat troops, civil defense must, in effect, tell people: "You will feel afraid when the first attack comes. So will everyone else, for attack is dangerous. There is no abnormality and no cowardliness in such justified fear. It is not whether you feel afraid, but what you do when you are afraid that counts. The fear you experience will make you more alert, stronger, and more tireless for the things that you and your neighbors can do to protect yourselves."[16]

The pragmatic nuclear fear advocated by *Project East River* is "healthy" for three reasons. It is a normal, indeed an inevitable, response to the dangers of nuclear war. Unlike nuclear terror, it can motivate appropriately trained citizens to take responsible positive steps to protect themselves from these dangers. Finally, the instrumentally rational behavior motivated by nuclear fear can be "channeled": if people have received proper training, they will be motivated by their own fear to respond to a nuclear attack in ways that conform to this training. Like soldiers who have been disciplined to take advantage of their fear of death in order to execute military assignments in spite of the hazards of combat – the "we've-got-a-job-to-do" work ethic of warfare – the American people can be trained to act on their fear of imminent destruction in order to perform tasks that will ensure their own survival as well as the national security. Therefore the lesson the public must learn is clear and simple. Nuclear terror is abnormal, irrational, and uncontrollable. Nuclear fear is a normal, rational, and manageable response to the bomb.

Under what conditions can the public be expected to respond to a threat of nuclear attack with nuclear fear rather than nuclear terror? According to *Project East River*, Americans will act in an organized and disciplined fashion only if they have been trained to do so. Training is the most powerful single measure to take against panic. In the same way that combat troops are rigorously trained to estimate dangers quickly and respond unreflectively with the most appropriate measures, so civil defense can be understood as the "intensive training of the public to recognize the main sources of danger in foreseeable emergencies and practice in effective actions to combat these dangers". By imposing a psychology of military training on the civilian population, civil defense strategists hoped to develop pre-attack habits and disciplines that would "resist disruption by emotion".[17] According to this view nuclear terror can be defeated only by careful civil defense planning, training, and discipline, which *Project East River* conceives as a program of emotion management: a psychological re-education of the public that stresses the appropriateness of a utilitarian fear as the preferred response to nuclear weapons, the deployment of such a measured fear as the primary means of motivating the public to participate in civil defense, and the use of civil defense as a therapy for panic control – the only method of mastering nuclear terror so that the absolute Soviet weapon in the Cold War could be neutralized.

Val Peterson provides a simplified, mass-market version of civil defense as emotion management in his *Collier's* article on panic. Because panic is the ultimate weapon in the Cold War, Peterson examines the failures of individual self-control that are allegedly responsible for panic. His purpose is to persuade *Collier's* readers that they are typical panic-prone Americans. Readers' fears of the dangers posed by their own panic would lead them to ask how they could manage their emotions. By employing techniques of emotional self-control, readers will learn how to defeat panic and foil any Soviet attempt to dominate the United States by exploiting the emotional weaknesses of the American people. These considerations lead Peterson to insist on the importance of becoming "panic proof". His article even includes a simple psychological test by means of which readers can measure their susceptibility to panic. The test includes ten questions on mathematical and logical relations to be answered within ten minutes, thus requiring the performance of unfamiliar quantitative operations under artificially imposed conditions of stress. It also asks examinees to undertake a brief self-evaluation of their tolerance for stress.[18]

Peterson claims that 83 percent of American men and 55 percent of American women can be made "reasonably panic resistant".[19] How can this be achieved? It is necessary to "make fear work for you". Readers are advised not to be ashamed of being afraid: "When you're under attack, fear is natural – even healthy".[20] The key is to use your fear to your best advantage instead of allowing it to use you. In the latter case, victims of fear will quickly find themselves in the grip of panic. In the former case, trained citizens, like trained soldiers, will employ their fear as a means of becoming more alert and emotionally more resilient, even under conditions of ultimate stress. According to Peterson, this requires systematic civil defense training: a comprehensive public education program that tells people what to expect and what measures to take in a nuclear attack and teaches them to develop the skills, resolve, and self-control to perform the tasks required. Readers are provided with a list of "panic stoppers": techniques of emotion self-management drawn from FCDA public information booklets that instruct middle-class householders on how to behave in a nuclear crisis. The performance of civil defense exercises – practicing drills at home, building a home shelter, taking a first-aid course, learning "fireproof housekeeping," storing food, water, and emergency supplies – provides, it was said, "insulation" against panic. It also enables family members to discharge their respective duties "like trained soldiers under fire".[21]

Thus, in the official view of the FCDA, civil defense can teach Americans how to control their emotions so they do not become victims of their own terror. Managing a nuclear crisis is achieved by careful planning, the acquisition of skills, and the development of discipline, all of which are intended to achieve emotional self-control. In the final analysis, mastery of a nuclear crisis is the product of self-mastery conceived as emotion management.

THE ROUTINIZATION OF ATOMIC ATTACK: AMERICAN SOCIETY IN THE THIRD WORLD WAR

In Wylie's story of the atomic bombing of Middle America in the 1950s, not all the citizens of Green Prairie and River City become victims of atomic blast, radiation, fire, panic, riot, murder, or rape. At the beginning of the novel the reader is introduced to the members of the Conner family of Green Prairie. The Conners live the American pastoral as depicted by Norman Rockwell on the covers of the *Saturday Evening Post*: a two-story white frame house on Walnut Street with front and back porches, clapboard siding, scrollwork around the eaves of the roof, a large lawn planted with spirea, forsythia, tulips, and dahlias, and a vegetable garden in the rear. The Conners are sitting down to Sunday dinner – roast beef, naturally, with mashed potatoes and gravy, fresh rolls with wild strawberry jam, pumpkin pie topped with whipped cream – when their repast is interrupted by the wailing of a siren summoning the civil defense organization of Green Prairie to an air-raid drill.

The father Henry is a district warden, responsible for coordinating civil defense in a residential neighborhood where he exercises authority over a thousand civil defense volunteers and supervises a team of block wardens. At the signal of the siren he dutifully interrupts his dinner and equips himself with his crimson CD arm-band, whistle, and First-World-War helmet and makes his way to another practice session in which the citizens of Green Prairie prepare to protect themselves from a Soviet nuclear attack. The mother Beth is a member of the civil defense first-aid group. The younger son Ted, a high-school student of 16 and a ham-radio buff, has joined the civil defense communication division. At the sound of the siren he rushes to his post in his attic bedroom and tunes in to the local civil defense headquarters for any information about an impending attack. The older son Charles, currently fulfilling his military obligations as an intelligence officer in the Air Force, is enjoying a 30-day leave at home. Of course there is a girl-next-door as well: Charles's sweetheart Leonore, the local beauty queen who lives directly across the privet hedge. Less plausibly, she is also a "Geigerman," outfitted in a yellow plastic "fire-resistant and chemical-proof" overall and "anti-contamination" suit. Armed with her Geiger counter, she monitors simulated blast sites for dangerous radioactivity.

On the Saturday afternoon before Christmas the Green Prairie civil defense organization receives a warning that waves of Soviet bombers have penetrated North American air space. The Conners respond quickly and efficiently by following standard civil defense procedures, their fear controlled by training and technique. Henry rushes from a pre-Christmas dinner to his district headquarters in the local high school, where the volunteers in his unit have assembled with grim determination. Ted drives to the empty family house and sits alone at his radio set, patiently collecting information on the nuclear destruction of San Francisco, Los Angeles, and Dallas, following security rules with steely self-control. When Leonore receives the coded telephone instruction informing her of the "red alert," she is having her hair done at the smartest hairdresser in the city as part of her preparations for a chic Christmas party. Without hesitating she rips herself in an untimely way from the hairdryer and bounds from the salon, at the same time maintaining ice-cold self-discipline and concealing news of the impending attack from the patrons and employees of the salon, and even from neighbors who offer to drive her home.

When the bomb falls, the citizens of Green Prairie who have learned correct civil defense procedure not only survive, but even manage to negotiate the hazards of the post-attack world without experiencing undue hardship. At the flash of the atomic blast Henry dives under a desk at his command post. In a few moments he emerges unscathed, brushes off a few bits of dust, and goes about his official business. Ted takes shelter under his radio equipment table and escapes with nothing more than a bruise and a cut leg. After dutifully checking the gas and electricity in the house, he calmly puts on his coat and makes his way through the nuclear debris to submit his report at civil defense headquarters. The attack catches Beth on foot, carrying a suitcase filled with first-aid equipment to a neighborhood church, now designated as an emergency hospital. When the bomb explodes she immediately drops to the ground at the foot of a neighbor's front lawn, picks herself up after the blast, and continues on her way to the church, not forgetting the suitcase.

As a result of preparations undertaken in the Conner's district, the well-trained civil defense organization brings fires under control, removes rubble from main thoroughfares, patrols the streets for looters, commandeers the remaining inventories of damaged food and clothing stores, organizes a systematic program for rescue, first-aid, and relief, and moves throughout the neighborhood to make sure that levels of radiation are "acceptable". Within hours of the attack life returns to the routines of the pre-attack world, demonstrating that for those who have made the requisite preparations, atomic warfare is not such a bad thing. Henry can relax his responsibilities as district warden and sit down to a hot corned-beef sandwich with baked beans and coffee. The plucky and undaunted Leonore tests a huge metal slag heap for radioactivity, judges it to be contaminated but "safe," lights a cigarette, inhales deeply, and takes a break to engage in shoptalk with a police lieutenant – insouciant, nonplussed, and self-possessed. The Conner home has, of course, been outfitted with a basement shelter, canned goods labelled on shelves, a portable sterno stove, and the regulation five gallons of distilled water. As a result Beth, in spite of a long night of first-aid service, is back at home making herself a cup of instant coffee in the first light of the first post-attack dawn, demonstrating that although war may be hell and nuclear war even worse, a nuclear attack leaves all things essentially the same in American life.

The moral of Wylie's story is clear. If you ignore civil defense procedures you can expect to suffer a terrible fate in a nuclear attack. If you are not killed instantly, you will die of injuries, bleed to death, succumb to exposure, go mad, or become a victim of murder or rape. However if you acquire the necessary civil defense skills you will be able to master a nuclear disaster, in which case a nuclear attack will produce no major changes in your life. Although

Wylie's novel is a nuclear fantasy, it reproduces without significant exaggeration the basic assumptions of Cold War emotion management. An intelligent fear of nuclear attack will motivate the public to take the steps recommended by the civil defense public education program. Civil defense training will lead to the acquisition of technical skills for self-protection as well as the moral discipline needed to practice these skills coolly and efficiently under conditions of maximum stress. Technical skill and moral discipline will produce emotional self-control. As the American people are repeatedly admonished, they must respond like soldiers in battle – good soldiers, naturally, who follow instructions competently, automatically, and unflinchingly, assuring that the objectives of their commanders are met. Civil defense militarizes life by nonmilitary means, using techniques of emotion management to train citizens to discipline and control themselves. As a result they will master their panic, at the same time mastering the nuclear crisis and fulfilling the domestic requirements of the American grand strategy for national security.

CONCLUSION: LIBERAL PROPAGANDA AND THE EXIGENCIES OF NATIONAL SECURITY

American civil defense in the 1950s rested on a propaganda strategy that shifted the crucial issue of civil defense from the question of how to protect the American people in the event of nuclear attack to the question of how to convince the people that they could protect themselves. Popular acceptance of deterrence as an admissible policy for achieving national security depended upon the credibility of the proposition that even if deterrence failed, the consequences would still be tolerable. Even if the American threat to counter Soviet provocations by employing nuclear bombs led the Soviets to respond in kind, the results would not be catastrophic. In the rhetoric of the time, if the price of freedom proved to be nuclear war, even this price was not too high. The federal civil defense programs of the 1950s represented an attempt to convince the American people to accept this proposition.

This attempt was undertaken by means of the Cold War system of emotion management, an audacious argument that maintained that although the state could not protect the American people in a nuclear attack, they could at least be persuaded to believe that self-protection was possible. Americans could indeed be convinced that they were capable of mastering the nuclear crisis, but only by means of the emotional discipline they would learn in civil defense training. Thus in the minds of civil defense strategists, planning for the Third World War was intimately linked to a politics of mass psychology and the project of controlling what was regarded as a potentially fatal weakness in the American determination to resist Soviet expansion and face the unparalleled dangers of nuclear war.

This propaganda strategy did not fail to generate paradoxical consequences. The civil defense establishment officially embraced a liberal conception of propaganda as public information. This conception may be reduced to two premises, both of which have their source in the Enlightenment: the idea that democracy depends upon truth; and the idea that the general will is a product of knowledge – on any issue the public will take the best course of action if it is properly informed. The first premise requires that propaganda be limited to an accurate representation of government policy and its intentions. Since democratic politics is based on the consent of the governed, the public must be persuaded to accept government positions by credible means. However credibility rests upon reputation, above all a reputation for veracity. This means that if the government fails to keep faith with the public and misrepresents policy, the public will withdraw its support because the government has proven itself untrustworthy. According to this view truth is a necessary condition for the acceptability of policy. The second premise assumes that if the American people are given the facts about nuclear war, they will do their part to support the grand strategy of national security. According to this view, truth is a sufficient condition for the acceptability of policy.

Given this conception of propaganda, the civil defense establishment was obliged to produce an accurate account of the facts of nuclear attack and the prospects for survival. However civil defense planners privately acknowledged that in an actual nuclear attack the project of emotion management was a vain illusion. Even President Eisenhower maintained this unofficial and secretly held position. In a nuclear attack neither ordinary citizens nor government officials can be expected to behave normally. People will be scared, even hysterical. As Eisenhower put it, they will go "absolutely nuts". Eisenhower emphasized that this characterization applies to everyone, including himself. According to this view a nuclear attack would be an emotionally shattering experience, and every man "will be beside himself with grief and apprehension about his family and his country". Under these conditions the main job of government will be "to preserve some common sense in a situation where everybody is going crazy" and the population is "completely bewildered".[22] Not surprisingly planners judged that propaganda as full disclosure of the facts would defeat the essential purpose of civil defense propaganda: to convince the American people that they can train and equip themselves to survive a nuclear attack. As a result planners sacrificed their liberal principles to their view of the exigencies of national security policy.

Notes

1. This essay is derived mainly from Guy Oakes and Andrew Grossman, "Managing Nuclear Terror: The Genesis of American Civil Defense Strategy," *International Journal of Politics, Culture, and Society*, vol. 5 (1992), pp. 361–403. Research was supported by a grant from Monmouth College and with funds provided by the Jack T. Kvernland Chair. For advice on sources, thanks are due to Dennis Bilger of the Harry S. Truman Library and Dwight Strandberg of the Dwight D. Eisenhower Library.

2. See Thomas H. Etzold and John L. Gaddis (eds), *Containment: Documents on American Policy and Strategy. 1945–1950* (New York: Columbia University Press, 1978); John Lewis Gaddis, *Strategies of Containment: A Critical Appraisal of American National Security Policy* (New York: Oxford University Press, 1982); Gregg Herken, *The Winning Weapon: The Atomic Bomb in the Cold War* (New York: Knopf, 1980); Steven Ross, *American War Plans, 1945–1950* (New York: Garland, 1988).

3. Walter Millis (ed.), *The Forrestal Diaries* (New York: Viking Press, 1951), pp. 350–1.

4. This Olympian and contemptuous view of the American public was part of the cultural capital of the early Cold War national security establishment, forming a compendium of assumptions that underpinned the planning of American national security after the Second World War. It was originally expressed in Henry L. Stimson's valedictory to the Truman cabinet as Secretary of War. See "Statement by the Secretary of War at the Cabinet meeting September 7, 1945 in re military training" in the Henry L. Stimson Diaries, vols 47–52, 1 May 1944–21 September 1945, Harry S. Truman Library. Even figures otherwise as antagonistic in their positions as John Foster Dulles and George F. Kennan shared this common body of positions about the moral infirmities of ordinary American citizens. See, for example, John Foster Dulles, "Thoughts on Soviet Foreign Policy and What to do about it," *Life*, 3 June 1946, pp. 112–26, and 10 June 1946, pp. 119–30; *War or Peace* (New York: Macmillan, 1950); George F. Kennan, *Memoirs*, 2 volumes (Boston: Little Brown, 1967, 1972).

5. Concerning the impact of nuclear weapons on American society, see Paul Boyer, *By the Bomb's Early Light* (New York: Pantheon, 1985); Elaine Tyler May, *Homeward Bound: American Families in the Cold War Era* (New York: Basic Books, 1988); and Spencer R. Weart, *Nuclear Fear* (Cambridge: Harvard University Press, 1988).

6. On the FCDA, see Thomas J. Kerr, *Civil Defense in the U.S.: Bandaid for a Holocaust?* (Boulder: Westview Press, 1983).

7. Philip Wylie, *Tomorrow!* (New York: Rinehart and Company, 1954).

8. Wylie's worries about the response of the American public in the face of a nuclear attack and his suggestions for controlling this response are fully documented in the Philip Wylie Collection, Firestone Library, Princeton University. The reviews of *Tomorrow!* from the FCDA were enthusiastic. See Philip Wylie Collection, Firestone Library, Princeton University, Box 224, Folder 4. In 1956 a paperback edition was published, with an initial printing of 250 000 copies priced at 35 cents. The publisher, Pines Publications, sent complimentary copies to all state governors as well as state and city civil defense directors. In addition the FCDA promoted the book in its public-information program. See "For Your Information," Education Services #284, Public Affairs (Battle Creek Michigan: Federal Civil Defense Administration, 1956).

9. Frederick "Val" Peterson, "Panic: The Ultimate Weapon?," *Collier's*, 21 August 1953, pp. 99–100. Ellipses in original. According to Peterson, less intelligent people are more panic-prone than the intelligent. Women are more panic-prone, by almost 30 percent, than men. The latter datum is explained by the routines of female life, which are said to pose fewer hazards than the work world of men. As a result women gain less experience in "conquering fear" (pp. 106–7).

10. Peterson, "Panic: The Ultimate Weapon?," p. 100.

11. Peterson, "Panic: The Ultimate Weapon?," p. 101. The doctrine that strategic bombing would panic urban populations and weaken

or destroy the popular will to wage war was not, of course, the product of the Cold War. The same fears were expressed by both British and German leaders during the infancy of aerial bombing in the First World War. The effect of aerial bombardment on· civilian morale was also an important strategic issue in the years immediately before the Second World War. War planners hypothesized that sudden, massive, and utterly catastrophic aerial bombing would produce panic, the collapse of public resolve to fight, and a swift surrender. See Michael S. Sherry, *The Rise of Air Power* (New Haven: Yale University Press, 1987), pp. 12–21, 64–9. On the private worries concerning the problem of panic expressed by national security officials during the Eisenhower presidency, see the following: the 28 January and 17 February 1954 meetings of the National Security Council, Papers of Dwight D. Eisenhower as President, Ann Whitman File, NSC Series, Box 5, Dwight D. Eisenhower Library; and the 12 July 1957 meeting of the cabinet, Papers of Dwight D. Eisenhower as President, Ann Whitman File, Cabinet Series, Box 9, Dwight D. Eisenhower Library. Civil defense planners were especially sensitive to the possibility that their own efforts to combat panic could be self-defeating. In emphasizing the dangers of nuclear war and its destructive effects, they might actually panic the public, leaving them with the impression that the situation was hopeless. As a result civil defense planners made a self-conscious attempt to manage their own public presentations with this problem in mind. See, for example, the suggestions of Charles Ellsworth, speechwriter and consultant in the public affairs office of the FCDA, to Katherine Howard, deputy administrator of the FCDA in 1953–4, concerning her television appearances: "You have a reflex tendency to smile when you refer to the atom bomb, or to death and destruction – probably in an instinctive attempt to avoid scaring people to death. A little serious matter-of-factness might be better at such times" (Letter of 19 June 1953, Katherine Howard Papers, Box 11, Television [1], Dwight D. Eisenhower Library).

12. On the management of emotions, see Arlie Russell Hochschild, *The Managed Heart: The Commercialization of Human Feeling* (Berkeley and Los Angeles: University of California Press, 1983); Carol Zizowitz Stearns and Peter N. Stearns, *Anger: The Struggle for Emotional Control in America's History* (Chicago: University of Chicago Press, 1986); Peter N. Stearns, *Jealousy: The Evolution of an Emotion in American History* (New York: New York University Press, 1989), and "Suppressing Unpleasant Emotions. The Development of a Twentieth Century American Emotional Style," pp. 230–61 in Andrew E. Barnes and Peter N. Stearns (eds), *Social History and Issues in Human Consciousness* (New York: New York University Press, 1989); and Peter N. Stearns and Timothy Haggerty, "The Role of Fear: Transitions in American Emotional Standards for Children, 1850–1950," *American Historical Review*, vol. 96 (1991), pp. 63–94.

13. On emotions as cultural artifacts, see E. Doyle McCarthy, "Emotions are Social Things: An Essay in the Sociology of Emotions,"

pp. 51–72 in David D. Franks and E. Doyle McCarthy (eds), *The Sociology of Emotions: Original Essays and Research Papers* (Greenwich, CT: JAI Press, 1989).

14. See the Papers of Katherine Howard, Project East River, Box 9, Dwight D. Eisenhower Library.

15. "Panic Prevention and Control," Appendix IXB of *Project East River*, Part IX, p. 64, Project East River File, Box 19, Record Group 304, National Security Resources Board, National Archives. On the genesis of the research on emotion management conducted by *Project East River*, see Papers of Harry S. Truman, Staff Member Office Files: Psychological Strategy Board Files, Box 34, Folder 348.51, *Project East River*.

16. "Panic Prevention and Control," Appendix IXB, *Project East River*, Part IX, p. 61.

17. "Panic Prevention and Control," Appendix IXB, *Project East River*, Part IX, p. 59.

18. Peterson, "Panic: The Ultimate Weapon?" See pp. 106–7: "Test Yourself: How Panic Proof Are You?"

19. Peterson, "Panic: The Ultimate Weapon?," p. 101.

20. Peterson, "Panic: The Ultimate Weapon?," p. 108.

21. Ibid.

22. Cabinet meeting of 25 July 1956, Papers of Dwight D. Eisenhower as President, Ann Whitman File, Cabinet Series, Box 7, Dwight D. Eisenhower Library. More than two years after these remarks, Eisenhower observed to the National Security Council that he had considered building a family fallout shelter at his farm in Gettysburg as a way of setting an example for the country. However he was reluctant to do so since the effect might be "to scare other people to death". See the 11 December 1958 meeting of the National Security Council, Papers of Dwight D. Eisenhower as President, Ann Whitman File, NSC Series, Box 10, Dwight D. Eisenhower Library.

Part III

The Ubiquity of Propaganda in Modern Society

14 Bureaucratic Propaganda: The Case of Battle Efficiency Reports*

David L. Altheide and
John M. Johnson

The application of rational efforts to depict efficiency, as well as to justify and present many individual efforts as though they were really part of a "system," has led many people to believe that official accounts can be assumed to reflect some action, even a very complex one. This chapter illustrates how a navy "weapon," the USS *Walden*, accomplished the task of presenting official reports about its overall effectiveness in combat. Reports about combat are of more significance for success, promotion, and general recognition and approval than are the events that occur. In short, reports are what count.

THE PURPOSE AND CONTEXT

The conflict in Vietnam was one of the United States's most sophisticated and rational attempts to destroy a foe with the aid of scientific technology and organization. Many new weapons were employed; in addition, improved communications capacity, along with more versatile hardware, including jet helicopters, were available to combine intellect and gauge reading with the blood and terror of the battlefields.

There was also another way in which the conflict in Vietnam differed from earlier campaigns. The success of the

---

* Reprinted from David L. Altheide and John M. Johnson, *Bureaucratic Propaganda* (Boston: Allyn and Bacon, 1980).

war effort was difficult to assess because of the enemy's guerilla tactics, elusiveness, and difficulty of identification. Bodies were hard to find; enemy stores seemed nonexistent; captured territory would return to enemy hands within days after American forces had secured it. Compared to earlier conventional wars, Vietnam seemed confusing. It was almost impossible to measure our effectiveness. For example, there was no scrimmage line that could bulge, as occurred in a famous European campaign in World War II. To the contrary, the enemy was sought through seek and destroy patrols. And there appeared to be no central enemy authority to provide documents that could be captured to reveal our effectiveness.

The difficulty in assessing success promoted more reliance on official reports about the number of bodies counted, expended ordnance, number of air strikes, and estimates of our domination of the seaways, especially offshore naval activity. These accounts came to be the foundation for actually deducing our effectiveness. The formula was quite simple: the more American troops in Vietnam, the more bombs dropped, the more air strikes flown, and the more shells expended became the basis for deducing the amount and character of damage to the enemy. Relatedly, the people inflicting the damage – dropping the bombs and firing the shells – were given credit for the presumed impact of these acts on "bringing Hanoi to its knees." Like all rational efforts, these acts were rewarded with prestige, careers, medals, and great attention via the mass media. This context changed the purpose from fighting an abstract war to showing what one's outfit was contributing to the war effort. The USS *Walden* was part of it all.

During the years of the Vietnam conflict the ships of this class were among the only ones that still possessed a capability for gunnery missions, which the newer, guided-missile destroyers could not perform. Thus, even though the "primary mission" of the USS *Walden* was officially that of antisubmarine warfare, it was scheduled to fulfill shore bombardment missions during the Vietnam conflict, as well as several other war-related activities. The priority of *Walden's* primary capability (ASW) had been replaced with that of gunnery operations in recent years.

DETERMINING BATTLE EFFICIENCY IN EASTPAC AND WESTPAC

Walden crew members perceived that the major criterion of success for their ship was its competition for the battle efficiency awards. The most prestigious award, the Battle E, was awarded to only one ship of squadron. In times of war, such as during Vietnam, this battle-related success generally involved some unusual or out of the ordinary mission while in Vietnam. To a large extent, the opportunity to engage in such an unusual activity was beyond the volition of the ship's commanding officer or operational commander.

Successful competition for battle-efficiency awards on a ship such as the USS *Walden* necessitated the construction of an immensely complex collection of records. The routine collection, production, and use of such records constituted one essential feature of the everyday activities of this organizational setting. Not all pieces of paper were regarded as being of equal importance, as we shall see. But, in one way or another, all of the paperwork collected and produced on the ship was seen as a part of the everyday working routine of the persons doing it. Personnel were typically evaluated in part by their ability to produce such documentation. The importance of a given report or other form of documentation is sometimes said to lie in the necessity for persons in high governmental positions to be informed about the operational status and battle readiness of the ships in the navy. But competent members in the lower echelons also understand that these reports also represent the organizational acumen of those producing them.

ACCOUNTS OF BATTLE EFFICIENCY FOR NAVAL GUNFIRE SUPPORT

Before deployment for its WestPac cruise, generally six to seven months in duration, the ship's personnel use a variety of inspections, drills, and exercises to construct their readiness. These preparations include a variety of predeployment inspections intended to insure that the ship, its personnel, and its materials are in satisfactory condition. The inspections and exercises, however, are also counted as fulfilling the requirements for the battle-efficiency awards. Personnel of the USS *Walden* called this "killing two birds with one stone."

Upon arriving in the West Pacific, when the ship was said to have chopped into the command of the operational commander of the Seventh Fleet, there were a variety of training sessions and briefings to familiarize everyone with the activities of the Vietnam conflict. During these discussions, those personnel permanently stationed in the West Pacific brought to the ship a variety of "Op Orders," which detailed the rules and procedures governing the activities of military units in the West Pacific. Op Orders may include detailed instructions for what will constitute compliance with an assigned mission. These missions include "plane guard," when a destroyer is assigned to an aircraft carrier to rescue any downed pilots; "search and rescue," which covers instances when the ship is detached for searching and/or rescuing a pilot lost in the ocean due to hostile fire or accident; "electronic intelligence," which includes instructions on how to monitor various electronic transmissions within a given geographical area; "antisubmarine warfare," which includes instructions for detecting and/or following enemy submarines; and naval gunfire support.

The USS *Walden* and similar ships were among those frequently used for providing naval gunfire support to ground and air forces in Vietnam. Three kinds of missions were classified as falling under the category of naval gunfire support. The first and most frequent was an "indirect firing mission." On a typical indirect firing mission, the ship would receive instructions on the locations and coordinates of targets or target areas within Vietnam. These targets were provided by a "spotter" who could be located in a small aircraft or on the ground. The ship would engage in firing missions at the direction of the spotter. These indirect firing missions were not in support of any American or Allied Forces in Vietnam. Closely associated with an indirect firing mission, the ship could be assigned "Harassment and Interdiction," which meant that the ship was provided targets on which to fire during the night at its own discretion. These

"H & I missions" also were not in the support of any American or Allied Forces, but were typically directed at areas near the coast where the Viet Cong were known to frequent. The third type of mission was known as a "direct firing mission." These assignments were rare, and the instructions for them were delivered on a situation-to-situation basis depending on the exigencies of a tactical advance by ground forces. Being assigned to a direct firing mission carried very great prestige for the "tin-can navy." This meant that one was firing in direct support of ground forces which afforded an unparalleled opportunity for the ship to demonstrate the accuracy and expertise of its gunnery operations. For a ship successfully to engage the enemy was typically sufficient for the awarding of some sort of commendation to the ship and its personnel, perhaps even the receipt of the Navy Unit Commendation Medal.

Upon arriving in the "battle zone" of Vietnam, a ship usually reported in to the task force commander. He controlled the movements and assignments of ships within a given geographical area; that is, within a subdivision of the battle zone. He was typically stationed aboard an aircraft carrier whose movements would revolve around a geographical point (such as "Point Yankee"), which, in reality, "moved" on a day-to-day basis to avoid enemy detection. On being detached by the task force commander for a shore bombardment assignment, a ship would steam to the designated area to report to the operational commanders located ashore in Vietnam. There were four areas designated in Vietnam: I Corps, II Corps, III Corps, IV Corps.

The officers and relevant gunnery personnel of the ship usually would meet with the various persons designated as "spotters" for that area on arrival. The spotters' task was to assign the ship an individual firing mission and to report to the ship the results of that mission. A spotter could be located on the ground, called a "ground spotter," or could be the pilot of a light single-engine aircraft, called "FACS." During this meeting, the spotters would inform shipboard personnel about the nature of their task, the kind and nature of targets to be fired on, and the nature of the geographical area (with special notes for any pertinent navigation information, any information about threats or contingencies one might expect while "on the gunline" in that area, and information pertaining to the coordination of the firing missions with other routines). Such routines included departing from an inland or off-shore station to an area further out at sea for the purposes of making water, dumping trash, or conducting underway replenishments with supply, fuel, or ammunition ships. These departures, necessary to maintain operational readiness, were often needed daily. Also, high ranking ship's officers informed spotters about the degree of training and experience of the shipboard personnel in fulfilling gunnery missions and perhaps about any special needs that the ship might have. The assignment of a ship to a shore bombardment mission was often strenuous for its personnel. They would often be required to remain at their battle stations for 16 to 20 hours a day. The typical period of time a ship was assigned to firing missions was 14 days.

Spotters usually informed the gunnery personnel that they would be firing on known enemy targets that were recorded in intelligence reports sometimes two to three weeks old. Such targets were usually designated as "base camps," "infiltration routes," "bunkers," "supply depots," "staging areas," "trails," "tree lines," and so on. Targets also were classified by several residual categories. One category was called an "area target," which meant the ship would fire into a specified area, but at no specific target. Another was a "target of opportunity," designed to include those rare occasions when an enemy unit may initiate some sort of firing action against a ship. With the exception of the Tonkin Gulf Incident and one other incident in 1966, destroyers rarely engaged fire with such targets of opportunity. But, as we shall see below, targets of opportunity could be used for other purposes.

During the initial briefings, spotters would also inform shipboard personnel about the relevant linguistic categories to report "battle damage assessment" for the firing missions. For example, upon completion of the firing of the specified number of "rounds" or "salvos" into a given area, spotters would indicate to the ship via radio transmission that one "infiltration route" had been "neutralized." Spotters would also inform the gunnery personnel about the current procedures for a "harassment and interdiction" mission. For these, the ship would receive a listing of targets during the latter part of a given afternoon and would be directed to fire on them during the night at the ship's discretion. Since "H & I" missions occurred at night, spotters reported battle damage assessment as, for example, that one "infiltration route" had been "interdicted."

The procedures discussed below were usually followed for a typical firing mission. At the beginning of the day, ship's personnel would contact the shore-based director of the firing mission via radio-telephone transmission on a preestablished frequency. After assuring that radio-telephone contact was established, the shore-based commander would then inform the ship when the spotter (who would direct the daily firing missions) would be airborne. When airborne, the spotter would establish radio contact with the ship on the same frequency and would transmit a listing of the geographical coordinates for the targets. The spotter would then direct the calls for fire at given targets. Calls for fire typically included the numerical designation of the target, a brief description (for example, a "base camp"), and its geographical coordinates. He would also instruct the ship about the type of ammunition to be used for a given target, for example, whether it was to be high explosive (HE), variable time fuse (VT), or "willy peter" (white phosphorous). The spotter then directed the ship to fire and also gave instructions regarding how many rounds of ammunition were appropriate to "neutralize" or "interdict" the target. Upon completion, the spotter would then fly over the target area and report the battle damage assessment. This assessment was then recorded, or "logged," and these records were accumulated throughout the day, or given period of firing, to construct the relevant reports. Such reports, detailing the successful completion and effectiveness of a ship's firing missions, were then transmitted to various task force, task group, and shore-based commanders.

REDEFINING BATTLE DAMAGE ASSESSMENT

For the most part, these procedures were sufficient for the practical purposes of completing a given firing mission.

Ambiguities of the procedures or certain situations that emerged but were not yet covered by any of the formal rules were ironed out between the shipboard personnel and the spotters during informal meetings. The procedures allowed for the spotter to designate a given area as a target, to direct the movements of the ship in completing a call for fire, and to provide battle damage assessment.

In spite of the clarity and explicitness of these procedures, however, there were many occasions when the spotter was unable to provide damage assessment. There were a variety of reasons for this: bad weather, the loss of fired rounds (which could result from navigational difficulties of the ship, an error or misunderstanding in the transmission of target coordinates, and other factors), and especially the inability of the spotter to detect battle damage through the dense jungle foliage. Before illustrating how some of these contingencies were managed, the following comments by one of the *Walden*'s officers (the officer responsible for submitting the official reports of the ship's gunnery missions) illustrate the general importance of battle damage assessment on missions such as these:

Author: Where did you get the information for the reports? I mean, how did you get it from the spotter?

S: From CIC [the ship's Combat Information Center].

Author: And where did they get it from?

S: From the spotters over the voice circuit. The firing was always controlled from CIC. For example, the spotter would say, 'good shoot, you got four bunkers, two hamlets, and five grave stones [laughs].

Author: Well, here, let's take this. Assuming that what came over the voice circuit was accurate, then...

S: Now that's one thing you can't assume, you know. They didn't care, they'd say – you know we talked to those spotters at the briefings – they'd say, they'd give you six bunkers if you shot up a mile of beach.

Author: Why? What did they...

S: Why? Because they had to; it was written in the regulations that damage assessment will be given at the completion of each mission. So even if there wasn't any damage, they'd give you some, because they had to justify – eventually the ship had to justify sending 300 shells onto a beach only to come back with no damage. I mean, no damage? The Type Commander is going to want to know why am I spending 18,000 dollars a shell, or whatever it is, and why are you firing 300 of these shells against no target? So they had to justify their sending rounds in there by faking some damage assessment. You follow me? You understand this?

Author: Yes.

S: They do the same thing with the aircraft carriers. Same thing. In other words, these planes take off at a monumental cost for an air strike, just like the B-52's from the shore facilities. They *have* to, they *have* to come back with significant damage. Otherwise their funds will be slashed. In other words, that's money. Damage is money. So, in order to get the money, if they don't have any real damage they gundeck it. Spotters do it; they do it all the time. In other words, take this. I fire a shell onto a beach. That shell makes a crater. The next shell hits that crater. That's one bunker destroyed. That's common; it's just accepted as common knowledge. It's common knowledge yet nobody ever says anything about it, right up through the Type Commander. It's the only way they can continue to fire shells and justify it. You read the news reports, don't you?

Author: Yes, I've gotten these...

S: Everyone knows it. He [the Type Commander] knows that it's the only way he can continue to get money from the government, from Congress. He can only justify it if he can show that shells are being fired at lucrative targets.

This comment documents the following: (1) the perceived importance attributed to battle damage assessment for recording one's success on a given gunnery mission; and (2) the black-and-white (or dichotomous) nature of the recording categories used by the members for ordering this feature of their work.

The following comments document one example of an instance in which the members' understandings of the formal procedures, even as elaborated through the ironing out processes of the informal briefings, are insufficient for preparing them for all of the contingent circumstances that they encounter in actual occasions. A former Gunnery Officer of the *Walden* comments:

> One time, I don't remember whether we had just arrived on the gun line in a particular area, or whether we'd been firing there for a couple of days, but anyway, this time we ran into a green spotter. This was his first time out although we didn't find this out until a couple months later in [the Philippines]. It was our first mission of the day, I think, and he came over the phone and said, due to the dense foliage, he couldn't give us any [battle damage] assessment. The Old Man [the Captain] told me to ask him again, to tell him that we *had* to have damage, but the spotter repeated the same thing again, that he couldn't give us any. Well, the Captain got on the circuit and gave a call to the spotter's CO [Commanding Officer] and said, very to the point I thought, no damage assessment for our rounds, and we pick up our marbles and go home. He didn't say it exactly that way, of course, but that was the message. Following this, we could hear the spotter's CO get on the same circuit, and he told him to fly a little lower over the target once again, to see if he couldn't find a few bunkers. The spotter could hear all of this, of course, and by this time he knew what it was all about. He found some, too.

The formal rules and procedures typically used for a given shore bombardment mission may not provide for all contingent circumstances. Such constructions of the organization *not only* implicitly assume a fully socialized organizational actor; they also assume that such organizational socialization includes more than merely being able to perform a given task. In this case, such competence includes knowing the various structures of relevance of *others* situated at diverse points within the organization and knowing exactly how one's specialized competence fits in with that of others. In this example, even if we assume that the airborne spotter had been competently trained to do the "spotting" aspects of his job, we can also see learning the expectations and structures of relevance of many others situated at other points, which is an equally crucial feature of organizational competence. As the construction of any large social order, such as that of the United States Navy or Vietnam conflict, depends necessarily on individuals' perceptions of the relevant features of the environment that constitute the social reality of that organization, such constructions are fundamentally problematic, even to people who are old hands at this sort of activity. Thus, when the Commanding Officer of the USS *Walden* redirected the attention of the spotter to the target area, we can see that competent members may use the procedures of the organization to indicate to others that such perceptions are "intended" or "called for" in the first place: their relevance is established reflexively by referring to the formal constructions of rules, procedures, and so on.

The following comments illustrate some of the features involved in an organizational education or competence and also some of the many problematics of generating the type of "knowledge" seen as relevant for successful gunnery missions. These are the comments of a navy officer who was stationed for one year with various United States Marines and ARVN (Army of the Republic of [South] Vietnam) forces as a ground spotter.

Author: I've already had a number of talks with people on various ships about their side of shore bombardment, and now I'd like to get the story from the other side, so to speak. I'd like to hear about shorbom from a spotter's point of view.

S: The whole show was a charade, strictly an exercise in you-scratch-my-back-and-I'll-scratch-yours. I'd give calls for fire, the ship would throw out a few salvos, and I'd give them a couple of bunkers, or whatever. It wasn't only a case of *them* needing some justification for firing, but so does the spotter, that is *me*. Took me some time to realize that, couple of weeks or a month maybe, but I soon realized where our bread was buttered.

Author: Now wait a minute, Bill, it doesn't even sound plausible that the whole thing was a charade. There's got to be more to it than that, I mean, what was the story with the targets? Were some of them erroneously plotted? Was the terrain so bad that you couldn't be sure of the coordinates? Were you always too far away to give an accurate assessment? I mean, there's got to be more to the story than that . . . .

S: Yeah, well, for one thing, well, I guess I was a bit oversimplifying with that first remark. It is much more complicated than that of course. Here, let me start at the beginning. Oh gee, okay, [pause] where did we get the targets in the first place? Now that makes a difference right off. First of all, all of the targets came from two places and were always two to three weeks old. Sometimes, every once in a while you'd get a target that was a couple of days old, that depending on what type of target it was. Well, it depended on a number of things, actually. Anyway, okay, we got our targets either from ARVN intelligence or reconnaissance units or patrols who'd stumbled across some VC bunkers or whatever, and they either didn't have the muscle to destroy it themselves, or didn't want to give their position away for some reason. So they'd give us the coordinates over the radio, or sometimes in a written report of some kind. The second source was the [indigent peasants on the payroll for supplying information for US or ARVN forces]. Now, in the case of the ARVN. Well, okay, I should say this. There were actually many more sources where we could get our targets: support planes flying over an area where they had been engaged by ground fire, gunboats, all sorts of sources. The ARVN and [the peasants] were the two major ones, though. Now, in the case of the ARVN – or any other military unit for that matter – the reports and coordinates were usually more or less accurate. By more or less I mean that they were as accurate as you could expect under the circumstances. In the case of [the peasants] you couldn't ever be sure of the exact location of the target; well, sometimes you could see them, but many times you couldn't, and we always wondered if about half the time whether there was anything there at all. Let's face it, that was their livelihood, at least for some of them.

Author: You mean that some of the peasants could get away with faking their sightings of VC camps or whatever?

S: No, not exactly. Sometimes there would be some way to check out the reports; in other situations there wasn't. It depended on a number of things, such as what area you were in. There was one hell of a lot of difference between the hills of 'eye corps' [I Corps] and all of that elephant grass the three-corps, you know what I mean? . . . Anyway, none of the [peasants] could've gotten by with any kind of complete fake job, but it was possible every now and then, and I'm sure many of them knew it. Anyway, I'd go out for shorbom missions and, let's face it, half the time I couldn't see the damn target even when figuring out the coordinates wasn't any trouble. Like most of those so-called bunkers were underground, remember, and who in the hell can pick out what was called a quote infiltration route unquote in a four canopy jungle when you're perched on top of some damn hill? And, of course, that's even easier than down in three-corps where you don't even have that many hills. Almost none, in fact.

Author: Now was it this way for all your spotting? I mean, is this peculiar to shore bombardment, or is the same thing true when you're spotting in company with some troops or ground forces?

S: Oh, that's different; that's a much different story altogether. No, it's not the same at all. I thought you just wanted to know about shore bombardment?

Author: Yes, let's stay with shore bombardment for the
moment. Let's see, so far you've mentioned that
the geographical area makes a difference in the
origin of the intelligence report. Anything else?

S: I guess I should've said that at the beginning.
The situation is completely different when you are
working with some troops. I was just talking about
shore bombardment with the ships, and I personally never had any experiences where I directed a
call-for-fire from a ship in support of ground troops.
Good God, heaven forbid. Anyway, when I first got
to Vietnam I'd only had my training, no previous
experience. The spotting in [the Philippines] was
the most realistic, but it still didn't prepare me
for anything like Vietnam. In the Philippines all
of our training was really more or less without
difficulty. I mean, we worked on the major problem of trying to give the correct spots [recom-
mendations to the ships for its fire control solution
of the computer] to the ships, and it never even
dawned on me that you'd ever have any trouble
finding the target *in the first place!* In Vietnam,
however, or in the real world, as they say, it was
much different than firing at [an island off the
coast of Southern California], or even in the Philippines. Most of the time I wasn't too sure where
the target was, anyway, and not that they were all
visible, anyway, understand, and so if the ship sent
a couple of salvos in the general area of where *I
thought* the target was, then I'd report back to
them they'd destroyed the target. As I said before, that was the name of the game. . . . If a given
ship got a lot of damage they'd send us a letter
of commendation through the chain of command,
and we'd do the same. . . .[1]

REDEFINING THE TARGET

Although naval gunfire support is widely acclaimed for its
accuracy among people in the various branches of the mili-

tary, such accuracy is highly dependent on the capability of ascertaining one's navigational position while either at anchor or at sea. When a destroyer conducted its naval gunfire support missions while at anchor, ascertaining its true navigational position was usually no problem. An exception to this was when the firing missions were located at the western edge of the four corps area, where the shoreline appeared very ambiguously on one's navigational radar and where there were few other geographical markings (such as islands) that could be used for establishing one's position. When a ship conducted its missions while steaming at low speeds, usually off shore at a distance of two to four miles, an accurate determination of true navigational position was more difficult, especially when weather made radar readings ambiguous and vague. To some extent, at least, such difficulties were seasonal; positions were more difficult to establish during the monsoon season.

The formal procedures of naval gunfire support did not provide for the possibility that a ship would fire at a target and miss it. If a ship had indicated that it was on station and ready to respond to the spotter's call for fire, then it was presumed that the target would be hit. Of course, there were many instances when the rounds fired did not hit the target exactly. On these occasions the spotter would inform the gunfire support vessel that they should check their solution (indicating that he desires certain recalculations of the inputs into the shipboard fire control computer – called a "spot"). Then the spotter would redirect the ship to fire additional rounds or salvos at the corrected target location. During those rare instances when a ship was firing in direct support of American or Allied ground forces, such recalculations were frequent and of great importance. It was understood by shipboard gunnery personnel that when firing in direct support of ground troops, it would be necessary to recalculate the computer solution several times for a given firing mission. This would mean that the ship's criterion of success for the battle efficiency awards, that is, the number of shells expended per target, would rise during these kinds of missions. But, on the other hand, this apparent cost was perceived to be offset by the greater importance of these missions in support of ground troops. On the more frequent indirect firing missions, which were not in direct support of ground troops, however, such recalculations were thought to constitute a self-labeling of one's command as lacking expertise in gunnery, or as incompetent. The reason for this was that shipboard personnel did not think that it was fair for the airborne spotter to request them to increase the number of shells expended per target when it could never be determined with certainty that the initial rounds' or salvos' inaccuracy had been due to a poor navigational fix, to inadequate computer inputs, or perhaps to inaccurate information supplied to the ship by the spotter himself.

Given such contingencies, there were often occasions when fired rounds of ammunition were "lost." In addition to the reasons, listed above, this could also happen as a result of human error, for example, when a spotter was looking for the rounds to engage target #3 and the ship was still firing at target #2. During times such as these, the spotter then redirected the ship to fire on the target that had been intended in the first place. On board the ship, to account for these rounds for one's battle efficiency reports shipboard personnel routinely used the category "target of opportunity" to indicate that their rounds had indeed fallen on target. By using this category, the members of the USS *Walden* systematically avoided the necessity of averaging the lost rounds into the overall calculation that would indicate number of shells expended per target, the operative criterion of competition for the battle efficiency award vis-à-vis the other ships in the division or squadron. A former gunnery liaison officer of the USS *Walden* comments on this procedure:

> Here's what I mean by 'lost rounds.' Now this wasn't too common, understand, but it wasn't rare either. That is, this was common if you ran into bad weather in four-corps, but other than that it wasn't too common. What happened here was that nobody knew what happened. I mean, we might be firing one day, perhaps we'd fire off a couple of salvos at a given target, wait for a couple of minutes, and the spotter would report back that he hadn't seen a damn thing. If the weather was no problem that

day, then my guess is that the spotter was looking at the wrong target, or maybe was doin' a little skylarking on the job. You have to understand this, though, that's only my side of the story. Jesus, I almost got into a fight over this one night in the Philippines. I was out drinking with a couple of spotters, and suggested that they were sometimes asleep at the switch, and one of them nearly clobbered me. From his opinion, he said [that when] such things like this happened it was all due to an incorrect input on board the ship. I must admit that's a possible answer, but it happened a little too often for me to accept it outright. . . . When we were in four-corps though, my God, the major problem was trying to figure out where we were. Sometimes the only definitive navigational fix would be forty or fifty miles from where we'd end up anchoring, and you know damn well that you cannot rely on that type of fix for any accuracy, unless you're just enroute somewhere, of course. . . . Over there [IV Corps], we'd often fire off several salvos which couldn't be spotted. If it didn't happen too often we'd log 'em on the same target, but if we had a pretty good idea that the trouble was with the spotter, then we'd use the old stand-by, target-of-opportunity. Why in the hell should we log in fifty rounds to destroy some measley bunker when the problem is the spotter who can't see over the elephant grass . . . you can't use that target-of-opportunity stuff too often, though, the Commodore's staff is pretty wise in seeing through that kind of thing.

These comments indicate that in situations in which one is accountable to various sets of rules and regulations of a large organization that do not seem to fit, or in situations in which the various rules or procedures may be in conflict with one another, the routine use of procedures that are sufficient for practical purposes most of the time may have to be modified or compromised in order to sustain the sense that the activities taking place within an organization are indeed a part of its unified program of action. These modifications to the procedures are sometimes deemed necessary by competent members when, in their judgments and reasoning, the goals or objectives of the organization at one time are deemed more important than other goals or other objectives of the organization. In this light then, the methodical use of the category "target of opportunity" is a kind of *minimax strategy* to construct the larger social order of the Vietnam conflict, one determined by the members' judgments of the priorities of the situation.

CREATING A TARGET

By using our commonsense notions of antecedent conditions, or cause and effect, the following reasoning might appear warranted. First, some feature of the environment defined as "a target" may be unproblematically perceived by competent organizational actors; that is, as an "objective feature" of that environment. Second, because of such an objective identification, and the concomitant knowledge that such entities are sometimes worthy of destruction, harassment, or interdiction, ships (or other military units) direct their gunfire at them. Third, since it is a target that one fires on, the effectiveness or efficiency of such an activity (however recorded or categorized) thus "reports on" (or "indexes") that activity. The following discussion will illustrate the limited utility of such commonsense notions for understanding these activities and will suggest the plausibility of the opposite sequence. That is, by desiring the submission of a certain kind of report on one's actions, rounds of ammunition are expended, which then define "the target." Stated differently, a target may become a target because it has been fired at, rather than being fired at because it was a target.

On one of the USS *Walden*'s deployments the following incident occurred. The *Walden* had been assigned shore bombardment missions for three or four periods of approximately two weeks each and had received many letters of commendation attesting to its expertise during these missions. It was commonly thought by many on the *Walden* that during this deployment the *Walden* had been assigned to more firing missions (than any other ship in the division or squadron), had successfully engaged more enemy targets, had expended fewer rounds of shells per target, and had generally gained wide recognition as a "Can-Do-Tin-Can" among military forces within the area. Accounts of the *Walden*'s successes had been trumpeted in various newspaper stories and press releases. Among those people who were interested in the competitive spirit of such activities, many thought the ship had demonstrated far greater expertise than two of the remaining three ships within the division. It was thought that there remained only one competitor (at least within this division) for the squadron battle efficiency award, the USS *Huff*.

The USS *Huff* was reported to have expended 3750 rounds of ammunition in support of American and allied forces in Vietnam as it departed from its final mission in the area. It had also established a reputable record for gunnery expertise. On the last day of its final assignment as a naval gunfire support ship, the USS *Walden* gunnery personnel determined that the ship had expended a total of 3952 rounds of ammunition at the conclusion of its final mission. Afterwards, when he learned of the total, the Commanding Officer of the *Walden* radioed the shore-base commander of the II Corps area in which the ship was located and requested that he designate an "area target" into which the *Walden* could "unload" 49 additional rounds of ammunition. The *Walden*'s Commanding Officer said to the II Corps Commander that such a designation was called for in order to "remove potential dangerous ammunition from the handling rooms." But he indicated to shipboard personnel that he wanted the *Walden* to be the only ship in the division to expend more than 4000 rounds of ammunition for the deployment. The shore-based commander (or his representative) designated such an "area target," and 49 additional rounds were expended into this area. For accounting purposes, it was recorded that 49 rounds had been "on target" for this "area target," one of the officially recognized residual categories mentioned previously. The *Walden*'s Gunnery Officer at the time commented on this occasion:

> So we unloaded the 49 rounds in some rice paddy or whatever. It wasn't any big deal really, wasn't any more of a waste of ammunition than those H & I [Harassment and Interdiction] missions, I'm sure. From my point of

view, it saved Second [Division] a lot of work. That's when accidents happen, having to strike below [return the shells to the magazines] ammunition after everyone is tired as hell and wants to rack it [go to bed]. So who knows, maybe unloading those rounds saved us from something that could've been worse. Anyway, the XO [Executive Officer] sure got a lot of mileage out of it in the plans of the day from then on, extolling the heroic feats of the so-called *Walden* Warriors, oh, my God, well, anyway, the XO had everyone thinking that we were the heroic warriors of Vietnam even though no one ever thought so before, when we were actually doing it.

In this situation, then, it can be seen that the formal organizational program can be used by the members as a sort of "secular canopy," or symbolic superstructure, under which the various activities taking place within the organization may be subsumed. In this illustration, the formal rules may be used in a systematic fashion to manage certain contingencies for which the formal schema could not possibly provide in its literal usage, such as the promotion and/or maintenance of the esprit de corps, or collective consciousness, of the USS *Walden* as an integral fighting unit. In situations such as these, the creation of an additional target can be seen to promote the members' sense of accomplishment in their tasks and even a sense of pride in having done them well.

REDEFINING THE RELEVANCY OF A MISSION

The prescriptions of the formal rules and the everyday use of them deemed no considerations more important than the fulfillment of a battle-related mission. There could be exceptions to this, although they were infrequent. The only exceptions accorded any "legitimacy" included equipment casualties to the ship's battle capabilities of one sort or another, or a serious accident (such as a fire). On the other hand, it was also widely known that the Commanding Officer is charged with the overall responsibility for the safety of the ship's personnel. The imputed importance of battle-related missions and the general responsibility of the Commanding Officer typically involved no conflict. On one occasion, however, the Commanding Officer of the USS *Walden* broke off a gunfire support firing mission and ordered his ship to sea. From his perspective, the perceived threat endangering the ship possessed a greater priority than the gunnery mission to which the ship was then assigned. The officer who was the Public Affairs Officer at the time commented on this situation.

S: We had one situation where we broke off a mission. We were anchored in the Saigon River where we had been firing for several days, between unreps [replenishments of supplies, fuel], that is. We, I'd say we were about three miles inland from Vung Tau [on the coast]. All of a sudden, and I had the watch at the time, the Old Man orders me to haul-in the anchor, and we steamed out of there all-ahead-full, you know, like twenty-seven knots. Broke off the mission just like that. Now the cause of all this, or supposedly, at least, was the Captain spotted a swimmer in the water. You know what that water's like? Like, man, first of all it's so damn muddy you couldn't see *anything* if you had to under the surface. And, second, there are so damn many jellyfish in that river no swimmer could ever survive it [intended as an exaggeration]. And not one person saw it other than the Captain, not one of the lookouts on the bridge, nobody on the main deck, the signal bridge, nobody, anywhere. But the Captain says he saw a swimmer, and so we give it all-ahead-full and put out to sea. Not only that, here, get this, he furnished a complete description of him [the swimmer] right down to the black shorts and black web belt. You believe that, a black web belt! So I went ahead and wrote up all of the news releases on it, two copies to the, well, practically to everyone in the world, the full shot, including the black web belt. Since we'd broken off a mission, our primary mission over there, we really had to do a job in

> the releases. The whole thing was completely gundecked from my opinion. There just ain't no way you could convince me there could've been a swimmer in that water, especially since I was standing right there. I must say though, the Captain, I don't think he was lying or anything like that. I actually think he thought he saw a swimmer, really...

Author: How do you explain it then? Was he...

S: I'm not really sure I can. [Pause] One thing that's related here, I think, oh hell, I don't know. Well, one thing, and I saw this with two different CO's, one thing is that that old saw about, you know, the general regulations, about the Commanding Officer being ultimately responsible for anything and everything that happens on the ship. I think it suddenly takes on a different slant when you're doing something like anchoring in the Saigon River, when the whole show could come to an end at any minute. It spooked me a couple of times, believe me. The only thing I know for sure is that I'm glad I didn't have that responsibility. If I'd been in his shoes, maybe I'd be seeing kamikazes...!

The above comments warrant our interest for several reasons. First, like the preceding illustration, they suggest that an assignment to a given mission is not one of the "givens" of the situation, but is fundamentally grounded in the members' choices, something involving situated judgments related to other priorities or structures of relevance. Second, these comments raise the issue of "the public-affairs angle" of the Vietnam gunnery mission. Decontextualized information often becomes reified as reality when the public hears, sees, and reads it as news. In the same interview, this officer commented further on this aspect:

S: ...now the Battle E, that's where you get it, in Vietnam, or at least the last couple of years that's the case. It's different than the Operations E, and the ASW E, and so forth. I think there are four possible E's all together which any given ship could win, depending on the readiness of each department. But the Battle E . . . that's only for one ship per squadron, and that's where my public affairs work came in. I wrote a story each day describing each day's missions. These weren't the same as the reports of the targets, rounds, and all that, though. I did usually glance at those to find out how many rounds we'd fired that day, and would usually begin with something about that. Not always, though. But the stories I wrote, the stories, they always left the ship at 1800 each evening in a message format and were always some kind of story about the firing that day. Here's an example, for example after telling what kind of mission it was, I might then go on to write a paragraph or two about some Seaman Deuce in Mount 53, and what he'd done that day to contribute to the day's mission.

Author: Were these always cleared by the Captain?

S: Oh, sure, anything leaving the ship in message form was approved by the Captain.

Author: Did he ever tell you what to write? In the stories?

S: No, never. He'd never tell me what to write, he'd just approve 'em. It was the XO. He'd completely . . .

Author: Did he edit the stories?

S: Sure. In fact, there were many stories that I couldn't recognize after he'd edit them and they went out. I'd see the . . .

Author: What do you mean? In what ways did he edit them?

S: Editing would be a euphemism for what he did to them. [Laughs] Completely rewrote them.

Author: Like what?

S: Well, in one case, let's say I'd write a perfectly good paragraph about Seaman Smith in Mount 53, what he'd done that day, what he said about it, stuff like that. What Seaman Smith would actually say about it, of course, would be unprintable. But I would create some statement that would make him out to be a nice guy, you know, a nice guy doing a dirty job in a gun mount, something like that. Usually pretty trite. Would've earned a flat F in any freshman composition class. [Laughs] And then, when I'd see the final draft of it after it would come out and I wouldn't be able to recognize any of it.

Author: What do you mean? Was it just a matter of style?

S: Well, to some extent. The XO would always begin by saying something like "The blazing guns of the *Walden* Warriors once again obliterated so many enemy targets. . . ." – you know, bullshit like that. He'd rewrite the whole story; not one sentence I'd recognize.

Author: You mean just a different style or the content?

S: Both. You know, standard naval sentence structure, standard inflation. All of it was inflated, to play it up bigger. . . .

Author: But did he actually change any of the facts, I mean like the type of mission or number of rounds, anything like that?

S: Oh no, at least not that I remember. It wasn't that kind of story, it wasn't. . . .

Author: Well, what was it used for? I mean, what was the use of writing them in the first place?

S: The use? Just publicity. Just publicity for the command, for the stateside papers. You've seen 'em, especially in [local paper].

These comments document another feature of many members' understandings within a large-scale (or bureaucratic) organization; namely, even when the formal rules are combined with the various kinds of practical arrangements within a setting, these various combinations rarely define but one objective environment of objects (or meanings). That is, as the comments illustrate, many members are very aware that their organizational activities are relevant (and in different ways) to different audiences. What constitutes the "objective facts" for one audience (as in a report of battle effectiveness within the organization) are not necessarily the same "objective facts" for another audience or for a different report (as in a news release). The great difficulty in transcending these barriers between the public and private are perhaps appropriately illustrated by the comments of one officer (cited earlier), when he began his account with the term "charade," readily admitted this as an "oversimplification," and proceeded to talk for several hours about the various activities and contingencies to which "charade" had previously referred.

This raises another set of issues: the various attempts by many of the members to explain, justify, or bring any sort of other rational understanding to their own activities. In several of the interviews conducted during this research, some of the members commented to the effect that some activities they had seen, witnessed or experienced, had rendered problematic the idea of "objective facticity." In two of the interviews, two different members tried to describe how they saw their own activities at the time they had accomplished them within the context of some practical activity and why they were subsequently led to "reinterpret" them in light of new knowledge or differing values. At one level, this is only to say that one's personal experiences (or personal biography) are continually renegotiable. But the members themselves also found such events problematical. They harbored uncertainty long after the practical accomplishment of their various tasks. A member comments:

I first arrived on the *Walden* in the fall of 1964. My first billet was Second Division [Gunnery Officer], where I spent my first twelve, maybe fifteen months. I'd never been to any one of the gunnery schools; a Boot Ensign in every sense of the word. During that first year, or however, I think it was a little over a year, actually, I became absolutely convinced that those guns couldn't hit the broad side of a barn under absolutely perfect conditions. I felt stupid as hell, but also thought it was quite a challenge to learn the system [the fire control system or various computer inputs, which controlled the movements of the guns]. I don't have to say that all during this time, however long it was, we never ran any of the really competitive exercises, had spent the whole first cruise without ever firing a shot. I really became quite fascinated with the whole system. [At this point, a long discussion of the various complexities of determining the various inputs to the gunnery systems on the ship]. . . .

Anyway, it wasn't until after I'd moved over to ASW [Officer] twelve or fifteen months later that [the guns] made a believer out of me. It happened one day during an air shoot; the first couple of rounds knocked off the sleeve [the metal target at the end of a long wire streamed behind a jet aircraft], and the rounds started to climb right up the wire towards the jet 'til he broke it off. Man, from my experiences as Weps I would have never even put a hundred-to-one bet on anything like that happening; really made a believer out of me. . . . The entire second cruise [this officer made only two cruises on the *Walden*] when we did all of the firing I was just an observer. I just watched the whole show from ASW Control [adjacent to CIC] but didn't play any part myself. During the whole show, though, it never even entered my mind that those rounds might actually kill someone. I know that sounds stupid as hell to say, but it was true. I just didn't see it in those terms. Didn't see it, that is, until that last day, or at least it was on one of the last days, of our gunfire support missions, when the spotter reported three KIA's [killed-in-action] and four whiskeys [WIA, or wounded-in-action] among some other damage. God, I'll never forget that day. I was standing right there in the doorway to CIC when the message came over the circuit, and all of a sudden everyone in CIC broke into this incredible cheering and shouting. I was absolutely terrified, I mean absolutely terrified. All before in my life, or at least since college, I'd always thought of myself as an idealist, and here I was, I'd been there doing war without any sense that people were getting killed until that particular day. . . . Well, I won't bother you with all the gory details of all the agony I've gone through about that, but I must admit, I've become terribly cynical about the possibility of eliminating wars once and for all time.[2]

BATTLE EFFICIENCY REPORTS AS PROPAGANDA

Battle efficiency reports do not reflect the reality they claim to; but they do tell us about the reality of official reports, and especially the practical and meaningful context that informs the activities of making war a rational endeavor. There is no reason to assume that these reports are atypical of all other military reports, although we do not claim that this is actually the case. Other researches will either support or reject these findings. What is more important is how war appears when viewed from the perspective of the officers and men of the USS *Walden*. Their war was inextricably anchored in a context broader than the murky waters of Vietnam, although their activities were very much influenced by this context. They had to account for their warfaring skills and to document, in a form acceptable to superiors, that they were not only doing their jobs, but also were being successful, and helping the war effort. This was what counted, even if it meant dumping thousands of rounds of ordnance on targetable areas. It was irrelevant whether an independent observer might or might not confirm that there was a stockpile of enemy supplies, and that the target might or might not have actually been destroyed. That is only one reality. From the perspective of the *Walden*, however, the targets existed because there were good reasons for them to be there.

From these illustrations, we have seen that "battle damage assessment" may be defined as a social phenomenon for the purposes of constructing an account of it. Such definitions are fundamentally problematic due to the adult socialization processes upon which they depend, processes that are necessarily open ended. From the second example presented here, it is clear that a "target" as a social definition may be redefined when, as a product of members' judgments of the priorities or relevancies of the situation, such a reinterpretation is conceived as following the *intent* of the organizational rules. In the third example, it was argued that an alternative to the commonsense understandings of antecedent and consequential (or cause and effect) conditions provides a more plausible understanding of the definition and redefinition of "a target" as a social phenomenon. In this example, it was asserted that the formal schema of the organization may be used for *symbolic purposes* for which no conceivable set of rules could possibly provide in any adequate fashion, independently of how such constructions were "interpreted" or "strictly enforced." And in the final example, we have seen that the very presence of the organizational personnel at the scene of a given mission is itself a product of commonsense situations of choice and may be changed or revoked by the use of different rules, understandings, or features of the formal organizational program seen as relevant for the situation at hand. This is not to imply that all parties are equally powerful to realize their own individual choices within a given situation, but merely to indicate the fundamental datum for any empirically adequate sociological theorizing.

In the situations analyzed here, the practical tasks of completing accounts of battle efficiency were seen to require the cooperation and/or co-ordination of many variously situated persons, although such co-ordinations are rarely unproblematic. Since such accounts are as much a function of the various audiences who receive them as of those who initiate them, it makes little sense to argue that such accounts are "structurally determined." Moreover, competent organizational members may use differing conceptions of the "objective facts" relevant for a given audience. Constructing such accounts, we have seen, involves presenting the appearance of orderly organizational situations (presumably, what the report is taken to stand for) by the members. But such accounts may also gloss over certain situated contingencies of action that could not possibly be provided for in any formal program of rules and regulations. Any given account, therefore, is necessarily problematic to those constructing it because of their *incomplete knowledge* of the reactions of the audiences (or various persons to whom a given account is sent). The people making the report can never be sure that its recipients will understand such situated contingencies in a similar manner to the members' understandings at the time the report was made.

The significance of reports cannot be divorced from the context and meanings of those who will learn of them. Military personnel, for example, who are not on the scene and who are unfamiliar with the practicalities of off-shore bombardment and its relevance for personal and group recognition, competition, and the practical "way to do your job," will not look beyond the statistical and rhetorical "data." If so, they may interpret such reports in terms of their understanding of what hitting a target means. If this interpretation is not informed by the considerations noted throughout this chapter, the recipients will be deceived. However, this is not likely to happen since the career route and experience of most military superiors likely to receive and assess such information readily informs them about what happened. This is useful since it means that they can then use the reports to reward their subordinates off the coast of Vietnam. The reports can also be used to compete with other representatives of the armed services and to join their colleagues in arms by citing objective evidence that "we're giving them hell." To this extent, everybody benefits – except the public.

Passing on versions of reports to the news media further distorts the original context. Now the public, and especially persons unfamiliar with the relationship between shelling and spotting procedures, career mobility, and military public relations efforts, are likely to deduce that a target in the *Walden's* terms is a target in his or her own terms; that a hit from one perspective is a hit from all perspectives. Such misinformation cannot be construed as a lie; it is more correctly regarded as reports without context. This is why we claim that the context of the information process must be clearly delineated.

The implications of all this for warfare and citizen involvement are perhaps evident. For one thing, fighting a war is less a result of overt feelings of "genocide," "racism," and "capitalistic exploitation," although such notions may account for its early history, definition, and public acceptance of it. There are good organizational reasons for carrying on a war in a certain way; simply defeating the enemy does not guarantee positive recognition of performance and does not ensure career and professional awards. Only record keeping based on rational procedures and assumptions can do these things. Beating one's competition and documenting it may encourage accidental killings of both soldiers and civilians who find themselves in officially sanctioned target areas. This will be inevitable when war is waged for good organizational reasons.

Notes

1. Harold Wilensky has noted that similar problems occurred with the identification of targets during the Second World War, especially when "area bombing" was involved. See *Organizational Intelligence* (New York: Basic Books, 1967), pp. 25–28.
2. Because of the rather limited interests of the research, a disproportionate number of commissioned officers was interviewed during the research. This comment, then, is not intended to be representative.

15 Making Products Heroes: Work in Advertising Agencies[1]*

Janice M. Hirota

Copywriters and art directors in advertising agencies are the paradigmatic mass symbol-makers of our time. Known in their occupational world as "the creatives,"[2] these men and women select, alter, and orchestrate a myriad of ideas and images while fashioning vocabularies of sentiment and motive meant to persuade mass audiences: they write the slogans, shape the visual images, and formulate the stories for mass advertisements. The products of creatives' work are everywhere in people's daily rounds. On a typical day, for instance, a person might see on television dozens, if not scores, of little narratives, often complete with wholly constructed pitchmen ranging from dogs in trench coats to raisins sporting dark glasses, dramatizing products, people, or causes of every sort, from beer to haute cuisine, from experts or clowns to presidential candidates, from AIDS-prevention messages to recruitment appeals for the priesthood, from pro-choice to right-to-life campaigns; hear on television or radio the catchy tunes, up-beat jingles, easily memorable slogans, and diversely applicable tag lines that enter, for a time, the popular vocabulary ("You make America work and . . ."; "Where's the beef?"; "When you care enough to send the very best"; "Reach out and touch someone"; "Just say no"; "To capture the hearts and minds . . ."; or "To make the world safe . . ."); might notice on billboards and in store windows, on buses or in subway stations glimpses of interesting lives and enticing situations meant to grab the attention of passers-by; or, in perusing

---

* Published for the first time in this volume.

any one of hundreds of magazines, newspapers, or journals of opinion, encounter highly stylized but compelling images of how life can and perhaps ought to be lived. In short there are few areas of people's personal lives, and certainly few issues facing our society, that are untouched by advertising, by the work and techniques of what one might call experts with mass symbols.

This essay explores the occupational world of art directors and writers[3] in American advertising agencies. It examines the structure of their work, as well as the experiences, habits of mind, and the peculiar images of the world generated by that work.[4] Through an analysis of the links between advertising work, on one hand, and the products of that work, on the other – that is, mass-communicated symbols, slogans, stories, and images – this essay considers the meaning and process of mass symbol-making itself.

It is critical, first, to grasp the organizational framework and dynamic structure of creatives' work. The advertising world is divided, essentially, into three parts: clients, account management at the advertising agency, and creatives.[5] The client is the "advertiser,"[6] that is, the group, person, or corporation that has a product, service, idea, or image to be sold or promoted. Clients buy advertising; therefore agencies work for clients. Men and women in advertising use the term "client" in many ways. For instance, client can refer to the entire entity buying the advertising, such as Proctor & Gamble or General Motors; or it can refer to a particular product division of a large corporation, such as Tasters Choice Coffee or Chevrolet. Even more specifically, client refers to the particular person with whom one interacts at the corporation, as when one says: "The client called." Moreover, while the term is usually employed in its singular form, its referent can be either singular or plural, as well as male or female. Thus a client meeting might involve six corporate men and women who are, interchangeably, both collectively and individually referred to simply as "the client".

Among themselves, admen and -women usually use "client" as a term of reference even when personal names are well known. Such usage focuses attention on the institutional relationship between the advertiser and the agency. In particular, the term refers to the work relationship between occupational groups, a relationship seen by creatives to have structural similarities from person to person, product to product, corporation to corporation, and agency to agency. This focus on the work relationship helps reinforce in creatives the habit of mind that defines the client as client, regardless of the corporation or product at issue. In this sense creatives see advertising in terms of servicing clients and not in terms of promoting any particular product, idea, company, or brand name. Further, the term's anonymity cuts through the idiosyncracies of a particular project and points to the critical factor for creatives: clients buy and therefore have ultimate decision-making power over the advertising that creatives fashion.

Yet most clients, buried in their own substantive expertise, have no understanding of how interpretive expertise works. As a result clients often see advertising, along with public relations, as magic of a sort, an alchemy capable of transforming the deadening rounds of bureaucratic life and the prosaic products it produces into glittering, glamorous cultural symbols. Clients believe that striking advertising helps them in the market; but more importantly they know that dramatic public posturing bolsters employees' internal organizational identification, thus affording opportunities for those who can claim credit for the advertising to gain ground within their own world.

It is against this backdrop, underlined by creatives' general perceptions of clients' lack of taste, knowledge, or grasp of middle-America audiences, that creatives see decisions made that can deeply affect their own work and careers. The issue for them becomes, then, how to maintain creative autonomy within a framework wholly dependent on others' wishes. Creatives' relationships with clients are thus always potentially antagonistic.

As a result agencies generally have clients interact principally with the business side of an agency, that is, with the men and women in account management. The terms "account executives" and "account people" refer to everyone on the account side, a usage that suppresses the hierarchical rankings in account management departments. The typical organizational ladder is trainee, account executive managing one account, account supervisor managing several account executives, and then a general manager or vice president in charge of several supervisors.

Account executives act as the liaisons between agencies and clients. With clients, they determine the target market to be addressed and map out the best advertising strategy to capture that market, a plan that includes a description of previous ad campaigns; perceived differences between a client's product and rival brands; the desired marketing approach, usually based on market survey data, to find and exploit a particular market niche; profile of the target audience; an outline of the product characteristics or image to be stressed; and the exact sorts of advertisements to be produced.[7] Account executives then explain both the target market and strategy to the creatives involved. Eventually they return to the client to help sell the advertising that creatives produce.

Account executives have day-to-day contact with clients. They "coddle the client," "hold the client's hand," and, in general, do all that is necessary to keep the client "happy," including buffering the interaction between clients and creatives. This means that account executives protect clients from "unpredictable and temperamental" creatives. But it also means that they protect creatives from importuning, meddling, and anxious clients, although the latter role is not generally appreciated by creatives. Indeed, although account executives see themselves as representatives of business rationality, creatives generally see account people as clients' lackies because of their constant attentiveness to clients' needs and whims.

As it happens the peculiar economic exigencies of advertising agencies help explain such attentiveness. Typically, a client assigns a piece of business exclusively to one agency, an assignment that may include all the advertising for a particular product, or the trade advertising for a product division, or, again, the corporate advertising for a company.[8] In this sense an agency works for a client and the client commits itself for that piece of business to the agency. However, unless special arrangements are negotiated beforehand, clients do not pay agencies unless and until they buy particular advertisements, regardless of the number of hours agency personnel spend on mandated projects. Of course creatives and account executives continue to receive salaries whether or not the advertisements they make or broker are sold. But no one survives or flourishes for very long at an advertising agency unless they work on ads that clients buy. Moreover it is an axiom in advertising that all clients, even well-served ones, eventually take their accounts elsewhere, wreaking organizational havoc at agencies as they leave. Account executives hold clients' hands not only to rekindle clients' hopes in the magic of symbols, but also to establish the face-to-face human contact that alone might ensure some advantage over competitors in difficult times.

The creative side of an agency usually has a flatter organizational structure than the account side. Typically, the head of the creative department oversees all the agency's creative work. Below the head are the creative group heads or supervisors who manage a group of creatives. The number of group heads varies from agency to agency. So does the size of their groups, even within agencies, from those of less than 10 people to others of more than 50. Group size depends, among other factors, on the total size of the creative department, the size and number of clients at the agency, and on agency philosophy. Overall an agency creative head allocates clients and their projects to the creative group heads. Within a group the lines of authority are also relatively flat and, in general, creative teams receive assignments from and take work to their group head.[9]

The fusion of verbal and visual expertise in equal work partnerships stands at the core of work with symbols in advertising, and indeed of modern mass symbol-making itself. Within their groups creatives almost always work in teams of two, with one art director and one writer paired for any given project, following the workplace innovation instituted by the advertising firm Doyle Dane Bernbach.[10] Some creative pairings are permanent partnerships, so strong on occasion that when one team member leaves an agency the other leaves as well. But sometimes group heads shift creatives around according to the project, whether by whim or for administrative convenience. In such situations, since people work on more than one project at a time, creatives may have a number of different partners simultaneously.

Creatives' work typically proceeds in stages. Initially, upon receipt of an assignment, partners "bounce ideas around" or "play ideas off" each other in a spontaneous, free-associational way. Ideas, images, or phrases from one teammate trigger responses, ripostes, jokes, and amendments from the other in a quickly-paced open-ended exchange. Sometimes the product, the client, the team's bosses, the entire agency, as well as celebrities and other public personalities who might figure in future advertising for the product become objects of ridicule, caricature, or raucous and obscene satire. The established roles of art director and writer collapse, with the art director freely suggesting copy and the writer imagining sets, props, and other visual details. Sooner or later one of the partners voices or sketches out an idea that "takes off" and the team subjects this to a more tempered, searching critique.

If the idea survives, it is altered and refined until it becomes a "concept," that is, a guiding theme symbolically linking the product to the needs, desires, or fantasies of the targeted market audience. At this point the concept is presented to the group head and subjected to an elaborate approval process that I discuss in detail elsewhere.[11] Briefly, however, the approval process in an agency brings together account executives, clients, and creatives in an organizational crucible out of which emerges the advertising we see. The process moves forward through "presentations," first to agency account executives and then, if approved, to executives up and down the ladder at the client, during which creatives must convince others of their own creative talents and of the merit of their work.

Creatives see their work roles and partnerships as oases in the bureaucratic desert of the modern workplace. While others, including clients, agency account executives, and friends in corporations, live by fixed procedures, creatives make and break rules at will. While others must constrain their behavior and wear public masks concealing all emotions and intentions, creatives set their own schedules, dress as they wish, and express themselves openly and without fear, at least to their teammates. But because "creativity" is antithetical to the rationalizing thrust of the modern workplace, creatives must continually lay claim to their distinctive occupational identity, principally by appearing to be "creative".

Art directors and writers thus act in ways that enhance their social identities as people who are creative. Such self-presentation of creativity cannot, of course, be totally idiosyncratic, but must fit the prevailing social image of what it means to be a creative and of how creatives act. Thus some creatives have "tantrums," that is, emotional outbursts, ranging from loud arguments to destructive behavior. While the term suggests the contemptuous impatience and suspicion that a world based on self-control feels for irrational and childish behavior, such outbursts are not only generally tolerated, they are in fact expected, since tantrums help assert and define the creative persona. Thus an art director, in a fit of frustration over a client's demands, walks into an agency men's room and sprays graffiti all over the walls, ceiling, and stalls with a can of red paint. Or a writer physically throws herself across a doorway to block an account executive from taking unfinished work to a client. Another, for a similar reason, challenges an account executive to a wrestling match that ends up on the floor. Another screams at her group head because other writers are getting all the plum assignments. An art director yells at a bewildered client. A writer stomps out of a meeting with clients, slamming the door as he leaves; another dumps soup into a client's lap during lunch. Of course, if tantrums repeatedly obstruct work in an agency or permanently damage client relationships, whole careers can be jeopardized. Yet the limits for such behavior are broadly set and only rarely result in firings or even reprimands. Instead the very irrationality of extreme emotional displays becomes proof of creativity, in the sense of an unwillingness to subject oneself to the humdrum rationality of the business world. Of course most creatives do not have tantrums. But the reputation of those who do colors the occupational group of creatives as a whole.

Such lore circulates throughout the advertising work world. Each occupational group, of course, interprets such behavior differently. Since they hunger for the great burst of inspiration that makes them and their products famous, clients are likely to see tantrums as evidence of artistic genius. But account people see tantrums as the products of overly sensitive, unreliable, childish, and generally unpredictable natures that need to be controlled in order to accomplish the pragmatic tasks necessary to serve and retain clients. And creatives, even those who do not indulge in public emotional displays themselves or who label tantrum-throwers as unprofessional, subtly countenance such behavior by proffering exculpating accounts or by defining tantrums as expressions of free and open natures. Moreover, when tantrums are triggered by corporate attempts to tamper with creative work, they are always taken by creatives as evidence of the deep gulf between the standards of creative people and those of account people and clients.

Creatives also present public faces that set them apart from the conventional appearances typical of the business world. While account executives (called "the suits" by creatives) wear standard corporate uniforms – worsted wool suits, pima cotton shirts, four-in-hand foulards or floppy polka-dot bow ties, understated jewelry, wingtip shoes or sensible pumps, all in quiet, conservative colors – attire in creative departments runs the gamut from old sweaters and running shoes to bold-colored designer dresses, dramatic accessories, and handmade boots. The dressed-down attire is said to help creatives work in a relaxed, unencumbered way, while the high-fashion look is taken as evidence of creatives' avant garde taste, flair, and general adventurousness.

Office decor also proclaims creativity. Creatives' offices range from rarified to homey, from sleekly elegant to zany. One might see an extremely cluttered office with ceiling-high stacks of papers and a window shelf lined with pots of dead plants; or a stark, nearly-empty room, just a bare desk, one chair, and three desk lamps in a row in the middle of the floor with necks turned up so that the light reflects off the ceiling (creatives dislike direct fluorescent lighting, it is said); or an office with neon signs and the occupant's name in lights; an office featuring items adorned with flamingos, including coffee mug, lamps, statuettes, ashtrays, and framed prints; another similarly decorated with black scotties; and others with antique furnishings or starkly modern, polished glass-and-chrome pieces. Everywhere one sees other idiosyncratic touches: shelves lined with plastic models of plates of food; a stuffed armadillo or mounted moose heads; a rubber chicken, plucked and beheaded; props from past shoots, including a sign from a mock store named after the writer on the project; a baseball autographed by the Red Sox (this in New York); signs from restroom doors and street corners; large company logos for products the names of which resemble the surnames of creatives; rows of chopstick wrappers; wind-up toys, board games, and frisbees held in ready for hallway sport; license plates personalized with puns; and the usual array of snapshots (sometimes blown up to poster size) of children, pets, families, and, of course, of creatives themselves, especially when out on shoots in exotic locales.

Such crafting of public behavior and appearance advertises one's unique qualities to others and helps carve out the freedom from bureaucratic constraints necessary to symbol-making. Self as product entails a self-proclaiming stance whereby creatives fashion advertising contexts in which to dramatize their own personae, a paradigmatic instance of the self-referential quality of advertising work. Self as product means the use of dress, office decor, personal styles, and interactional behaviors to promote a creative persona. It also means, of course, self as hero of the stories that creatives promulgate and that make the round of agencies, stories that dramatize themselves as witty, adventurous, open men and women with glamorous, exciting lives.

In self-advertising the two sides of a self-promotional stance – as both fabricator and product – come together in the most critical role for creatives' success: that of salesperson. Selling oneself and one's ideas entails many overlapping public faces. These include a knack for entertaining clients with clever casual conversation; a graceful acceptance of being the focus of attention; a talent for thinking on one's feet; a willingness "to star" at client presentations, throwing oneself with verve into proposed commercials and dramatizing children, animals, experts, housewives, talking fruit, and celebrities alike. It also requires a pose that allows creatives simultaneously to mystify the "creative leap," logically "talk the client through the creative process," and emphasize the essential difference between creatives and others. As successful salespeople, art directors and writers must project creative personae but they must also know when and how to switch to more rational modes of discourse. Moreover the tactics of salesmanship are important to protect one's ideas without seeming to be obstinate, temperamental, or unreasonable. "Going to the wall" for one's ideas always entails career risks.

In all of this, "enthusiasm" and the ability to generate enthusiasm in different audiences is crucial. Enthusiasm is the social face of creatives' attitude toward themselves and their work. Enthusiasm means a generally up-beat, energetic self-presentation; a can-do optimism; great self-confidence; and zeal about advertising in general and the immediate project in particular. Enthusiasm means communicating and generating excitement about one's self and one's ideas. Art directors and writers know the value of projecting enthusiasm since they often argue that unless one is enthusiastic about one's own work – no matter what the product or who the client – no one else will be. It is not surprising, then, that subordinates highly value supervisors who can spark this kind of excitement. Such bosses, after all, not only recharge creatives with the emotional energy critical to their work but help them develop the guises necessary to keep others off balance.

At the same time art directors and writers generally take a cool, distanced stance toward the creative personae that they fashion, one tinged both with self-mockery and with the kind of gleeful thrill that accompanies thumbing one's nose at established conventions. In private they laugh uproariously at gawking prospective clients being given a tour of the creative warrens by account people who point out idiosyncratic office arrangements as evidence of the creativity that clients want in their advertisements. Or Sam and Harry, a famous pair of creatives, make a presentation on "The Creative Process" as part of an in-house training session for new account people. The creatives begin their talk, when suddenly a professional striptease artist dances through the audience to loud, brassy music. With exaggerated bumps and grinds, she flings articles of clothing into the audience of predictably clean-cut, conservatively dressed young men and women. She leaves the stage dressed only in pasties and G-string, amidst uncertain laughter, while Sam and Harry start to run a film that reveals, they say, the "real creative process". The film stars Sam and Harry, who walk toward the camera down a long empty corridor, their footsteps echoing loudly. The camera then follows them into a men's room where they enter adjoining stalls. The camera focuses steadily on the closed stall doors, while the partners carry on a muffled conversation through the walls. A short time later they emerge from the stalls and continue their indecipherable mumbling to each other as they wash their hands. The film concludes with Sam and Harry announcing that this is how they create award-winning advertising.

The performance warns future bureaucrats that all their efforts to rationalize creativity will come to naught. Moreover it celebrates the distinctive stance of ironic skepticism that writers and art directors take toward everything, even toward their own craft. Such a stance has its practical uses: it permits creatives to manipulate freely the trappings of the creative image to dazzle, outwit, or befuddle audiences as the situation requires, in order to sell themselves and their work to other creatives, account people, and clients alike.

Such ironic skepticism breeds a habit of mind essential for symbol-making work itself, namely a detachment that enables creatives to step back and observe dispassionately the foibles, mannerisms, public sentiments, and popular trends of social life for use in their advertisements. Cultivating the detachment of the social observer demands, of course, a high degree of self-rationalization, the systematic streamlining of self characteristic of all bureaucratic structures. Creatives' behavioral freedom in the workplace in comparison with account executives or corporate clients actually conceals this self-discipline at the core of their craft.

Creatives try to develop a methodical social attentiveness, one that continually forces them out of the rounds of their own milieux. Such detached social alertness underpins creative work in advertising, since one achieves resonance with mass audiences only by making advertisements "reflections of what life is like out there," that is, only by incorporating familiar and realistic elements into mass symbols. To this end creatives are alert to people's manners, gestures, and interactional activities. Wherever possible they eavesdrop on the conversations of people in different social classes, both to get a sense of their concerns and especially to hear their use of language. They watch people closely, particularly in public places such as airports and subways, to understand the subtle rules of crowd protocol or avoidance mannerisms. They go to trendy bars and museums with the explicit purpose of observing unusual behavior or dress, knowing that, in American society, today's idiosyncracy is tomorrow's orthodoxy. Some adventurously plunge into wholly unfamiliar activities such as hot-air ballooning, both to gain new experience and to meet people with different viewpoints. In their attentiveness to social activity, and perhaps especially in their willingness to enter new social worlds, creatives are commercial urban ethnographers of a sort whose subjects are the demeanor, idioms, interplay, and foibles of other people. Whatever one's own viewpoints, one learns to discern the settled, taken-for-granted expectations of particular audiences, the commonplace cultural narratives that provide their frameworks of meaning and the familiar details that symbolize shared assumptions. One does not dabble in the experimentally esoteric, or the alien or mysterious, or, worst of all, the "offensive," until these have become familiar to the target audience.

Of course ascertaining the familiar in our kaleidoscopic culture has become an increasingly difficult task. As a result art directors and writers take popular cultural forms as the most reliable index of the currently familiar. They keep up, therefore, with all the swirling fads and newest slang expressions in our society, the shifting celebrity scenes, the current films, plays, and musicals, the fashion changes, the museum shows, the latest best sellers, and the ever-changing varieties of music. They watch television by the hour. They see themselves as "flypaper for what's going on" and expect their colleagues to recognize and respond to their popular cultural allusions. Such knowledge of popular cultural lore becomes, in fact, a principal criterion for selecting new creative recruits; no one wants to work with a creative who, like account executives and clients, is slow on the uptake. Creatives puzzle over the meanings of such lore to various audiences, appropriating insights for their own work. In this regard the workplace becomes a forum for the systematic and ongoing assessment of taken-for-granted cultural lore, a locale that distills everyday knowledge into an occupational virtue.

Perhaps most importantly, creatives keep alert to the quintessential popular cultural form, namely advertisements themselves. They avidly watch the work of their peers, both to gauge the shifting norms of their own world and to garner clues about how best to cast either central themes or detailed images for their audiences. Advertising, like all popular culture, thus has a highly self-referential quality, a circularity that makes *déjà vu* a normal and indeed expected part of everyday life.

Creatives also strive to make advertising as realistic as possible, even while they attend to the enormous premium on "freshness" in their world. Advertising plays back to audiences already existing, enduring preoccupations, pointedly concretizing people's everyday concerns within a commercial context. To be effective the familiar details of people's lives must look and sound as wholly plausible as possible,[12] an objective that requires close attention to extremely mundane aspects of events. But advertising's focus on products always introduces the danger of strained false notes, however realistic the details. In most diners, for instance, customers do not witness paper-towel absorption tests; shoppers rarely run into Mr Whipple in supermarket aisles; nor do roommates, husbands and wives, parents and children, co-workers, neighbors, lovers, and friends converse endlessly about toilet-bowl cleaners or frozen dinners, except at the risk of interpersonal mayhem or social isolation. Creatives address the dilemma by endlessly searching for fresh ways to make products heroes, even as they provide a backdrop of convincing realism.

The stance of dispassionate observer that continually seeks to unpack the taken-for-granted and to discern precisely which details make for realism in situations has consequences for one's own life. One stops interjecting one's personal views into conversations because this colors others' spontaneous expressions that might contain useful social clues or even specific phrases for adoption; one suppresses one's urge to joke about everything because joking often subverts social reality instead of allowing one to absorb it; one develops a high degree of self-consciousness that others find discomforting, but increasingly is central to one's self-image. One turns one's relentless eye in every direction, including toward one's own most intimate experiences and relationships. Thus a writer in a nostalgic longing for his own father conceives an advertisement where a boy is brought by his father to Barney's for his first suit; another presents his social rejection by classmates as the first act of a minidrama of sweet revenge following the transformation of his lunchbox from an object of ridicule to one of envy with the inclusion of packaged cupcakes; and still another, in a commercial for dark glasses, recalls a blind date that blossomed into love at first sight. Personal experiences thus become rich bottom-land for producing symbols with deep emotional resonance. All of one's life becomes material for one's work.

In short, with a kind of sanctioned occupational promiscuity, creatives become willing to appropriate and alter material from any source and from any sphere of experience, whether public and secular or private and sacred, and apply that material to whatever project and for whatever client is at hand. In the process, of course, creatives' detachment continuously distances them from the experiences they seek or those they recall or imagine.

Yet whatever vitality advertisements have comes largely from the way creatives draw on contemporary cultural, social, and personal material. And clearly there are times when advertising does resonate with the collective fantasies, desires, and shared understandings of the broader viewing audience. One need only mention the enduring popularity of such images as the hearty conviviality of Miller Time, the independent tough maleness of the Marlboro Man, the up-beat social enthusiasm of the Pepsi Generation, and the joyfully flippant style of the Virginia Slims woman. As Joseph Bensman has pointed out: "Advertising simply accepts the world as it is, and then makes it even more so."[13]

But I mean here not just a reflection of social reality, a recycling of images from social life through advertising production and back out to the public. Rather, creatives' heightened sensitivities and insights into American culture enable them to pick out and absorb potentially useful and usable material. Then, through the process of production, advertising people – particularly creatives – select, edit, intermix, emphasize, and distort this material. In the process, extant images and ideologies, such as the recent vague sense of nationalism, are embedded in and made manifest through such lines as "You make America work and this Bud's for you," or the financial service branch of General Motors is an "Official Sponsor of American Dreams," or Miller is "Made the American way," or Plymouth is "Born in America," or *The Wall Street Journal* is "The Daily Diary of the American Dream," or "Today's Chevrolet" is "The Heartbeat of America." They take the disparate, decontextualized bits and fragments that they have gleaned and transform them into vocabularies of sentiment – widely available and easily accessible vocabularies that help organize and give expression to meanings, emotions, and experience.

Yet these vocabularies of sentiment are meant to promote particular ideas, candidates, products, or corporations. Creatives take the raw stuff of their culture and society and organize it into internally coherent messages, little stories in which products are heroes. In large and small agencies, those known for hard-sell advertising as well as those with more creative reputations, art directors and writers see themselves writing little stories, scenarios that cast "products as heroes" protecting and rescuing men, women, and children from unwarranted fates, messy situations, tangled relationships, and even from dull careers and all too mundane lives. Thus Colt 45 Malt Liquor invariably snares luscious, long-maned women for Billy Dee Williams; Certs ignites close encounters of a romantic kind by destroying bad breath; Whisk banishes "ring around the collar"; Volvo is "a civilized car for an uncivilized world"; AT&T not only rescues business deals but allows friends, lovers, and families to "reach out and touch" each other from afar; IBM personal computers turn small-business chaos into rationalized triumph; Windsong perfume keeps a woman on her lover's mind by tantalizing his nasal capillaries; Cascade saves social face by making unsightly spots on glassware disappear;

Mr Clean and Glade alike dispel musty household odors and the presumed shame they create; 9 Lives tempts even bossy, finicky cats into canine docility; and Hefty bags hold and conceal all the debris from overstuffed lives.

The construction of images, vocabularies, and interpretive frameworks that allow products to shine requires and promotes certain occupational habits of mind. Art directors and writers are commercial experts with symbols who, for instance, must be able to dispense with traditional notions of "truth" and employ instead a notion of "story," a habit of mind that obtains whether one is fashioning advertisements for a detergent, a presidential candidate, a corporate image, or a public service safety campaign. The notion of story requires creatives to dramatize and vitalize any product by highlighting and framing whatever seems to provide a salable edge. This means at times extending product traits to oversized proportions and endowing them with larger-than-life impact. The product packaged as hero performs extraordinary acts.

Advertising storytelling requires a certain circular cast of mind that underpins a talent for exploiting equally product attributes or deficiencies. Advertising, of course, celebrates the product at its core; the point is to find the right angle for applause. Knowing that celebration is a given, creatives look to products not with investigative or questioning minds, but pragmatically, simply to find handles upon which to hook praise. Product attributes merely provide the necessary means, and not the cause, for advertising celebration. For example, creatives construct links that mesh a product trait with perceived needs or concerns of the buying public. Such construction elicits the interpretation of broad themes through the narrow focus of a product, sometimes entailing the use of "borrowed interest" to hook products onto larger fads or issues. Thus advertisements for caffeine-free soft drinks suddenly begin to tout this previously ignored feature when a general concern with preventive health care helps make it a market asset. Or, again, advertising singles out wholly peripheral features to help distinguish a product from its competitors; the packaging of cigarettes or the literal weight of magazines supersede an emphasis on their actual value or utility. Indeed advertising lauds anything thought to be viable, even a marginal or invented product feature such as the color of a pill ("It's orange!"). Here, storytelling requires the reflexive perspective of funhouse mirrors as creatives continually magnify, distort, and extol a product's uniqueness even, perhaps especially, when its singularity is based only on the slightest of differences, "even... just its name – anything that distinguishes it from comparable products".

Advertising storytelling also requires a knack for symbolic inversion. This is the ability to turn symbols, images, or rationales upside down and make perceived weaknesses in a client's product, service, or image appear to be strengths; or deficiencies appear to be virtues. At the same time one must be able to undermine the credibility of an opponent's position. An advertising campaign regarded as classic by many creatives clearly illustrates this approach. In the late 1950s Volkswagen launched a print campaign for its Beetle, mimicking standard automobile advertisements dominated by large pictures of glossy cars. Indeed the Volkswagen advertisements featured a stark picture of the Beetle, emphasizing precisely its oddity and downright ungainliness. Moreover the campaign underlined the issue of appearance with one of its headlines: "It's ugly, but it gets you there." The symbolic inversion went beyond the in-joke use of a standard advertising format for a nonstandard car. The campaign turned the image of big, sleek automotive beauty, and its symbolic psychosexual meanings, upside down by graphically highlighting and applauding the Beetle's smallness, ugliness, and practicality. Or, again, the beefy sports heroes of Miller Lite commercials move the beer's image away from a light "pansy's beer" to that of a "real man's" beer while playing precisely on its lightness but in the context of raucous male camaraderie.

As an extreme case, "image advertising" demonstrates how advertising focuses on any product aspect that appears potentially viable. Generally speaking, image advertising fabricates user images, that is, images of the kind of person who uses the product. Imagery forms, of course, an important aspect of all of creatives' efforts. But campaigns for certain products, specifically cigarettes, liquor, and cosmetics, consist almost entirely of imagery. Thus, advertisements are peopled by Marlboro's macho loner, or Virginia Slim's liberated woman, or Satin's sensualist. Others feature men who take Martell "of course," or know that Hennessey is the "civilized way to call it a day," or count themselves among Cutty Sark's "leaders" who have "the right stuff". Still others parade women who allow Vanderbilt perfume to "release the splendor" of themselves, or announce that they are Charlie, Scamp, or "Shalimar, all over," or have a place among Revlon's "most unforgettable women in the world".

Some creatives find image advertising to be "the quintessence of advertising" because their efforts are totally unrestricted by real or constructed product features or brand differences. Rather, the reliance on fabricated images makes working on, say, cigarettes "pure advertising" because it is based on nothing but a talent for literally "blowing smoke," that is, storytelling. Image advertising essentially consists of fashioning frameworks that turn the wispy, ephemeral clouds of a cigarette into a rugged or independent image, a perfume's elusive fragrance into "a promise of getting laid," and the taste of an alcoholic beverage into a symbol of cultivated good breeding. Through various symbolic acrobatics, including a knack for puffery, inversion, and imagery, advertising stories present viewers with ways of enmeshing products into their daily lives and self-presentations.

Advertising embodies the promotional stance required by its production. It invites audiences to participate in the indiscriminate celebration of products and their attributes; to accept tenuous, shifting fabricated links between products and various images, symbols, and fads; and to imbibe its models of how life can and perhaps ought to be lived. At the same time creatives' self-advertising relies on the same storytelling turn of mind and expertise in, for example, symbolic inversion, magnification of product features, use of borrowed interest, and imagery built on smokey air, as required by the fabrication of advertising for clients' products. Creatives' detached habit of mind, with its skeptical, ironic perspective, distances them from even their own self-advertisements, even as it facilitates their advertising efforts. The endless storytelling, promotion, dramatization, and symbol manipulation that permeate advertising's structure, also disseminate to mass audiences the ethos of advertising work itself. As it happens, this ethos celebrates the manufacture of image, the adroit framing of perspectives and issues, and the style of presentation – that is, how one tells a story – far more than it celebrates the content of a tale, the substance of an issue, or, indeed, the reality of experience.

Notes

1. A grant-in-aid from the Wenner-Gren Foundation for Anthropological Research helped support the original fieldwork for this project. Later fieldwork both in advertising and in public relations was supported by the National Endowment for the Humanities, Division of Research, Interpretive Research Grant #RO-21493-87, "Experts with Symbols: Advertising, Public Relations, and the Culture of Advocacy" (with Robert Jackall).
2. The term "the creatives" is used formally and informally throughout the world of advertising. As do all social labels, "the creatives" acts to circumscribe the group to which it refers, defining art directors and writers as a cohesive occupational group found across agencies. At the same time it distinguishes the group from other agency groups, such as account people and researchers, and from clients who buy advertising. My use of the term reflects this social usage and does not, of course, imply any evaluation of talent, aesthetic taste, or imagination.
3. The formal title for those who write advertising copy is "copywriter"; within the advertising world, however, the word "writer" is almost always used for identification and self-identification when referring both to individuals and to the occupational group, and I follow this usage here.
4. For a three-year period from July 1982 to June 1985, I did ethnographic fieldwork in 20 advertising agencies in New York City, studying the occupational community of art directors and writers. During the field research, I conducted intensive interviews with more than 110 men and women. By intensive interviews, I mean semistructured, open-ended interviews that are generally conducted in the workplace during regular work hours. Such interviews range in length from single meetings of at least an hour, to those of several hours in length conducted over two or more meetings, to those lasting scores of hours and conducted over months and years. In addition, I undertook extensive participant and nonparticipant observation in creatives' work world. Such fieldwork ranged, for example, from being on location during the shooting of television commercials, the taping of radio spots, and the photographing of print advertisements; to watching material being shaped in film editing houses; to trading

information and perspectives over meals; to attending formal meetings and informal huddles; to sitting in on gossip sessions; to observing telephone interaction; to watching casting sessions; and to reviewing a great many reels of commercials and scores of books of print advertisements, all accompanied by self-critiques and the critiques of observers. Throughout, of course, I observed and participated in creatives' interactions with, among others, their creative peers, supervisors, agency account people, agency producers, production-house representatives, directors, editing-house technicians, actors, photographers, and clients.

Agencies vary in size and in image within the world of advertising. Generally speaking, agencies that are perceived as more creative tend to be the smaller ones while larger agencies are seen as more conservative. I did fieldwork in a wide variety of agencies across this spectrum and I also studied selected agencies in depth at different points on the spectrum in order to gain as representative a view of creatives' work world as possible. Despite differences in size and image, however, the structure and work processes of advertising production are in general fairly similar from place to place.

5. In addition to the main groups treated in the text, various other occupational groups, both inside and outside the agency, also participate in advertising production. I can only briefly point to some of these here; for a fuller discussion, see Janice M. Hirota, *Cultural Mediums: The Work World of "Creatives" in American Advertising Agencies*, PhD dissertation, Department of Anthropology, Columbia University, 1988. For example, an agency research department, and sometimes one at the client, may be involved in a project from beginning to end. Agency media research and buying people also participate in advertising projects from the start, making up media plans that most effectively utilize a client's budget.

Once a client has approved an advertisement for production, various other groups of workers become involved. For a print advertisement, these might include a photographer, models, graphics artists, and technicians at the printer. For a television commercial, other workers might include, for example, agency casting staff and an agency producer who acts as the liaison between the agency and a production house, the organizational base for the director. In addition to the director who actually shoots the film footage, production workers might include stylists, technicians, and special-effects specialists. Commercials might also require actors or models, known as "the talent". After the shoot, technicians at an editing and mixing house work on the footage with the creatives, the agency producer, and often the client. Together they select frames for the "final cut," edit the footage, and match the sound track to the visual images. Art directors and writers usually remain involved in the "production end" of projects until clients accept the final advertisements.

6. Creatives use the term "client" all the time; they almost never use the term "advertiser" in conversation. But whenever the term is

used, it always refers to the client. A quick way to spot someone who knows nothing about the advertising world is to see how they use the word "advertiser". If the term is used to refer to people at an agency, whether account people or creatives, one can be certain that that person has never set foot inside an agency.

7. "Advertising" and "advertisements" are generic terms that refer to both print and electronic advertising. Advertising that appears in print is generally specified as "print advertisement" or "print ad". The term "commercial" always refers to broadcast advertising and, when used alone, always means advertising that appears on television; a radio commercial is always so specified.

8. Trade advertising is generally print ads that appear only in trade publications, as distinct from, say, national advertising appearing in the mass media. Corporate advertising, which is actually a form of public relations, presents a desired corporate image rather than selling a particular product or service. The oil companies have specialized in corporate advertising, including what are sometimes called "advertorials". See, for example, Texaco's campaign emphasizing the company's efforts to find new sources of oil and thus decrease America's dependence on Middle Eastern sources or Mobil's regular think pieces on the Op-Ed page of *The New York Times* that try to position the company as a thoughtful contributor to public discourse on a wide range of issues.

9. This is generally true for creatives from junior to senior status, although one finds variations on this work arrangement. For instance some groups have assistant group heads, with some supervisory authority over particular accounts or over other, more junior creatives. Such supervisory relationships may be perceived by both the senior and junior creatives involved as tinged with mentor–apprentice overtones. A few creative departments are not organized into creative groups headed by group heads. Rather creatives are simply members of the creative department and creative supervisors select the creatives they want to work on particular projects. Such a situation is meant to permit the greatest flexibility in pairing teammates and therefore in bringing together the most creative potential. Theoretically at least, partners may shift constantly just as creatives on a particular account may be continually changed. Creative supervisors who have long-term affiliations with accounts provide stability and continuity in such situations.

10. Doyle Dane Bernbach (DDB) was founded in 1949 and became the spearhead of the fabled "creative revolution" that swept American advertising in the 1960s. Before DDB, most advertising firms separated writers and artists. Writers wrote copy for advertisements and then passed it on to a "bullpen" of anonymous artists who drew visual images to match the words. DDB instituted two-person teams of writers and artists, renamed "art directors," to work together on advertisements from start to finish. The actual authorship of this workplace innovation is obscure since it seems that several firms used writer/artist teams at different times, depending largely on

whether and how particular talents jelled. But there is no question that once DDB made the work teams the centerpiece of its creative operation, the practice spread quickly throughout the industry. One of DDB's founders, Bill Bernbach, claimed credit for the workplace innovation itself, a claim that, whatever its merits, is widely honored.

11. Hirota, "The Structure of Work in the World of Advertising," in *Cultural Mediums*, chapter 2.

12. There are, of course, different genres of advertising. Some, such as comedy, fantasy, parody, and what is called "new wave," are not meant to be literal reflections of everyday life. In this sense they are less realistic than more straightforward advertisements such as those called "slice of life," typified by the cosmetician giving advice at the beauty shop, or direct comparisons of one product to another, or testimonials. However even in less realistic advertisements, recognizable and realistic components may be presented, though often in caricature. Thus the stereotypical hapless functionary who has forgotten important papers for a board-of-directors meeting only to be saved by Federal Express reminds audiences of the well-known perils of big organizations. Here the realistic details of typical bureaucratic dress, setting, and props heighten the comedy, sharpen the parody, and make more enticing the fantasy of rescue. Even when advertisements do not directly present manifest social life, they reflect viewers' anxieties, daydreams, desires, and senses of whimsy or nostalgia.

13. Joseph Bensman, "The Advertising Man and His Work," *Dollars and Sense* (New York: Macmillan, 1967), p. 68.

16 The Magic Lantern: The World of Public Relations*

Robert Jackall

The need for symbolic dexterity, particularly the ability to fashion, quickly and readily, appropriate legitimations for what must be done, intensifies as one ascends the corporate ladder. Since the success of large commercial bureaucracies depends to a great extent on the goodwill of the consuming public, ambitious managers recognize that great organizational premiums are placed on the ability to explain expedient action convincingly. Public opinion, of course, constitutes one of the only effective checks on the bureaucratic impulse to translate all moral issues into practical concerns. Managers not only face the highly specific and usually ideological standpoints of one or another "special-interest" group but, even more fearsome, the vague, ill-formed, diffuse, highly volatile, and often irrational public opinion that is both the target of special-interest groups and the lifeblood of the news media. Those imbued with the bureaucratic ethos thus make every effort to mold public opinion to allow the continued uninterrupted operation of business. Moreover, since public opinion inevitably affects to some extent managers' own conceptions of their work and of themselves, public goodwill, even that which managers themselves create, becomes an important part of managers' own valued self-images. In this sense, both moral issues and social identities become issues of public relations.

Public relations serves many different functions, some of them overlapping. Among the most important are: the systematic promotion of institutional goals, products, images,

---

* Reprinted from Robert Jackall, *Moral Mazes: The World of Corporate Managers* (New York: Oxford University Press, 1988).

and ideologies that is colloquially called "hype," a word probably derived from hyperbole or, perhaps, from hypodermic; the direct or, more often, indirect lobbying of legislators, regulators, special publics, or the public at large to influence the course of legislation; the creation, through a whole variety of techniques, like matchmaking money with art or social science, of a favorable awareness of a corporation to provide a sense of public importance to otherwise anonymous millionaires; and the manufacture and promulgation of official versions of reality or of benign public images that smooth the way for the attainment of corporate goals or, in special circumstances, that help erase the taint of some social stigma affixed to a corporation. In short, the goal is to get one's story out to important publics. In such ways, managers can at least try to shape and control the main dimensions of public opinion in an unsettled social order where values, leadership, and even the direction of the society itself often seem up for grabs. This attempt to establish some sort of rationality and predictability over potentially tumultuous public opinion parallels exactly the corporate rationalization of the workplace itself through the techniques of scientific management and the rationalization of employee relationships through the human relations movement and its latter-day progeny.

Most corporations try to get their stories out on a regular sustained basis, intensifying their efforts, of course, during crisis periods. For the most part, corporations allot this work to special practitioners of public relations within the firm who consult regularly with the highest officials of the organization. These practitioners, and quite often the highest officials themselves, also employ public relations specialists in agencies. With some important differences that I shall discuss later, the views of public relations specialists both in corporations and in agencies correspond closely with those of corporate executives and managers, though typically the outlook of specialists is more detached. In particular, public relations work gives its specialists a fine appreciation of how the drama of social reality is constructed because they themselves are usually the playwrights and the stage directors. Public relations specialists may then be considered sophisticated proxies for those corporate managers sensitive to public opinion. Their work, which consists essentially of creating and disseminating various ideologies, the ethics that they fashion, and in particular the basic habit of mind that underpins all of their efforts, provide some insight into how moral issues get translated into issues of public relations.

From the modern beginnings of their occupation, men and women in public relations have been acutely aware that social reality and social reputations are not given but made. Modern public relations began with the ballyhoo of the circus and carnival barkers whose job it was to pull crowds into the big tent or the sideshow or point out to the assembled multitude the derring-do of performers. Some carnival barkers had to dazzle crowds long enough – by keeping, for instance, everyone's neck craned while the crowd looked up at the high diver poised before flight – in order to allow the pickpocket concession time enough to work their light-fingered magic.[1] Later, press agents built on the simple and effective messages of propaganda that P. T. Barnum enunciated in his autobiography.[2] They developed a wonderworld of publicity stunts that delighted, amazed, and amused millions of people and drew public attention to clients or to other wares. Harry Reichenbach, by his own admission the greatest publicist of them all, tells in his autobiography, among a great many other tales, the story of how he elevated, on a wager, "an unknown girl with hardly any ability and in ten days had her name in electric lights on Broadway at a star's salary,"[3] and how he arranged to have Rudolph Valentino's beard shaved off at a national barbers' convention and the remains deposited in a museum, thereby benefiting both the barbers and Valentino's sagging popularity.[4] His promotional work for the infant motion-picture industry consumed a great part of his career. In pushing one movie or another, he organized a delegation of Turkish notables (actually recruited from the Lower East Side) to visit New York on a secret mission to find the "Virgin of Stamboul," a fabled heiress who had been whisked from her native land on an American freighter in a romantic intrigue.[5] He arranged for a lion to be smuggled into a posh New York hotel in a piano case and appear later with its "owner," one T. R. Zann.[6] In two other stunts, both unfortunately aborted, he organized a cannibal tribe in Tarrytown, New York,[7] and had the ossified salt body of Lot's wife, complete with a certifying letter from an English archaeologist in Egypt, discovered by a night watchman in a vacant field.[8]

It is worth looking past what seem today to be sophomoric stunts to dwell briefly on Reichenbach's career. Behind his disarming optimistic ingenuousness, itself an occupational characteristic of public relations practitioners, lies a hard appraisal of the malleability of social reality and of people themselves that is also typical of the occupation. Reflecting, for instance, on how he had arranged for an oversized orangutan dressed in a tuxedo and high silk hat to drop in on New York's 400 at the Knickerbocker Club, Reichenbach says:

> The idea that it would be possible for a monkey dressed in natty clothes to crash into society was something unusual, unbelievable, and when it happened, it furnished front-page material. The fact that I had planted this episode and used it to promote the Tarzan picture, established more firmly in my mind that the whole difference between the things one dreamed about and reality was simply a matter of projection. Many publicity stunts that occurred later on in my work took on this magic-lantern effect. An idea that would seem at first flush, extravagant and impossible, became by the proper projection into life, a big item of commanding news value.[9]

He observes that some kinds of fabricated episodes, like that of the Turkish sheiks searching for the lost heiress, exert a powerful hold on the public mind:

> There was that quality of fascination about the incident that made it almost better than truth. It had become romance, illusion. It was one of those episodes which gave public and press alike the feeling that if it didn't happen, it should have happened![10]

The news media collaborate with publicists to exploit these kinds of public fancies.

Wish-news is a type of publicity that nearly always breaks on the front page. It is news so thrilling, melodramatic and heart-gripping that every city editor wishes it were true. There was a time when publicity men would concoct this kind of news in dark corners for fear of being exposed. Today some tabloids don't wait for publicity men to concoct it. They make it up themselves.[11]

Playing with the magic lantern demands, of course, a pliable audience, and Reichenbach discovered at an early age the seemingly inexhaustible gullibility of the crowd and, indeed, its complicity in its own deception. Professional solicitors of the crowd's approval were not much different. Even a boy from Frostburg, Maryland, like Reichenbach, could concoct stories from "simple backwoods recipe(s)" that "wise newspapermen" from the "mighty cosmopolitan press" would eagerly devour.[12] In time, even those whose fame had been entirely fabricated with skillful artifice came to believe their own press clippings.

[T]he irony of all publicity [is that] . . . [n]o matter how fantastic the ruse by which an unknown actor was lifted to fame, he'd come to believe it was true and the poor press agent would be shocked to find that he had never told a lie.[13]

Reichenbach came to see himself at the center of a vast matrix of influence. Given what he saw as the gullibility of most people, this had broad ramifications.

Publicity is the nervous system of the world. Through the network of press, radio, film and lights, a thought can be flashed around the world the instant it is conceived. And through this same highly sensitive, swift and efficient mechanism it is possible for fifty people in a metropolis like New York to dictate the customs, trends, thoughts, fads and opinions of an entire nation of a hundred and twenty million people.[14]

In this view, "the mass is always a magnified reflection of some individual."[15]

Take apart the average individual, dissect his mind, his manner, his attitudes and you will find that every idea, every major habit and trend in his makeup is a reflection of the fifty outstanding personalities of the day.[16]

In the average person's mind, Rockefeller's new dimes exemplify thrift; Ziegfeld's Follies girls female beauty; and Irving Berlin's latest tune the standard of popular music.[17] The wise publicist need only find the right personalities of the moment and tie his client's needs to their luster.[18] Moreover, Reichenbach saw publicity as a wholly neutral tool, a "blind disseminating force" that worked for anyone who knew how to use it, as effective for inspired reformers as for racketeers. He noted that the latter, in fact, had come to appreciate the value of a good front and the great utility for business of being well-dressed, living a genteel lifestyle, and of being known as a good family man.[19] In such a view, reality dissolves into appearances and becomes chimerical. Notions of substance get lost in a welter of shadowy images, of staged events, of carefully arranged fronts. The publicist sits in the wings of a theater he has fashioned, amidst all the rigging and props, and watches with detached bemusement and eventually with a growing private cynicism,[20] masked always by public ingenuousness, the plays he has written, the actors he has put on stage, and the warm appreciation of an audience he has assembled precisely by creating illusions.

In time, the circus barker and the ballyhoo expert became transformed into the more dignified public relations counsel. Other writers have detailed the main stages and themes of what was a tangled and uneven development.[21] I shall mention here only some highlights of the main drift of this history.

1. To counter the moralistic antibusiness broadsides of muckraking journalists early in this century, businesses began to hire their own press agents to plant favorable stories in newspapers and magazines, both with and without attribution. Businesses also withdrew advertising revenues from leading muckraking journals, forcing some to cease publication.[22] At the same time, some enlightened business leaders and their counselors, led by the Guggenheims and the Rockefellers, began to develop the more sophisticated techniques of the frank open statement toward one's enemies and the grand conciliatory gestures like benefices to the public, that preempt all discussion.[23] The leading public relations man of the pre-First-World-War era, Ivy Lee,

counselor to the Rockefellers, advocated in fact the supremacy of public opinion in a democracy and the necessity for corporate leaders to court it in a rational open way, with the public relations counselor as an interlocutor.[24] In this view, public relations could play a useful role in persuading business to make actual substantive reforms rather than merely paper over real concerns with talk and gestures. Though Lee's public philosophy was not entirely consistent with his actual practice, this idealized image of the profession persists today among some public relations practitioners and it is occasionally fulfilled.

2. The crucible of the First World War saw the melding of the three emerging professions of symbol manipulation and management – journalism, public relations, and advertising – through the institutional mechanism of the Committee on Public Information, headed by George Creel. This vast sprawling propaganda organization brought former muckraking journalists, like Creel himself, together with promoters of corporate privilege, like Harry Reichenbach and Ivy Lee, in the higher cause of mobilizing ideas to carry the "Gospel of Americanism to every corner of the globe."[25] A whole generation of opinion-shapers, storytellers, publicity experts, and image-makers honed their already well-developed skills in symbol manipulation to a fine point in selling the war to end all wars to the American people, the idea of America to the world, and the idea of surrender to enemy soldiers.[26] As Richard Tedlow has pointed out,[27] many of the participants in Creel's committee went on to become leaders in public relations and related fields.

The apparent success of wartime propaganda heightened interest in the professional possibilities of molding public opinion in peacetime. One of Creel's committee, Edward Bernays, the man who displaced Ivy Lee and became the prototype of the 1920s public relations man, commented later on how key figures perceived the successes of First-World-War propaganda and its possible lessons:

It was, of course, the astounding success of propaganda during the war that opened the eyes of the intelligent few in all departments of life to the possibilities of regimenting the public mind.... [T]he manipulators of patriotic opinion made use of the mental cliches and the emotional habits of the public to produce mass reactions against the alleged atrocities, the terror and the tyranny of the enemy. It was only natural, after the war ended, that intelligent persons should ask themselves whether it was not possible to apply a similar technique to the problems of peace.[28]

Where Ivy Lee had advocated, at least in public, the desirability of open rational discourse, Bernays, at least at this stage of his career, straightforwardly adopted simply a more genteel version of Reichenbach's notion of impressionable masses. Dim conceptions of the masses were in the air at the time. In 1925, Walter Lippmann critically analyzed a public's ability to appreciate the intricacies of any issue or indeed to keep its attention on anything but crises. He adds:

> [S]ince [a public] acts by aligning itself, it personalizes whatever it considers, and is interested only when events have been melodramatized as a conflict.
>
> The public will arrive in the middle of the third act and will leave before the last curtain, having stayed just long enough perhaps to decide who is the hero and who the villain of the piece.[29]

Around the same time, advertising began to emphasize nonrational appeals to consumers. Many advertising men came to feel that their craft had to be based not so much on reasonable grounds but on suggestive appeals to the unconscious.[30] Bernays echoed all of these theories. His early work in particular is pervaded with the imagery of herds of people shepherded by those expert in the "mechanisms and motives of the group mind."[31] The public relations counselor was a creator of events, a man in a position to make things happen.[32] Bernays favored indirect ways of appealing to the public, and he developed many of the tactics and devices that are now stock in trade for public relations practitioners. These include third-party endorsements by authoritative figures; the identification and cultivation of "opinion leaders" or "trend setters"; the use of public events – for example, contests or displays – that highlight one thing, like beautiful women or great art, and simultaneously sell another, like floppy hats on beautiful women or the corporate sponsor of the art exhibit; pretesting public opinion with psychological tests and surveys; and the thoughtful speech by the corporate or political leader that makes private interests appear to be public goods.

3. The Depression and all the ills that accompanied it – economic catastrophe, the growing success of the labor movement in presenting its own case to the public, the spectre of leftist political radicalism, the appeal of cooperative enterprise, and the gigantic apparatus of the New Deal spearheaded by a president who was himself a master publicist – led key business leaders to launch a massive public relations counterattack so that business could tell its story. The campaign was centered in a newly revitalized National Association of Manufacturers (NAM) and it evinced in nearly classical form what has been called the "American business creed."[33] The espousal of the classical business creed was not restricted to the NAM campaign. Individual corporations, particularly giants like General Motors, U.S. Steel, Dupont, and Ford, expanded their own internal public relations staffs and launched their own campaigns reiterating or echoing the same kind of message. The extent and range of all of these efforts were impressive. They included extensive institutional advertising campaigns extolling in various ways free opportunity, initiative, and competition; a massive advertising campaign entitled "Prosperity Reigns Where Harmony Dwells"; special editions of in-house magazines designed for public distribution; the placement of probusiness editorials in small dailies across the country; the syndication for several hundred papers of a cartoon series with a probusiness stance; the sponsorship of radio programs of every variety, complete with probusiness homilies; and the massive production of short motion pictures telling the story of one or another industry for distribution as trailers to movie theaters or to educational or recreational organizations.[34] It was during this period too that businesses began to develop systematic internal communication efforts directed at their own employees; well-informed workers with correct perspectives were deemed a company's best ambassadors to the world.

NAM and its allied adherents to the classical business creed were not, of course, the only corporate petitioners for the public ear. During the Second World War and after, more liberal business voices, often identified with those segments of managerial capitalism that appreciated the great economic opportunities presented by the adoption of Keynesian economic policies, began to find expression principally through the public relations campaigns of the Committee for Economic Development (CED).[35] Not long after, the NAM campaign was ridiculed by William H. Whyte, then an editor for *Fortune* magazine.[36] These particular ideological splits between different wings of the business elite centered on the proper role of government in economic affairs. One may notice similar ideological clashes in more recent years, say, on the issue of the social responsibility of business. The CED campaign is important in another respect. Reflecting perhaps the improving fortunes of its own constituency, it dropped the somewhat defensive tone that had marked the NAM effort; its optimistic buoyancy and assertiveness restored to public relations its historical and, one might argue, proper role – that is, as "prophet of good fortune."[37]

4. During the Second World War and in the postwar years, public relations became and has remained a major institutional force in American society. There are no systematically compiled data to support such a claim;[38] one must rely rather on a number of disparate though related indices. For instance, corporate and trade association expenditures on what is called corporate or public relations advertising – that is, advertisements that do not sell a particular brand of product but rather try to establish a good image for a company or for a generic product, like milk or cotton – seem to be on the rise. Moreover, the number of public relations agencies has grown, the revenues of the largest public relations firms have kept abreast of economic growth, many colleges and universities across the country now offer degrees or courses in public relations, and virtually every large organization in all orders of our society – whether business, government, religious, educational, or military – now has a public relations division.[39] Finally, attempts at professionalization of the field, while less than

successful because of the peculiarities of the occupation, especially the sharp competition for clients between agencies, have nonetheless been regularly renewed. In the last decade, probably in response to the opportunities presented by the growth and consolidation of the electronic media, many public relations firms have been acquired by large powerful advertising houses that wish to provide their clients with wholly coordinated double-barreled offensives. The new alliance between these twin but historically somewhat antagonistic sources of image management might signal a whole new phase in public relations history.

It is, in any event, no exaggeration to say that public relations practices and techniques pervade every nook and cranny of our social order. In the course of a single day, the average middle-class citizen might easily hear on radio snatches of several speeches given by government or corporate officials but ghostwritten by a public relations wordsmith; tune in to the plethora of staged media events that dot his television screen, for instance, press conferences, talk-show panel discussions, celebrations of achievement such as the Emmy presentations or the Academy Awards, the pregame, postgame, and even midgame interviews with players and coaches that have transformed sporting events, or interviews of "spokesmen" or "spokeswomen" for books, companies, self-improvement courses, social causes, or even scientific theories; see in passing on the screen a few of the thousands of "news clips," the electronic descendants of press handouts that report feature stories related to a company's business – like a feature on daylight saving time by a watch company, or a series on the medical uses of procedures utilizing small amounts of radioactive materials by a group of nuclear physicians; visit a museum to see an exhibit of, say, Egyptian art sponsored by a design corporation that, coincidentally, has just released its latest line of apparel featuring the new Egyptian look; receive newsletters from some of the thousands of organizations, public or private, politically conservative, liberal, or radical, eleemosynary, educational, or religious, that routinely manufacture official or counterofficial versions of reality suiting their needs; read in *The Wall Street Journal* or *The New York Times* accounts of specific events or larger trends attributed to "informed sources," the code name for public relations men and women; or see in the same journals the results of the latest public opinion poll on the most serious or the most banal topic conducted by an "independent research firm," actually a wholly owned subsidiary or a subcontractor of a public relations agency. Such a welter of images and ideologies even comes to assume for many men and women in our society a comfortable air of solidity, a development that would not, of course, have surprised Harry Reichenbach. Paradoxically, the more artifice used in constructing social reality, the more does that reality come for many to seem commonplace, natural, and taken for granted.

Men and women in public relations are not generally taken in by their own artifice. Rather, the very nature of their work continually reminds them that the world is put together, often in the most arbitrary fashion. Whether in a corporation or an agency, a public relations practitioner, in addition to meeting the normal bureaucratic fealty requirements of his station, must above all satisfy his clients' desires to construct the world in certain ways.[40] Clients always want certain versions of reality propagated. These should: enable them to accomplish whatever practical tasks are at hand as expeditiously as possible; and convey a favorable public image, and implicitly a preferred self-image, to some crucial publics. The organizational success of public relations practitioners depends on remaining attentive to clients' desires. As one vice-president at Images Inc. says: "Even if your viewpoint is 180 degrees from his [the client's], you have to see which track his mind is on." In general, moreover, clients want to believe the best about themselves; in this sense, they, rather than targeted publics, become the public relations practitioner's best customer.

There are, of course, good clients and bad clients. A good client keeps his public relations specialists adequately informed, provides "feedback" and "constructive criticism," and recognizes that public relations depends on time-billing rather than on product billing and provides enough funds to do the job properly. A good client "takes stock of himself," that is, dispassionately objectifies his company's products, his company's organizational structure and personnel, and, say, in the case of a top corporate official, himself, to make them all more readily manipulable and therefore marketable commodities. Above all, a good client is flexible and therefore able rapidly to shift ground and actual policies as well to meet new needs or new pressures. A bad client, by contrast, either does not understand or chooses to ignore the peculiarly indirect approach of public relations and wants immediately observable results in terms of press clippings or TV time; uses a public relations program as a vehicle for self-aggrandizement within his own corporation, placing the public relations specialist in danger of "getting caught in a pissing contest between executives"; demands the release of press statements that are only marginally "newsworthy" and then blames the public relations specialist when nothing at all gets printed or aired; conceals crucial aspects of his story from his public relations advisers and refuses them adequate access to his staff and facilities to get the full story; comes to the public relations agency with trumped-up data and fake photographs – as happened, for instance, at Images Inc. when a client falsely claimed the efficacy of a product to remove tar from despoiled beaches – and ends up declaring bankruptcy, leaving the public relations agency liable for a multimillion-dollar lawsuit; wants the public relations agency, as in the case of some single-party foreign governments, to put a good public face on practices like the "persuasion" and "elimination" of opponents; expects the public relations agency to be the "bag man" to pay off government officials or newspaper editors; and, perhaps especially, insists on an indefensible or totally unbelievable version of reality or expects the public relations specialist to tell outright lies.

Agency personnel are the most vulnerable to clients' wishes. Typically, work in agencies is organized around accounts, with teams of practitioners with particular expertise, often drawn from different lines of authority, being assigned to service an account; or, if an account is large and diversified, various specialists deal with particular needs of a client. In an agency, interesting work, prestige, money, perquisites for oneself and one's friends, like tickets to the opera, ballet, theater, symphony, and major sporting events, as well as invitations to the chic receptions where businessmen mingle socially with figures from the literary and artistic worlds, all depend on holding and satisfactorily servicing lucrative accounts. To some extent, working for a prestigious client even if the account itself is not lucrative – being, for instance, the spokesman on a specific issue for a well-known international watch manufacturer – can be a source of internal organizational leverage for a practitioner, but only because one's colleagues assume that an account with such a well-known and respected company very likely involves big money.

When big accounts, or portions of them, "take a walk," agency staff quite often are asked to follow them out the door. As it happens, accounts in the public relations world circulate continually and only sometimes because of actual or alleged dissatisfaction with public relations service. The pattern of continual mergers, upheavals, and power struggles in corporations, that is at the core of American corporate life, directly affects public relations agencies. When a new CEO or divisional president assumes power in a corporation, he will quite often change public relations and advertising agencies as part of a larger strategy of shedding the past or to assert his own "new vision" of the future. When this occurs, almost invariably, he will move his account to an agency whose leaders he knows and with whom he feels comfortable. This continual circulation of accounts means that agency personnel are constantly searching for new accounts and constantly devising ways to hold present clients, despite the knowledge of the inevitability of their eventual departure. Both exigencies create the fundamental condition of public relations work, that is, the necessity to be continually attentive to clients' desires. An anecdote from Images Inc. illustrates the point. One day, an executive vice-president in the agency was lavishly praising a bright young man who was currently "on a roll." When I asked if this person would be promoted because of his work, the executive vice-president looked at me with some surprise and said: "Well, just because he's great today doesn't mean he'll be great tomorrow. Anything can happen. He has to keep his clients happy if he wants us to stay happy with him." One's future, at least in public relations agencies, depends almost entirely on creating and sustaining particular versions of reality.

As a rule, corporate public relations specialists lead somewhat more secure lives. However, during the controversies endemic to the great industries today, their positions can also become suddenly precarious. It is they who have to hammer out and offer to the public the customarily bland and delicately phrased versions of reality thought necessary to dampen public ire or at least keep special-interest groups at bay while corporate leaders grapple with exigencies in back rooms. The very pace of events, however, and the choices events demand often leave corporate public relations specialists scrambling to invent appropriate ways to explain what has to be done.

Such enforced attentiveness to others' desires to portray the world a certain way breeds a distinctive habit of mind that characterizes the ethos of public relations and, through the influence of public relations, the ethos of American business. In the world of public relations, there is no such thing as a notion of truth; there are only stories, perspectives, or opinions. One works, of course, with "facts," that is, selected empirically verifiable statements about the world. But as long as a story is factual, it does not matter if it is "true." One can feel free to arrange these facts in a variety of ways and to put any interpretation on them that suits a client's objectives. Interpretations and judgments are always completely relative. The only canons binding this process of interpretation are those of credibility or, more exactly, of plausibility. If an interpretation of facts, a story, is taken as plausible by a targeted audience, it is just as good as "true" in any philosophical sense, indeed better since it furthers the accomplishment of an immediate goal. Insofar as it has any meaning at all, truth is what is perceived. Creating the impression of truth displaces the search for truth.

Since all events are stories, one must develop a sensitivity to the nuances of language and to the familiar twists of plot that allow these stories to be told as simple, living dramas. This does not require a meditative reflectiveness or, least of all, any historical inquisitiveness about the origins of events. Indeed the past is useful only insofar as a selective recasting of it might help one to grasp and present events as popular novelists do, that is, in broad brushstrokes.

Avoiding undue complexities, one learns to craft the little stories that will engineer at least acquiescence if not consent and allow a client's operations to proceed without undue interruption. After all, most people's understanding of the world consists precisely of such little stories, pieced together or accepted outright from a myriad of other constructions of reality.

Men and women in public relations are, of course, acutely aware that their advocacy of certain positions makes them somewhat suspect to an increasingly media-savvy public, a suspicion that they feel is unwarranted. In their view, the public has been unduly influenced by, if it has not swallowed whole, the occupational ideology of the journalistic media, an ideology that they know well both because of their continual interaction with journalists and especially because many people in public relations have "crossed the street" from journalism, to, of course, a mixed chorus of envy and contempt from their former colleagues. From the standpoint of public relations, the journalistic ideology closely resembles the social outlook of most college seniors – a vague but pious middle-class liberalism, a mildly critical stance toward their fathers in particular and authorities in general; a maudlin championship of the poor and the underclass; and especially the doctrine of tolerance, open-mindedness, and balance. In fact, public relations people feel, the news media are also constructing reality. They are always looking for a "fresh" and exciting angle; they have an unerring instinct for the sentimental that expresses itself in a preference for "human interest" rather than substance; and they arrange facts in a way that purports to convey "truth," but is in fact simply another story. In reality, news is entertainment. And, despite the public's acceptance of journalistic ideologies, most of the public watch or read news not to be informed or to learn the "truth," but precisely to be entertained. There is no intrinsic reason, therefore, why the constructions of reality by public relations specialists should be thought of as any different from those of any group in the business of telling stories to the public. Everyone is telling stories and everyone has a story to tell. Public relations men and women are simply storytellers with a purpose in the free market of ideas, advocates of a certain point of view in the court of public opinion. Since any notion of truth is irrelevant or refers at best to what is perceived, persuasion of various sorts becomes everything.

Before discussing some of the particular persuasive techniques of public relations, two general remarks are in order. First, the essential task of public relations in all of its operations is to invent better ways and especially to devise better explanations and accounts for what has to be done; in short, its role is to transform expediency into altruism or even statesmanship. Second, the genius of public relations, a gift that is shares with advertising, consists to a great extent in its dexterity at inverting symbols and images. Whether it is hyping products, influencing legislation, transforming reputations, or erasing stigma, public relations tries to transform actually or potentially perceived weaknesses into strengths and subvert or at least call into question the strengths or particularly the credibility of opponents. Thus, the lowly bottom-feeding catfish, a food for generations of poor southern whites and especially blacks, when commercially farmed, is promoted as the "cultivated catfish," complete with a long-tailed tuxedo and starched shirt. Or, in an era dominated by television, radio executives launch a campaign to alter the idea of radio as a nonvisual medium by emphasizing the power of the imagination; they distribute posters showing a fish smoking a pipe or a banana dancing, both with the tagline, "I just saw it on radio." The textile industry, under great market pressure from well-made and cheaper Asian imports, pushes for restrictive tariffs, extolling the virtues of traditional American craftsmanship. A diversified conglomerate seeking a "unified corporate identity" commissions a major pathbreaking study on what is actually an inversion of a somewhat embarrassing private obsession of the chief executive officer. The CEO's house, it is said, in the aftermath of a mugging of a friend, is an arsenal stocked with weapons and booby-trapped against the night when some unfortunate burglar wanders into his yard. A public relations firm fashions a study on how the quality of American life is affected by the fear of crime and names the report and the corporation itself after the CEO. An asbestos manufacturer declares bankruptcy and changes its name to end a flood of worker compensation suits arguing that, far from being an avoidance of responsibility, such a strategy is actually the first step in establishing an industry and government fund that will ensure equity in payments to all, not just those disabled workers who are first in line. And a corporation that produces plastic containers, regularly under assault from various groups for littering the environment, considers a public relations communications program to explore and extol the role of packaging goods throughout human history. The subversion of an opponent's credibility takes various forms but, generally speaking, it tries to undercut the legitimacy of opposing claims. The most common example is to question the particular scientific data that underpin a position that counters one's own interests.

Both the general aim and the genius of public relations may be observed in its persuasive techniques. As it happens, following the legacy of Edward Bernays, indirect means of persuasion are thought to be particularly effective ways of reaching deeply into the many publics that can influence a business. In this, public relations contrasts sharply with the direct hard sell of advertising. By all odds, the classical indirect method of public relations is the creation of a corporate persona, a kind of fictive reality, known colloquially in the field as a "front." This technique helps mobilize or defuse public support for a position while concealing or at least obscuring the principal interests initiating action.

An example from Alchemy Inc. illustrates how the front works. The chemical company is one of the leading producers of chlorofluorocarbons (CFCs), extremely useful inert chemicals that have wide applicability both for industrial and consumer use. In 1974, a major scientific controversy developed about the possible erosion by these chemicals of stratospheric ozone, a broad zone of the earth's atmosphere that extends from about 8 and 30 miles above the earth and that filters out cancer-producing and otherwise harmful ultraviolet solar rays. Aerosols using CFCs were banned by regulation in 1978, causing substantial losses to the big producers of the substances, among them Alchemy, and wiping out in the process the whole industry that produced aerosols. In 1980, a new Advanced Notice to Propose Rulemaking (ANPR) was issued by the Environmental Protection Agency (EPA) proposing a further regulation of CFCs, this time capping production at certain levels, utilizing a market share allocation mechanism to determine the maximum amount of CFCs a firm would be allowed to produce in a year. The aim of the proposed legislation was to create artificial shortages, drive up prices for the chemicals, and finally to control what was termed the "banking" of CFCs. Because CFCs are inert and have extremely long life, they would in time, it was argued, when released from millions of refrigerators, foam cushions, car or home air conditioners, or as waste after use as industrial solvents, find their way into the stratosphere and attack the ozone. Great arguments raged in the scientific community about the ozone depletion theory. For instance, in the course of eight years, the National Academy of Sciences issued several reports alternately supporting the theory, having second thoughts, and then retreating from the field in ambiguity. Advocates of the ozone depletion theory were quite forceful in pushing the proposed regulation. Some went so far as to assert that the continued unregulated production of CFCs was laying the groundwork for a new and even more catastrophic Love Canal. Advocates for the business position argued that, in the absence of scientific surety, production should continue unabated while further research proceeded. In fact, some scientists in the business community worked on developing early warning systems that would signal a worsening of ozone erosion and provide ample lead time for response. At the chemical company, line managers directly charged with or familiar with CFCs privately scoffed at the ozone depletion theory and argued that the scientists who cooked it up had their own eyes on the main chance. Up the ladder, key business leaders felt that the real issue in the whole dispute was the proposed market share allocation device that might served as a model for still other and possibly more damaging regulation in different areas.

With the help of a public relations firm and together with another principal producer of CFCs, Alchemy Inc. created a group called the Alliance for Responsible CFC Policy. On the surface, the Alliance seemed to be a coalition of the industrial consumers of CFCs, that is, small manufacturers who used the substances to produce commodities like polyurethane foam, plastics, and air conditioners. In reality, the chemical company and the other big producers of CFCs bankrolled and controlled the whole operation, made and broke different executive directors of the Alliance, organized speaking tours of young, personable, and attractive managers armed with "speaking packages" with multicolored tabs for quick reference during question periods, and coordinated a national campaign of sober scientific dissent and of outraged letters to congressmen and regulators protesting the proposed regulation. Near the end of the initial period of comment to the ANPR, managers at Alchemy gleefully congratulated each other on their efforts – an entire room at the EPA was said to be overflowing with the mountain of paper generated by their write-in campaign. It would be a long time, they said, before anybody heard or even saw the relevant program officer at the agency. In the end, shortly after President Reagan's appointee took over the EPA, the regulation was quietly buried, although the Alliance failed in its attempt to drive a stake through the ozone depletion theory itself and thus forestall possible future regulation.[41]

Of course, none of the major players in such a drama – that is, regulators, environmental activists, politicians, or businessmen themselves – are really fooled by such a classic maneuver. One should note, however, that the heat of battle, the continual necessity to act in public forums outside the corporation as if a particular front were indeed an independent entity, and the sometime requisite stance of indignation toward one's opponents, sometimes cause many businessmen to half-believe realities they know to be fictive. In any event, one's direct opponents are not the target of fronts. Rather, fronts are devised for the broader public whose support is deemed crucial in the struggle against opponents. In this arena, the most credible or plausible organizational public face is thought to have the best chance of winning the day. Practically speaking, this means finding and marketing the most salable organizational image while simultaneously undermining or at least calling into question the image of one's chief adversaries. In the CFC case, managers and their public relations advisers calculated correctly that, among those images available, the one with the widest public appeal and with the best chance of striking terror into the hearts of regulators and congressmen alike was that of small businessmen, rather than corporate giants, valiantly joining forces to struggle against bureaucratic tyranny, regulators who precipitously jump to conclusions before all the scientific data are assessed, and self-promoting professors of chemistry whose ambition clouds their scientific objectivity.

Fronts are particularly suited to furthering private interests under the guise of another organizational image, that of the "constructive alternative." For instance, Images Inc. worked for a coalition of manufacturers and small grocery store owners who were fighting a bottle bill referendum requiring a deposit on beverage containers. The firm organized a committee of eminent, well-known, and well-placed people that: invoked a variety of appeals, including hidden costs and inconvenience to the consumer and the likelihood of an explosion of pests in the small stores and bodegas that under the proposed bill would have to receive returned containers; and worked for a Total Litter Control program, advertised with the acronym TLC, instead of "focusing narrowly" on bottles and cans. As it happens, the committee existed only on expensive and well-illustrated stationery. The multitudinous press releases warning of the horrors that would follow public approval of the referendum, the red-and-white, heart-adorned TLC stickers that began to litter building walls and subway cars, and the spokesmen and women with high-sounding, but in one case wholly fictional, academic degrees who trooped the talk show circuit, were all products of the public relations imagination. Apart from the creation of fictitious credentials, one should note that this use of the front differs not at all from the way the device is employed by thousands of political, social, cultural, and religious organizations of every ideological and social stripe. Public relations men and women, whether on the right, center, or left, whether in the service of God, the state, art, human rights, or commercial gain, know that in a society of media markets the magic of a glittering name, respected accomplishment, and the cultural authority that accompanies established professional or institutional position are far more persuasive than reasoned arguments.

Finally, a very frequently encountered organizational image among front groups in these days of heated scientific controversy is that of the disinterested scientific institute. For instance, the Formaldehyde Institute, basically a trade association of formaldehyde producers and industrial users of the chemical, was formed in 1979 to counter growing public and scientific concern about the chemical. Formaldehyde is a highly reactive, colorless, and low-cost substance that has widespread applicability in a great number of industries – for instance, in cosmetics, explosives, paints, leathers and furs, and medicines to name only a few. Serious problems had emerged with urea formaldehyde foam insulation in homes, and some studies strongly suggested the possibility of nasal cancer in humans exposed to the substance for prolonged periods. At the time, regulation governing the foam insulation was pending before the Consumer Product Safety Commission, and the big fear was that other industrial users of the chemical might be regulated by still other agencies. The textile industry, in particular, which relies wholly on a formaldehyde-based resin to produce permanent press polyester/cotton fabrics, feared that OSHA would impose a standard reducing workers' allowable time-weighted average (TWA) exposure to the chemical from the current two to three parts per million (ppm) to one ppm, a reduction that would cause severe operating problems in finishing plants.[42]

The stated purpose of the Formaldehyde Institute "is for the sound science of formaldehyde and formaldehyde-based products and to ensure that the data are used and interpreted properly."[43] To this stated end, the Institute has, among other activities, amassed a variety of independent studies on formaldehyde, collaborated with various regulatory agencies and groups like the National Cancer Institute on other related research, compiled an extensive bibliography of studies on the chemical, held workshops and seminars on formaldehyde, sent out mailings with summary results of data to directors of health departments in all fifty states, and published a wide variety of pamphlets and brochures for the general public on the benefits to society of this "building block" chemical. The themes in all this literature constitute a paradigm of sorts of the basic message of other disinterested scientific institutes focusing on similarly complex scientific issues:

1. There is no scientific evidence that formaldehyde causes cancer in humans.
2. Animal tests on rats that have shown incidences of nasal cancer are inapplicable to humans. First, rats have a predisposition to nasal irritations. Second, the extremely high levels of exposure to which test rats are subjected span almost the whole lifetime of a rat, an unrealistic test that cannot be extrapolated to humans.
3. The only reliable data are long-term epidemiological studies of workers regularly exposed to formaldehyde. The only major study of this kind provides no evidence that formaldehyde causes cancer in humans at the levels of exposure to the chemical experienced in the workplace, let alone the much lower levels of the chemical released in such consumer products like textiles or pressed wood.
4. Regulation must be based on firm, generally accepted science. In the absence of such science, any interference with the production and use of formaldehyde constitutes unwarranted restriction and betrays, in fact, an unscientific cast of mind.
5. Our society cannot live without formaldehyde. Without it, not only would more than a million American workers directly involved in making formaldehyde and formaldehyde-based products, in industries earning more than $18 billion a year, be thrown out of work, but many other crucial industries, like textiles, the automotive and machine industries, and the construction industry, would be severely curtailed with direct economic penalties to individuals and society as a whole.
6. Besides, a multitude of natural as well as man-made sources produce massive amounts of formaldehyde, including the human body, vegetation, and automobile emissions. The chemical is, in fact, essentially part of the natural environment of any society, particularly an industrial social order.[44]

Scientific fronts thus gather together under the rubric of science a host of arguments that try to discredit opponents' positions while establishing the reasonableness and plausibility of scientific interpretations favorable to a certain practical application of knowledge. Of course, the Institute does not discourage somewhat more colorful and pointed arguments to the public made by various users of the chemical. Opponents of regulation on formaldehyde often point out, for instance, that morticians who use a lot of formaldehyde suffer not from an excess of nasal cancer but rather from cirrhosis of the liver, an ailment caused by other pickling substances. Executives at Weft Corporation argue that permanent-press shirts are the mother of women's liberation and that banning formaldehyde would result in sending newly career-minded women back to their ironing boards. They also argue that they feel caught in a double bind. The industry has moved as far as consumer preferences will allow it to polyester blends, at least partly because of the cotton dust issue. But polyester blends require treatment with formaldehyde to meet consumer preferences. Do government threats to regulate formaldehyde mean that it wants the industry to move back to the use of more cotton?

Scientific fronts often conceal complicated political strategies. For instance, the Edison Electric Institute, an umbrella organization for energy producers and consumers ranging from the very conservative National Independent Coal Operators' Association to the moderate National Association of Manufacturers, recently formed the Alliance for Balanced Environmental Solutions. The Alliance's principal task is to counter the growing domestic and international public concern about acid rain, that is, the deposit of harmful chemical pollutants through precipitation that alters the pH balance in soil and bodies of water. A principal, though by no means the only, source of acid rain in the eastern part of North America seems to be the airborne transmission of sulfur dioxide from coal-burning electrical plants. As it happens, these plants are located in the midwestern United States. However, because of extremely high smokestacks installed in the 1950s, precisely to carry pollution away from local communities, and because of the vagaries of wind patterns, air-borne sulfates from these plants are, apparently, helping to "acidify" and thus to despoil the lakes, streams, and forests of the northeastern United

States and southern Canada. The situation raise complicated jurisdictional disputes and particularly questions of
interregional equity and liability. Put simply, the real issue is: Who pays for other people's troubles when responsibility is blurred? Through a series of reports, conferences,
and newsletters, the Alliance is making *mutatis mutandis*
essentially the same arguments as the Formaldehyde Institute. In particular, it stresses the need for continued scientific
research into the origins of acid rain, the actual extent of
supposed damage, and the harmfulness of any regulatory
or legislative solutions before scientific certitude is established.[45] In reality, it is likely that the Edison Electric Institute is playing for time through the Alliance. First, the
future direction of national energy policy is deeply uncertain in the wake of the operational mishaps and financial
disasters suffered by the nuclear energy industry in recent
years. Second, the massive coal-burning electrical plants in
the Midwest have many years to go before exhausting the
huge investments made in them after the Second World War.
The rhetoric of the quest for scientific surety helps to post-
pone political choices until money already spent is well used
and until investment alternatives become clear.

One can scarcely dispute the importance of reliable science as a basis for regulation. As noted earlier, the whole
framework of our society depends on rational scientific inquiry and its technological application. Faulty or fraudulent science can only impede the quest for what one might
call a civic rationality. Most men and women cannot make
informed assessments of scientific data. Moreover, when they
try to make such judgments, they rarely have a forum within
which to articulate their appraisals. Still further, if articulated, their judgments are likely to be dismissed as being
insufficiently expert. Men and women in public relations know
therefore that, as a rule, science is as science seems. By
their nature, scientific data are always tentative and subject to revision. And, in fact, practical men and women who
understand the pivotal role of public opinion welcome
scientific ambiguity unless they themselves can claim certainty
to their own benefit. Uncertainty provides the requisite space
to maneuver, provided that one invokes the hallowed canons
of science in a measured and respectable way and provided,

of course, that one surrounds oneself with a group of experts, preferably with impeccable credentials, who will testify to the probity of one's position. Since credentials influence credibility, they must include not only proper certification and established position but also freedom from ostensible conflict of interest that might allow others to interpret scientific judgment as biased.

An example from Images Inc. brings these themes together. Images Inc. represented for a time a pharmaceutical firm that was under criticism for a weight-control pill that in certain cases, it was charged by a well-known public health group, had the unfortunate side effect of death. Executives at the pharmaceutical firm cited their own experts to argue that such charges were not only absurd but malicious. Executives at Images Inc. had no interest whatsoever in trying to master the chemical complexities of the dispute. Here, as in many other cases, they threw up their hands and argued that their own lack of expertise meant that they certainly could not adjudicate any scientific ambiguities. However, one PR executive who was troubled by the public health group's evidence, investigated the issue on her own and reached a negative judgment about the drug. She voiced her concern at a meeting that I attended and urged the agency to consider resigning the account. A top agency official pointed out that, although she was entitled to her private and individual viewpoint, experts disagreed about the drug. The real problem facing Images Inc., he went on to say, was the public image of the head scientist at the pharmaceutical firm. The man's slight public awkwardness underlined his lack of established professional achievement; regrettably, he was also the brother-in-law of the drug firm's president. The chief order of business for Images Inc. was not therefore to discuss complicated scientific quandaries but to persuade the president to dump his brother-in-law and to figure out which articulate experts could be lined up to convince the public that the weight-control pill posed no unnecessary or unreasonable dangers to health.

Closely related to fronts are other methods of persuasion that promote products, causes, people, or organizations in a similarly indirect way. Thus, one creates marathon and cross-country events to promote running shoes and children's bubble-gum blowing contests with school scholarships as prizes to push bubble gum. In the aftermath of a series of politically motivated murders of tourists, one plants articles in key upscale magazines on exotic birds, summer camping, tropical fruits and vegetables, and native cuisine to stimulate tourist interest in a Caribbean island, as well as arranging well-publicized celebrity visits to the "resort paradise." Or one produces short news features giving a behind-the-scenes look at how the commercials for a client's products are made and arranges for such films to be shown to captive audiences on airplanes at no charge.

"Landmark studies" of various sorts constitute another crucial indirect public relations device today. At the suggestion of a public relations firm, a corporation will commission a study to be carried out by the PR firm's research wing. Most commonly, these focus on issues directly related to a company's marketing areas. Thus, a PR firm does an analysis of American reading habits for a book industry group, a study of fashion consciousness for a leading clothes store, studies of changing perceptions of women's roles both for a feminine hygiene products firm and for a cigarette company out to capture the young female market, and an appraisal of sports in American life for a beer firm that advertises heavily during sports events. Often, too, "path breaking" studies that are designed to put corporate leaders "out in front" of important public issues are commissioned. For instance, an insurance company funds a study of changing values in American life that argues, with an assurance that only comes with a certain innocence of historical knowledge, that the level of an individual's religious commitment more strongly determines personal values than economic status, age, sex, race, or political belief and that the "increasing impact of religion on social and political institutions may be . . . a trend that could change the face of America"; and a leading producer of office furniture funds a study of how the tastes and styles of the baby-boom generation are shaping "corporate cultures" and the environment and decor of the contemporary office. Such reports are always conducted "under the aegis of a distinguished advisory panel" of both men and women of affairs and particularly of the higher reaches of the academic world who help legitimate the entire enterprise, win accolades for the public spiritedness, social vision, and social sensitivity of corporate leaders, and, of course, gain more extensive name recognition for the sponsoring organization.

Typically, such studies use the standard polling techniques developed and perfected since the mid-1930s by the Gallup, Roper, and Harris organizations. As it happens, the methodology of polling techniques ideally matches the underlying habit of mind of public relations. Public relations studies dip into the rapidly moving stream of public opinion. Since the premium, especially as established by clients, is always on current opinion, the studies are either ahistorical or use historical facts in a highly selective way. They make only low-level empirical generalizations uninformed by any clear theoretical position. Public opinion itself becomes both the primary datum and the interpretive yardstick of material. The notion of historical structures or continuities has no significance nor, for that matter, do shifts in public opinion except for the assumption that today's poll results erase and invalidate yesterday's opinions. Without a historical consciousness and some firm criteria to locate materials and to help make discerning judgments, the wheat and chaff of "the million bits of information," the "hard data" produced by "sophisticated statistical techniques," are not separated and are presented with equal seriousness or equally cheerful, upbeat blandness.

It is somewhat inaccurate to say that there are no firm criteria in public relations with which to assess public opinion data. One framework that always matters is the client's assessment of what data mean or, more precisely, should mean. As a general rule, few clients wish to be associated with "gloomy" reports unless, in so doing, they can stake out positions of corporate leadership and point to clear programmatic solutions for the problems noted. Such solutions should not, it goes without saying, upset too many people. Further, few executives will sponsor a report that counters their own organization's interests or for that matter their own personal ideologies. Clients' desires thus place some strictures or "parameters" on the interpretations of data available to public relations practitioners.

An example from Images Inc. illustrates the way such interpretive parameters work. In the early 1980s, the agency talked one of its big clients, a major container producer, into sponsoring a "breakthrough" study on perceptions of the "trade-offs" between environmental protection and economic growth. Data were to be gathered from the public at large, avowed environmentalists, top corporate executives, small businessmen, and several communities facing specific tensions between the environment and economy. In the heady days of neoconservative triumph following President Reagan's first election, executives at the container corporation fully expected to receive a report that highlighted the public's abandonment of the environmentalist sentiments of the 1970s and an espousal of a "new realism" about the regrettable exigencies that inevitably accompany economic growth. After analyzing the data, however, the research group and account team at the public relations agency felt compelled to write a draft arguing that although the public wanted a return to economic growth, it did not want, in any event, growth at the expense of environmental decline. In fact, the draft said that the country seemed gripped by a pervasive "earth concern" that put economic growth in a distinctly secondary role. As it happened, the draft provoked such consternation at the highest levels of the container corporation that the entire project and future projects as well were jeopardized. Top officials at the public-relations firm became more actively involved at this point. After several rewritings, a much blander document emerged that stressed the public's desire for a finely poised balance between growth and preservation of the environment. Rumors circulated freely in the public relations firm about the near reversal of emphasis, and both junior and senior people said privately that whole sections of data contrary to the thesis of balance had either been omitted or reported in an undecipherable way in the final version. The chief researcher for the project and a top official both adamantly deny this and argue that all the data were reported. The researcher, however, allows that "a lot of soul-searching was necessary in order to achieve the broadest perspective possible on this issue." The top official, in a written document prepared for a meeting to discuss the issue, argued that:

[T]he final report was better than it would have been if it had not gone through [the] process of reexamination. It was stronger, it was more important, it was more constructive. ... At the same time, there is no doubt that pressures were brought on us to come to the kind of conclusions we finally reached.

At the meeting, he added, somewhat more pithily: "We tried to be honest but, believe me, it wasn't easy."

In this context, the notion of honesty becomes ambiguous and elusive since it is unclear by what standards honesty is being measured. Here the notion of truth treated earlier becomes crucial. The same top executive defines truth:

I sometimes sit back and think that if we could make up a list of all the viewpoints of all our clients and somehow fit them together, then that would be truth. That would be what we are as a firm.

Another executive in the same agency says:

Everyone out there is constructing reality. We and our clients have perceptions too. Who is telling the truth? Is there anyone out there who has the time and the inclination to sit down and truly evaluate the many situations?

Yet another executive from the same firm puts a fine point on the issue when one of his colleagues raised a question about the truth of a position advocated by one of the firm's clients:

Truth? What is truth? I don't know anyone in this business who talks about 'truth'.

To some extent, these views simply reflect the particular habit of mind, the kind of marked relativism, already described, that undergirds public relations work and the ethos that public relations helps shape for corporate managers. This relativism has, as it happens, a close though largely unappreciated affinity with views currently propagated in literary and philosophical circles. Here truth is also either an irrelevant concept or one that is wholly kaleidoscopic. It is pointless to seek for underlying structural unities or even determinate partial truths, because there are only differences. The objective world dissolves into subjective consciousness and is projected outwards. Just as Harry Reichenbach came to see things, reality consists precisely of projected perspectives. Law, for instance, becomes literature; morality becomes public convention; social life becomes a text subject to infinite hermeneutical exegesis.[46] As one public relations executive puts it, in commenting on another rearrangement of data to move closer to a client's viewpoint: "It's called 'interpretation.'" As long as a kind of plausibility is maintained, one perspective is as good as any other. In discounting in advance any intrinsic significance of ideas or, one might add, of moral values that flow from them, this habit of mind meshes nicely with the bureaucratic virtues of adeptness at inconsistency and alertness to expediency. Within such a framework, public relations specialists usually conclude very pragmatically that one might as well "sing whatever song the client wants to hear."

Public relations work both demands and fosters in its practitioners a characteristic occupational virtue, that is, a highly self-conscious, reflexive ability to "doublethink," to borrow Orwell's term, to hold in one's mind and be able to voice if necessary completely contradictory versions of reality. Successful doublethinking demands, first, a talent for the intricate casuistry needed to broker whatever differences may exist between one's sense of self and the exigencies of immediate situations and, second, the ability to externalize one's casuistic ability to help others invent better reasons for doing what has to be done. One should note that this occupational virtue is a highly refined version of the adeptness at inconsistency that marks the symbolic dexterity of successful corporate managers and to the extent that corporate managers rely on public relations practitioners, it is one seedbed of that adeptness.

Public relations practitioners sometimes define their ability to doublethink as a personal hazard of sorts even as they recognize its professional value. They see, for instance, the systematic distancing of oneself both from the symbols that one manipulates and from the people that one serves – a distancing that they know makes doublethink possible and effective – as a kind of cynicism. The aphorism in the field is: "You come into this business an idealist; you leave a cynic." Practitioners' view of the malleability of truth is the touchstone for their recognition of the hazardous virtue that their work requires. One public relations executive explains:

> Most PR people are very cynical indeed. For them, truth is relative, completely relative. They can see relativity in any situation. They can look at truth from many different angles and switch viewpoints often and rapidly.

One must, of course, bring form out of such plasticity in order to accomplish the practical goal of helping clients forge a particular public stance. But even as one doublethinks to help others rationalize themselves, one becomes drawn deeper into an ambiguity where nothing is certain and where nothing commands, or can command, a lasting commitment. The same executive says:

> You have to be able to understand how people think. To really do this, you have to objectify people; you have to be able to press people and go deeper into their motives than you normally would. You have to be able to recognize the diversity of perspectives on things and you have to be able to say the opposite point of view from what you might have yourself.

Like the notion of truth, ideas as such are irrelevant or only become useful and important when they have an immediate practical use. For this reason, even more than in other areas of business, deeply held convictions, whether political, religious, or moral, can only be a hindrance to big success in public relations. However, Images Inc., and some other public relations firms as well, do not require their executives to work on accounts with which they feel "uncomfortable." Such a policy honors individuals' private reservations whatever their source. It also prudently recognizes that psychologial discomfort could undermine the emotional conviction, or its convincing semblance, thought necessary to sell a client's viewpoint to a public. Such a separation of individual conscience from corporate action institutes a particular kind of casuistry, one that allows individuals to enjoy the benefits of corporate responses to exigencies while permitting personal feelings of moral purity. As it happens, the peculiar angle of vision that public relations work affords its practitioners demands continual casuistry. Greater proficiency in doublethink not only increases the ability to shape usable practical ideas but it also increases the sense of distance that practitioners experience between themselves and their occupational roles. Practitioners come to see how their own carefully crafted rationales cloak self-interest even as they, like Harry Reichenbach before them, see their clients coming to believe the promotional stories that they fashion. They see too the propensity and willingness of large sectors of a presumably literate public to "believe in the tooth-fairy" and they often ask themselves: If the public will accept, say, this, what won't they accept? In this sense, the more successful one becomes at public relations, the greater the likelihood of seeing oneself as cynical, though, as suggested earlier, any such self-conception is always, except perhaps to some close colleagues, masked with public faces of optimistic ingenuousness and buoyant vitality. Moreover, as also mentioned earlier, public relations practitioners, attuned as they are to public opinion, are acutely aware of the often pejorative public views of their profession. Both because they see their own virtues as hazardous and know that others see their profession as suspect, they apply their abilities of inventing better ways of legitimating what has to be done to their own work. It is worth noting some of the main directions such legitimations take.

Public relations practitioners sometimes claim an identification with the interests of their clients, say, advocacy of textile tariffs or construction of a political action committee. Here, the situation of corporate in-house public relations practitioners differs somewhat from those in agencies. Continual efforts for a unitary set of interests can provide corporate practitioners with a readier basis for organizational faith than the necessarily variegated advocacies of men and women in agencies. The depth of such faith depends largely on the extent to which corporate practitioners help make the decisions they have to defend publicly, that is, on the extent to which they take on the managerial role and become liable to its cognitive consequences. Agency practitioners not only defend multiple interests but face repeatedly the experience of even well-served clients switching agencies. Especially unsettling are the departures of clients who decide that, since they are as they have been portrayed, they have no future need to construct reality. The continual circulation of client accounts in agencies diminishes the possibilities of comforting, long-held allegiances to organizations, products, or causes.

Alternatively, and by contrast, practitioners in both settings sometimes justify their efforts by appealing to a professional ethos that celebrates the exercise of technical skill separated from any emotional commitment to one's clients. A dignified version of this legitimation is the often repeated analogy between public relations practitioners and lawyers; both occupations, it is argued, fulfill important advocacy roles in a free society. Only the practice of the professional virtue of public relations, however hazardous to individual practitioners, can assure the continued diversity of opinion that marks our democracy. Practitioners evince a somewhat more direct version of this stance when they refer to themselves as "hired guns," a characterization often accompanied with sardonic irony. For instance, when his firm had just taken the account of a corporation engaged in a widely publicized ploy to thwart workers' attempts to gain compensation for debilitating occupational illnesses by declaring bankruptcy, one executive says: "Well, after all, these bastards have got a story too!" Another executive muses: "I often ask myself: 'What is the going price for my soul today?'" Here, verbal irony symbolizes and expresses the professional virtue of cynicism but more in celebration than in defense. For the most part, hired guns accept the world as it is, without qualms, and tell stories for those who can pay the storytellers. As one executive explains:

> That's the *reality* of our society. There's no question that their story is being told because they have the money and power. I've got to recognize that I'm part of this society and just come to live with that. Our society *is* the way it is. It's run on money and power, it's that simple. Truth has nothing to do with it. So we just accept the world as it is and live with it.

on a large screen where they can see all the ploys they use to manipulate others in the little dramas of their own lives. They see all the duplicity and all the storytelling of their own lives writ large. It makes them very uncomfortable because we remind them of themselves.

Men and women in public relations simply utilize their own intuitive and experiential understandings of the quandaries, negotiations, and brokered and bungled solutions of private lives as the stuff to shape the scripts of public drama. They succeed precisely when the stories they fashion have emotional resonance in the private lives of broad sectors of the public, even though such resonance might precipitate a recoiling jolt of self-recognition and consequent antagonism toward the storyteller. In this sense, public relations performs a quasireligious symbolic role, most closely approximated by the traditional role of priest or minister or in our more secular world by the psychotherapist. This quasireligious function reconciles business to the public by providing businessmen with acceptable vocabularies to confess their sins and do repentance if necessary and with the opportunity to receive from the public, regulators, and legislators alike, a kind of absolution.

However, I should reiterate that, because of the occupational role structure that binds them together, the most important audience and customer for public relations are managers themselves. The premium on alertness to expediency demands, of course, an ability and readiness to doublethink one's way through the contradictory irrationalities of everyday problems. But standing at the middle of events grappling with exigencies, especially in a hierarchical milieu that requires authorities to display sincere conviction in their actions, seems to foster at least a kind of half-belief, and sometimes more, in one's efforts to do what has to be done. In helping managers invent better reasons for expedient action, public relations counselors, and less directly the techniques and the casuistic habit of mind they institutionalize in management circles, reduce the distance managers experience between requisite moral flexibility and the occupationally induced urge to believe sincerely in the value of one's own actions. The central institutional mechanism in managerial circles for this process, from the middle levels to the very top of the corporation, is what might be called a rehearsal.

Rehearsals mark all of social life. I shall focus here only on a special kind of rehearsal, that is, the rehearsal of legitimations for what has to be done. Within their own organizational circles, managers regularly rehearse their explanations and accounts for actions decided upon. On one hand, such rehearsals may prepare one principally for the ongoing internal organizational drama. In this case, rehearsals often focus on developing "defensible" rationales for action which can, of course, assume widely varying forms depending on which criteria and ideologies hold sway in an organization at a particular time. Alternatively, rehearsals may be geared to honing rationales for the broader extra-organizational audiences that managers at certain levels and in particular positions must sometimes address. But whether rehearsals of legitimation are designed to prepare managers for internal or external audiences, they typically go through a three-stage sequence. First, managers cast around a variety of perspectives in order to "cover all the bases" and see the situation at hand from many angles of vision. In this stage, there is little formality and often a fair amount of levity, usually in the form of parody by offering, for instance, burlesque rationales for action with mock seriousness. Certain viewpoints fall of their own weight, others get discarded as wholly implausible, and still others are entertained for long periods but in a provisional manner.

The second stage of such a rehearsal begins when it becomes clear, often but not always by the edict of the presiding authority, that certain explanations rather than others should be the point of focus. Given managers' sensitivity to interactional and verbal cues, particularly from bosses, the shift to a more focused discussion is not usually precipitous or forced. Rather, one or more possible rationales become subject to a kind of devil's advocacy in which potential weaknesses of arguments are explored. The manner of discussion shifts during this stage toward a more formal etiquette of debate. One manager will say, for instance, "Well, we could say that . . .," elaborating a set of reasons for action. Another manager will counter, "But, if you say that, it could be argued that. . . . Why not put it this way . . .?" And still another will say, "But if we say that, how do we explain . . .?" Except during a precipitous crisis, this second stage of a rehearsal can last for long periods and extend over many meetings until viewpoints begin to crystallize.

The final stage of a rehearsal of legitimations begins, almost imperceptibly, when a certain viewpoint seems convincing to a circle and begins to assume coherent and elaborate form. Sometimes an individual manager will articulate a rationale in a manner that suddenly "puts all the pieces together"; sometimes a public relations counselor assumes this interactive symbolic role. However, the decisive moment in the third stage of a rehearsal and, in fact, the point of the whole process comes when a managerial circle, or key members of it, decide that a certain rationale "is the way to go," one with which they "feel comfortable." Here morality becomes one's personal comfort vis-à-vis the anticipated views of others. The measure of that comfort becomes a confidence in the casuistry necessary to persuade others that one's stories are plausible and one's choices reasonable. Such anticipatory confrontations with the viewpoints of certain publics make rehearsals, on one hand, a forum for a kind of accountability. On the other, in helping managers master the public relations technique of playing with the magic lantern, rehearsals also encourage the most subtle form of hype, namely convincing oneself of one's own rectitude.

Despite their thoroughgoing skepticism, even public relations men and women can become dazzled by their own technique. The magic lantern produces both light and shadows. What matters on the screen are convincing impressions of reality, plausible representations, and a conformity to conventional manners, faces, and tastes. The images cast upon the screen do not so much displace substance, notions of truth, and principles as leave them in the dim periphery of the theater. Public relations becomes public-relations-mindedness, a circuitous institutional logic that makes placating various publics the principal and, at times, the only goal. Some years ago, Images Inc. came under vigorous journalistic and public assault for some questionable practices of its own. The firm's instinctive institutional response suggests the habit of mind that public-relations-mindedness creates. Executives at the firm held, of course, their own rehearsal to frame appropriate responses to the charges being made. As public pressure mounted, the public relations firm created a position and then appointed a director of public relations.

Notes

1. See Harry Reichenbach, *Phantom Fame,* as told to David Freedman (New York: Simon and Schuster, Inc., 1931), pp. 46–47.
2. Phineas T. Barnum, *Barnum's Own Story: The Autobiography of P. T. Barnum, Combined & condensed from the various editions published during his lifetime by Waldo R. Browne* (New York: The Viking Press, Inc., 1927). For a thoughtful and provoking essay on the social significance of Barnum's art and ideology, see Neil Harris, *Humbug* (Boston, Mass: Little, Brown and Company, 1973).
3. Reichenbach, *Phantom Fame* (New York: Simon and Schuster, Inc., 1931), p. 8.
4. Reichenbach, pp. 203–204.
5. Reichenbach, pp. 106–113.
6. Reichenbach, pp. 55–58.
7. Reichenbach, pp. 178–183.
8. Reichenbach, p. 184.
9. Reichenbach, p. 29. The first magic lantern was a simple projective device consisting essentially of a box with a concave mirror at the rear, a candle for a light source, an aperture to insert silhouette slides, and a lens to magnify the image. Later, slides mounted in a circle or in an enclosed mobile cylinder enabled motion to be simulated on the screen. The motion picture is the direct descendant of the magic lantern. A Jesuit priest, Athanasius Kircher, invented the magic lantern around 1644; he was considered by many to be engaged in necromancy because he could make images and shadows appear where none had been before. For a fascinating treatment of the whole history of magic lanterns, see Martin Quigley, Jr., *Magic Shadows: The Story of the Origin of Motion Pictures* (Washington, D.C.: Georgetown University Press, 1948).

   One should note that extravagant stunts, like those concocted by Reichenbach, are still used by public relations firms. Television coverage, of course, provides an even greater magic lantern effect than Reichenbach could have imagined. The following item appeared in the in-house newsletter of Images Inc.:

   > [S]taffer [Jim Jenkins] recently assisted in the coordination of a "hanging" by . . . a dance troupe out of Japan, on behalf of [a major Japanese corporation]. Prior to a performance at the Warner

Theater in the Nation's Capital, the troupe performed a "hanging" from the National Theater . . . [as] four members, with their ankles bound, were lowered by ropes, from the top of the building. Dressed in white, and with their heads shaven, the dancers stopped traffic during the noontime event as they performed a brief dance, suspended in the air. The event received extensive network and local affiliate attention.

10. Reichenbach, p. 112.
11. Reichenbach, p. 123.
12. Reichenbach, pp. 99, and 113.
13. Reichenbach, p. 92.
14. Reichenbach, p. 165.
15. Ibid.
16. Reichenbach, p. 166.
17. Reichenbach, p. 167.
18. Reichenbach, p. 169.
19. Reichenbach, pp. 168–169.
20. Reichenbach, p. 173.
21. One should examine in particular Leila A. Sussmann, *The Public Relations Movement in America*, unpublished M.A. Thesis (University of Chicago, Department of Sociology, March 1947); Richard S. Tedlow, *Keeping the Corporate Image: Public Relations and Business, 1900–1950* (Greenwich, Conn.: JAI Press Inc., 1979); and Alan R. Raucher, *Public Relations and Business, 1900–1929*, (Baltimore, Md.: The Johns Hopkins Press, 1968).
22. See C. C. Regier, *The Era of the Muckrakers* (Chapel Hill, N.C.: The University of North Carolina Press, 1932), pp. 173 ff. Regier's work is a good social history of the whole era.
23. In 1912, for instance, Daniel Guggenheim testified before a hostile industrial relations commission in the aftermath of fierce strikes by workers in Guggenheim mines who claimed a number of abuses, including twelve-hour work days, low wages, poor living conditions, and an extremely high rate of disabling injuries. Under the guidance of Bernard Baruch and Sam Untermeyer, Guggenheim told an astonished commission and audience of labor organizers and socialists that workers are justified in organizing, entitled to more material goods, entitled to a greater voice in determining work conditions, and entitled to share in industry's profits. Guggenheim went so far as to assert that the government should facilitate these goals by taxing the estates of the rich. The last sentiment outflanked Miss Ida Tarbell, the woman considered, to her own chagrin, the scourge of the Rockefellers. She criticized Guggenheim's proposal for inheritance taxes as somewhat too radical, though she lauded him as a fine captain of industry. See Harvey O'Connor, *The Guggenheims: The Making of an American Dynasty* (New York: Covici-Friede Publishers, 1937), pp. 314–323. Ida M. Tarbell was, of course, the author of *The History of the Standard Oil Company*, 2 vols (New York: McClure, Phillips & Company, 1904), one of the earliest and most

important muckraking tracts. As Richard Hofstadter points out, Tarbell, the daughter of an oil-rich Pennsylvania family whose fortunes suffered from Rockefeller's push for monopoly, was an accidental muckraker of sorts, as was true of many of her colleagues. She ended her career publishing a hagiography of the industrialist Judge Gary. See Richard Hofstadter, *The Age of Reform: From Bryan to F.D.R.* (New York: Vintage, 1955), pp. 193–194.

In 1914, the Rockefellers, under great public criticism because of the massacre of striking workers and their families at Ludlow, Colorado, hired Ivy Lee, then a counsel with the troubled Pennsylvania Railroad. Shortly thereafter, John D. Rockefeller, Jr., toured the strike areas of Colorado, spoke with the workers, an event that received wide press coverage, and later shook hands with the fabled Mother Jones before the same labor commission that Guggenheim had outmaneuvered. Both the Guggenheims and the Rockefellers, of course, also developed wide-ranging philanthropic programs. See Alan R. Raucher, *Public Relations and Business, 1900–1920*, pp. 25–27, and Leila A. Sussman, *The Public Relations Movement in America*, p. 16. See also the account in the biography of Lee by Ray Eldon Hiebert, *Courtier to the Crowd* (Ames, Iowa: Iowa State University Press, 1966), pp. 97–108.

24. See, for instance, Ray Hiebert, *Courtier to the Crowd*, p. 12. Throughout his career, Lee adopted the public stance that leaders should be frank and direct with the masses. See, for instance, Ivy Lee, Occasional Paper-No. 3, *The Problem of International Propaganda*, An Address by Ivy Lee Before a Private Group of Persons Concerned With International Affairs, in London, July 3, 1934 (New York?: 1934).

25. George Creel's autobiography *Rebel At Large* (New York: G. P. Putnam's Sons, 1947) describes his early career, which included campaigns against child labor, bribery of public officials, and Rockefeller's difficulties at Ludlow, Colorado. Louis Filler, *Crusaders for American Liberalism* (Yellow Springs, Ohio: Antioch Press, 1961), among others, notes the irony of the wholesale incorporation of the muckrakers into the Committee on Public Information. Creel's own unofficial recounting of the CPI is *How We Advertised America: The First Telling of the Amazing Story of the Committee on Public Information That Carried the Gospel of Americanism to Every Corner of the Globe* (New York: Harper & Brothers, 1920).

In a short eighteen months, among other activities, the CPI published large numbers of pamphlets for worldwide distribution; commanded the services of 75,000 speakers in 5,200 communities giving 755,190 speeches, each of four-minutes duration; mobilized artists and advertising men both to produce pictorial publicity and to disseminate it in every conceivable way; issued a daily newspaper to 100,000 people; produced a wide range of feature and shorter length films, as well as photographic and slide displays; gathered together the "leading novelists, essayists, and publicists of the land" who produced articles on the war and American life for press syndication; established a Bureau of Cartoons that mobilized and directed the cartoonists of the country for constructive war efforts; and supervised the censorship of newspapers, periodicals, cables, and films to ward off any misleading impressions of American life. For some general treatments of the work of the Committee on Public Information, see U.S. Committee on Public Information, *The Creel Report* (New York: DaCapo Press, 1972); Detlef R. Peters, *Das "US-Committee on Public Information"* (Inaugural-Dissertation, Freie Universität, Berlin, 1964); and James R. Mock and Cedric Larson, *Words That Won the War* (Princeton, N.J.: Princeton University Press, 1939). For an inside understanding of the organizational workings of the CPI, one should consult the correspondence of Carl Byoir, Creel's associate chairman. The vast part of the daily business of the CPI went through Byoir, and it is in his letters and directives that one can begin to sense the sprawling nature of the organization, the inevitable petty bickerings, the currying of political favor, and the development of the often ingenious methods used to develop public support for the war. See National Archives, Record Group 63, *Records of the Committee on Public Information.* CPI 1 A-4, CPI 1 A-5, CPI 1 A-6, and CPI 1 A-7. Byoir, of course, went on to found a prosperous public relations agency that bore his name until late in 1986, when it was absorbed by Hill and Knowlton, another large public relations firm.

26. Harry Reichenbach, a member of Creel's Committee, describes some of the techniques used to demoralize the enemy and encourage surrender. These included sending a million letters to Italian soldiers at the front telling them that their wives were adulterously involved with those exempted from armed service, dropping "diplomas" over German lines that qualified any German private to go over to the Allies and be immediately promoted to office status, and smuggling small pocket Bibles into Germany that contained propaganda tracts inside. See Reichenbach, *Phantom Fame*, pp. 236 and 246–248.

27. Richard Tedlow, *Keeping the Corporate Image*, p. 40.

28. Edward L. Bernays, *Propaganda* (New York: Liveright, 1928), pp. 27–28. Harry Reichenbach also comments on his own realization of the importance of propaganda during the war:

> The vast extent of propaganda only dawned on me now. It was almost as much a war of printing presses as of machine guns. Instead of one spieler on a platform in front of the Koutch tent, there were a hundred and fifty thousand spielers, – spielers as far as the eye could reach, spielers that could show you black is white and night is day without stumbling a single word or interrupting the smooth and glossy flow of their language: "Come here folks! The greatest war on earth! We've got the deadliest gases, the biggest cannons, the most tangled barbed wire, the fastest aeroplanes, the surest torpedoes, the finest soldiers to send over the top – and what is more, the enemy is all wrong!" (Reichenbach, *Phantom Fame*, p. 240.)

29. Walter Lippmann, *The Phantom Public* (New York: Harcourt, Brace and Company, 1925), p. 65.
30. See Merle Curti, "The Changing Concept of 'Human Nature' in the Literature of American Advertising," *Business History Review*, Vol. 41, No. 4 (Winter 1967), pp. 335–357, especially p. 356. See also Daniel Pope, *The Making of Modern Advertising* (New York: Basic Books, 1982), pp. 237–251.
31. Edward Bernays, *Propaganda*, p. 47.
32. Edward Bernays, *Propaganda*, p. 152.
33. See Francis X. Sutton, Seymour E. Harris, Carl Kaysen, and James Tobin, *The American Business Creed* (New York: Schocken Books, 1962). Stated briefly, some of the main themes of the NAM campaign were:

    – Business has been systematically misrepresented to the American people by self-interested groups – labor, radicals, and those bent on socialism. This misinformation has created a serious misunderstanding of the vital role that business plays in the American system.
    – No matter how bad things are at the moment, Americans still enjoy the best standard of living on earth, and this is a direct result of the genius of American business. Moreover, the great political freedom we enjoy here is inextricably tied to our economic freedom; only the free market system can provide political freedom. We cannot deceive ourselves with the idea that government encroachments on the economy can be allowed without endangering our basic political rights.
    – Moreover, Americans are all in this together. Business, labor, and government are not, at bottom, antagonists. They all share the common interest of rebuilding America. Businessmen want and need to be successful for everyone's benefit. What hurts business hurts everyone.
    – The real leaders of our country are therefore businessmen and business managers. It is they who are seeking harmony and progress and working for everyone's interests. People should not impede them in this task but rather assist them. Businesses need to make a fair profit to continue their work on behalf of the society.

    See Sutton et al., pp. 19–52. See also S. H. Walker and Paul Sklar, *Business Finds Its Voice* (New York: Harper and Bros., 1938), pp. 1–16.
34. See Walker and Sklar, *Business Finds Its Voice*, pp. 19–40.
35. Richard Tedlow, *Keeping the Corporate Image*, pp. 122–125, gives a good description of the split between the NAM and the CED.
36. William H. Whyte, *Is Anybody Listening?* (New York: Simon and Schuster, Inc., 1952).
37. The term is Max Weber's to describe one of many types of ancient prophets, specifically those whose predictions "evoked timely expectations" in royal court circles. See *Ancient Judaism*, translated by Hans Gerth and Don Martindale (Glencoe, Ill.: Free Press, 1952),

p. 325 and *passim*. In our era, public relations is, of course, only one of the many professions that act as prophets of good fortune. In this category, one must also include any group that puts its empirical and interpretive legerdemain at the disposal of established authority. See Joseph Bensman, "Hans Gerth's Contribution to American Sociology," in *Politics, Character and Culture: Perspectives from Hans Gerth,* edited by Joseph Bensman, Arthur Vidich, and Nobuko Gerth (Westport, Conn.: Greenwood Press, 1982), pp. 221–274. See especially p. 247.

38. Exact data on public relations are hard to obtain because the indirect character of the public appeals that mark the field obscures the real extent of public relations activities. Corporate budgets for the salaries of internal public relations staff are, for instance, a poor index of the real amount of money spent on public relations work. That same staff may be coordinating portions of various budgets, such as those allocated for government lobbying, corporate donations to the arts, and advertising.

39. From 1974 to 1984, corporate expenditures for what is called corporate or public relations advertising in the six main media outlets (consumer magazines, newspaper supplements, network television, spot television, radio, and outdoor) rose by 249 percent to total $782,985,000 in 1984. Trade association advertising of the same sort showed an even larger increase, rising 397.4 percent over the same period; associations spent $435,168,500 in the same six media in 1984. See Josephine Curran, "The 14th Annual Review of Corporate Advertising Expenditures," *Public Relations Journal,* Vol. 41, No. 12 (December 1985), p. 28 ff. One should note that some people in public relations would dispute using any advertising figures to measure public relations. But public relations personnel are often involved in planning out this particular kind of advertising.

Gross revenue figures for the largest public relations firms are perhaps a better index of the growth of the field. *Jack O'Dwyer's Newsletter,* the most widely read publication in the field, publishes annually a list of the top public relations firms and their gross fee income. For the top 15 firms in 1969, the total combined fee income was $46,215,000; in 1983, it was $265,223,000 (my calculations, rounded and unadjusted figures). The growing educational respectability of public relations is another measure of the field's growth. Albert Walker, *Status and Trends in Public Relations Education in United States Senior Colleges and Universities* (New York: Foundation for Public Relations Research and Education, 1981) lists more than 300 colleges and universities that offer courses in public relations; 65 of these offer degrees in public relations or in closely related fields with a public relations emphasis.

40. The word "client," as used in both the public relations and advertising worlds, has a multitude of meanings depending on the context. It is used to refer variously to a corporation whose account one services, one's opposite number at the corporation, or an entire group of individuals at the corporation charged with overseeing

and evaluating agency work. It can also describe a generalized other with whom one has a sometimes friendly, sometimes antagonistic, but always dependent relationship. The best treatment of the multi-faceted and inferential use of the word, as well as of the far-reaching consequences for agency personnel having multiple interpretive arbiters of one's work, has been done by Janice M. Hirota in her analysis of the "approval process" in advertising agencies. See her "Cultural Mediums: The Work World of 'Creatives' in American Advertising Agencies," unpublished Ph.D. Diss., Department of Anthropology, Columbia University, 1988.

41. The scientific literature on the ozone depletion controversy is vast and highly technical. However, one can grasp the main dimensions of the issue by examining the principal reports that have come out of the National Academy of Sciences on the issue. These are National Research Council, Committee on Impacts of Stratospheric Change, *Halocarbons: Effects on Stratospheric Ozone* (Washington, D.C.: National Academy of Sciences, 1976); National Research Council, Committee on Impacts of Stratospheric Change, *Halocarbons: Environmental Effects of Chlorofluoromethane Release* (Washington, D.C.: National Academy of Sciences, 1976); National Research Council, Committee on Impacts of Stratospheric Change and Committee on Alternatives for the Reduction of Chlorofluorocarbon Emissions, *Protections Against Depletion of Stratospheric Ozone by Chlorofluorocarbons* (Washington, D.C.: National Academy of Sciences, 1979); National Research Council, Committee on Chemistry and Physics of Ozone Depletion and the Committee on Biological Effects of Increased Solar Ultraviolet Radiation, *Causes and Effects of Stratospheric Ozone Reduction: An Update* (Washington, D.C.: National Academy of Sciences, 1982); and National Research Council, Committee on Causes and Effects of Changes in Stratospheric Ozone, *Causes and Effects of Changes in Stratospheric Ozone: Update 1983* (Washington, DC.: National Academy Press, 1984).

As it happens, a hole in the ozone the size of the continental United States was only recently discovered above Antarctica. A multination meeting sponsored by the United Nations Environmental Program agreed in principle (in April 1987) to freeze and eventually to reduce the production and consumption of chlorofluorocarbons and other industrial chemicals that purportedly attack the ozone. See Thomas W. Netter, "U.N. Parley Agrees to Protect Ozone," *The New York Times*, Friday, May 1, 1987, A1, col. 1 and A10, cols. 3–4. In an interview in late 1986, an Alchemy executive commented on the finding in Antarctica: "We weren't aware that penguins used that much hairspray."

42. At Weft Corporation's huge finishing plant, the obstacles to reducing workers' exposure to formaldehyde do indeed seem to be formidable. At that plant, Weft applies a formaldehyde-based resin to raw cloth, along with a variety of other mixtures such as blueing agents and softeners, depending on customer specifications, on nineteen finishing ranges located in the middle of the plant. The ranges

are between 150 and 200 feet in length and handle fabric up to 200 inches wide. Each range is fed by two feeder vats located in an enclosed room above the ranges; these vats themselves are fed from a warehouse through a piping system.

The problem of workers' exposure to free formaldehyde – that is, formaldehyde that has escaped the resin and returned to a gaseous state – occurs in the upstairs room as well as downstairs at each range. The vats upstairs could be totally encased without too much trouble, but only the few workers who mix the resin work around them. The real problem is in the downstairs ranges, which because of their size cannot be easily or inexpensively encased. Moreover, in order to get exposure down to one ppm, the level that Weft executives at the time of my field research feared OSHA would impose, the present four exhaust systems that carry off fumes and emissions from production would have to be dramatically improved. Essentially this would require the erection of a massive smokestack to eject the hot moist air from production high enough above the plant to prevent any recirculation of ejected air while at the same time pumping enough fresh air into the plant to prevent a quasivacuum from being created. But another entire manufacturing operation is located in the same building, on the floor directly above the finishing ranges. This would have to be closed down or moved to another location. In effect, were the exposure to formaldehyde to be lowered to one ppm, the real choices facing Weft would be to build a new plant with both completely encased machinery and a wholly new ventilation system, or to find a substitute for formaldehyde. Similar dilemmas face other manufacturers. The textile industry has been scrambling to find a substitute for formaldehyde, but no really cost-effective one has yet been discovered.

43. James W. Giggey, "Chairman's Report," *1983 Annual Report, Formaldehyde Institute* (Scarsdale, N.Y.: Formaldehyde Institute, 1983), p. 3.

44. See Formaldehyde Institute, *Formaldehyde Information Kit* (Scarsdale, N.Y.: Formaldehyde Institute, no date), *passim*. In the last several years, there have been several studies done by different groups on the health dangers posed by formaldehyde. Evidence for the carcinogenicity of formaldehyde was first presented in 1979. See Chemical Industry Institute of Toxicology, *Statement Concerning Research Findings*, Docket No. 11109 (Research Triangle Park, N.C.: CIIT), October 8, 1979. These data and other evidence are reviewed in Joint NIOSH/OSHA Current Intelligence Bulletin 34, *Formaldehyde: Evidence of Carcinogenicity* (Cincinnati, Oh.: National Institute for Occupational Safety and Health, April 15, 1981). More recently, OSHA issued a notice prior to rulemaking that further reviews previous studies and proposes lowering permissible exposure levels to the chemical. See "Occupational Exposure to Formaldehyde," *Federal Register*, Wednesday, April 17, 1985, Vol. 50, No. 74, pp. 15179–15184. On December 10, 1985, OSHA proposed a final rule with two regulatory alternatives, depending on whether it decided

finally whether formaldehyde is an irritant or a carcinogen. The Formaldehyde Institute, of course, took the position that its members should support the notion that the chemical is an irritant; this would involve lowering the permissible exposure limit to between one and two ppm. The Institute told its members to urge OSHA "not to conclude that low levels of exposure (3 ppm 8-hour TWA) of formaldehyde should be regulated as a potential occupational carcinogen unless there is evidence of occupational cancer in man as opposed to laboratory animals under high dose conditions." See Formaldehyde Institute, *Formaldehyde Newsletter*, Vol. VI, No. 1 (March 3, 1986), p. 1. (The newsletter and other materials are available from the Institute at its current address, 1330 Connecticut Avenue, N.W., Washington, D.C. 20036.) The Institute received a big boost for its position with the release in June 1986 of a long-term epidemiological study conducted by the National Cancer Institute together with a consortium of producers and users of formaldehyde. The study concluded that the data from its historical cohort study of 26,561 workers in ten formaldehyde-producing or using facilities "provide little evidence that mortality from cancer is associated with formaldehyde exposure at levels experienced by workers in this study." (p. 1071). See Aaron Blair *et al.*, "Mortality Among Industrial Workers Exposed to Formaldehyde," *Journal of the National Cancer Institute*, Vol. 76, No. 6 (June 1986), pp. 1071–1084.

But subsequent studies, including another by Dr. Blair (see Aaron Blair *et al.*, "Cancers of the Nasal Pharynx and Oral Pharynx," *Journal of the National Cancer Institute*, Vol. 78, No. 1 [January 1987], pp. 191–192), have left the matter still very controverted. In the late spring of 1987, the Environmental Protection Agency issued a risk assessment of formaldehyde saying that there is limited evidence that exposure to formaldehyde causes cancer in humans. There was, of course, a chorus of scoffs and boos from segments of the business community. See, for instance, the editorial "Scaring the Public" in *The Wall Street Journal*, July 7, 1987. The Formaldehyde Institute's position remains unchanged. A final OSHA rule on workplace exposure to formaldehyde is expected late in 1987, with implementation due sometime in 1988.

45. For an overview of the acid rain dispute, see Congress of the United States, Office of Technology Assessment, *Acid Rain and Transported Air Pollutants: Implications for Public Policy* (Washington, D.C.: Government Printing Office, 1984); National Research Council Committee on Atmospheric Transport and Chemical Transformation in Acid Precipitation, *Atmospheric Processes in Eastern North America: A Review of Current Scientific Understanding* (Washington, D.C.: National Academy Press, 1983). See also Robert H. Boyle and R. Alexander Boyle, *Acid Rain* (New York: Schocken Books, 1983).

The Alliance's viewpoint is put forward in a series of newsletters. The moderate, genteel tone of these newsletters shows sophisticated public relations work. Exactly the same arguments, expressed, however, much more crudely, may be found in *The National Independent Coal Leader*, the monthly publication of the conservative National Independent Coal Operators' Association. See, for instance, "Acid Rain: VPI Professor Says Coal Is Not to Blame," Vol. 15, No. 8 (March 1981), p. 27; "Many Reputable Scientists Disagree on the Acid Precipitation: Coal is Not the Culprit," Vol. 16, No. 3 (October 1981), p. 1 ff.; "Cause and Effect of Acid Rain Needs Research," Vol. 16, No. 11 (June 1982), p. 14; "Experts Question Acid Rain Theories," Vol. 17, No. 4 (October 1982), p. 14 (issue misnumbered; should be No. 3); "Acid Lakes Traced to Soil, not Rain," Vol. 17, No. 8 (March 1983), p. 16; "Acid Rain Bill Would Harm Industry, Economy," Vol. 17, No. 10 (May 1983), p. 16; "Acid Precipitation and Acid Lakes; Is Coal the Whipping Boy for Oil's Pollution Contribution?" Vol. 18, No. 4 (November 1983), p. 1 ff.; "Expert Says Acid Rain Issue Distroted [sic] by Press," Vol. 18, No. 6 (February 1984), p. 1 (issue misnumbered; should be No. 7); "Environmentalists Accused of Trying to Kill Mining," Vol. 18, No. 5 (December 1983), p. 6; "Based Entirely on Theory: Acid Rain – Fact or Fiction?", Vol. 18, No. 6 (January 1984), p. 1 ff.; "Ky. Official Sees Little Benefit From Acid Rain Controls," Vol. 19, No. 6 (March 1985), p. 20; and "Studies Find No Acid Precipitation," Vol. 20, No. 2 (September 1985), p. 8.

46. The literature of poststructuralist, postrealist criticism is enormous and covers a variety of fields. For a few salient examples, see Stanley Fish, *Is There a Text in This Class? The Authority of Interpretive Communities* (Cambridge, Mass.: Harvard University Press, 1980); Mark C. Taylor, "Deconstruction: What's the Difference?", *Soundings*, Vol. LXVI, No. 4 (Winter 1983), pp. 387–403; and Sanford Levinson, "Law As Literature," *Texas Law Review*, Vol. 60, No. 3 (March 1982), pp. 373–403. For some counterviews, see Gerald Graff, *Literature Against Itself* (Chicago, Ill.: The University of Chicago Press, 1979); Steven Knapp and Walter Benn Michaels, "Against Theory," *Critical Inquiry*, Vol. 8 (Summer 1982), pp. 723–742; and Gene Bell-Villada, "Northrop Frye, Modern Fantasy, Centrist Liberalism, Anti-Marxism, Latin Leftism, Passing Time, and Other Limits of American Academic Criticism," *Berkshire Review*, Vol. 19 (1984), pp. 40–55.

17 The Persuasive Functions of Slogans*

Charles J. Stewart, Craig Allen Smith, and Robert E. Denton, Jr.

The drastic increase in social activism within the United States since 1960 has been accompanied by such memorable and sometimes infamous, slogans as: "Hey, Hey, LBJ, How Many Kids Have You Killed Today"; "Hell No, We Won't Go"; "Fuck the Draft"; "Freedom Now"; "Free Huey"; "Dare to Struggle, Dare to Win"; "Black Power"; "Don't Trust Anyone Over 30"; "America, Love It or Leave It"; "America, Change It or Lose It"; "Gray Power"; and "Black Is Beautiful." Protestors have chanted, shouted, and sung slogans; printed them in leaflets, pamphlets, and social movement newsletters and newspapers; worn them on buttons, tee-shirts, jackets, and the seats of their pants; and have written, painted, or pasted them on billboards, posters, banners, automobile bumpers, buses, subways, sidewalks, and walls. But in spite of the use and visibility of slogans, they have received little attention in studies of strategies, tactics, and communication channels employed by social movements.[1]

THE NATURE OF SLOGANS

"Sloganeering" did not originate in the 1960s. The term has a rich history. It originated from the Gaelic word *slaughgharim*, which signified a "host-shout," "war cry," or "gathering word of phrase of one of the old Highland clans; hence the shout or battle cry of soldiers in the field."[2] English-speaking people began using the term by 1704. The term at that time meant "the distinctive note, phrase or cry of any person or body of persons." Slogans were com-

* Reprinted from Charles J. Stewart, Craig Allen Smith, and Robert E. Denton, Jr., *Persuasion in Social Movements*, 2nd edition (Prospect Heights, Ill.: Waveland Press, 1989).

mon throughout the European continent during the middle ages, and they were utilized primarily as "passwords to insure proper recognition of individuals at night or in the confusion of battle." The American revolutionary rhetoric would not have been the same without "the Boston Massacre," "the Boston Tea Party," "the shot heard around the world," and shouts of "no taxation without representation."

John Bowers and Donovan Ochs define slogans as "imperative statements ... single words or short phrases with the imperative mood strongly implied."[3] But slogans are more than "imperative statements" – commands, decrees, edicts, or fiats; they also invoke impressions and elicit emotional responses. George Shankel defines a slogan as "some pointed term, phrase, or expression, fittingly worded, which suggests action, loyalty, or which causes people to decide upon and to fight for the realization of some principle or decisive issue."[4] This definition recognizes that slogans perform a variety of persuasive functions. Murray Edelman has discussed the "dynamic" function of language in stimulating mental or behavioral action. For him, this dynamism is the key to understanding the persuasive use of symbols such as slogans within the realm of politics:

> The employment of language to sanctify action is exactly what makes politics different from other methods of allocating values. Through language a group cannot only achieve an immediate result but also win the acquiescence of those whose lasting support is needed. More than that, it is the talk and the response to it that measures political potency, not the amount of force that is exerted.[5]

Thus, slogans operate in society as "social symbols" and, as such, their intended or perceived meanings may be difficult to grasp and their impact or stimulation may differ between and among individuals and groups. Edelman notes that "Because language is so efficient a tool for reifying the abstract, it is central to the practice endemic in contemporary culture of dealing in abstractions."[6] Hugh Duncan emphasizes that "it is the ambiguity of symbols which makes them so useful in human society. Ambiguity is a kind of bridge that allows us to run back and forth from one kind of meaning to another, until we take firm resolve to cross the bridge into new, and fixed meanings."[7] From this "new and fixed meaning," we think, we feel, and ultimately we may act.

Robert Brooks demonstrated the phenomenon of symbolic bridge crossing in his investigation of how three groups – black college students, white college students, and white policemen, interpreted the meaning of the slogan "Black Power."[8] He discovered three dominant dimensions in the meaning of "Black Power." The first dimension was "aggression." Whites, more frequently than blacks, perceived aggression, violence, confrontation, and racial domination inherent in the concept of "Black Power." The second dimension was "goals." Blacks, more frequently than whites, tended to associate various political goals such as equal rights and equal opportunity with the slogan. And the third dimension, "mystique," referred to endowing the slogan with nonmaterial attributes such as self-identity, pride, and awareness. The words "black power," therefore, had different meanings for different groups, ranging from positive notions such as political goals and pride to negative notions such as aggression, confrontation, and violence. Slogans, then, may serve as the symbolic justifications for feelings and actions and provide a bridge or direct link to social action. Hugh Duncan concludes:

> Symbols, then, create and sustain beliefs in ways of acting because they function as names which signify proper, dubious, or improper ways of expressing relationships. As we are taught in the Bible, we act in the name of the Father, the Son, and Holy Ghost.[9]

Because slogans may operate as "significant symbols" or as key words that have a standard meaning in a group, they serve both expressive and persuasive functions. Harold Lasswell recognized that the influencing of collective attitudes is possible by the manipulation of significant symbols such as slogans.[10] He believed that a verbal symbol might evoke a desired reaction or organize collective attitudes around a symbol. Murray Edelman writes that "to the political scientist patterning or consistency in the contexts in which specific groups of individuals use symbols is crucial, for only through such patterning do common political meanings and claims arise."[11] Thus, the slogans a group uses to evoke specific responses may provide us with an index of the group's norms, values, and conceptual rationale for its claims.

SLOGANS AS TOOLS OF PERSUASION

Slogans are so pervasive in today's society that it is easy to underestimate their persuasive power. They have grown in significance because of the medium of television and the advertising industry. Television, in addition to being the major advertising medium, has altered the nature of human interaction. Political images are less personal and shorter. They function as summaries and conclusions rather than bases for public interaction and debate. The style of presentation in television is more emotional, but the content is less complex or ideological. In short, slogans work well on television.

The advertising industry has made a science of sloganeering. Today, communication itself is a problem because we live in an "overcommunicated" society. Advertisers have discovered that it is easier to link product attributes to existing beliefs, ideas, goals, and desires of the consumer rather than to change them. Thus, to say that a cookie tastes "homemade" or is as good as "Mom used to make" does not tell us if the cookie is good or bad, hard or soft, but simply evokes the fond memories of Mother's baking. Advertisers, then, are more successful if they present a product in a war that capitalizes on established beliefs or expectations of the consumer. Slogans do this well by crystallizing in a few words the key idea or theme one wants to associate with an issue, group, product, or event. "Sloganeering" has become institutionalized as a virtual art form, and an advertising agency may spend months testing and creating the right slogan for a product or a person.

Slogans have a number of attributes that enhance their persuasive potential for social movements. They are unique and readily identifiable with a specific social movement or social movement organization. "Gray Power," for instance,

readily identifies the movement for elderly Americans, and
"Huelga" (strike in Spanish) identifies the movement to aid
Mexican-American field workers in the west and the south-
west. Slogans are easy to say and to remember, but they
are difficult to imitate. In the abortion controversy, for
example, the "right to choose" does not sound as potent
and urgent as the "right to life." Slogans are often fun
because they contain active verbs and adjectives, are witty,
and rhyme. Examples of slogans with these characteristics
are: "Make Love, Not War" (anti-Vietnam War movement);
"Keep Your Morality Off My Body" (pro-choice and gay rights
movements); "Not the Church, Not the State, Women Must
Decide Their Fate" (women's liberation movement); and "We
Are Here and We Are Not Going to Disappear" (Gray Panthers). Slogans are often repetitious or are designed to be
repeated or chanted. The Black Action Movement at the
University of Michigan chanted "Open It Up or Close It
Down" during demonstrations demanding an open admis-
sions policy and an active minority recruitment program at
the University. Demonstrators and participants in mass rallies
shouted "Free Huey" again and again in their efforts to obtain
the release of arrested Black Panther Party leader and Minister of Defense Huey P. Newton from jail. Slogans may
serve as a way to release pent-up emotions and frustrations
and, like name-calling and obscenity, may act as a verbal
surrogate for physical aggression. And finally, slogans may
create a "blindering" effect by preventing audiences from
considering alternative ways of thinking, feeling, and/or
acting.[12] Slogans tend to be definitive, Platonic statements
of the social movement's "truths" and rely on audience predispositions to achieve expected responses.

Three things should be evident about slogans. First, they
are more than a mode of expression or information; they
are *persuasive* in nature. Second, by recognizing the "symbols" to which audiences have been conditioned to respond,
social movement persuaders may formulate slogans that will
have profound, persuasive, organizing effects. And third,
the analysis of slogans of various social movements and social
movement organizations (such as the John Birch Society,
the Black Panthers, and the American Indian Movement)
may reveal their implicit norms, values, and claims.

TYPES OF SLOGAN

There appear to be three types of slogans in the persuasion of social movements. *Spontaneous slogans* tend to be "original" and to rely upon individual protestor initiative for their creation and use during demonstrations and movement meetings. Spontaneous slogans are often short, rhythmical chants such as "Shut It Down" (anti-war protestors in Chicago during the 1968 Democratic National Convention); "Freedom, Freedom, Freedom" (civil rights movement); "ROTC Has to Go" and "Pigs Off Campus" (anti-war demonstrations at Kent State University); and "Viva La Causa" (Chicano movement). Other spontaneous slogans are longer, sometimes more issue-oriented, and appear on signs carried by protestors. Examples are "Don't Cook Dinner, Starve a Rat Today" and "Housewives Are Unpaid Slaves" (women's liberation movement); "We Have Our Bible, We Don't Need Your Dirty Books" (movement to censor school textbooks and books in public libraries); "The Racist Pigs Must Free Huey or the Sky's the Limit" (Black Panther Party demonstration for Huey Newton); and "We Build Up, We Don't Tear Down" (pro-Vietnam War movement).

Sanctioned slogans are "official" slogans of social movements or ones adopted by the movement or a specific social movement organization. They are placed on movement produced buttons, leaflets, posters, and newsletters, and are often chanted at movement meetings. Examples are pro-life's "Give to the Unborn Child Their First Civil Right – Life," "Never to Laugh or Love," and "We Are Protestants, Protesting Abortion." The counter-culture movement employed such slogans as "Don't Trust Anyone Over 30" and "All Power to the People." The official slogan of the Knights of Labor was "An Injury to One Is an Injury to All." Highly organized social movements that publish their own newspapers, magazines, and pamphlets tend to use an official slogan or motto on the front pages or the covers of publications, and these slogans may accompany or be part of the official logo. For example, the masthead of *The Call*, published by the Marxist–Leninist October League, contains the slogan, "People of the World Unite to Defeat Imperialism." The native American newspaper *Wassaji* uses the slogan "Let My People Know." *The*

Table 1   Distribution of slogans in this study

Social movement	Sample of slogans
Anti-nuclear power movement	32
Anti-nuclear weapons movement	6
Anti-Vietnam War movement	79
Black rights movement	66
Ecology movement	21
Gay rights movement	14
Gray power movement	15
Kidvid movement	4
Native American movement	19
Movement to reform marijuana laws	3
Pro-choice movement	19
Pro-life movement	38
Pro-nuclear power movement	8
Radical left movement	45
Radical right (resistance) movement	114
Save the whales movement	3
United Farm Workers/Chicano movements	28
Women's liberation movement	71

Rebel Worker, published by the radical left Workers Party and Rebel Worker Organization, has the slogan "Freedom, Justice, Social Equality" on a banner held in the beak of a Bald Eagle. And publications of CARE (Citizens Against a Radioactive Environment) has a circular logo with a half-sunburst in the top part and the words "No Nukes" in the bottom part.

Advertising slogans are found most frequently on buttons, bumperstickers, and tee-shirts. They tend to be short statements that emphasize a single demand or remind us of the social movement or a particular social movement organization. "Issue" examples are "Recall Ralph Nader" (radical right resistance groups); "Employ, Don't Destroy" (anti-nuclear power and weapons groups); and "Solar Employs, Nuclear Destroys" and "Don't Waste America" (anti-nuclear power). "Organizational" slogans are "Black Panthers," "Gray Panthers," "Right to Life," and "The Wobblies Are Coming" (Industrial Workers of the World).

Let us turn now to a discussion of the persuasive functions that these three types of slogans perform for social movements.

PERSUASIVE FUNCTIONS OF SLOGANS

In the remainder of this chapter, we attempt to determine the persuasive functions that social movement slogans perform. Our analysis is based on a sample of 585 spontaneous, sanctioned, and advertising slogans used by 18 contemporary American social movements.[13] We selected contemporary social movements so that we would be aware of how, when, where, and by whom the slogans were used – all important factors in determining the persuasive functions of such brief and ambiguous messages as slogans. The movements and samples of slogans are shown in Table 1.

Let us turn first to a discussion of how social movement slogans attempted to transform perceptions of history: past, present, and future.

Transforming Perceptions of History

The Past. Not one of the 585 slogans included in this study attempted to transform perceptions of the past. Social movements tend not to dwell on the past in their persuasive efforts, and the simplicity of slogans would seem to make them an inappropriate source for treating any event, issue, or concept that requires explanation. Audiences must be able to attach instant meanings to the slogans that they see, hear, or say.

The Present. Only 16 percent of the selected slogans portrayed the present, and these slogans tended to appear in a few social movements that felt an urgent need to transform perceptions of "reality." Eighty-nine percent of the slogans that dealt with the present were efforts to make audiences aware of intolerable situations. Typical examples were: "No playing today kids – smog by General Motors" (ecology); "Abortion: The American Holocaust (pro-life)"; "Housewives are unpaid slaves" (women's liberation); "War is not healthy for children and other living things" (anti-Vietnam War); "How can we make ends meet?" (Gray Panthers); and "You can't be free in St. Louis with slavery in Birmingham" (black rights).

Protestors often included graphic pictures with their slogans to enhance their persuasive impact. For instance, the

Table 2   Devil appeals in slogans (in percent)

Most devil appeals		Fewest devil appeals	
Radical right	29	Gray Panthers	7
Anti-Vietnam War	23	Native American	5
Gay rights	21	Pro-life	3
Radical left	20	Pro-choice	0
United Farm Workers	18	Anti-nuclear power	0

ecology movement's slogan "Ecology is for the birds" was accompanied by a picture of an oil-soaked duck. The anti-Vietnam War slogan "The real tragedy of war is its survivors" was accompanied by a picture of crippled Vietnamese children. And the United Farm Worker slogan "Every grape you buy keeps this child hungry" was accompanied by a picture of a starving child in filthy surroundings. Some social movements have attempted to "redefine reality" through such slogans as: "Fetus is Latin for child" (pro-life); "Peace is more than the absence of war" (anti-nuclear weapons); "Porn is violence disguised" (women's liberation); and "Abortion is something personal – not political" (pro-choice). The pro-choice slogan "If men could get pregnant, abortion would be a sacrament" seems to have been an attempt to redefine abortion and the motives of the male-oriented opposition to it.

The Future. Only 4 percent of the 585 slogans studied attempted to transform perceptions of the future, and these slogans (unlike social movement songs) attempted to create negative expectancies in the minds of readers and listeners, expectancies that would come about unless a change was initiated or stifled. The anti-nuclear weapons movement declared that "nuclear war is nuclear suicide" and the ecology movement pleaded, "Save our grandchildren now, not when it's too late." Some movements seemed to play verbal ping-pong with their adversaries. For example, pro-life warned that "Abortion today justifies euthanasia tomorrow" while pro-choice asked "Do you want to return to the butchery of back-alley abortion?" And anti-nuclear power advised, "Better active today than radioactive tomorrow" while pro-nuclear power warned, "No nukes, no heat, no lights."

Most social movement slogans were brief and seemed to emanate during the stage of enthusiastic mobilization when movements were preoccupied with demands and confrontations with established institutions. Thus, social movement slogans dwell little on history and, when doing so, tend to be negative and to expound upon an intolerable present.

Transforming Perceptions of Society

The Opposition. Only 15 percent of the selected slogans identified the social movement's devil – its major antagonist. Slogans of movements that engaged in frequent conflicts with institutions and other social movements and were generally regarded as "radical" and "revolutionary" contained the most devil appeals (Table 2).

These figures reveal that devil appeals appear far less often in slogans than in songs. And, in contrast to songs, only a simple majority of slogans identified nebulous, unnamed evil forces, groups, or things such as men, anyone over 30, communism, the rich, capitalists, oil profiteers, and blacks. On the other hand, nearly half of the selected slogans identified specific devils such as Ronald Reagan, Lyndon Johnson, Richard Nixon, Anita Bryant, Jane Fonda, the SDS (Students for a Democratic Society), Gallo Wines, General Electric, and the National Council of Churches. Unlike songs, slogans (especially spontaneous ones) are often created for specific situations or events and may become dated or obsolete within hours, days, or weeks. It is not surprising, then, that they would be more specific than songs. None of the slogans contained conspiracy appeals or used the word conspiracy.

The selected slogans employed surprisingly mild language toward the opposition. Only about 4 percent (compared to 27 percent for songs) used invective or name-calling. The following were some of the more colorful slogans: "Don't cook dinner – starve a rat today (women's liberation)"; "Boycott Campbell's Cream of Exploitation Soup" (United Farm Workers); "Let's stop supporting the bandit state of Israel" (radical right); "Pill-em or kill-em groups make $'s from abortion" (pro-life); "Green Pigs" (anti-Vietnam War protest at Kent State University); and "Anita Bryant – Empress of the bigots" (gay rights).

Table 3 Slogans dealing with self-concept (in percent)

Most frequent		Least frequent	
Gay rights	43	Pro-choice	5
Gray Panthers	33	Pro-life	3
Native Americans	31	Anti-Vietnam War	2
Women's liberation	22	Anti-nuclear power	0
Radical right	17	Ecology	0

Only about 2 percent of the 585 slogans (compared with 10 percent for songs) employed ridicule. Typical examples were: "The SDS is a social disease" (radical right); "The peace dove is a chicken" (radical right and pro-Vietnam War); "Judas William Foolbright" (radical right and pro-Vietnam War protest against anti-war Senator William Fulbright); "Why can't white men act like human beings?" (Native American); "Bless those who declare war, they're usually too old to fight and die" (anti-Vietnam War); "If you liked Hitler, you'll love Wallace" (black rights protest against Alabama Governor George Wallace, who was running for President).

The brevity of slogans may explain the near-absence of ridicule and satire in social movement slogans, but brevity would not explain the mild language of slogans. Perhaps during the enthusiastic mobilization stage of movements, protestors are preoccupied with making demands and pressuring the opposition rather than identifying devils and calling names, a rhetoric more appropriate for earlier stages of protest and less confrontative times.

Social movement slogans tend to have more specific targets than do protest songs, but they tend to be less abrasive in language than songs. These are interesting contrasts when we consider that songs are generally sung in safe surroundings somewhat removed from both the public and opposition, while slogans are usually displayed, chanted, or shouted in public places or in the face of the opposition and on the opposition's territory.

The Self. A surprisingly small 12 percent of the 585 selected slogans dealt with self-concept. As expected, the slogans of social movements that have felt a critical need to establish or to defend the "self" included the most frequent appeals to self-concept (Table 3). The selected social movement slogans contained only about one-third as many appeals to self-concept as did the social movement songs. Slogans appear to be used less often than songs to transform perceptions of society.

The most common appeal was to self-worth, proclaiming that "I am somebody," "I am important," "I am of value," or "I should be in a position of authority." Typical of these slogans were direct appeals, such as "Women are not chicks" (women's liberation); "A woman's place is in the house – and in the Senate" (women's liberation); "We build the city up, not burn it down" (radical right); "Discover America with real Americans" (Native American); "Seniors count too" (Gray Panthers); "Say it loud, I'm Black and I'm Proud" (black rights); "God loves Gays" (gay rights); and "I am special, I am me" (women's liberation).

Less direct, but clever, attempts to enhance self-concept were the women's liberation slogan "Trust in God, *She* will provide" and the gay rights slogan "I am your worst fear, I am your best fantasy."

Another common appeal was to feelings of power and strength. The simple but persuasive slogan "Black power" generated a host of imitations: "Brown power," "Red power," "White power," "Gray power," "Woman power," "Senior power," "Poor power," "Gay power," and "All power to the people." Other slogans expressed the strength of movement members of their capacity to bring about change. For instance, a women's liberation slogan declared, "The hand that rocks the cradle should rock the boat;" a Chicano slogan stated, "We are not a minority;" a NORML (National Organization for Reform of Marijuana Laws slogan) assured audiences that "You can change the world;" and a Gray Panther slogan declared, "Panthers on the prowl." Such slogans as these appear to be designed to alter the image of movement members as well as to give them feelings of strength and the will to act. There were only 28 appeals to power and strength among 585 selected slogans. This small figure, however, does not reveal the frequency with which protestors used specific slogans. Undoubtedly the slogan "black power," for example, was more significant in both

Table 4   Demands and solutions in slogans (in percent)

Most often		Least often	
Anti-nuclear power	74	Women's liberation	38
Black rights	64	Radical left	33
Pro-choice	53	Gay rights	28
Native American	53	Ecology	24
Radical right	47	United Farm Workers	0

frequency and impact than dozens of other black rights slogans combined.

Twenty percent of appeals to self-concept dealt with self-identity. These slogans seemed to reflect a need among protestors to express who they were. Examples were: "I'm proud to be an American" (radical right); "Meet a woman who's had an abortion" (pro-choice); "I am a [sic] Indian and I am pretty dam [sic] proud of it" (Native American); "Vietnam vets for peace" (anti-Vietnam War); and "I am a lesbian and I am beautiful" (gay rights). These slogans exuded pride, a declaration of beliefs or support for a cause, and the willingness to reveal one's self for a cause.

Other slogans identified persons with specific groups or organizations: "Feminism lives" (women's liberation); "I am a secret member of the John Birch Society" (radical right); "I am an American Nazi" (radical right); "We care, we love, we are Pro-life" (pro-life); "We are pro-choice and we vote" (pro-choice); and "Young Americans for Freedom" (radical right).

As we will see later, slogans such as the above serve important organizational and unifying functions as well as the need to enhance self-concept.

Only 12 percent of the selected slogans (compared with 22 percent of songs) attempted to "activate" audiences by challenging them to act through appeals to self-concept. The following examples were typical of such slogans: "Don't be half a man, join the Klan" (radical right); "Whose side are you on... theirs [soldiers] or Nixon's" (anti-Vietnam War); "Be counted this time, march to end the war" (anti-Vietnam War); "Why shop where you can't eat?" (black rights); and "Dare to struggle, dare to win" (radical left).

Although the importance of creating we-they distinctions through social movement persuasion is undisputed, few social movement slogans seem to be designed either to attack the "they" or to enhance the "we." Slogans do a better job of attacking others than enhancing the self.

Prescribing Courses of Action

The What. Demands and solutions appeared in 43 percent of the slogans, and they tended to dominate the slogans of several contemporary social movements. Notice in Table 4 that the percentages are fairly high (with the exception of the United Farm Workers whose slogans tended to urge action) for all the contemporary social movements included in this study.

Many slogans made vague references to equality, happiness, free speech, freedom, justice, rights, and peace, but 37 percent of all demands and solutions were quite specific. For example, a radical right slogan demanded "Freedom for Rudolf Hess" (the former German Nazi leader); a black rights slogan urged institutions to "Ban the Krugerrand" (a South African gold piece being sold in America); a native American slogan demanded that authorities "Free the Wounded Knee 300"; and anti-nuclear power advocates chanted "Close Indian Point" (a nuclear power plant) while pro-nuclear power advocates tried to prevent the closing of a nuclear power plant with the slogan "Save No. One." Nearly all slogans that addressed demands and solutions were what Bowers and Ochs have referred to as "imperative statements" – commands, edicts, or fiats.

One of the most important persuasive functions of slogans is their simplification of complex issues, problems, solutions, and relationships. Thus, some of the selected slogans polarized complex issues: "America – love it or leave it" (radical right and pro-Vietnam War); "Make love not war" (anti-Vietnam War); "Abortion kills babies – choose life" (pro-life); "Employ: don't destroy" (anti-nuclear power); and "Separation or death" (radical right and KKK).

Other slogans proposed simple solutions without recognizing the complicated steps involved or the ramifications of implementation: "No more nukes" (anti-nuclear power); "Save the whales"; "Dump Israel" (radical right and

American Nazis); "Humanize America" (radical left); and "Get out of Vietnam" (anti-Vietnam War).

Many slogans revealed the impatience of movement members and leaders during the enthusiastic mobilization stage. In John Wilson's words,[14] protestors had grown "tired of being sick and tired"; "Enough! Out now" (anti-Vietnam War); "End the arms race now" (anti-nuclear weapons); "Equal rights now" (women's liberation); "Jobs or income now" (radical left); "Abortion rights now" (pro-choice); and "We demand an FEPC law now" (black rights).

Other social movement slogans espoused vague dreams, hopes, or visions, such as the following: "Peace on earth, good will to people" (women's liberation); "Every child a wanted child, every mother a willing mother" (women's liberation and pro-choice); "For a bicentennial without colonies" (native American); "What if they gave a war and nobody came?" (anti-Vietnam War); and "Live and let live" (pro-life).

Slogans allow social movement members and leaders to simplify and "package" their pictures of the world – their ideologies – that produce "impressions" of action, direction, analysis, and thoroughness.[15] If, as Joseph Lelyveld claims, television has reduced the "attention span of the ordinary viewer" to "fractions of minutes" and "has made political communication a matter of fleeting impressions," then social movement slogans would seem to be important persuasive vehicles for contemporary social movements.[16]

The Who. Only 4 percent of the 585 selected slogans addressed who must bring about or stifle change, including mentions of movement organizations (e.g., "Gray Panthers: age and youth in action"; "Young Americans for Freedom"; and "The KKK likes Cubans, if they are in Cuba") and the naming of social movement leaders (e.g., "Viva Chavez," "We stand with Fr. Dan Berrigan," and "We protest the arrest of Rev. Dr. King in Birmingham"). An important persuasive characteristic of such slogans is their potential for creating a strong personal identification with and commitment to a cause, particularly when protestors wear these slogans on buttons or tee shirts, place them on their automobiles, or carry them on placards. The following examples reveal this persuasive potential: "I am an American Nazi" (radical right); "Nurses for Life" (pro-life); "We are Protestants protesting abortion" (pro-life); "Pro-family, pro-choice" (pro-choice); "Panthers on the prowl" (Gray Panthers); and "Americans *FOR* nuclear power" (pro-nuclear power).

Thus, slogans provide both an opportunity for self-expression of beliefs and membership and a means of exhibiting or communicating these to a variety of audiences. Too few contemporary slogans take advantage of this opportunity.

The How. Only three slogans addressed how (strategies, tactics, and communication channels) movements should accomplish their goals. The United Farm Workers slogan "No violencia es nuestra fuerza" urged non-violence; the radical right (pro-Vietnam War) slogan "Why be violent – debate" chided the anti-Vietnam War movement for resorting to violence when it opposed violence in Vietnam; and the anti-Vietnam War slogan "No negotiations" inveighed against negotiation as a means of resolving either the protest or the military conflict. Slogans are obviously not used for prescribing or discussing tactics.

Mobilizing for Action

Calls to Action. Twenty-seven percent of the selected slogans called upon audiences to act. Some were ambiguous pleas to repent, fight, picket, support, wake up, vote, help, "do it," "do your part," and encouragements such as "Right on sister." Unlike musical calls to action, many slogans prescribed specific actions: "Boycott Chiquita bananas" (United Farm Workers); "Sign here to keep Taiwan free" (radical right); "Be the voice of the unborn – vote no on B" (pro-life); "Vote yes: change the abortion law – November 7" (pro-choice); "Occupy Seabrook" (anti-nuclear power); and "Support 'Operation Shutdown'" (black rights).

Calls to action were second only to courses of action in frequency of appearance in slogans. Very small percentages of slogans called upon audiences to join the cause, to unite, or to organize. Although slogans are personal expressions of self, belief, commitment, and action, they rarely proclaimed actions in the first person. A rare exception was radical right's "I think it's time for us to stand up and be counted."

Appeals Beyond the Movement. Unlike protest songs that are largely in-group persuasive activities, slogans appeal implicitly and explicitly to a variety of audiences: the un-committed "oppressed," the "people," "legitimizers," and the mass media. When the United Farm Workers demonstrated in front of supermarkets and liquor stores, for example, they carried and chanted such slogans as "Don't buy Red Coach Iceberg lettuce," "Help the grape workers win their strike," and "Don't swallow Gallow's wine." Their appeals were primarily to the public, customers, and the media, not to movement members. The same was true when save-the-whales protestors used the slogan "Wake up! to the alarming facts"; and when the ecology movement urged people to "Breathe deeply, then revolt." Many slogans urged audiences to get involved. A black rights slogan protesting the control of local schools asked black people on the streets of New York, "Do you want your child to be a big dummy?" An anti-nuclear weapons slogan pleaded, "Americans unite and disarm." And a pro-choice slogan entreated readers, "Don't stand by silently and let outrage become law – fight back."

Slogans are a primary means of getting attention and making people conscious of a problem. Claus Mueller has noted that:

> Articulated dissent presupposes that political symbols (terms, concepts, and ideological interpretations) be attached to subjectively experienced conditions that do not correspond to expectations or needs. Political consciousness is perforce bound to a symbolic interpretation of socio-political experience. . . . as long as no political interpretations were attached to deplorable conditions, these conditions remained inert, posing no threat to the status quo.[17]

The save-the-whales slogan "Our look can kill," for example, attempted to make people aware that whales were being slaughtered to provide cosmetics. The NORML slogan "This little plant can turn your life upside down" warned audiences that violation of unfair marijuana laws could cost them their money and their freedom. In 1966 Stokely Carmichael, chairman of the Student Nonviolent Coordinating Committee, began to contemplate a slogan and an act that would capture the attention of the mass media, instill new life into the black rights movement, and redefine the image of blacks, their demands, and their allies. On June 5, 1966 James Meredith undertook a one-man voting rights pilgrimage from Memphis, Tennessee to Jackson, Mississippi, but he was ambushed and shot on June 6. Numerous black rights leaders, including Carmichael, immediately took over the march. The SNCC group led by Carmichael chanted the new slogan whenever marchers met hostile treatment along the way. On the evening of June 17, about halfway through the march, Stokely Carmichael introduced the new slogan to the nation in a speech at Greenwood, Mississippi. He stated in part: "The only way we gonna stop them white men from whuppin' us is to take over. We been saying 'freedom' for six years and we ain't got nothing. What we gonna start sayin' now is Black Power!" "Black power" quickly became one of the best known, most controversial, and more influential slogans in American history. It monopolized the attention of the mass media for weeks, became a rallying cry and ego-enhancer for blacks, catapulted Stokely Carmichael into the top echelon of black leaders, divided the black rights movement into "civil rights" and "black power" factions, purged the movement of unwanted white liberals, and threatened a variety of institutions.

Slogans can unite, or at least create a perception of unity among people "with widely varying motives and beliefs," by focusing upon a common characteristic, value, belief, or goal.[18] This is particularly true, Murray Edelman writes, when political and social issues are unclear – as is the case with most social movements.[19] An obvious example of a unifying slogan is the native American movement's adoption of the classic slogan, "All for one, one for all." The women's liberation movement reaches beyond its membership with the slogan, "Rape is a crime against *all* women." In a similar fashion, the pro-life movement attempts to appeal to all women with the slogan, "Unborn women have rights too." And the anti-nuclear power slogan, "In case of nuclear accident kiss your children goodbye" appeals to parents and to the universal love of children and the motive to protect them at all costs. Slogans such as these allow people to rally around a common belief or value when they might disagree over many specific aspects of a social movement.

Pressuring the Opposition. The majority of the 585 selected slogans, unlike social movement songs, applied direct or indirect pressure against other movements, institutions, or agents of institutions. Nearly every demand, for example, was phrased as an imperative statement and shouted or displayed in public or on location: state legislatures or Congress, corporations, churches, court houses or chambers, colleges, stores, beauty contests, and so on. Such slogans as "Ratify ERA now" (women's liberation), "No bus for us" (radical rights), "Convert Rocky Flats" (anti-nuclear power), and "Free Huey" (black rights) applied at least indirect pressure on the opposition. The same is true for expressions of power such as "Black power," "White power," "We are everywhere" (gay rights), "We are back: National Socialist White People's Party" (radical right), and "Feminism lives" (women's liberation). When social movements call upon people to act or to unite, they pose threats to oppositions, and these oppositions cannot remain indifferent when movements employ such slogans as "talk about what we can do, do what we talk about" (women's liberation), "Books are weapons, use them" (radical right), "Support Indian resistance" (native American), and "Buy war guns" (black rights).

Some social movements applied direct pressure upon oppositions through calls to action against them or overt threats. Not surprisingly, social movements involved in confrontations resorted most often to overt threats. The most common threats were calls for action against various oppositions: "Tell him what to do with the broom!" (women's liberation); "Look for the label, boycott scab grapes" (United Farm Workers); "Don't trade here! Owners of this business surrendered to race mixers" (radical right); "Shut it down" (radical left); "Kill the pigs" (anti-Vietnam War); and "Stop Diablo – join the blockade" (anti-nuclear power).

As Bowers and Ochs have pointed out, oppositions, particularly established institutions, cannot afford to take threats lightly.[20] If they are caught unprepared, they may experience loss of sales, votes, property or, most importantly, the support of "the people." Over-preparation or over-reaction, however, may make institutions look foolish or ugly or lead to tragedy. The morning after students at Kent State

University tried to burn down the ROTC building and before the fatal shooting of four students, a large banner hanging from a tree asked, "Why is the ROTC building still standing?" Undoubtedly such slogans added to the atmosphere that prompted National Guardsmen to fire upon the students.

Some social movement slogans applied direct pressure through questions and threats: "Would you be more careful if it was you who got pregnant?" (women's liberation); "Hey, hey, LBJ, how many kids have you killed today?" (anti-Vietnam War); "We will remember" (United Farm Workers); "Niggers beware! Hands off whites or die" (radical right); "Keep your laws and your morality off *my* body" (pro-choice); and "Free Huey now or the sky's the limit" (black rights).

Thus, social movement slogans, unlike songs, were not merely or primarily for in-house consumption. They appealed to a variety of audiences, applied both direct and indirect pressure upon oppositions, and talked more *to* than *about* their opponents.

Victory is near. Not one of the 585 selected slogans predicted that victory was at hand. Most slogans tended to be neither optimistic nor pessimistic about ultimate victory.

Sustaining the Movement

Since most slogans addressed the "here and now" during the mobilization stage, they did not refer to setbacks or delays (brevity would prevent explanations of either) and did not urge followers to remain committed. A few slogans assured audiences that victory would come ultimately for their efforts. Examples were "Failure is impossible" (women's liberation), "We shall overcome" (United Farm Workers and black rights), and "When women decide this war should end, this war will end" (anti-Vietnam War).

A small percentage of slogans referred to hero-victims, victories, or tragedies to sustain commitment and the movement's forward progress. Examples included: "Remember the Augusta Six" (black rights); "Tyrone had a right to live" (radical left); "We got the Rosenbergs" (radical right); "Remember Kent [State] and Jackson [State]"

(Anti-Vietnam War); and "Remember 3 Mile Island" (anti-nuclear power).

It appears that most slogans are created during the enthusiastic mobilization stage before most tragedies and victories take place and before heroes and martyrs are enshrined. Few new slogans appear during the maintenance stage when demonstrations and confrontations, dwindle or disappear.

CONCLUSIONS

Slogans, with us for centuries, act as social symbols and symbolic justifications. Social movements employ them to create impressions, to alter perceptions, to elicit emotional responses, to make demands, and to pressure oppositions. The ambiguity of slogans enable them to serve as verbal bridges from one meaning to another and allow individuals and groups to interpret them according to their own perceptions and needs. They simplify complex problems, solutions, and situations while demanding instant corrective actions. Many slogans are unique to and readily identifiable with specific social movements or social movement organizations.

All of the general and most of the specific persuasive functions appeared in at least a few of the 585 social movement slogans analyzed for this study. Slogans, particularly spontaneous ones, were created during the enthusiastic mobilization stage of movements. Thus, they tended to reflect concern for the moment rather than for the past or the future. They made uncompromising and often highly specific demands and urged immediate action rather than attacking the opposition or enhancing the self. They appealed to a variety of audiences (movement sympathizers, "the people," legitimizers, and the mass media) rather than to the in-group as social movement songs do. And they applied both indirect and direct pressures upon oppositions. Although many of the 585 slogans were imperative statements, a small percentage of them used name-calling or abrasive language. A large percentage of the selected slogans were situation or event specific and became obsolete once a strike or a campaign ended, an opposition leader left office, or a movement leader was released from prison. A number of slogans, particularly sanctioned and advertising slogans, such as "black power," "Gray Panthers," and "I am an American Nazi" appealed to feelings of power and strength and created a personal identification with and commitment to a cause. Slogans tend to be a highly personal form of protest because individuals wear them, carry them, shout them, and place them on possessions such as automobiles.

Notes

1. Robert E. Denton, "The Rhetorical Functions of Slogans: Classifications and Characteristics," *Communication Quarterly*, vol. 28 (spring, 1980), pp. 10–18.
2. George E. Shankel, *American Mottoes and Slogans* (New York: Wilson, 1941), p. 5.
3. John W. Bowers and Donovan J. Ochs, *The Rhetoric of Agitation and Control* (Reading, MA: Addison-Wesley, 1971), p. 22.
4. Shankel, p. 7.
5. Murray Edelman, *The Symbolic Uses of Politics* (Urbana, IL: University of Illinois Press, 1967), p. 114.
6. Edelman, p. 117.
7. Hugh Duncan, *Symbols in Society* (New York: Oxford University Press, 1968), p. 8.
8. Robert D. Brooks, "Black Power: The Dimensions of a Slogan," *Western Speech*, vol. 34 (spring, 1970), pp. 108–14.
9. Duncan, p. 22.
10. Harold D. Lasswell, "The Theory of Propaganda," *American Political Science Review*, vol. 21 (1927), p. 627.
11. Edelman, p. 115.
12. John Makay and William Brown, *The Rhetorical Dialogue: Contemporary Concepts and Cases* (Dubuque, IA: W. C. Brown, 1972), p. 374.
13. The 585 slogans were obtained from social movement buttons, posters, bumperstickers, newspapers, journals, leaflets, pamphlets, books, photographs of slogans being displayed during demonstrations, and accounts of social movements and their actions.
14. John Wilson, *Introduction to Social Movements* (New York: Basic Books, 1973), pp. 89–90.
15. Nelson Polsby and Aaron Wildavsky, *Presidential Elections* (New York: Scribners, 1971), p. 178.
16. Joseph Lelyveld, "The Selling of a Candidate," *New York Times Magazine*, 18 March 1976, p. 16.
17. Claus Mueller, *The Politics of Communication* (New York: Oxford University Press, 1973), p. 113.

18. George F. Rude, *The Crowd in History* (New York: Wiley, 1964), p. 246.
19. Murray Edelman, *Politics as Symbolic Action* (Chicago: Markham, 1971), p. 119.
20. Bowers and Ochs, p. 40.

18 Politics and the English Language*
George Orwell

Most people who bother with the matter at all would admit that the English language is in a bad way, but it is generally assumed that we cannot by conscious action do anything about it. Our civilisation is decadent, and our language – so the argument runs – must inevitably share in the general collapse. It follows that any struggle against the abuse of language is a sentimental archaism, like preferring candles to electric light or hansom cabs to aeroplanes. Underneath this lies the half-conscious belief that language is a natural growth and not an instrument which we shape for our own purposes.

Now, it is clear that the decline of a language must ultimately have political and economic causes: it is not due simply to the bad influence of this or that individual writer. But an effect can become a cause, reinforcing the original cause and producing the same effect in an intensified form, and so on indefinitely. A man may take to drink because he feels himself to be a failure, and then fail all the more completely because he drinks. It is rather the same thing that is happening to the English language. It becomes ugly and inaccurate because our thoughts are foolish, but the slovenliness of our language makes it easier for us to have foolish thoughts. The point is that the process is reversible. Modern English, especially written English, is full of bad habits which spread by imitation and which can be avoided if one is willing to take the necessary trouble. If one gets rid of these habits one can think more clearly, and to think clearly is a necessary first step towards political regeneration: so that the fight against bad English is not frivolous and is not the exclusive concern of professional

---

* Reprinted from George Orwell, *Shooting an Elephant and Other Essays* (New York: Harcourt, Brace and Company, 1946).

writers. I will come back to this presently, and I hope that by that time the meaning of what I have said here will have become clearer. Meanwhile, here are five specimens of the English language as it is now habitually written.

These five passages have not been picked out because they are especially bad – I could have quoted far worse if I had chosen – but because they illustrate various of the mental vices from which we now suffer. They are a little below the average, but are fairly representative samples. I number them so that I can refer back to them when necessary:

1. I am not, indeed, sure whether it is not true to say that the Milton who once seemed not unlike a seventeenth-century Shelley had not become, out of an experience ever more bitter in each year, more alien [sic] to the founder of that Jesuit sect which nothing could induce him to tolerate. (Professor Harold Laski, essay in *Freedom of Expression*)

2. Above all, we cannot play ducks and drakes with a native battery of idioms which prescribes such egregious collocations of vocables as the Basic *put up with* for *tolerate* or *put at a loss* for *bewilder*. (Professor Lancelot Hogben, *Interglossa*)

3. On the one side we have the free personality: by definition it is not neurotic, for it has neither conflict nor dream. Its desires, such as they are, are transparent, for they are just what institutional approval keeps in the forefront of consciousness; another institutional pattern would alter their number and intensity; there is little in them that is natural, irreducible, or culturally dangerous. But *on the other side*, the social bond itself is nothing but the mutual reflection of these self-secure integrities. Recall the definition of love. Is not this the very picture of a small academic? Where is there a place in this hall of mirrors for either personality or fraternity? (Essay on psychology in *Politics* (New York).

4. All the 'best people' from the gentlemen's clubs, and all the frantic Fascist captains, united in common hatred of Socialism and bestial horror of the rising tide of the mass revolutionary movement, have turned to acts of provocation, to foul incendiarism, to medieval legends of poisoned

wells, to legalise their own destruction to proletarian organisations, and rouse the agitated petty-bourgeoisie to chauvinistic fervour on behalf of the fight against the revolutionary way out of the crisis. (Communist pamphlet)

5. If a new spirit *is* to be infused into this old country, there is one thorny and contentious reform which must be tackled, and that is the humanisation and galvanisation of the BBC. Timidity here will bespeak canker and atrophy of the soul. The heart of Britain may be sound and of strong beat, for instance, but the British lion's roar at present is like that of Bottom in Shakespeare's *Midsummer Night's Dream* – as gentle as any sucking dove. A virile new Britain cannot continue indefinitely to be traduced in the eyes, or rather ears, of the world by the effete languors of Langham Place, brazenly masquerading as "standard English". When the Voice of Britain is heard at nine o'clock, better far and infinitely less ludicrous to hear aitches honestly dropped than the present priggish, inflated, inhibited, school-ma'amish arch braying of blameless bashful mewing maidens! (Letter in *Tribune*).

Each of these passages has faults of its own, but, quite apart from avoidable ugliness, two qualities are common to all of them. The first is staleness of imagery; the other is lack of precision. The writer either has a meaning and cannot express it, or he inadvertently says something else, or he is almost indifferent as to whether his words mean anything or not. This mixture of vagueness and sheer incompetence is the most marked characteristic of modern English prose, and especially of any kind of political writing. As soon as certain topics are raised, the concrete melts into the abstract and no one seems able to think of turns of speech that are not hackneyed: prose consists less and less of *words* chosen for the sake of their meaning, and more of *phrases* tacked together like the sections of a prefabricated hen-house. I list below, with notes and examples, various of the tricks by means of which the work of prose construction is habitually dodged.

Dying metaphors. A newly invented metaphor assists thought by evoking a visual image, while on the other hand a metaphor which is technically "dead" (e.g. *iron resolution*) has in effect reverted to being an ordinary word and can generally be used without loss of vividness. But in between these two classes there is a huge dump of worn-out metaphors which have lost all evocative power and are merely used because they save people the trouble of inventing phrases for themselves. Examples are: *Ring the changes on; take up the cudgels for; toe the line; ride roughshod over; stand shoulder to shoulder with; play into the hands of; no axe to grind; grist to the mill; fishing in troubled waters; rift within the lute; on the order of the day; Achilles' heel; swan song; hotbed.* Many of these are used without knowledge of their meaning (what is a "rift", for instance?), and incompatible metaphors are frequently mixed, a sure sign that the writer is not interested in what he is saying. Some metaphors now current have been twisted out of their original meaning without those who use them even being aware of the fact. For example, *toe the line* is sometimes written *tow the line.* Another example is *the hammer and the anvil,* now always used with the implication that the anvil gets the worst of it. In real life it is always the anvil that breaks the hammer, never the other way about: a writer who stopped to think what he was saying would be aware of this, and would avoid perverting the original phrase.

Operators, or *verbal false limbs.* These save the trouble of picking out appropriate verbs and nouns, and at the same time pad each sentence with extra syllables which give it an appearance of symmetry. Characteristic phrases are: *render inoperative; militate against; prove unacceptable; make contact with; be subjected to; give rise to; give grounds for; have the effect of; play a leading part (rôle) in; make itself felt; take effect; exhibit a tendency to; serve the purpose of;* etc etc. The keynote is the elimination of simple verbs. Instead of being a single word, such as *break, stop, spoil, mend, kill,* a verb becomes a *phrase,* made up of a noun or adjective tacked on to some general-purposes verb such as *prove, serve, form, play, render.* In addition the passive voice is wherever possible used in preference to the active, and noun constructions are used instead of gerunds (*by examination of* instead of *by examining*). The range of verbs is further cut down by means of the *-ise* and *de-* formations, and banal statements are given an appearance of profundity by means of the *not un-* formation. Simple conjunctions and prepositions are replaced by such phrases as *with respect to, having regard to, the fact that, by dint of, in view of, in the interests of, on the hypothesis that*; and the ends of sentences are saved from anticlimax by such resounding commonplaces as *greatly to be desired, cannot be left out of account, a development to be expected in the near future, deserving of serious consideration, brought to a satisfactory conclusion,* and so on and so forth.

Pretentious diction. Words like *phenomenon, element, individual* (as noun), *objective, categorical, effective, virtual, basic, primary, promote, constitute, exhibit, exploit, utilise, eliminate, liquidate,* are used to dress up simple statements and give an air of scientific impartiality to biassed judgements. Adjectives like *epoch-making, epic, historic, unforgettable, triumphant, age-old, inevitable, inexorable, veritable,* are used to dignify the sordid processes of international politics, while writing that aims at glorifying war usually takes on an archaic colour, its characteristic words being *realm, throne, chariot, mailed fist, trident, sword, shield, buckler, banner, jackboot, clarion.* Foreign words and expressions such as *cul de sac, ancien régime, deus ex machina, mutatis mutandis, status quo, Gleichschaltung, Weltanschauung* are used to give an air of culture and elegance. Except for the useful abbreviations *i.e., e.g.* and *etc,* there is no real need for any of the hundreds of foreign phrases now current in English. Bad writers, and especially scientific, political and sociological writers, are nearly always haunted by the notion that Latin or Greek words are grander than Saxon ones, and unnecessary words like *expedite, ameliorate, predict, extraneous, deracinated, clandestine, sub-aqueous* and hundreds of others constantly gain ground from their Anglo-Saxon opposite numbers.[1] The jargon peculiar to Marxist writing (*hyena, hangman, cannibal, petty bourgeois, these gentry, lackey, flunkey, mad dog, White Guard,* etc) consists largely of words and phrases translated from Russian, German or French; but the normal way of coining a new word is to use a Latin or Greek root with the appropriate affix and, where necessary, the *-ise* formation. It is often easier to make up words of this kind (*deregionalise,* *impermissible, extramarital, non-fragmentatory* and so forth) than to think up the English words that will cover one's meaning. The result, in general, is an increase in slovenliness and vagueness.

Meaningless words. In certain kinds of writing, particularly in art criticism and literary criticism, it is normal to come across long passages which are almost completely lacking in meaning.[2] Words like *romantic, plastic, values, human, dead, sentimental, natural, vitality,* as used in art criticism, are strictly meaningless, in the sense that they not only do not point to any discoverable object, but are hardly even expected to do so by the reader. When one critic writes, "The outstanding features of Mr X's work is its living quality", while another writes, "The immediately striking thing about Mr X's work is its peculiar deadness", the reader accepts this as a simple difference of opinion. If words like *black* and *white* were involved, instead of the jargon words *dead* and *living*, he would see at once that language was being used in an improper way. Many political words are similarly abused. The word *Fascism* has now no meaning except in so far as it signifies "something not desirable". The words *democracy, socialism, freedom, patriotic, realistic, justice,* have each of them several different meanings which cannot be reconciled with one another. In the case of a word like *democracy*, not only is there no agreed definition, but the attempt to make one is resisted from all sides. It is almost universally felt that when we call a country democratic we are praising it: consequently the defenders of every kind of regime claim that it is a democracy, and fear that they might have to stop using the word if it were tied down to any one meaning. Words of this kind are often used in a consciously dishonest way. That is, the person who uses them has his own private definition, but allows his hearer to think he means something quite different. Statements like *Marshal Pétain was a true patriot, The Soviet press is the freest in the world, The Catholic Church is opposed to persecution,* are almost always made with intent to deceive. Other words used in variable meanings, in most cases more or less dishonestly, are *class, totalitarian, science, progressive, reactionary, bourgeois, equality.*

Now that I have made this catalogue of swindles and perversions, let me give another example of the kind of writing that they lead to. This time it must of its nature be an imaginary one. I am going to translate a passage of good English into modern English of the worst sort. Here is a well-known verse from *Ecclesiastes*:

> I returned, and saw under the sun, that the race is not to the swift, nor the battle to the strong, neither yet bread to the wise, nor yet riches to men of understanding, nor yet favour to men of skill; but time and chance happeneth to them all.

Here it is in modern English:

> Objective consideration of contemporary phenomena compels the conclusion that success or failure in competitive activities exhibits no tendency to be commensurate with innate capacity, but that a considerable element of the unpredictable must invariably be taken into account.

This is a parody, but not a very gross one. Exhibit 3, above, for instance, contains several patches of the same kind of English. It will be seen that I have not made a full translation. The beginning and ending of the sentence follow the original meaning fairly closely, but in the middle the concrete illustrations – race, battle, bread – dissolve into the vague phrase "success or failure in competitive activities". This had to be so, because no modern writer of the kind I am discussing – no one capable of using phrases like "objective consideration of contemporary phenomena" – would ever tabulate his thoughts in that precise and detailed way. The whole tendency of modern prose is away from concreteness. Now analyse these two sentences a little more closely. The first contains 49 words but only 60 syllables, and all its words are those of everyday life. The second contains 38 words of 90 syllables: 18 of its words are from Latin roots, and one from Greek. The first sentence contains six vivid images, and only one phrase ("time and chance") that could be called vague. The second contains not a single fresh, arresting phrase, and in spite of its 90 syllables it gives only a shortened version of the meaning contained in the first. Yet without a doubt it is the second kind of sentence that is gaining ground in modern English. I do not want to exaggerate. This kind of writing is not yet universal, and outcrops of simplicity will occur here and there in the worst-written page. Still, if you or I were told to write a few lines on the uncertainty of human fortunes, we should probably come much nearer to my imaginary sentence than to the one from *Ecclesiastes*.

As I have tried to show, modern writing at its worst does not consist in picking out words for the sake of their meaning and inventing images in order to make the meaning clearer. It consists in gumming together long strips of words which have already been set in order by someone else, and making the results presentable by sheer humbug. The attraction of this way of writing is that it is easy. It is easier – even quicker, once you have the habit – to say *In my opinion it is a not unjustifiable assumption that* than to say *I think*. If you use ready-made phrases, you not only don't have to hunt about for words; you also don't have to bother with the rhythms of your sentences, since these phrases are generally so arranged as to be more or less euphonious. When you are composing in a hurry – when you are dictating to a stenographer, for instance, or making a public speech – it is natural to fall into a pretentious, latinised style. Tags like *a consideration which we should do well to bear in mind* or *a conclusion to which all of us would readily assent* will save many a sentence from coming down with a bump. By using stale metaphors, similes and idioms you save much mental effort, at the cost of leaving your meaning vague, not only for your reader but for yourself. This is the significance of mixed metaphors. The sole aim of a metaphor is to call up a visual image. When these images clash – as in *The Fascist octopus has sung its swan song, the jackboot is thrown into the melting-pot* – it can be taken as certain that the writer is not seeing a mental image of the objects he is naming; in other words he is not really thinking. Look again at the examples I gave at the beginning of this essay. Professor Laski (1) uses five negatives in 53 words. One of these is superfluous, making nonsense of the whole passage, and in addition there is the slip *alien* for akin, making further nonsense, and several avoidable pieces of clumsiness which increase the general vagueness. Professor

Hogben (2) plays ducks and drakes with a battery which is able to write prescriptions, and, while disapproving of the everyday phrase *put up with*, is unwilling to look *egregious* up in the dictionary and see what it means. (3), if one takes an uncharitable attitude towards it, is simply meaningless: probably one could work out its intended meaning by reading the whole of the article in which it occurs. In (4) the writer knows more or less what he wants to say, but an accumulation of stale phrases chokes him like tealeaves blocking a sink. In (5) words and meaning have almost parted company. People who write in this manner usually have a general emotional meaning – they dislike one thing and want to express solidarity with another – but they are not interested in the detail of what they are saying. A scrupulous writer, in every sentence that he writes, will ask himself at least four questions, thus: What am I trying to say? What words will express it? What image or idiom will make it clearer? Is this image fresh enough to have an effect? And he will probably ask himself two more: Could I put it more shortly? Have I said anything that is avoidably ugly? But you are not obliged to go to all this trouble. You can shirk it by simply throwing your mind open and letting the ready-made phrases come crowding in. They will construct your sentences for you – even think your thoughts for you, to a certain extent – and at need they will perform the important service of partially concealing your meaning even from yourself. It is at this point that the special connection between politics and the debasement of language becomes clear.

In our time it is broadly true that political writing is bad writing. Where it is not true, it will generally be found that the writer is some kind of rebel, expressing his private opinions, and not a "party line". Orthodoxy, of whatever colour, seems to demand a lifeless, imitative style. The political dialects to be found in pamphlets, leading articles, manifestos, White Papers and the speeches of Under-Secretaries do, of course, vary from party to party, but they are all alike in that one almost never finds in them a fresh, vivid, home-made turn of speech. When one watches some tired hack on the platform mechanically repeating the familiar phrases – *bestial atrocities, iron heel, blood-stained tyranny, free peoples of the world, stand shoulder to shoulder* – one often has a curious feeling that one is not watching a live human being but some kind of dummy: a feeling which suddenly becomes stronger at moments when the light catches the speaker's spectacles and turns them into blank discs which seem to have no eyes behind them. And this is not altogether fanciful. A speaker who uses that kind of phraseology has gone some distance towards turning himself into a machine. The appropriate noises are coming out of his larynx, but his brain is not involved as it would be if he were choosing his words for himself. If the speech he is speaking is one that he is accustomed to make over and over again, he may be almost unconscious of what he is saying, as one is when one utters the responses in church. And this reduced state of consciousness, if not indispensable, is at any rate favourable to political conformity.

In our time political speech and writings are largely the defence of the indefensible. Things like the continuance of British rule in India, the Russian purges and deportations, the dropping of the atom bombs on Japan, can indeed be defended, but only by arguments which are too brutal for most people to face, and which do not square with the professed aims of political parties. Thus political language has to consist largely of euphemism, question-begging and sheer cloudy vagueness. Defenceless villages are bombarded from the air, the inhabitants driven out into the countryside, the cattle machine-gunned, the huts set on fire with incendiary bullets: this is called *pacification*. Millions of peasants are robbed of their farms and sent trudging along the roads with no more than they can carry: this is called *transfer of population* or *rectification of frontiers*. People are imprisoned for years without trial, or shot in the back of the neck or sent to die of scurvy in Arctic lumber camps: this is called *elimination of unreliable elements*. Such phraseology is needed if one wants to name things without calling up mental pictures of them. Consider for instance some comfortable English professor defending Russian totalitarianism. He cannot say outright, "I believe in killing off your opponents when you can get good results by doing so". Probably, therefore, he will say something like this:

While freely conceding that the Soviet regime exhibits certain features which the humanitarian may be inclined to deplore, we must, I think, agree that a certain curtailment of the right to political opposition is an unavoidable concomitant of transitional periods, and that the rigours which the Russian people have been called upon to undergo have been amply justified in the sphere of concrete achievement.

The inflated style is itself a kind of euphemism. A mass of Latin words falls upon the facts like soft snow, blurring the outlines and covering up all the details. The great enemy of clear language is insincerity. When there is a gap between one's real and one's declared aims, one turns as it were instinctively to long words and exhausted idioms, like a cuttlefish squirting out ink. In our age there is no such thing as "keeping out of politics". All issues are political issues, and politics itself is a mass of lies, evasions, folly, hatred and schizophrenia. When the general atmosphere is bad, language must suffer. I should expect to find – this is a guess which I have not sufficient knowledge to verify – that the German, Russian and Italian languages have all deteriorated in the last ten or fifteen years as a result of dictatorship.

But if thought corrupts language, language can also corrupt thought. A bad usage can spread by tradition and imitation, even among people who should and do know better. The debased language that I have been discussing is in some ways very convenient. Phrases like *a not unjustifiable assumption, leaves much to be desired, would serve no good purpose, a consideration which we should do well to bear in mind*, are a continuous temptation, a packet of aspirins always at one's elbow. Look back through this essay, and for certain you will find that I have again and again committed the very faults I am protesting against. By this morning's post I have received a pamphlet dealing with conditions in Germany. The author tells me that he "felt impelled" to write it. I open it at random, and here is almost the first sentence that I see: "[The Allies] have an opportunity not only of achieving a radical transformation of Germany's social and political structure in such a way as to avoid a nationalistic reaction in Germany itself, but at the same time of laying the foundations of a co-operative and unified Europe." You see, he "feels impelled" to write – feels, presumably, that he has something new to say – and yet his words, like cavalry horses answering the bugle, group themselves automatically into the familiar dreary pattern. This invasion of one's mind by ready-made phrases (*lay the foundations, achieve a radical transformation*) can only be prevented if one is constantly on guard against them, and every such phrase anaesthetises a portion of one's brain.

I said earlier that the decadence of our language is probably curable. Those who deny this would argue, if they produced an argument at all, that language merely reflects existing social conditions, and that we cannot influence its development by any direct tinkering with words and constructions. So far as the general tone or spirit of a language goes, this may be true, but it is not true in detail. Silly words and expressions have often disappeared, not through any evolutionary process but owing to the conscious action of a minority. Two recent examples were *explore every avenue* and *leave no stone unturned*, which were killed by the jeers of a few journalists. There is a long list of fly-blown metaphors which could similarly be got rid of if enough people would interest themselves in the job; and it should also be possible to laugh the *not un-* formation out of existence,[3] to reduce the amount of Latin and Greek in the average sentence, to drive out foreign phrases and strayed scientific words, and, in general, to make pretentiousness unfashionable. But all these are minor points. The defence of the English language implies more than this, and perhaps it is best to start by saying what it does *not* imply.

To begin with, it has nothing to do with archaism, with the salvaging of obsolete words and turns of speech, or with the setting-up of a "standard English" which must never be departed from. On the contrary, it is especially concerned with the scrapping of every word or idiom which has outworn its usefulness. It has nothing to do with correct grammar and syntax, which are of no importance so long as one makes one's meaning clear, or with the avoidance of Americanisms, or with having what is called a "good prose style".

Seeing oneself as a hired gun extols technical virtuosity while affording the emotional distance that allows the thorough, rational application of that virtuosity to clients' interests. At the same time, it guards one against the wounded idealism that seems to make requisite cynicism emotionally corrosive.

Public relations practitioners also justify their work by pointing to the social goods that are the by-products of the corporate stories that they fashion. Images Inc., for instance, regularly arranges corporate sponsorship of a variety of art, sculpture, and photography exhibitions and collaborates as well in publishing books on them. The agency literally creates these realities by matchmaking artistic talent and accomplishment with money. In the process, up-and-coming junior corporate executives get the kind of exposure to refined, sophisticated artistic and intellectual circles that will help prepare and polish them for higher posts. Artists, in turn, as long as their work is not too avant-garde, receive the benefits of a latter-day Medici-like patronage. Public relations people claim a double accomplishment – they help civilize businessmen, not least by inspiring in them a "passion for greatness" rather than self-interest as the important motive for patronage of the arts; and they provide the public with access to high culture. The same firm has also arranged corporate sponsorship of dance and musical performances, helped develop important educational programs such as one on infant nutrition, conducted some useful surveys such as one on the problems facing ethnic minorities, and done a lot of *pro bono* work for philanthropic, community, and public service organizations in the bargain. One tries, then, to move some clients in directions that seem socially desirable while at the same time playing with the magic lantern to serve their interests. Sometimes, too, the ability to accomplish any good at all in this world seems to depend on the willingness to serve even clients with no apparent redeeming features in order to seize capricious opportunities to channel other clients' resources into work deemed socially worthwhile.

Sometimes, finally, men and women in public relations legitimate what they have to do with virtuoso displays of their special legerdemain in symbolic reversal. By definition, public relations is concerned with actions and particularly language in the public sphere of social life, with professional and institutional performance in somewhat ritualized social drama. However, public relations practitioners often argue that their real concern is simply "basic human interaction, helping people to communicate with one another," that is, sharpening the most rudimentary and ordinary human skills. In this view, what is important in the wholly secular sphere of public social life are abilities originally shaped in intimate, private, and somewhat sacred social settings. Historically, of course, public relations has been at the forefront of the many social forces breaking down the separation between public and private in our society. Public relations has, for instance, furthered the already strong democratic impulse to level social distinctions by encouraging both political and corporate leaders to appear before the public as "regular guys." Moreover, its many promotional techniques have been responsible to an important extent for the celebrity phenomenon in this century, which depends largely on creating and fostering a ravenous public appetite for glimpses of intimate details of the private lives of the rich, famous, and powerful. The legitimation at issue appeals precisely to such a merger of public and private. In this view, public relations simply embodies in a professional way the intricate subterfuges, the explanations, excuses, and justifications that mark all social intercourse. What seems to be public and peculiarly professional is at bottom private and universal, that is, part of human nature. In discussing why public relations is often viewed by the public with suspicion, one executive says, for example:

You know, PR is dealing with all the things that we deal with every day in our private lives, but on a much larger level. I mean, there is a certain beauty to it. It's reflective of what we all do each day. We do something wrong and we try to explain it. We get drunk and we act badly; we have a fight and we use abusive language. Well, [Company X] got drunk, drunk with money and power and abused its employees and then covered it up. That's a terrible thing, but it's not all that different from what we all do. I think that what people don't like about PR is that we remind them of themselves, on a grand scale,

On the other hand it is not concerned with fake simplicity and the attempt to make written English colloquial. Nor does it even imply in every case preferring the Saxon word to the Latin one, though it does imply using the fewest and shortest words that will cover one's meaning. What is above all needed is to let the meaning choose the word, and not the other way about. In prose, the worst thing one can do with words is to surrender to them. When you think of a concrete object, you think wordlessly, and then, if you want to describe the thing you have been visualising, you probably hunt about till you find the exact words that seems to fit it. When you think of something abstract you are more inclined to use words from the start, and unless you make a conscious effort to prevent it, the existing dialect will come rushing in and do the job for you, at the expense of blurring or even changing your meaning. Probably it is better to put off using words as long as possible and get one's meaning as clear as one can through pictures or sensations. Afterwards one can choose – not simply *accept* – the phrases that will best cover the meaning, and then switch round and decide what impression one's words are likely to make on another person. This last effort of the mind cuts out all stale or mixed images, all prefabricated phrases, needless repetitions, and humbug and vagueness generally. But one can often be in doubt about the effect of a word or a phrase, and one needs rules that one can rely on when instinct fails. I think the following rules will cover most cases:

1. Never use a metaphor, simile or other figure of speech which you are used to seeing in print.
2. Never use a long word where a short one will do.
3. If it is possible to cut a word out, always cut it out.
4. Never use the passive where you can use the active.
5. Never use a foreign phrase, a scientific word or a jargon word if you can think of an everyday English equivalent.
6. Break any of these rules sooner than say anything outright barbarous.

These rules sound elementary, and so they are, but they demand a deep change of attitude in anyone who has grown used to writing in the style now fashionable. One could keep all of them and still write bad English, but one could not write the kind of stuff that I quoted in those five specimens at the beginning of this article.

I have not here been considering the literary use of language, but merely language as an instrument for expressing and not for concealing or preventing thought. Stuart Chase and others have come near to claiming that all abstract words are meaningless, and have used this as a pretext for advocating a kind of political quietism. Since you don't know what Fascism is, how can you struggle against Fascism? One need not swallow such absurdities as this, but one ought to recognise that the present political chaos is connected with the decay of language, and that one can probably bring about some improvement by starting at the verbal end. If you simplify your English, you are freed from the worst follies of orthodoxy. You cannot speak any of the necessary dialects, and when you make a stupid remark its stupidity will be obvious, even to yourself. Political language – and with variations this is true of all political parties, from Conservatives to Anarchists – is designed to make lies sound truthful and murder respectable, and to give an appearance of solidity to pure wind. One cannot change this all in a moment, but one can at least change one's own habits, and from time to time one can even, if one jeers loudly enough, send some worn-out and useless phrase – some *jackboot, Achilles' heel, hotbed, melting pot, acid test, veritable inferno* or other lump of verbal refuse – into the dustbin where it belongs.

Notes

1. An interesting illustration of this is the way in which the English flower names which were in use till very recently are being ousted by Greek ones, *snapdragon* becoming *antirrhinum,* *forget-me-not* becoming *myosotis,* etc. It is hard to see any practical reason for this change of fashion: it is probably due to an instinctive turning-away from the more homely word and a vague feeling that the Greek word is scientific.

2. Example: "Comfort's catholicity of perception and image, strangely Whitmanesque in range, almost the exact opposite in aesthetic compulsion, continues to evoke that trembling atmospheric accumula-

tive hinting at a cruel, an inexorably serene timelessness. . . . Wrey
Gardiner scores by aiming at simple bullseyes with precision. Only
they are not so simple, and through this contented sadness runs
more than the surface bitter-sweet of resignation." (*Poetry Quarterly.*)
3. One can cure oneself of the *not un-* formation by memorising this
   sentence: *A not unblack dog was chasing a not unsmall rabbit across a
   not ungreen field.*

Acknowledgements

Propaganda originated as a course at Williams College and I wish to thank my students whose insights helped shape the framework of this book. A faculty seminar on the ethics of mass persuasion with my colleagues Thomas Kohut, Clara Park, and James Wood greatly enriched my thinking in this area. Special thanks to Janice M. Hirota for her careful editorial suggestions on the original essays presented here and to Paul Cantrell for his work on the index. The National Endowment for the Humanities provided me with funds for two different research projects that contributed to the making of this volume. I am also grateful to Francis C. Oakley, former President of Williams College, for his long-time support of my work. Funding from the Willmott Family Chair at Williams College helped launch the *Main Trends of the Modern World* series.

The following essays are reprinted with the permission of their original publishers.

Chapter 1, "Propaganda" by Harold D. Lasswell, reprinted with the permission of Macmillan Publishing Company from Edwin R. A. Seligman (Ed. in Chief), *Encylopaedia of the Social Sciences*, 1st edition, vol. XII, pp. 521–7. Copyright © 1934, renewed 1962, Macmillan.

Chapter 2, "The Rise of Public Opinion" by Hans Speier, reprinted with the permission of the University Press of Hawaii from H. D., Lasswell, D. Lerner and H. Speier (eds), *Propaganda and Communication in World History*, vol. 2, pp. 147–67. Copyright © 1980, University Press of Hawaii.

Chapter 3, "The Phantom Public" by Walter Lippmann, reprinted with the permission of Macmillan Publishing Company from Walter Lippmann, *The Phantom Public*. Copyright © 1925, renewed in 1953 by Walter Lippmann.

Chapter 4, "Towards a Sociology of Expertness" by Israel Gerver and Joseph Bensman, reprinted from *Social Forces*, vol. 32 (March 1954), pp. 226–235. Copyright © The University of North Carolina Press.

Chapter 5, "The Mass Society" by C. Wright Mills, reprinted with the permission of Oxford University Press from C. Wright Mills, *The Power Elite*, pp. 298–323. Copyright © 1956, Oxford University Press, renewed in 1984 by Yaraslava Mills.

Chapter 6, "The Machinery of Propaganda" by Cate Haste, reprinted with the permission of Cate Haste and Curtis Brown Group Ltd from Cate Haste, *Keep the Home Fires Burning*, pp. 21–48. Copyright © 1977, Allen Lane.

Chapter 8, "The State and Propaganda" by Z. A. B. Zeman, reprinted with the permission of Oxford University Press from Z. A. B. Zeman, *Nazi Propaganda* (1964). Copyright © 1964, 1973 (new edn), Oxford University Press.

Chapter 9, "Goebbels' Principles of Propaganda" by Leonard W. Doob, reprinted with the permission of The University of Chicago Press and Leonard W. Doob from *Public Opinion Quarterly*, vol. 14 (Fall 1950), pp. 419–42. Copyright © 1950, The University of Chicago Press.

Chapter 12, "Mass Persuasion: A Technical Problem and a Moral Dilemma" by Robert K. Merton, reprinted with the permission of Robert K. Merton from Robert K. Merton, *Mass Persuasion: The Social Psychology of a War Bond Drive*, pp. 2–3, 175–89. Copyright © 1946, Robert K. Merton.

Chapter 14, "Bureaucratic Propaganda: The Case of Battle Efficiency Reports" by David L. Altheide and John M. Johnson, reprinted with the permission of Allyn and Bacon, Inc., and David L. Altheide and John M. Johnson from David L. Altheide and John M. Johnson, *Bureaucratic Propaganda*, pp. 205–27. Copyright © 1980, Allyn and Bacon, Inc.

Chapter 16, "The Magic Lantern: The World of Public Relations" by Robert Jackall, reprinted with the permission of Oxford University Press from Robert Jackall, *Moral Mazes: The World of Corporate Managers*, pp. 162–90. Copyright © 1988, Oxford University Press.

Chapter 17, "The Persuasive Functions of Slogans" by Charles J. Stewart, Craig Allen Smith, and Robert E. Denton, Jr., reprinted with the permission of Waveland Press from Charles J. Stewart, Craig Allen Smith and Robert E. Denton, Jr., *Persuasion and Social Movements*, 2nd edition, pp. 233–52. Copyright © 1989, Waveland Press, Inc.

Chapter 18, "Politics and the English Language" by George Orwell, reprinted with the permission of Harcourt, Brace & Company and the estate of the late Sonia Brownell Orwell and Martin Secker & Warburg Ltd from George Orwell, *Shooting an Elephant and Other Essays*. Copyright © 1946, Sonia Brownell Orwell, renewed in 1974 by Sonia Orwell.

Notes on the Contributors

SERIES EDITORS

Robert Jackall is Willmott Family Professor of Sociology and Social Thought at Williams College. His most recent book is *Moral Mazes: The World of Corporate Managers.*

Arthur J. Vidich is Senior Lecturer and Professor Emeritus of Sociology and Anthropology at the Graduate Faculty, New School for Social Research. He is the co-author of *Small Town in Mass Society* and *American Society: The Welfare State and Beyond.*

AUTHORS

David L. Altheide is Regents' Professor of Sociology at Arizona State University. He is the author of *Creating Reality: How TV News Distorts Events* and *Media Power.*

Joseph Bensman was Distinguished Professor of Sociology at the Graduate Center of the City University of New York. He is the author of *Dollars and Sense* and the co-author of *Craft and Consciousness.*

Robert E. Denton, Jr. is Professor and Head of the Department of Communication Studies at Virginia Polytechnic Institute and State University. His books include *The Primetime Presidency of Ronald Reagan* and *The 1992 Presidential Campaign.*

Leonard W. Doob is Sterling Professor Emeritus of Psychology at Yale University. During the Second World War, he served as Policy Coordinator for the overseas branch of the Office of War Information. He is the author of *Public Opinion and Propaganda* and the co-author of *Propaganda: Its Psychology and Technique.*

Israel Gerver taught sociology at the John Jay College of Criminal Justice of the City University of New York. During the 1960s he was Director of Research and Evaluation for the Office of Juvenile Delinquency and Youth Development and for the National Commission on the Mental Health of Children.

Cate Haste works as a director and producer of political and historical documentaries for British television. She is the author of *Rules of Desire*, a social history of British sexual mores since the First World War.

Janice M. Hirota is an urban anthropologist who has studied occupational communities of mass media professionals, social service workers, and community activists, as well as homeless populations in New York City. She is currently Research Associate at The Chapin Hall Center for Children at the University of Chicago. She is the co-author (with Robert Jackall) of the forthcoming *Experts with Symbols: Advertising, Public Relations, and the Culture of Advocacy.*

John M. Johnson is Professor of Justice Studies and Women's Studies at Arizona State University. He is the author of *Doing Field Research* and the co-editor of *Crime at the Top* and *Official Deviance.*

Harold D. Lasswell was Professor of Political Science at the University of Chicago and Yale University. His many works include *Propaganda Techniques in the World War, Psychopathology and Politics,* and *Politics: Who Gets What, When, How.*

Walter Lippmann, a major journalistic commentator on politics, economics, and philosophy, was a co-founder of *The New Republic.* His books include *A Preface to Politics* and *Public Opinion.*

Robert K. Merton is University Professor Emeritus at Columbia University and Foundation Scholar of the Russell Sage Foundation. He is the author of *Social Theory and Social Structure* and *On the Shoulders of Giants.*

C. Wright Mills was Professor of Sociology at Columbia University. He is the author of *White Collar* and *The Sociological Imagination.*

Jessica A. Meyerson is a doctoral student in history at Princeton University. In addition to her interest in American film, she is engaged in a study of race relations during the 1950s on the Lower East Side of New York City.

Guy Oakes is Jack Kvernland Professor of Philosophy and Corporate Social Policy at Monmouth College, New Jersey. He is the author of *The Soul of the Salesman* and *The Imaginary War: Civil Defense and American Cold War Culture.*

George Orwell was a British journalist and man of letters renowned for his many essays and for his cautionary tales *Animal Farm* and *Nineteen Eighty-Four.*

Craig Allen Smith is Professor of Communication Studies at the University of North Carolina, Greensboro. He is the author of *Political Communication* and *The White House Speaks: Presidential Leadership as Persuasion.*

Hans Speier was Professor Emeritus of Sociology at the Graduate Faculty, New School for Social Research. He is the author of *German White-Collar Workers and the Rise of Hitler* and the co-author of *German Radio Propaganda.*

Charles J. Stewart is Professor and Head of the Department of Communication at Purdue University. His research focuses on the persuasive efforts of social movements.

Z. A. B. Zeman is Research Professor in European History and Professorial Fellow of St Edmund Hall, Oxford University. His books include *Selling the War: Art and Propaganda in the Second World War* and *Heckling Hitler: Caricatures of the Third Reich.*

Index

Meredith, James: shooting of, 417
Metaphor: use in language, 425–26
Military: and propaganda, 17,
  22–23, 324–27; field tactics of,
  39–40; and secrecy, 120–21;
  kinds of support missions,
  302–03; battle zone procedures
  of, 303–06; and damage
  assessment, 306–12, 325; and
  target redefinition, 312–16,
  325–26; and target creation,
  316–18; and mission relevance,
  318–24; and construction of
  reports, 326–27
Mobility: in careers, 61–62
Mobs: and images of nuclear war,
  284–85
Morale: and propaganda, 124–28,
  194–95, 196–97, 210–15
Mueller, Claus: on political symbols,
  416
Museum of Modern Art: film library
  of, 257n.2

Name calling: in propaganda,
  218–19
National Association of
  Manufacturers: advertising by,
  359–60, 394n.33
Nationalism: and propaganda, 17;
  and war, 40–41; and symbols of
  purpose, 265, 268, 269. *See also*
  Americanism
Necker, Jacques: and public
  opinion, 31–33
Newspapers: as mass media,
  113–14, 149, 180–83, 186–87,
  197–98; and censorship,
  114–22, 130; and propaganda,
  149, 165n.22; in Nazi
  Germany, 180–83, 186–87,
  197–98
Nuclear terror: and social theory,
  275, 278–80, 283; and emotion
  management, 275–76, 281–88;
  and internalization, 282; as
  irrational, 285

Ochs, Donovan: on slogans, 401
Opinion leaders: and advertising,
  358–59
Opinion-makers: and publics,
  79–80; and institutional scale,
  86; crackpot realism of, 89;
  and mass media, 92–93,
  145–48; intellectuals as,
  108–11, 132, 137, 139,
  169n.47
Office of Strategic Services: and
  war films, 230–31
Operators: as elements of language,
  426–27
Organization: and mass society,
  83–86; of propaganda, 137,
  149–61, 162n.5; of public
  relations, 352–53, 363–64, 387
  See also Joseph Goebbels

Pamphlets: as propaganda, 109–11
Panic: social theory of, 275,
  278–80, 283, 286–87, 294n.9,
  295n.11
Parsons, Talcott: on professions,
  69n.3
Parties: and the public, 75; and
  Nazi organization, 175, 176
Peterson, Frederick (Val): on
  collective panic, 279–80,
  286–87, 294n.9
Plain folks device: in propaganda,
  220–21
Poetry: as propaganda, 111
Politicians: and mass society, 82
Politics: and the decline of
  language, 423; and bad writing,
  431–33
Popular will: and government, 48.
  See also Public opinion
Power: of experts, 65–66; and the
  public, 74; and mass society, 84,
  86, 100; and mass media, 91
Power elite: and mass society, 100
Pretentious diction: as needless in
  language, 427–28
Private: and public relations, 386
Private opinion: and communication,
  22, 26
Professionals: as independents,
  66–67, 72n.31; Parsons on,
  69n.3
Propaganda: history of, 1, 9n.3–4,
  13–14; characterized, 2, 16, 22,
  138; and war, 4–7, 17, 20, 105–
  34, 137–61, 196–97, 262; and
  interest groups, 4, 14–17;
  defined, 13, 105; international,
  15, 23, 123; intragroup, 15–16;
  and social theory, 20–21, 225;